Ethnic Relations in Canada

165701

Ethnic Relations in Canada

Institutional Dynamics

RAYMOND BRETON

Edited and with an Introduction by
JEFFREY G. REITZ

McGill-Queen's University Press
Montreal & Kingston · London · Ithaca

© McGill-Queen's University Press 2005
ISBN 0-7735-2957-8 (cloth)
ISBN 0-7735-3021-5 (paper)

Legal deposit third quarter 2005
Bibliothèque nationale du Québec

Printed in Canada on acid-free paper that is 100% ancient forest free
(100% post-consumer recycled), processed chlorine free.

This book has been published with the help of support from the
Department of Sociology and the R.F. Harney Program in Ethnic,
Immigration, and Pluralism Studies at the University of Toronto.

McGill-Queen's University Press acknowledges the support of the Canada
Council for the Arts for our publishing program. We also acknowledge
the financial support of the Government of Canada through the Book
Publishing Industry Development Program (BPIDP) for our publishing
activities.

Library and Archives Canada Cataloguing in Publication

Breton, Raymond, 1931–
    Ethnic relations in Canada: institutional dynamics / Raymond Breton;
edited and with an introduction by Jeffrey G. Reitz.

Includes bibliographical references and index.
ISBN 0-7735-2957-8 (cloth)
ISBN 0-7735-3021-5 (paper)

1. Canada – Ethnic relations. 2. Ethnicity – Canada. I. Reitz, Jeffrey G.
II. Title.

FC104.B747 2005   305.8'00971   C2005-902231-0

Typeset in New Baskerville 10/12
by Infoscan Collette, Quebec City

Contents

Figures and Tables

Acknowledgments

Publication of these essays by Raymond Breton has been made possible through support from the Department of Sociology and from the R.F. Harney Program in Ethnic, Immigration and Pluralism Studies, at the University of Toronto. The excellent editorial assistance of Elizabeth. Thompson, Harney Program Administrator, was essential to the preparation of the manuscript. Ron Gillis provided helpful comments as well. All this support is greatly appreciated. The specific impetus for the publication came from Dennis Magill and Lorne Tepperman, who at the time were co-chair and chair of the Department, respectively. The current chair, Blair Wheaton, was also extremely supportive. They, and I, hope that the book will, in addition to its academic purposes, provide a fitting tribute to the many and highly valued contributions Professor Breton has made to the Department, to the University, and to the discipline over the course of his career. I also wish to thank Professor Bretonhas for personally reviewing the manuscript, providing comments, and helping to ensure the appropriateness and accuracy of the information contained in the book. Of course, responsibility for any errors remains with the editor.

Jeffrey G. Reitz
University of Toronto
3 November 2004

Raymond Breton's Institutional Analysis of Ethnic Relations in Canada

JEFFREY G. REITZ

Raymond Breton is one of the foremost scholars on the subject of the ethnic and linguistic diversity of Canadian society. His sociological works on Canadian diversity are extensive and varied; they include major studies of immigrant communities and English-French relations, as well as significant consideration of aboriginal peoples. Over the course of a career extending from the late 1950s to the present, he has produced more than fifty publications on these subjects, including seven authored or co-authored books, four edited books, sixteen journal articles, and twenty-nine book chapters. Given the centrality of the subject of ethnic and linguistic diversity to the Canadian experience, particularly during the present era, and given Breton's stature in the field, it is important for scholars to have access to the essential components of his work. This collection of essays is intended to address that need and to bring together the most crucial contributions, certain items of which are not readily available except in large libraries.

Breton's work articulates a distinctive institutional perspective on ethnic relations in Canada. This perspective is a unifying theme in much of the analysis, providing highly original insights into Canadian diversity and an agenda for future research. An important objective of this book is to focus attention on Breton's institutional perspective and to promote its critical appreciation. Breton has provided his readers with the basic materials necessary for this task: monographs and articles presenting original theory and research; broad theoretical statements; and overview chapters for books designed as textbooks. What is needed, and what this books seeks to provide, is a publication that encompasses the work as a whole, identi-

fying Breton's distinctive theoretical framework, pointing towards underlying and unifying theoretical themes, and illustrating their application in
his empirical work. A presentation with such a structure should prove
useful as a textbook on ethnic relations in Canada, accessible to advanced
undergraduate and graduate students.

   Breton's institutional analysis began in 1964 with his article "The Institutional Completeness of Ethnic Communities and the Personal Relations
of Immigrants." The concept of the "institutional completeness" of immigrant ethnic communities had an enormous initial impact. The article
became an internationally acclaimed classic, one of those rare scholarly
works that continues to be read and cited decades after its initial appearance. The article introduces an analytic framework with far-reaching implications, which Breton has pursued and developed over much of his later
work. This framework posits that inter-group relations must be understood
in terms of their institutional context, and that social, economic, and political institutions structure individual options and choices in a variety of very
significant ways. Ethnic relations are "embedded" within their institutional
framework, so to speak, and, to borrow Granovetter's (1985) language,
applied here to ethnic relations rather than economic phenomena (for
discussions of the impact that institutional analysis has come to have in
many fields of sociology since the 1980s, see Powell and DiMaggio 1991,
and Brinton and Nee 1998). Breton's application of this institutional perspective has provided insights not only into ethnic community attachments,
the focus of the original article, but also into ethnic inequality, ethnic
conflict, and change in the lives of immigrant minorities. Importantly, the
institutional perspective frames a thorough analysis of French-English relations in Canada, including the "Quiet Revolution," conflict over language
and culture, the politics of Quebec sovereignty, and constitutional change.

   The essential nature of institutional analysis is clearly illustrated by
Breton's concept of institutional completeness. The key insight is that the
strength of an ethnic community is affected not only by the strength of the
commitment of individual members, or by the resources they may have to
contribute, but also by the range and diversity of the institutional sectors
existing within the community. The reason for this "institutional completeness" effect is that an institutionally-complete community offers its members the opportunity to live their lives completely within the framework of
the ethnic community – in work, shops, schools, and elsewhere in the
community, as well as in religious participation. The existence of these
options within the community reduces dependence on institutions dominated
by other groups, thus providing a powerful reinforcement for individual
ethnic commitment and a significant resource for ethnic organizations
seeking a clientele. In effect, the more institutionally complete ethnic
communities generate greater cohesion because of the greater extent to

which individuals may pursue their objectives within the context of the ethnic community. Because of the institutional structure of this community, the ethnicity of individuals becomes a personal asset rather than a liability, as it might be in the mainstream institutional setting.

Institutional completeness is an eminently sociological concept. Breton's insight captures a way in which the social dynamics of human behaviour operate within institutional settings *having a life of their own that "extends beyond the life of participants"* (to quote from the 1964 article). Institutions create alternatives and opportunities for individual choices, making certain kinds of actions more likely, and leading variously to group formation, conflict, and efforts at change. The phrase "institutional completeness" captures the power of social structures to shape individual behaviour and has become an important addition to the lexicon of scholars of immigrant ethnic communities.

Since that early publication, Breton has produced a steady stream of additional theoretical and empirical studies on immigrant ethnic communities, pursuing the theme of the centrality of social institutions and the value of insights derived from their systematic analysis. These consider a range of issues including ethnic community attachments, ethnic inequality, social exclusion and discrimination, ethnic conflict, development of ethnic politics, and the role of other institutions, including government, in society. Regarding government, he has particularly focused on the origins and impact of Canadian multiculturalism and related policies. Perhaps his most significant books are *Ethnic Identity and Equality* (1990), a comparative study of immigrant communities based on a survey in Toronto (a co-authored work in which he was the leading force), and *The Governance of Ethnic Communities* (1991), but he has written a number of influential articles and book chapters on these and related subjects. Significantly, a list of the seven most important English-language articles in twentieth century Canadian sociology, compiled by Hiller and Langlois (2001), includes two by Breton on ethnicity. Both are included in this volume: "The Production and Allocation of Symbolic Resources" as chapter 4, and "Institutional Completeness" as chapter 10.

Despite the influence of his work on immigrant communities, arguably Breton's most important contribution to scholarship concerns French-English relations in Canada; this work shares the thematic emphasis on institutional analysis found in the studies of immigrants. His 1972 article, "The Socio-political Dynamics of the 'October Events,'" applies an institutional perspective to an analysis of the crisis created by the Front de Libération du Québec (FLQ) hostage-taking incident and its aftermath; it is a seminal essay containing, as it does, the kernel of a broader analysis of French-English relations in Canada. Then in a series of studies, including *Cultural Boundaries and the Cohesion of Canada* (1980), *Why Disunity?*

(1980), co-authored with his brother, the economist Albert Breton, "From Ethnic to Civic Nationalism" (1988), and *Why Meech Failed: Lessons for Canadian Constitutionmaking* (1992), he provides a comprehensive sociological understanding of the true nature of the "two solitudes" in Canada.

This book presents Breton's institutional analysis in its most comprehensive form and illustrates its application to specific aspects of ethnicity. The fifteen essays – articles, chapters, and book excerpts – are presented in four parts. The first part contains four essays outlining broad theoretical and orienting concepts, which identify various institutional dimensions of Canadian diversity and examine a number of theoretical propositions. The next two parts contain five essays each, on French-English relations and on immigrant ethnic communities, respectively. These present more specific hypotheses, often backed by more intensive empirical work. The final part is a concluding chapter discussing recent trends in Canadian diversity.

This structure of presentation represents a bit of "editorializing." An editor who wished to let his subject simply speak for himself might have presented the essays as they were written, in proper chronological order, likely starting with the original "institutional completeness" article. However, while a reader is free to read the essays this way, I suggest that the essays may be read as components of a larger project – the systematic institutional analysis of inter-ethnic relations – which has evolved over time but which has an underlying unifying structure. This structure and its significance will be emphasized in the description below. Then, to help understand the significance of context and chronology, I will comment on the evolution of Breton's ideas over time.

I. ETHNICITY AND CANADIAN SOCIETY: GENERAL PROCESSES

Breton's institutional perspective is perhaps best articulated in his most theoretical essays; a selection from these opens this collection as Part I. These articles suggest that the institutional structure of ethnic groups is multi-dimensional and variable in ways critical to an appreciation of its impact on individuals. This theoretical discussion also posits the linguistic duality of Canada as a primary axis of ethnic differentiation, hence the division into two substantive sections: French-English relations and immigrant communities.[1]

The most elaborate theoretical statement of Breton's institutional perspective is provided in chapter 1, "Types of Ethnic Relations: Segmentation and Heterogeneity," originally written for a text edited by Leo Driedger (1978). Here, Breton states explicitly that while considerable attention has been given to the phenomena of ethnic inequality and conflict, "relatively little has been done toward the development of conceptual

frameworks that could be used for the analysis of various types of collectivities found in Canadian society ... Attention needs to be given to the
variations in institutional arrangements that emerge (or fail to emerge)
to accommodate the existing ethnic diversity, and to the various forms of
the institutional accommodations. It is such arrangements that structure
and regulate inter-ethnic relationships; it is also such arrangements that
become at times the object of inter-ethnic conflicts and social change"
[55, in original; 4, this volume]. In other words, inter-ethnic inequalities
and conflicts are embedded in an institutional context and can be usefully
understood in terms of that context.

This formulation was intended to place French-English relations and all
types of immigrant ethnic communities within a single conceptual scheme.
The former may be thought of as an instance of what Breton calls "ethnic
segmentation" (later called "ethnic parallelism") and the latter as "ethnic
heterogeneity." The former, plural societies arising from the political amalgamation of contiguous territories, exists as potentially independent societies with their own institutional systems. The latter arises from migrations in
which the migrants are intent on integration into the destination societies;
these involve the creation of institutional structures that are limited in scope
and function, and operate within the context of the institutional systems of
the destination society. The situation of native or aboriginal peoples, arising
when migrants are more powerful than the indigenous groups and well-
organized for the purpose of domination, is identified as a distinct type as
well. Ethnic segmentation and ethnic heterogeneity are "ideal typical" categories, in the sense in which Max Weber used the term, so the specific
empirical cases of English-French relations and immigrant communities in
Canada are examined as approximations to the theoretical categories.

While the discussion of the distinction between ethnic segmentation and
ethnic heterogeneity borrows from earlier articles on types of inter-ethnic
encounters by Stanley Lieberson (1961) and on plural societies by Pierre
van den Berghe (1969), it is also an extension of Breton's own "institutional
completeness" variable. In Breton's application, an ethnically segmented
or plural society is one in which the institutional system is sufficiently complete to admit of an entirely separate society. Segmentation vs heterogeneity
becomes a kind of "master concept," explored in terms of its relevance for
understanding ethnic inequality, ethnic cohesion, ethnic conflict, and the
role of government in the management of inter-group relations. In effect,
the analysis of institutional completeness is extended in two directions: first,
to encompass plural societies as a more extreme case of institutional development; and second, to show implications beyond community attachments
to include such variables as inter-group inequalities and conflict.

In chapter 2, "Implications for Ethnic Inequality and Conflict" (1978), one
hypothesis is that the higher the degree of parallelism (or heterogeneity),

the greater the degree to which inequalities will be affected by the ranking of organizations of each ethnic community. Interestingly, although inequality is often a basis for conflict, Breton suggests that higher degrees of parallelism generate an expectation of conflict, regardless of degrees of inequality: parallelism entails organizational rivalries which, in turn, fuel concerns about threats that each group poses for the other.

The institutional analysis explains the complexity of the relation between ethnic cohesion and equality, with implications for John Porter's discussion in *The Vertical Mosaic*. Porter's monumental study, published in 1965, remains the single most influential publication in the history of Canadian sociology. It presents a path-breaking and somewhat iconoclastic analysis of inequalities of social class and power in Canada, and their interrelation with ethnicity. A cornerstone of his argument is that ethnic boundaries represent barriers to the achievement of equality in Canada, and that progress towards greater equality requires the reduced salience of ethnicity. Yet Breton's theoretical discussion shows how and why this need not be the case.

The institutional perspective suggests that with a greater degree of parallelism, the attainment of equality by a previously disadvantaged ethnic group may increase its cohesion, because of greater opportunities created within its institutional system. This echoes forward to results in studies both on French-English relations and on immigrant communities (to be discussed below and in the final chapter of this volume, where Breton makes similar points).

Sources of "Economic and Instrumental Aspects of Ethnic Inequality" (1979) are pursued in chapter 3, where emphasis is placed on the relevance of sociological theories focusing on individual competition, social class structure, and group competition or "social closure." Debate among these perspectives, particularly between the first two, was in the forefront of sociology throughout the 1970s; Breton, however, shows how each may be useful. He makes a point relevant to his own theoretical scheme, namely that his discussion applies to ethnic heterogeneity, not ethnic segmentation: in other words, a partial discussion of ethnic inequality. This poses the challenge of applying the three theoretical perspectives to ethnic segmentation. Breton examines instances in which ethnic groups gain control of certain domains and may engage in conflict with other groups over such control. Hence, the group competition and social closure approaches may be particularly relevant to the case of ethnic segmentation.

The final chapter in this introductory group, chapter 4, "Symbolic Resources and Status Inequality" (1984), adds two themes that pervade Breton's empirical studies. The first is the importance of "symbolic resources," in addition to instrumental or material resources, in the analysis of ethnic inequality. The second is the significance of state institutions and their interventions in processes involving both symbolic and material resources. The "symbolic order" in Breton's discussion includes processes of identity formation, culture, and language. His distinction between symbolic and instrumental resources brings into play two Weberian distinctions. One is the relation between material and ideal interests, with Breton's emphasis on the significance of ideal interests being analogous to Weber's emphasis in *The Protestant Ethnic and the Spirit of Capitalism*. The other is between class and status or social honour. Ethnic differences in status[2] are a primary subject for analysis in the field of inter-group relations and are seen as affected by stereotypes, prejudice, and racist thinking. But Breton's analysis of the symbolic order makes the point that the allocation of symbolic resources affects social rankings. Breton further suggests that in Canada, state policies (and therefore state institutions) have affected the symbolic order, and therefore have had a significant impact on the allocation of status among ethnic groups. These processes are more salient in instances of ethnic segmentation than in those of heterogeneity, and one of the primary themes in Breton's later discussions of French and English nationalism, language policy, and multiculturalism, is that these policies are interrelated in their impact on processes of inequality and conflict.

II. INSTITUTIONAL PERSPECTIVES ON FRENCH-ENGLISH RELATIONS IN CANADA

The five selections in Part II provide an application of the institutional perspective to French-English relations at two levels: a general historical overview; and a more detailed analysis of a series of critical events in recent decades. These include divergent forms of nationalism emerging in English and French Canada; strategies of the Quebec independentist movement with its various components, including the terrorist element in the late 1960s and early 1970s; the relation of linguistic and regional conflict in Canada; and the most recent constitutional crises. In each case, Breton's institutional perspective offers fascinating insights into what is one of the most profound issues confronting Canadian society.

Essentially, Breton's institutional approach examines French-English conflict as a feature of relations between institutional systems. A key aspect is the power struggle among institutional elites, arising as industrialization and urbanization have altered traditional political relations. These elites initiate and carry on conflicts, and mobilize the support of group members whose jobs, careers, and well-being generally depend on the condition of the institutions and the opportunities offered by the institutions. To the extent that they succeed in mobilizing support, the struggle becomes an intergroup one, led by elites. Such processes occur *between* French and English elites within Quebec and across Canada, and *within* the francophone and anglophone elites. The evolution of this web of conflicting group interests over time is understood in terms of the specific resources available to these groups, and their capacity to manage the political process in relation to these resources.

Chapter 5, "Social History of French-English Relations in Canada (1988), examines the history of French-English relations in Canada – from initial seventeenth century settlements to Confederation, through the period up to World War II, and into more recent times, including the Quiet Revolution – through the lens of institutional analysis. It is, in effect, a social and political history of the development of Canada's parallel institutional systems. The historical roots of institutional parallelism in Canada are illuminated by Breton's focus on separate yet related French and English activities – exploitation of North American resources, conflicts over key political acts such as the Quebec Act of 1774, Confederation, and so forth. Breton presents this history as the emergence of two institutional systems, their interinstitutional relations, and the over-arching federal system; he explains how events have largely favoured English Canada and assesses the forces underlying the Quiet Revolution and the independentist movement, emphasizing that industrialization and urbanization have formed the institutional structure of Quebec society while preserving its institutional parallelism.

The development of political culture within each of the two institutional systems is the subject of chapter 6, "From Ethnic to Civic Nationalism in English Canada and Quebec" (1988). The essay has been influential because of its distinction between ethnic and civic nationalism. Breton spells out different forms of nationalism, and argues that while both English Canada and Quebec have adhered to ethnic nationalism, in English Canada a transition to civic nationalism has been under way for more than a half century. This transition has entailed certain tensions, which may be expected in Quebec as well, as that province undergoes a parallel transition.

In chapter 7, "The Quebec Independentist Movement and Terrorism in Quebec in the 1970s" (1972), Breton shows how an institutional perspective helps us to understand both the elite power struggles accompanying the Quiet Revolution in Quebec and the not-so-quiet character of the strategies of the FLQ in the 1960s and early 1970s. First, since separatism questions the legitimacy of established federal institutions, political authorities have more difficulty linking political symbols to behaviour within the rules of normal politics. Next, Breton suggests one should consider the difficulties that mainstream or non-violent separatists have in controlling their more radical elements. One of the key difficulties is the working-class composition of FLQ extremists, and the barriers, including class barriers, to influence within the Parti Québécois (PQ) and other mainstream separatist organizations. Finally, pressures within the FLQ to produce "results" led to the adoption of increasingly radical tactics, including robberies, bombings, kidnappings, and murder. At this point (see n16, chapter 7), Breton emphasizes the difference between social science explanation and moral justification: as a social scientist, he is engaged in explanation, which in no way involves moral justification for violence. In particular, he does not shift blame for FLQ violence to the separatist leadership. Yet it becomes clear why the election of the PQ in Quebec contributed to the reduction in violence by helping the separatist movement to incorporate radicals.

The issue of national unity in Canada is examined further in chapter 8, "Relation between Linguistic and Regional Cleavages in Canada" (1980). This essay puts forward the view that linguistic and regional cleavages may be seen as part of a complex struggle for organizational power among elites in Canada. Viewing national unity in this way helps explain similarities in the positions of the disadvantaged linguistic group (French Canadians, based primarily in organizations within Quebec) and the disadvantaged regional groups (Western Canada, Eastern Canada). Both demand power concessions from the Ontario-based centre.[3] It also explains the "legs" of the issue, the fact that it remains endemic in Canadian politics to an extent seemingly out of proportion to the views of ordinary Canadians, who may have to be prodded to support various elites in this struggle; and perhaps most importantly, it explains both the recurring nature of the constitutional crisis and the failure to resolve it.

The constitution is the topic of the final chapter in this group, chapter 9, "Symbolism and Constitutional Change: The Meech Lake Confrontation" (1992). The failure of the constitutional referendum containing the provision recognizing Quebec as a "distinct society" illustrates the elite nature of the conflict and the difficulties encountered by elites when the wider population enters the discussion through processes such as a referendum. But the crux of the matter is that in the on-going struggle, governmental power is only one element and constitutional issues are only one feature affecting the distribution of power within government. Hence, the analysis suggests that constitutional debates are largely symbolic. If constitutional discontent in the population is useful to elites seeking to advance their position, then the failure to resolve the constitutional debates may actually benefit various actors in the struggle. Thus, on the one hand, a major symbolic resource remains available for future use; but on the other hand, resolution of the constitutional problems would require a search for other issues to mobilize popular discontents.

III. IMMIGRATION AND ETHNIC RELATIONS IN A PLURAL SOCIETY

Part III begins with the classic essay on institutional completeness, "The Institutional Completeness of Immigrant Ethnic Communities" (1964), and then turns to later work applying an institutional perspective to

immigrant ethnic communities. Chapter 10's study of institutional completeness is based on survey research conducted in the late 1950s in
Montreal for Breton's doctoral dissertation at Johns Hopkins University.
The sample size was small, and the data analysis not overly complex, but
the elegant use of data to powerful effect serves as a reminder that small-
scale surveys need not limit the substantive value of the research.

Whereas the chapter on institutional completeness focuses on implications
for the personal relations of immigrants, chapter 11, "Immigrant Ethnic
Groups and Social Incorporation" (1990), examines the question of equality within the broader society. This is drawn from the book *Ethnic Identity
and Equality*, the primary product of a major survey of immigrant ethnic
communities conducted in Toronto by a research team led by Breton (and
including W.W. Isajiw, W.E. Kalbach, and J. Reitz). The selection here is
from the introduction and conclusion to the book, drafted chiefly by
Breton to summarize and integrate the findings of the various authors.
Breton's institutional perspective is reflected in the concept of ethnic
incorporation (rather than simply ethnic inequality), which includes the
complex array of relations across a range of economic, political, social,
and cultural institutions. Equality is a key aspect, but unlike the usual
connotations of the term "equality" in relation to processes of individual
competition, social incorporation of immigrant minorities includes the
possibility of equal access to resources through various institutional means.
The process of incorporation may be reflected, in part, in the relation
between ethnic institutions and those of the mainstream society. An institutional perspective is reflected in the overall findings of the study: namely
that where incorporation occurs, it is not necessarily accompanied by the
disappearance of ethnic identity or ethnic community relationships.
Instead, the findings are variable across groups, and the variation is
largely associated with institutional formations within the immigrant communities, as is illustrated in various ways across the groups included in
the study: Chinese, German, Italian, Jewish, Portuguese, Ukrainian, and
West Indian.

Another incorporation issue concerns the incorporation of ethnic
diversity in public institutions. In a paper entitled "The Vesting of Ethnic
Interests in State Institutions" (1989), Breton addresses this issue from two
perspectives: the shaping of the cultural-symbolic character of these institutions and the formation of structures and processes for the representation
of the various interests of ethnic groups.

Breton's own analyses in the Toronto project concerned political institutions, and led to two further articles also included here: chapter 12,
"The Ethnic Community as a Polity" (1991, from a separate publication,
The Governance of Ethnic Communities), and chapter 13, "Ethnic Organizations and Political Action: An Analysis of Public Opinion" (1990, Breton's

empirical chapter in *Ethnic Identity and Equality*). In the former, the focus is on the structures and mechanisms through which ethnic communities govern themselves. The institutional perspective is revealed in the use of what he calls the "demand" and the "supply" approaches. In analysis of demand, organizational actors respond to political interests articulated by community members; in the supply approach, organizations within the community become an "arena of entrepreneurial activity," because they constitute or embody resources that may become the object of political action on the part of institutional elites. Then in the latter, "Ethnic Organizations and Political Action," Breton uses survey data to show that individuals look to ethnic organizations, not only to the extent that they experience problems associated with their ethnic background (the demand side), but also in terms of the degree of involvement in the ethnic community and the perceptions of the community and its organizations. These perceptions relate to various qualities of leaders, their efficacy, and their accessibility to the community.

An important theme in Breton's analyses of immigrant communities is the impact of French-English relations, and the location of the immigrant group in English Canada as opposed to Quebec; chapter 14, "Social Origins of Multiculturalism in Canada" (1986), is representative of these analyses. Breton notes that the roots of multiculturalism in Canada are various, and include the decline of British influence, as well as a heightened need to recognize cultural contributions of immigrant-origin groups as part of the process of legitimating special language rights for both French and English Canadians.

IV. ETHNICITY AND CHANGE IN CANADA

The final chapter 15, "Ethnicity and Change in Canada" (1998), was written for the volume assessing the work of another exemplary Canadian sociologist, John Porter: *The Vertical Mosaic Revisited*, edited by Rick Helmes-Hayes and Jim Curtis. Breton's contribution reviews relevant changes in Canadian society and ethnic relations between 1965 and the end of the century, and discusses how subsequent experience has either confirmed or contradicted Porter's basic assertions, or has suggested the importance of other images of Canada. In addition, it contains an extended and useful discussion of changes in the position of aboriginal peoples in Canada.

Chapter 15 provides an occasion to consider how Porter's basic understanding of Canadian society might be modified in the light of Breton's analysis. In many respects, Breton finds that Porter's analysis has been confirmed; for example, the proposition that ethnic differentiations reflecting inequalities among immigrant groups have faded over time. Elsewhere, however, he finds that the theoretical model of the "vertical mosaic" must be altered. Breton's institutional analysis highlights the continuing impact of ethnic differentiation on social organizations, sustaining ethnic commitments related to both language and culture, and generating conflicts even where inequalities in income or other individual resources are not a serious issue. Forces such as industrialization have generated institutional changes in English and French Canada alike, altering their relations to each other. Porter's analysis needs amendment to account for historical changes he could not have anticipated, including the increased racial diversity in Canada since 1965.

CONCEPTUAL AND THEORETICAL EVOLUTION OF IDEAS OVER TIME

The underlying theoretical unity of Breton's institutional analysis is remarkable and, as explained earlier, is the reason for the conceptual ordering of chapters in this book. Yet the various contributions were written in a quite different sequence from the one seen here, more or less independently of one another, and evidently not according to any pre-set plan. This raises some legitimate questions. If there were no explicit plan, what accounts for the thematic unity in Breton's work? What is the origin of the emphasis on institutional context and on differences between ethnic segmentation and heterogeneity? How did Breton come to examine institutional dynamics as the agent of ethnic change – as opposed to the more usual attention to culture and cultural assimilation? In what ways have the ideas developed and evolved over time?

To answer such questions properly would require a detailed intellectual biography, which is well beyond the scope of this discussion. Nevertheless, it may be appropriate to suggest how Breton's perspective and the evolution of his ideas over time have been shaped by his personal background, early life experiences, and education. Let me put forward two tentative hypotheses. One is that Breton's background well positioned him to appreciate the nature and significance of the complex institutional dimensions of ethnic relations. The other is that, because of his wide-ranging interests and likely for other reasons as well, Breton was actually somewhat ambivalent towards the study of ethnicity, and always maintained an open critical agenda. These two aspects – Breton's personal exposure to institutional dimensions of ethnicity and his ambivalence towards making a long-term commitment to its study – underscore the conceptual and theoretical evolution of his ideas.

Of particular significance is that Breton is a francophone Canadian who defies stereotypical categories. He was born (in 1931) and raised not in Quebec but in a small prairie town deep in the anglophone centre of the country. A solidly French enclave in a sea of English, this was a uniquely Canadian place, as is reflected in the name: Montmartre, Saskatchewan.

Saskatchewan was, of course, thoroughly anglophone. Although it had many immigrants and immigrant communities, almost all were European and almost none French. Montmartre's population, then about 500, was a definite contrast. It was overwhelmingly French, mostly people who had migrated from Quebec, encouraged to settle there to create a francophone presence in Saskatchewan.

One can see how a francophone growing up in such a situation might well appreciate the complexity of inter-ethnic relations. This goes beyond the most obvious: being a member of a small ethno-linguistic minority, with all that entails in terms of interpersonal relations and identity. It also includes the features of the Montmartre French situation that were different from what might be experienced by other minorities. Not only was the actual existence of the town a consequence of the broader position of the French in Canadian society but many of its experiences were affected by that fact. Local manifestations included conflicts over control of the public schools. Public schools in Saskatchewan were required by law to offer instruction in English only, and parents wishing to have their children educated in French faced the alternative of private schools. Breton's parents took advantage of this alternative for all of their six children. But in prairie francophone communities generally, a complex struggle for power over schools as a key *institutional* sector emerged as a main feature of inter-group relations. Moreover, the way these events played themselves out in the local context was affected by the fact that the availability of public services in French was then emerging as one of the most significant issues in French-English relations across Canada. As well, the subsequent decline in the French community in Montmartre reflected its institutional weaknesses.

Even given this personal background, the idea of devoting a professional career to the study of inter-ethnic relations was initially not on Breton's mind. This focus emerged slowly, as the result of a series of opportunities arising somewhat by chance. After secondary school, Breton completed a degree in liberal arts and sciences at the Collège Saint-Boniface (affiliated to the University of Manitoba) in 1952. From there, he proceeded to McGill with the intention of earning a graduate degree in mechanical engineering. Only after being launched on this course did it become clear to him that he was not prepared to devote his life to engineering. At the same time, and by sheer chance, an employment opportunity arose in a research organization called the Social Research Group (Le Groupe de Recherches Sociales), and Breton took this up as a short-term expedient. This group included such talented persons as Fernand Cadieux (the founder of the organization), Sally Cassidy, and Paula Verdet. During that year, Breton was the only junior member of the group.

His experiences in Montreal during the 1950s involved studies on immigrants and laid the foundation for his professional interests in ethnicity and in the social sciences generally. Formal aspects of training were based entirely in the United States, because of its weight of social science expertise in the 1950s, and with the support of senior researchers in Montreal, Breton entered the graduate program in sociology at the University of Chicago. This was not the "Chicago school" period focusing on immigration, but rather the modern period in which broad theoretical concerns were closely linked to survey and other empirical research, with leadership from figures such as W.W. Warner, Everett Hughes, David Reisman, Peter Rossi, Peter Blau, Anselm Strauss, Donald Bogue, and James Coleman. In 1958 Breton completed his master's thesis on residential mobility in a Chicago neighborhood in racial transition (supervised by Warner), and all requirements for the doctorate except the thesis. He then moved to Johns Hopkins in Baltimore, where a department of social relations was newly established under the direction of James Coleman (who was his thesis supervisor) and included another innovative empirical theorist, Arthur Stinchcombe (who served on his thesis committee). He earned the doctorate in 1961.

Throughout this period, Breton's base in Montreal was easily as important an influence as his graduate training in the US. Experiences in Montreal awakened his interest not only in social science but also in various aspects of ethnicity in Canada. Breton maintained his academic affiliations in Montreal and held appointments at both the Université de Montréal and McGill. His doctoral research, based on studies conducted in Montreal, led to his first publication on institutional completeness. He also met his wife Lily – a native of Cap-de-la-Madeleine, Québec – in Montreal.

At the same time, despite his early success in the study of ethnicity, Breton had reason to avoid charting a career built exclusively on developing the subject. In the first place, his interests were quite varied. This was reflected in his early inclination towards fields in engineering and in his later academic interest in the related study of education, careers, work organizations, and bureaucracies, among other subjects. Throughout his formal education, he never took any courses in ethnic or race relations. The first major postdoctoral study for which he took sole responsibility concerned education and career choice, and was funded by the federal Department of Manpower. In addition, there may have been a degree of ambivalence or avoidance regarding the subject of ethnicity itself, or at least to the thought of a long-term commitment to it. After all, the very circumstances that provided the basis for some of Breton's insights into ethnicity might also have made him uncomfortable with aspects of the subject related to social marginality. There were multiple dimensions to this, because if French status was marginal in Saskatchewan, prairie origins implied marginality in Québec.

Despite the significance of his experiences in Montreal and the centrality of Montreal in the changing climate of French-English relations in Canada, after 1964 Breton developed his work mostly in an anglophone context.

After several years at Johns Hopkins, he accepted a faculty position at the University of Toronto, where he remained for twenty-three years, until his retirement in 1992. From this vantage point, he was free to set his own agenda, which included, but was definitely not exclusive to, the study of ethnicity. He conducted major studies on a variety of other topics, including education, career choice, organizations, and employment. During the period 1976–81, he did return to Montreal in a joint appointment as Program Director at the Institute for Research on Public Policy, but there he was involved in studies on a number of topics.

Overall, Breton's work on ethnicity arises in the context of his broad interests. It has progressively become broader and more ambitious, both theoretically and empirically. New dimensions – such as the emphasis on symbolic dimensions of institutional processes – have been added. But the essential theoretical framework has remained consistent. In sum, Breton's institutional perspective had a solid foundation in personal experience, and once articulated in terms of sociological theory, did not require major revision. Instead, it was applied to an ever-expanding range of issues pertinent to inter-ethnic relations in Canada. Over time, this has covered a substantial portion of the available intellectual terrain. At the same time, although Breton's ideas were comprehensive, he did not follow a systematic agenda in his own work. Rather, many of his specific projects arose as a result of circumstance or opportunity, such as invitations to make presentations or to contribute chapters to textbooks. Personally, he maintained an open agenda, and pursued a number of topics, as circumstances permitted.

Currently Emeritus Professor of Sociology at the University of Toronto, Breton has continued to pursue a diverse research agenda since his formal retirement. Two books appeared in 2003, each of which focuses on broader issues, while including the subject of ethnic diversity. One is a study of the social foundations of Canadian society called *A Fragile Social Fabric? Fairness, Trust and Commitment in Canada* (McGill-Queens University Press, written in collaboration with Norbert Hartmann, Jos Lennards, and Paul Reed). The other is based on a conference held in his honour at the University of Toronto, *Globalization and Society: Processes of Differentiation Examined* (Praeger, in collaboration with J. Reitz). He also chaired the Statistics Canada Advisory Committee for the development of the Ethnic Diversity Survey, recently released as a major new data source.

A FEW MINOR DIFFICULTIES IN CONCEPTUAL (RATHER THAN CHRONOLOGICAL) GROUPING OF CHAPTERS

Although readers are encouraged to consider these various contributions as they are grouped conceptually in this book, rather than in the chronological sequence in which they were written, the ordering creates certain

difficulties which, though relatively minor, should be kept in mind. These
are difficulties related to terminological changes, historical anachronisms,
and selective chapter cross-references.

The most important terminological issue relates to institutional variables
themselves. In some places Breton uses the term "ethnic segmentation"
(chapter 1), whereas in others he speaks of institutional "parallelism" or
of "plural" societies (chapter 2), which perhaps more clearly emphasizes
the co-existence of two competing institutional systems. The terms have
essentially the same reference: to institutional structures with particularly
high degrees of – that other term – "institutional completeness." And yet
that latter term was introduced mainly in connection with immigrant communities, which are termed instances of "ethnic heterogeneity," and hence
are actually less institutionally complete. Still, it was undoubtedly intentional not to use the term "institutional completeness" in connection with
French-English relations. Thus, in a seemingly experimental way, Breton
chooses words that are helpful in a particular context and in a particular
paper. The resulting terminological inconsistencies should not cause
confusion, nor do they reflect significant shifts of meaning.

Readers will notice occasional historical anachronisms, because the
ordering of chapters is not quite in step with historical change. For example, chapter 7 on the independentist movement refers to the low proportion of Quebec immigrants speaking French. Yet chapter 6 includes there
is a reference to how subsequent legislation has changed this. The chapter
on nationalism is placed first for thematic reasons: it examines a broader
sweep of historical change. As it was written later, however, it encompasses
more recent trends.

Another type of difficulty leads to a certain selectivity of chapter cross-
references. In the original versions of the various papers, Breton often
cites other related papers that he had published recently or on which he
was working at the time. Such self-citations are a useful form of chapter
cross-referencing in a book such as this. But Breton's citations to recent
or parallel work are not necessarily most appropriate in retrospect. For
example, chapter 2 contains a discussion of inter-ethnic power struggles
in plural societies, with a reference (n7) to the forthcoming book *Why
Disunity?*, an excerpt from which appears as chapter 8. This is a useful
chapter cross-reference, albeit highly selective, as such power struggles are
discussed throughout Part II and not only in chapter 8. This selective
reference occurs simply because Breton was working on *Why Disunity?* at
the time he drafted what was to become chapter 2 in this volume.

TASKS FOR THE FUTURE

Breton's writings are theory-driven, and inevitably contain hypotheses and
empirical generalizations that go beyond currently available data. Breton's

thinking has a resolutely scientific style that causes one to pose questions about how social organizations actually operate – as opposed to how they are commonly thought to operate – and that encourages further discussion and analysis.

Throughout his career, Breton has encouraged his sociological colleagues to extend the scope of their analyses and to consider the impact of the broader institutional context. It is hoped that by bringing together selections from his work to date and by pointing towards certain unifying themes, this collection will contribute to the further development of Breton's institutional analysis and to the dissemination of his social scientific style to a new generation of students.

PART ONE

Ethnicity and Canadian Society:
General Processes

CHAPTER ONE

Types of Ethnic Relations: Segmentation and Heterogeneity*

There are several dimensions to the structure of relationships between ethnic collectivities. One dimension that has received considerable attention, and rightly so, is the degree of inequality and the occurrence of conflict among people of different ethnic or racial origins. But there are three other dimensions that have perhaps not received the attention they deserve. First, it is quite evident that ethnic collectivities differ considerably from each other in their social organization. But relatively little has been done toward the development of conceptual frameworks that could be used for the analysis of the various types of collectivities found in Canadian society, and of how such variations affect the ways in which the ethnic collectivities relate to one another. Second, we know little about the conditions under which people establish relationships and form groups on an ethnic basis. In a way, our ethnic origin is always with us, but it is not always operative in determining social behaviour and in shaping social organization. Third, attention needs to be given to the variations in institutional arrangements that emerge (or fail to emerge) to accommodate the existing ethnic diversity, and to the particular forms of the institutional accommodations. It is such arrangements that structure and regulate interethnic relationships; it is also such arrangements that become at times the object of interethnic conflicts and of social change.

---

* "The Structure of Relationships between Ethnic Collectivities," in *The Canadian Ethnic Mosaic: A Quest for Identity*, edited by L. Driedger (Toronto: McClelland and Stewart, 1978), 55–73.

In the following pages, these three issues are explored. Only selected aspects of the issues are discussed, however. In the first section, an attempt is made to contrast two basic kinds of situations, that of ethnic segmentation and that of ethnic heterogeneity. Next, the question of ethnic group formation is examined, or more generally, the conditions under which ethnicity becomes a basis of social organization as a phenomenon which is important for the structure of interethnic relationships. Finally, three social movements are discussed – social movements which are an expression of ethnic aspirations and which have implications for the possible restructuring of the institutional arrangements within which interethnic relationships take place. The movements in question are the multiculturalism movement, the "red power" movement, and the Quebecois independentist movement.

ETHNIC HETEROGENEITY AND ETHNIC SEGMENTATION

One way of approaching situations of ethnic diversity is to examine the circumstances at the origin of the diversity. First, a distinction can be made between situations arising from migrations and those arising from the amalgamation of contiguous territories either from the drawing of or changes in political boundaries. For example, when European states established their colonial empires in Africa, "they subdivided the whole continent arbitrarily among themselves, usually proceeding from the coast and its natural harbors into the interior, cutting across all traditional boundaries" (Duchacek 1970: 25). As a result, the units formed tended to enclose different African ethnic groups. And these units, which initially represented zones of European sovereignty and colonial administration, provided, in many cases, the territorial basis of multi-ethnic independent African countries. The Austro-Hungarian Empire is an example of ethnic diversity resulting from annexation of contiguous territories through dynastic agreements and marriages, and through wars of conquest (Jaszi 1929).

An essential characteristic of amalgamation of contiguous territories is that it is a process that brings together groups that already exist as societies, each having their own social and institutional systems (Hughes and Hughes 1952). In such situations, the character of the interethnic relationships – at the political, economic, social and socio-psychological levels – is likely to be substantially different than in other types of diversity.

On the other hand, ethnic diversity which arises out of migrations can be quite varied, depending on factors such as the motives for migration, the intentions of the migrants with respect to their new environment and its native population, the socioeconomic characteristics of the migrants, and the mode of implantation into the new environment.

One set of characteristics of migrants are those that pertain to their capacity to create the political and economic milieu suitable for establishing their own institutions. Lieberson identifies a number of variables in this connection, but two appear particularly important: "When the population migrating to a new contact situation is superior in technology (particularly weapons) and more tightly organized than the indigenous groups, the necessary conditions for maintaining the migrants' political and economic institutions are usually imposed on the indigenous population" (1961b: 12–13). By means of such assets and other factors such as a substantial flow of immigrants, the migrants establish their own social organization parallel[1] to the ones already existing on a given territory. Canada offers a good example of such a process, first with the French establishing an institutional system parallel to that of the Indians, and then the English establishing a third institutional structure.[2] "Migrant superordination," to use Lieberson's expression, is a situation that resembles amalgamation of contiguous territories in at least one respect: in both instances, the resulting diversity involves groups that tend to be institutionally complete, that is to have their own institutional systems.

The other type of migration is characterized by the fact that the migrants are not in a position to set up a full-fledged institutional structure, or may not wish to do so. They may have migrated with the intention of integrating as rapidly as possible into the receiving society. Sometimes, the migrants do not wish to integrate, or are prevented from doing so by various kinds of circumstances, e.g., language difficulties or rejection by members of the receiving society. In such instances, some sort of community will form itself, but it will tend to be limited in scope and function. By and large, except for British immigration, immigration in Canada since the conquest has been of this type.[3] British immigration, at least up to well into the nineteenth century, has been "settlement immigration" aimed at establishing and expanding an English institutional system; that is to say, it was part of the process of establishing a parallel and dominant institutional system.

The first type of diversity can be referred to as segmentation and the latter as heterogeneity. Canadian society contains both types of diversity.

Ethnic Segmentation

Although agreement is not complete as to what constitutes a segmented or "plural society," as opposed to unitary social systems, there seems to be a certain consensus with regard to two points. Societies are segmented insofar as they exhibit, to a greater or lesser degree, 1) an enclosure of social networks along ethnic lines; and 2) "a social structure compartmentalized into analogous, parallel, non-complementary but distinguishable sets of institutions" (van den Berghe 1969: 67).

Social enclosure, in the present context, refers to the structure of social relations among the members of a society; to the existence of separate networks of social relations. It refers to the existence of social boundaries between groups and to mechanisms for the maintenance of these boundaries.[4] It also refers to a particular pattern in the contours of such boundaries. Indeed, enclosure involves a certain superimposition of social boundaries, or, perhaps more accurately, the containment of the many networks of social affiliations within the boundaries of an inclusive system of ethnic boundaries. In an ethnically segmented society, the limits of various social networks tend to coincide with the more inclusive ethnic boundaries. Group memberships may overlap considerably within the segments, but the resulting criss-crossing of social affiliations does not extend over the basic ethnic line of social division.

Again, as Barth mentions (1969: 9–10), the existence of a boundary does not mean that there is no interaction between the members of each segment, nor does it mean that there is no mobility between them. What enclosure means is that the interaction and mobility that takes place is regulated in such a way as to preserve the boundaries between the segments.

If enclosure· refers to the structure of social relations, compartmentalization refers to the related structure of institutions and corresponding organizations.

Each segment has a set of institutions of its own. This does not necessarily imply culturally distinct institutions and practices. For example, both English and French in Canada operate within a variant of the British parliamentary system. Compartmentalization is not a statement about cultural pluralism; rather, it is a statement about the locus of the institutional authority and clientele. For example, parallel educational structures refers to the fact that there are at least two sets of educational organizations serving different clienteles and under the control of different elites, not to their cultural differences. Since both the clientele and the elite are defined in terms of the lines of social segmentation, the processes of institutional compartmentalization and of social enclosure reinforce each other. Of course, both aspects of segmentation are a matter of degree; they are not all-or-none phenomena.

Ethnic Heterogeneity

The situation of ethnic heterogeneity, on the other hand, is quite different. It is a differentiation that does not entail the degree of social enclosure and of institutional compartmentalization discussed above. Rather, this type of ethnic differentiation tends to occur within the social and institutional systems common to the society.

One approach to the phenomenon of ethnic heterogeneity draws – implicitly or explicitly – from the sociological analysis of a more general phenomenon, namely the difference in the patterns of social affiliations in different types of social structures. In the more "traditional" society, persons tended to identify themselves as members of a group, their "people," and "this 'peoplehood' was, roughly, coterminous with a given rural land space, political government … a common culture …" (Gordon 1964: 23). On the other hand, in medieval society, according to Simmel (1955), the individual is enveloped in a set of concentric circles. That is to say, participation in the smallest social unit implied participation in larger ones as well. Such a pattern:

had the peculiarity of treating the individual as a member of a group rather than as an individual, and of incorporating him thereby in other groups as well … In the Middle Ages affiliation with a group absorbed the whole man. It served not only a momentary purpose, which was defined objectively. It was rather an association of all who had combined for the sake of that purpose while the association absorbed the whole life of each of them. If the urge to form associations persisted, then it was accompanied by having whole associations combined in confederations of a higher order. [Thus] cities allied themselves first of all with cities, monasteries with monasteries, guilds with related guilds. (Simmel 1955; 139, 149)

One feature of the "traditional" and of the "medieval" patterns is that social relationships within them tended to be involuntary. There is little room for individual choice in social structures based on localized relationships, on kinship ties or on groupings which do "not permit the individual to become a member in other groups, a rule which the old guilds and the early medieval corporations probably illustrate most clearly" (Simmel 1955:140).

Furthermore, in such social structures, the individuals tend to act as whole persons. Of course, people perform different types of activities and, in this sense, perform different roles. But since the various role relationships tend to involve the same set of persons, there is little discontinuity in their social lives. As a consequence, their identities do not tend to be compartmentalized on the basis of different roles and role relationships.

The so-called "modern" type of society, on the other hand, is characterized by a structure of social relations that is highly differentiated and consists of juxtaposed groups: instead of exhibiting a pattern of concentric circles, social affiliations follow a pattern intersecting circles, with the individual at the point of intersection. What we have is a "social organization based on roles rather than on persons" (Coleman 1970: 163). Modern social structure involves a large number of organizations which structure the different segments of our lives: work, recreation, religion, politics, and so on. Our social personalities are thus segmented into roles and role relationships occurring in a series of organizational domains. And even within the organizations, the relationships through which the organization functions are to a substantial extent "relationships between roles, not the persons who occupy them" (Coleman 1970: 163). In short, we have a kind of social organization in which people perform more or less segmented roles, usually involving relationships with different sets of people. In Simmel's terms, "the groups with which persons affiliate are juxtaposed and 'intersect' in one and the same person" (150).

Moreover, in a differentiated social structure, roles and role relationships involve an element of individual choice. For instance, a person's network of relationships is not completely determined by the kin groups in which he happens to be born or by the guild to which he belongs. Relationships are formed on affection, necessity, or interest rather than being "given" (Geertz 1963; Simmel 1955).

In such a structural situation, a person's identity tends to be fragmented or "partialized" rather than unitary and total. Mazrui illustrates the difference between a total and a partial identity in the following way:

A tribe in a relationship of bare coexistence with other tribes has a total identity of its own. But the Hotel Workers Union in Uganda or the American Political Science Association is only a partial form of identity. The process of national integration is a partialization of group identities – as the tribes or communities lose their coherence as distinct systems of life. (Mazrui 1969: 335)

The situation of ethnic heterogeneity (as opposed to segmentation) is one in which the ethnic grouping tends to involve "a partial form of identity." The question can be explored further by examining the differences between ethnically homogeneous and heterogeneous societies. A *homogeneous* society, ethnically speaking, is one in which virtually everyone shares the sense of a common origin, the sense of belonging to the same "people." In such a society, ethnicity takes the form of nationalism. Fishman points out that "nationalism is made up of the stuff of primordial ethnicity; indeed, it is transformed ethnicity with all the accoutrements for functioning at a larger scale of political, social and intellectual activity" (1965: 72–3).

There are two kinds of nationalism: territorial and ethnic. Territorial nationalism occurs when the relevant collectivity is defined in terms of a territorial unit, while ethnic nationalism "seeks to extend the ethnic by securing economic integration and political rights, through self-government and autonomous legislation" (Smith 1972: 14). Nationalism in a homogeneous society is both ethnic and territorial; the boundaries of the ethnic national collectivity and of the territorial national collectivity are the same.

In such a situation, ethnic identity is a "total identity" – total in the sense that it is supported by all the cultural and organizational components of the society. It is total in the sense that there is a continuity of identity throughout all the spheres of social relationships and activities, and in the sense that there is no institutional domain, social activity, or network of relationships in which people have to meet different ethnic assumptions for the definition of the situation. In both the "traditional" and the "modern" homogeneous society, then, ethnicity is a total, all-encompassing phenomenon, although in different ways in the two types of situations.

In the ethnically *heterogeneous* society, ethnicity tends to become fragmented or partialized rather than being total. And this tends to be the case, but in varying degrees, at the cultural, relational, and organizational levels as well as at the level of the individual identity. Only certain areas of a person's life involve his or her ethnicity. Ethnically specified social expectations tend to be restricted to a few limited aspects of behaviour such as, for example, those pertaining to the role of spouse or parent.

Ethnicity becomes partialized as a result of the process of social differentiation which involves, as we have seen, a social organization based on roles. Individuals behave differently in different roles and in different contexts; they change "social personality" from one to the other. In this kind of social organization, it is primarily roles and role relationships rather than entire institutional domains that become ethnically defined. Some segments of the lives and identities of individuals become "de-ethnicized," while others remain within the confines of ethnic definitions and expectations. In this kind of social organization, a person's identity or position in the system becomes a divisible quality in the sense that identity choices are not mutually exclusive or in opposition to each other. In Parenti's (1969: 283) words, "A person experiences cumulative and usually complementary identifications, and his life experiences may expose him to some of the social relations and cultural cues of the dominant society while yet placing him predominantly within the confines of a particular minority subculture." The reverse may occur: a person may be exposed to some of the social relations and cultural cues of a particular ethnic sub-culture while placing him predominantly within the mainstream society.

As far as the structure of social relations is concerned, it tends to consist in "individual-based coalitions" (Wolf 1966) rather than in closed ethnic networks. Friendships, marriages, business relationships, and so on, are formed in a multiplicity of directions; "members of the ethnic group cease to have a single focus of alliance with their fellow-members" (Zenner 1967: 111). Ethnic ties characterize a limited number of the "intersecting circles" to which a person belongs. Ethnicity may characterize, for example, his kinship and friendship ties, but not his occupational, religious, and political affiliations. A person's ethnic ties may be even further specialized in the sense of being limited to membership in ethnocultural associations. In such instances, ethnic networks are virtually completely dissociated from other types of social affiliation.

At the institutional level, a parallel phenomenon occurs: the network of organizational structures is fragmented or partial. It involves structures for limited aspects of social life (e.g., religious, recreational, professional services).

The fragmentation of ethnicity is a phenomenon that occurs in ethnically heterogeneous societies. But it is important to note that ethnic heterogeneity, as opposed to segmentation, is possible only to the extent that a society is differentiated; that is, to the extent that certain roles are performed in separate organizational contexts. A "social organization based on roles" is a type of social organization that allows ethnic heterogeneity because it permits its members to establish at least a few basic functional role relationships independent of their ethnic identities. A social organization based on whole persons could not enclose members of different ethnic groups without assimilating them completely, or treating them as strangers existing at the periphery of the group.

Heterogeneity involves some degree of fragmentation whereby the cultural, social, and institutional elements of ethnicity become dissociated from each other (at the individual and collective levels), and whereby some of the elements lose their importance and even disappear. But all groups in a heterogeneous society are not equally subject to the process of partialization. The ethnicity of dominant groups, for instance, usually maintains a higher degree of integration, in the sense discussed here, than that of subordinate groups. As Zenner points out, "one development in the modern world has been the constitution of the dominant ethnic group in a state as a corporate ethnicity" (1967: 110). Corporateness pertains to the capacity of a collectivity to maintain its social and institutional boundaries, and to define the rules and conditions of membership. Dominant corporateness is a characteristic that tends to prevent the partialization of the ethnicity of the group.

Finally, the fragmentation of ethnicity varies not only in degree but also in the particular combinations of areas of social life. which remain subject to ethnic expectations and social definitions, and of those who become "de-ethnicized."

The situations of heterogeneity and of segmentation are structurally quite different. Because of this, we would expect the character of inter-ethnic relationships also to be quite different under the two types of situations. For instance, the institutional forms of economic equality and inequality would differ as well as the institutional expressions of differentials in political power. The condition of socioeconomic mobility would be somewhat different under the two structural conditions. The issues over which conflict would occur as well as the forms of the conflict would also differ.[5] In short, the nature of the relationships between ethnic collectivities cannot be properly understood without taking account of the overall structural context in which they occur.

It should be emphasized by way of conclusion that this section deals with overall patterns of ethnic differentiation. There is a need to identify and analyze the variety of subpatterns that can occur within each of these broad patterns. Moreover, these two patterns are not exhaustive of all the possible broad patterns of ethnic differentiation.

ETHNICITY AS A BASIS OF SOCIAL ORGANIZATION

In order to understand the structure of relationships in a multi-ethnic community or society, another question that must be raised is the extent to which, and the ways in which, ethnicity becomes a criterion of group formation, that is, the ways in which it delimits the boundaries of social networks. Much of our thinking about interethnic relationships assumes the existence of ethnic groups. That is to say, the very phenomenon that is problematic is frequently taken as a given. Fishman has pointed out that we "all too frequently ask *which* ethnic *groups* exist in a particular area (or what is the ethnic background of informant X) rather than inquire of the extent to which ethnicity is apparent in behavior" (1965: 78), and in the institutional structure. In the previous section, the concern was with two societal patterns of ethnic differentiation. But within these broad patterns, certain social relationships and structures are defined as ethnic while others are not; or a given role relationship (e.g., employer-employee) is sometimes defined in its non-ethnic and sometimes in its ethnic dimensions. These patterns of variation need to be accounted for.

The variations are considerable: variations for people with different objectively defined ethnic backgrounds; variations from one institutional context to another; variations from one historical period to another; variations from one social situation to another.

It is important not to restrict the question of ethnic group formation to the formation of ethnic associations within the so-called ethnic communities. Group formation, or the establishment of social relationships on an ethnic basis, can occur in many other circumstances: commercial networks may be formed along ethnic lines; financial transactions can occur within ethnic channels;[6] contracts and subcontracts can be negotiated within particular ethnic networks; informal work groups in an organization can follow ethnic identifications; levels of authority can be defined in ethnic terms;[7] political parties or subgroups within parties can have an ethnic basis; and so on. In fact, it is possible to imagine a society in which ethnicity permeates the entire social organization but which has very few specifically ethnic voluntary associations.[8]

In a way, ethnicity is always there in the sense that we all have an ethnic origin. As van den Berghe points out, "ethnicity is an absolutely fundamental and ineluctable aspect of social reality. We are all human, not in the abstract or by virtue of our membership in a biological species but as carriers of a specific culture, speakers of a specific language, and so on" (1971: 41). But ethnicity, or at least several elements of one's ethnicity, can remain latent; it may have little significance in defining one's identity and behaviour and no relevance for the structuring of social relationships. On the other hand, under certain kinds of circumstances, it may acquire meaning for certain categories of people and become relevant for the organization of their personal lives, of their occupational activities and networks, of their communities, or of the institutions of the society. A basic question, then, is under what conditions or in what circumstances does ethnicity acquire such a role in behaviour and social organization?

In order to deal with such a question, a few propositions need to be taken into consideration, even though they are almost truisms. First, depending on the circumstances, ethnicity may be an asset or a liability, or it may be indifferent for those involved. In other words, it may be to one's advantage to keep one's ethnicity latent, hidden in the background, or it may be to one's advantage to do the very opposite, to bring one's origin and identification to the fore, to define the relationship, the social situation, in ethnic terms. When I say an asset or a liability, I do not mean in economic terms necessarily; it may well be so in psychic, social, political, or economic terms.

It is important to emphasize that ethnicity may or may not be consistently a liability or an asset for a particular category of people. It can be a liability in particular roles and social contexts and an asset in others. It can be a liability in relation to certain categories of people or an asset in relation to others. For most people, there is a lack of complete consistency in this area, and because of this, I would hypothesize that a considerable number of people are to some degree ambivalent about their own ethnicity: in some ways, they see it as a positive element in their lives; in other ways, it is something they would prefer be ignored.

Second, particular categories of people may or may not have much choice in the definition of their behaviour and social relationships in ethnic terms. This depends on the character of the social climate in the community-at-large, or in particular contexts; it also depends on the definitions that other parties bring into the situation.

Multiculturalism as a government policy has been criticized on grounds related to the question of choice. It has been argued by some that an official policy fostering the maintenance of ethnicity is likely to make it more difficult for individuals to keep their ethnicity latent if they so wish. Others argue the opposite: that the policy makes it easier for people to define themselves ethnically if they so choose. Whatever the case may be, this debate suggests that the social context is very much related to the degree of choice that particular categories of people may have in manifesting or keeping latent their ethnic identifications, whether this context has been defined historically, or defined by official policies, by ethnic group leaders, by the activities of certain organizations, by the mass media, or otherwise.

Of course, there may be some degree of ambiguity as to whether or not ethnicity is an asset or a liability, or as to the degree of choice that can be experienced in particular contexts. There may be uncertainty as to the advantages and disadvantages of defining the situation in ethnic terms.

The variations on the extent to which ethnicity is an advantage, or on the extent to which it is a matter of choice, depend on several factors:

a) The condition of segmentation that I have described above leaves less choice than a situation of heterogeneity. When people from different segments interact, the situation tends to be defined in ethnic terms, at least to some degree. A cabinet minister from French Quebec is likely to be seen not as a cabinet minister, but as a French cabinet minister, that is, one acting as a representative of the ethnic segment with which he is identified. Also, under conditions of segmentation, ethnicity is more likely to be consistently either an asset or a liability; in situations of heterogeneity, it will vary much more with the position one occupies in the social structure, with the role relationships involved, with the organizational context, and so on.

b) It also depends on the particular ethnic origins involved and the historical antecedents each carries with it. The weight of the historical background should not be underestimated in the definition of contemporary ethnic configuration of assets and liabilities, and the degree of choice in resorting to one's ethnicity.

c) The extent to which a collectivity is given an explicit, formal recognition in society will also affect the configuration of advantages and disadvantages and the extent of choice in making reference to one's ethnicity.[9]

d) It depends on the particular institutional context and the person's location in it. As a result, people of the same ethnic origin may experience a different set of advantages and disadvantages, and a different amount of choice depending on the circumstances.

What the foregoing comments are intended to underscore is that the structure of interethnic relationships in particular social contexts can be best understood through an examination of the conditions under which people form groups, associations, or organizations on an ethnic basis, and the conditions under which their ethnicity remains latent or is kept in the background. People form groups in order to deal with problems they are encountering or in order to take advantage of certain opportunities. People attempt to define situations to their advantage and to resist the definitions that they perceive as being to their disadvantage. When does ethnicity come to define the configuration of problems and of opportunities?

In this perspective, interethnic relationships are not necessarily the relationships between ethnic communities. Rather, interethnic relationships are those that occur between whatever ethnic groupings happen to be formed in particular institutional contexts or social situations.

SOCIETAL ORGANIZATION AS AN OBJECT OF SOCIAL ACTION

In recent years, Canada has witnessed the emergence of three sets of social groupings organized on an ethnic basis, articulating ethnic interests and advocating types of policies bearing on the condition of ethnic collectivities. These three sets of groupings can be referred to as the Québécois independentist movement, the multiculturalism movement, and the "red power" movement. Even though each set is heterogeneous, it is possible to refer to them as movements because of their overall thrust. For example, there were at one time over a dozen separatist organizations in Quebec, each with its own political philosophy and program of action. Since the formation of the Parti Québécois, the number appears to have decreased, but there is still not a unique organization representing a unique approach. Even within the Parti Québécois there are factions with differing views as to what the orientation of the party should be. But in spite of this diversity, the groupings are related to each other at least in their basic definition of the problem, and on overall orientation to its solution. Because of this, we can refer to the set as a movement.

The situation is similar in the case of the multiculturalism and "red power" movements. They also involve a variety of groups and associations in different parts of the country. From the point of view of the rest of the society, they do not constitute a series of isolated groups with activities occurring at random. Each has in common a problem and a general thrust.

Each of the three movements represents a mobilization designed to modify or transform the social order in certain ways.[10] There are perhaps more differences than similarities among the three movements in their societal situation and in the modifications they advocate. For instance, two of the movements are occurring within a "societal segment" which, historically, has had a very different relationship with the dominant segment. Both show a certain mobilization towards redefining that relationship. On the other hand, the multiculturalism movement is occurring in the context of heterogeneity rather than in the context of segmentation. Also, as indicated above, there are considerable differences of orientation within each movement. But in spite of their diversity, there is one factor that they appear to have in common: they represent the beginning of a basic change in orientation vis-à-vis the institutional system.

Touraine has indicated that such an orientation toward the social organization is a phenomenon that appeared with the advent of industrial civilization, in which economic achievement and growth became a paramount goal to the pursuit of which the institutions of the society had to be used and thus shaped to satisfy such a requirement. The very organization of the society, and of its institutions, came to be seen as objects of invention, experimentation, and social action (1965: 119–32).

A similar kind of orientation may now be slowly appearing in regard to the role of ethnicity in social organization. That is to say, political rules and structures, educational organizations and programs, mass communication facilities, and even occupational and economic organizations are beginning to be seen as being modifiable in such a way as to take account of ethnic diversity and even facilitate its expression. Traditionally, the institutional order was taken as given; the questions raised had to do with the integration or assimilation into it of newcomers or of people who were somehow defined as alien (e.g., because of their colour, language; or culture); the view was the adaptation of people to the existing structures. The functionalist and conflict approaches did not differ markedly in this regard: both took the institutional system as given; they differed especially in the ways in which individuals and groups increase their participation in it, one approach stressing value consensus, the other the confrontation between established and emerging interests.

The traditionally dominant ideology in our society, an ideology which is far from having disappeared, views the institutions of the society as functioning better if ethnic differences are ignored, and preferably eliminated. In this perspective, ethnicity is relegated to the private sphere – to family life, interpersonal relationships, and voluntary associations. It is interesting to note that the trend toward the de-ethnicization of the social organization appears to have paralleled the trend toward secularization in which religion was also relegated to the private sphere.

One variation of this traditional view has been analyzed in a very insightful fashion by Blumer (1965). In this variation, the modern industrial personality is essentially non-ethnic; whatever ethnicity remains is a remnant of a traditional past and will eventually disappear under the powerful forces of the industrial and post-industrial civilization whose institutional forms are based on rationality, something seen as almost the opposite of ethnicity. If ethnic elements remain, it is only the result of a cultural lag. Blumer argued that this view constituted an ideology with little basis in reality. Industrialization may be a solvent of pre-established patterns of ethnic organizations and social relations, but with it, ethnic boundaries assumed new social forms and frequently lines of ethnic differentiation that were not salient before industrialization appeared in social organization.[11]

Industrialization was pushed forward on an individualistic ideology in which the attachments to one's ethnic origin, one's religion, one's community of origin were seen as detrimental to the mobilization of labour for economic development. They were also seen as detrimental to the formation of the nation-state. Indeed, the ideology underlying the nation-state held that only one kind of nationalism was valid: territorial nationalism. Nationalisms based on culture or region were seen as a threat to the nation-state, as a menace to the integration of the political community. The social philosophy that accompanied these developments was one in which individuals, not collectivities, had rights.

In this context, ethnicity is also considered as an essentially individual attribute. Ethnicity and ethnic identity are seen as a "heritage," as "cultural baggage," as a set of values and sentiments, as a feeling of common origin. Of course, many people may have these attributes, share in the heritage, and have a sense of common origin; but these attributes are individual. Under a philosophy of individual rights, they have to be respected. But they are not attributes that could serve as a basis of social organization, except perhaps in the private sphere. Ethnicity should intrude as little as possible in the organization of public institutions.

The prevalence of this ideology is not an accident. Its role in the institutional evolution of our society is certainly very complex. But an important aspect of this phenomenon should be alluded to. It appears that the prevalence of this ideology accompanied the appropriation by one ethnic collectivity – the English – of as large a portion as possible of the institutional system of our society. It is also striking that in the process, that particular ethnic group has, by and large, succeeded in defining itself as "non-ethnic." In other words, it appears that the ideology of an ethnicity-free social organization played an important role in the process whereby an ethnic collectivity assumed the control of the major social institutions, a process requiring that it define itself as non-ethnic.

Historically, the attempt was to make Canada an English society, to give its institutions and way of life a definite ethnic (English) character.[12] This involved a valuation of English culture and language and a devaluation of other cultures and languages as "alien," "minority," "traditional," and less adapted to the industrial civilization. It also involved a particular usage of the word "ethnic" – a word which became part of the very language of devaluation. The success of this ideology in organizing our way of thinking is reflected in the fact that a substantial proportion of Canadians find it impossible to think of the English in Canada as an ethnic collectivity and of an important segment of the Canadian institutions as institutions which, to a large extent, were moulded by and reflect the culture of a particular ethnic group.

What has been happening in recent years is the emergence of a different view concerning the relationship of ethnic diversity and social organization – a view in which it is possible to mould the institutions of the society to take into account ethnic differences. Rather than seeing the ideal social organization as ethnicity-free, social institutions are seen as objects of creativity and experimentation for the purpose of best incorporating ethnic diversity. This is the basic significance of the three social movements that have emerged recently.

I am not saying that this orientation is well established; on the contrary, it is only an emerging one. I am not saying either that it will eventually become the prevailing attitude in our society; it may be a temporary, transitory phenomenon. Certain groups may perceive its results as having such high social and economic costs for themselves that they will oppose it with varying degrees of success. The potential implications of this social perspective for the patterns of interethnic relationships are such that it is a phenomenon that we cannot ignore; nor is it a phenomenon we can be content to be for or against. We need to study its dynamics and the ways in which it is affecting the structure and functioning of our institutions.

We need to study the specific orientations of the movements, the social forces underlying them, their internal organization and conflicts, and the social and institutional responses to them. For instance, Touraine (1965: 151–63) points out that a social movement involves a principle of identity that is a definition of its interests, goals, and character; a principle of opposition that is a definition of the obstacles that have to be overcome, obstacles that are usually embedded in conditions controlled by other groups in the society; and, finally, a principle of totality that is a view of the place that the group or collectivity is to have in the organization of the society.

It would be quite worth while to compare the three movements in regard to these three parameters: identity, opposition, totality. For example, if we consider the principle of totality, we sense that the independentist movement does put forward a model of organization of the socio-political system, although the model does evolve with time. The "red power" movement is now in the process of formulating its own model of how it is to fit in the institutional system of the society as a whole. It represents a dissatisfaction with the present arrangement and a rejection of the individualistic integration model which negates ethnic communal values and structures. The multicultural movement, however, does not offer as clear an image as to which ethnic collectivities are to be incorporated in the social organization and in what institutional form they would be.[13] It represents a certain dissatisfaction with the place that has been given to the "other" groups in our society; but it is not clear what institutional arrangements are contemplated. There is a good deal of uncertainty and concern about multiculturalism in Canada. The most frequent questions raised about it are "What does it mean in practice? What does it mean other than folklore?" Such questions may appear superficial, but I think they are quite fundamental. What is asked is what does multiculturalism imply for the organization of society and of its institutions? These questions reflect an uncertainty as to the kind of institutional arrangements – at school, at work, in politics, and so on – that are intended or that are implicit in the orientation of the multicultural movement.

In short, we need to study carefully the theory or theories concerning the way the society as a whole, or particular institutions, should be organized and put forward by each social movement either implicitly or explicitly. It is essential to analyze theories if we are to understand the role of the movements in generating social change, in restructuring the relationships between ethnic collectivities in our society. We also need to study the internal organization and dynamics of movements as well as the social and institutional responses to them. Such responses are crucial in determining the kind of impact, if any, that the movements will eventually have.

In short, these movements represent attempts to modify, in varying degrees, the institutional arrangements that define the position of the ethnic segments vis-à-vis each other and regulate their interaction, as well as the arrangements that determine the modes of incorporation into our society of the existing ethnic heterogeneity.

CONCLUSION

The aim of this paper is to show that the structure of interethnic relationships is the result of at least three broad categories of factors. One pertains to the socio-historical circumstances at the origin of interethnic contact and to the type of ethnic differentiation that emerges. Two types were discussed: segmentation and heterogeneity. Another stems from the notion that although categories of people may be identifiable in terms of their ethnic origin, it does not mean that groups are necessarily formed and social relationships established on an ethnic basis. That is, ethnicity may or may not be a basis of social organization. The conditions under which it does must be studied. Also, ethnicity may take many different social forms, and such variations must be accounted for.

The third class of factors has to do with the theories and designs that groups generate for the structuring or restructuring of institutional arrangements in which interethnic relationships take place, with the organizations that set up to pursue those clear objectives, and with the response that other groups and institutional elites make to them.

CHAPTER TWO

Implications for Ethnic Inequality and Conflict*[1]

All sorts of transformations have been taking place in Canadian society and have been doing so at an accentuated pace in recent years: in the economic and industrial structure, the educational institutions, the sex structure, marriage and family patterns, and so on. The structure of the relationship among the ethnolinguistic groups that constitute Canadian society is also in the process of being transformed. The discussion that follows is offered as one possible way of looking at the underlying dynamics of these transformations and of the conflicts through which they occur (or fail to occur).

Ethnolinguistic groups in Canada differ considerably in their social organization and in other characteristics such as size, geographical concentration, and distinctive cultural traits. The starting point of the analysis to be presented is as follows: if the ethnolinguistic groups in a society differ in some important respects, the character of the relationships between pairs of different kinds of groups must also differ. Thus, a society can contain many types of intergroup relationships. Viewed from the standpoint of the society as a whole, the complexity of network of intergroup relations depends on the number of groups involved. The society and its institutions are affected by this complexity; so are particular groups that as a result of the complexity find themselves in a web of intergroup relations as, for example, in the case of the French in relation with the British

* "Stratification and Conflict between Ethnolinguistic Communities with Different Social Structures," *Canadian Review of Sociology and Anthropology* 15, 2 (1978): 148–57.

group, Native peoples, and immigrant groups, each relationship having its particular features and dynamic processes.

An important reason for paying attention to variations in types of ethnic communities and to the resulting variations in intergroup relationships is that these variations have consequences for two related classes of phenomena: the production and distribution of societal values, both material and symbolic, and the degree and character of social integration. In other words, variations in types of intergroup relationships have relevance for the degree and patterns of inequality among communities, as well as for the extent and mode of incorporation of the communities (or community) in the society and its institutions.[2]

There are two broad classes of characteristics of ethnic communities that are particularly important, at least in the present context. One pertains to the pattern of differentiation between ethnic communities. It is crucial: it is indeed difficult to understand the processes of intergroup relations unless the analysis takes account of the ways in which ethnic communities are structurally differentiated from one another. The second set of characteristics pertains to the group's capacity for concerted action; that is, to its capacity to act collectively either in relation to internal circumstances or in relation to circumstances in its socio-political environment. This set of factors constitutes the dynamic component of intergroup relations.

The present essay deals primarily with the first set of characteristics – patterns of differentiation – and its implications for ethnic stratification and for societal integration. In the concluding section, some observations will be made on the second class of characteristics and its relevance.

PARALLEL SOCIAL NETWORKS AND INSTITUTIONS

A critical discussion of ethnic differentiation has to do with the extent to which the ethnic communities have parallel social networks and institutions. This dimension has to do with the character of the social and institutional boundaries between groups. We will refer to the two aspects in question as the degree of social enclosure and of compartmentalization that exists between ethnic communities.[3]

Enclosure refers to the structure of social relations among the members of a society; to the existence of separate networks of social relations. It refers, first, to the existence of separate networks of social boundaries between groups and to mechanisms for the maintenance of these boundaries. Second, it refers to a particular pattern in the contours of such boundaries. Indeed, enclosure involves a certain superimposition of social boundaries, or perhaps more accurately, the containment of the many networks of social affiliations within the boundaries of an inclusive system of ethnic boundaries. The limits of various social networks tend to coincide with the more inclusive ethnic boundaries.

If enclosure refers to the structure of social relations, compartmentalization refers to the related structure of institutions and organizations, to the extent to which each ethnic community has a set of institutions of its own. It refers to its degree of institutional completeness (Breton 1964 [editor's note: see Chapter Ten in this volume]). This does not necessarily imply culturally distinct institutions and practices. Compartmentalization is not a statement about cultural pluralism; rather, it is a statement about the locus of the institutional authority and clientele. For example, parallel educational structures refer to the fact that there are at least two sets of educational organizations serving ethnically different clienteles and under the control of ethnically different elites. Since both the clientele and the elite are defined in terms of the lines of ethnic segmentation, the processes of compartmentalization and of enclosure reinforce each other.

The degree of parallelism in societal networks and institutions can vary considerably: when it is very high, we essentially have sub-societies in relation to one another; when it is very low, we have ethnic social formations on a purely situational basis. The communities existing as sub-societies tend to have continuity and tradition, autonomy, organization, and common affairs (Smith 1974: 93–4). Those existing as situational formations tend to be based on personal experience and therefore lack historical continuity; they also tend to exist within larger units and therefore to lack autonomous organization and to have few, if any, common affairs. There are perhaps few ethnic communities to be found at each of these extremes; but most tend to come closer to one of the polar types than to the other.

Parallelism, on the other hand, may exhibit more than variations in degree; it may vary in the range of areas of social life involved, as well as in the particular mix. Few or many of the different types of social relations may be segmented; few or many of the different domains of organizational activity may be compartmentalized.

It should be noted that, seen from the point of view of the individuals involved, the degree of parallelism has to do with the extent to which a person's life can, potentially at least, be absorbed in his own ethnic community. The greater the parallelism, the more of a person's life can be lived in one of the ethnic communities without contact with individuals or organizations in the other.

IMPLICATIONS FOR ETHNIC STRATIFICATION

The degree of segmentation has several implications for the structure and processes of intergroup relations. In a very general way, these implications have to do with the fact that a high degree of parallelism entails interaction between institutions and their organizational apparatus in some domains of social activity, while a low degree involves the interaction between individuals, small groups, or cohorts of individuals within various social and institutional contexts. Those variations manifest themselves in varying degrees and forms; they also manifest themselves in different components of social activity and organization. In this section, I will explore briefly some of the implications of a high and of a low degree of parallelism for certain aspects of stratification between groups.

The Stratification of Individuals or of Organizations

A basic difference between high and low degrees of segmentation has to do with the unit of stratification: under low parallelism, it is primarily individuals or cohorts of individuals that are being ranked within the institutional system, while under high segmentation, it is also the organizations that are being ranked. That is to say, the greater the degree of parallelism in a particular domain of activity (economic, political, educational, etc.), the more issues of inequality will tend to involve the relative status of the organizations of each ethnic community and their position in the over-all institutional structure. Conversely, the lower the parallelism, the more the issues of inequality will tend to have to do with the status of individuals in the society at large and in its institutions and with the conditions for individual participation and advancement in the institutional systems. It is not that the units of stratification are entirely different under high and low parallelism; the difference, rather, is in their relative importance.

The socioeconomic status of an individual is always the function of his own position with regard to dimensions of stratification such as occupation, property, education, as well as of the position of the organizations to which he belongs in the institutional system. By virtue of his occupation, a university professor occupies a certain position in the social hierarchy; but his position also depends on the status of the department in which he is teaching and on the status of the university in which the department is located. Thus, in order to improve his situation, the professor can change jobs; but he may also try to raise the status of his department; or he may do both. As will be seen later, those two problems require different types of strategies and resources.

In the present context, the situations considered are those where the organizational differentiation is along ethnic lines, in contrast with those where it is not; that is, situations of ethnic institutional parallelism and situations involving a unique institutional structure (in particular domains of social activity). When there is ethnic parallelism, a member of an ethnic community may attempt to improve his status by moving up the occupational hierarchy; but if his ethnic group is relatively disfavoured, he will be limited by the status of its organizations and face the prospect of having to change the condition of the organization in order to improve his own status any further.

The Segmentation of Labour Markets[4]

It is not only that there may be parallel ethnic organizations in which people work, but also that the pools in which these organizations find their members may be segmented along ethnic lines. Parallel ethnic labour markets may exist with their own set of institutions and networks through which information and influence flow: newspapers, placement agencies, social clubs, professional associations, "old boy networks," and so on.[5]

One of the important characteristics of labour market networks (personal and organizational) is that they tend to ramify throughout a wide range of segments of the social structure: an occupationally relevant contact may occur at church, in the extended family, in professional meetings, on the golf course, in voluntary associations, in the neighbourhood, and so on. If then, the degree of institutional and social parallelism is high, the two (or more) labour markets may hardly intersect at all; that is, they will also tend to be parallel to each other. In such a situation, the members of the different ethnic communities are connected to different sub-markets and as a result benefit from different flows of information and influence. Conversely, if parallelism is low, the members of the different communities will tend to participate in a unique labour market or in different labour markets with many points of intersection. Another way of putting it is to say that in the first instance, the cost of getting information about and access to certain opportunities, is highly associated with one's ethnic identification, while in the other, the costs tend to be associated almost exclusively with non-ethnic factors.

Race and Language as Compounding Factors

If some degree of parallelism of organizations or of labour markets exists in a society, it may be to the advantage of a particular individual to orient himself towards one set of organizations or one labour market and to avoid the other. That is to say, in relation to a particular organizational network and labour market, a person's ethnicity may be more or less an asset or a liability; it may be useful or harmful for connecting and integrating oneself to a particular ethnic sub-system.

An important circumstance in this regard is the degree of choice a person has in concealing his ethnic identity or in relegating it to the private sphere of his life. The degree of choice may be determined through legally

imposed restrictions, through informal social processes, or through the use
of ideological weapons. It may also depend on features of the differentiating characteristics: visible physical characteristics of significance in a culture and linguistic ability[6] (if the parallelism involves language differences)
can reduce considerably the person's possibilities of manœuvre in connection with his ethnic identification. As a result, differences in physical characteristics and in language may reinforce the parallelism and its impact.

Types of Factors Related to Mobility

Social mobility under high and low degrees of parallelism does not depend
on the same kinds of factors and processes (although there is some overlap).
When parallelism is high, the concern is with those factors affecting the
status of organizations and organizational systems; when it is low, it is with
the factors affecting the status of individuals within an institutional system.
   The position of an individual in the stratification system depends on
factors such as his social origin, his educational attainment, his mental
and social abilities, his personality attributes, his connections, and the
interaction of these personal attributes with the various kinds of opportunities and constraints to which he becomes exposed at one point or
another of his career. The person is involved in the labour market and is
subject to the structure of that market and to the mechanisms operating
in it. Ethnic stratification in this context refers to the situation of members
of different ethnic groups in relation to the structure of the labour market
and to the resources that determine one's position in it.
   The position of an organization in the institutional structure, however,
depends on somewhat different sets of resources. One of the most important determinants is the extent of its access to the capital market; another
is its access to technology and to means of technological innovation. The
situation of the organization also depends on its relation to the labour
market as a buyer of labour (rather than as a seller as in the case of individuals) and on its position in the structure of the market for the distribution of products and services. Ethnic stratification in such a context refers
to the differential access to resources that determine the formation of organizations, their growth, and their position in relation to other organizations.
   Under high parallelism, the interest would tend to be in organizational
control rather than in the conditions of individual mobility as such.[7] The
concern is at least with organizational survival if not with organizational
growth. Basically an ethnic sub-society tends to concern itself with the
control and growth of the means for generating wealth, prestige, and
power. On the other hand, in a community with little or no parallel institutional system, the concern will be with the position of its members in
the over-all occupational structure and income distribution.[8] In short, in

one instance the problems are those of economic development of different ethnic communities; in the other, they are those of the social mobility in an institutional system of people of different ethnic origins.

In Canada, communities such as the French in Quebec, the Acadians, those of British origin in Quebec and in the rest of Canada, and the Native peoples represent fairly high degrees of parallelism – social and institutional – relative to one another. In contrast, most other ethnic communities constituted through the usual processes of individual or family migration involve few degrees of parallelism. The problems of stratification and mobility would then be quite different for these different communities.

These problems can be looked at from the point of view of the communities or from the point of view of the individuals involved. From the point of view of the community, one problem is the choice between more or less parallelism; should it build and expand its institutional system or not? Should it attempt to build it in all spheres of activity or limit itself to a few? The issue is one of great controversy in the case of the Native peoples, some arguing that Native peoples' communities are not really viable except as cultural communities, and that the improvement of their conditions should be through individual mobility into the mainstream institutions of the society. Others argue that they have the potential to develop both political and economic organizations of their own, and that this is the means through which their life conditions should be improved. The issue is also debated in the case of the Acadians and of the French in Quebec.

Once parallelism has been opted for, at least to a degree, then the relevant questions are those that pertain to the acquisition of control over the means necessary for the formation and expansion of organizations and organizational systems: access to capital and markets for goods and services, required institutional autonomy, political and economic conditions for taking advantage of the resources of one's territory, and so on.

These issues are somewhat different when looked at from the point of view of the individuals involved. One consequence of organizational parallelism and of segmented labour markets along ethnic lines is that the socioeconomic status of an individual is tied to the status of the ethnic community to which he belongs – more so than is the case under conditions of low parallelism. And this for two reasons. First, as indicated above, one can raise one's status by contributing to an improvement in the socio-economic condition of one's organization (e.g., increased productivity, expansion), because one's status depends in part on the status of one's organization and of the economy of the community as a whole.

The second reason is related to the segmentation of the labour market. Suppose an individual is dissatisfied with his present position. If he imputes his relatively poor condition to the particular job in which he is and how it fits his tastes and potential, he will try to change jobs. In order to change jobs, he will first use the resources available to him through the networks to which he is connected. This exploration may have different results: (a) he may find what he is looking for – thus reinforcing the parallelism; (b) he may find this network unsatisfactory in the sense that it leads to limited opportunities and try his chance in the "other" labour market. If successful, he will integrate into the other network and contribute to reduce the parallelism, but this may trigger reactions on the part of institutional elites and on the part of those remaining in the community who see the overall strength of their institutions being slowly eroded; (c) but if the "other" network is relatively closed, there is a relatively low probability of such an integration. In such an event, the individual would have an interest in supporting activities aimed at reinforcing or expanding the institutional system to which he is already (or best) connected and hence increase his own (or his children's) life chances. If this appears to have a low probability of success, he would then have an interest in supporting activities aimed at breaking open the relatively closed labour market under the control of the "other" group.

IMPLICATIONS FOR SOCIETAL INTEGRATION

Conflict Between Ethnic Communities

Variations in the degree of parallelism among ethnic communities affect not only the dimensions of the stratification among them but also the character of the power and conflict interactions that occur among them. In order to formulate hypotheses on this aspect of intergroup relationships, it is useful to distinguish, as Bachrach and Baratz (1962) argue should be done, the two faces of power, namely the structuring or definition of the issues and alternatives, and the conflict over those alternatives.

Briefly, Bachrach and Baratz argue that the analysis of the socio-political process should, on the one hand, deal with what becomes a matter for decision-making and with the alternatives selected for consideration. What kinds of questions become objects of controversy and collective decision, and through what processes? On the other hand, once a question has become a matter of controversy, the exercise of power has to do with the bargaining over the various alternatives and the resulting outcome. Of course, both the structuring of issues and conflict and bargaining over the outcomes can occur through either very formal, routinized procedures, or through informal, unstructured social mechanisms.

The general hypothesis I am formulating is that the degree of parallelism has an impact on the kinds of matters that become issues between ethnic communities, as well as on the character of the accompanying social bargaining processes taking place between them. The following are a few hypotheses in this regard:

Hypothesis 1   The greater the parallelism (that is, the more institutionally complete an ethnic community), the more it is likely to represent a threat to other communities and, as a consequence, the more the existence of a parallel institutional system or the conditions necessary for its maintenance or expansion become objects of conflict between the communities involved and an area for the exercise of power between them. That is to say, the legal and administrative arrangements and the social organizations that prevent, hinder, or facilitate the organization and expansion of the institutional system can become matters of controversy and power conflicts between ethnic communities. This, of course, is especially the case if, for example, because of its large size, the development of an institution on the part of a community would imply the social, economic, or political ascendancy of that community in the society as a whole, or in a particular area of activity. This is the case in South Africa, in Rhodesia, and in a number of southern states in the US. It has also been the case in Canada, especially during the period of our history where the French were a numerical majority: in those instances, the conflicts are basically over the attempts on the part of one of the communities to maintain or expand its institutional system on the one hand and the attempts on the part of others to weaken the other group's organizational strength or to hinder its further development.

There are several conditions that a collectivity can attempt to affect in order to maintain or expand the institutional system that it controls. Among those conditions are the following:

(a) The conditions related to gaining access to resources that can be used for the formation or expansion of organizations, that is capital resources as opposed to consumer resources. The case of the Dene nation in the Northwest Territories is a good illustration of this: there has been a dramatic shift in their concern from an emphasis on various forms of social and economic assistance to individuals to an emphasis on benefits from natural resources that can be used for further economic development. A number of illustrations could also be drawn from the Quebec scene, where more or less successful attempts have been made in the same direction.

(b) Since language is an instrument of institutional control, he who imposes the linguistic rules in a particular situation has established ascendancy in that situation. Modifying the linguistic rules of the game can be seen as an attempt on the part of a linguistic community to maintain or expand its institutional domain. This is usually what language legislation is fundamentally about. This is not to minimize the cultural role of language nor its importance as a symbol of group identification. But culture and social symbols do not exist in the abstract; nor do they exist only in the private lives of individuals. They become embedded in and sustained by the institutional system of a community. The linguistic dimension serves to illustrate that maintaining or expanding the control of an institutional system (or segments of it) is related to both the material and symbolic aspects of ethnic stratification.

There are also a multiplicity of ways in which an ethnic community can attempt to prevent or hinder the institutional development of another. It is beyond the scope of this paper to explore all the mechanisms used. By way of illustration, however, three types of procedures can be mentioned:

(a) Eliminating or restricting the right of association. This rather direct mechanism has been frequently used, either by passing legislation to that effect, or by the threat or use of economic, social, or physical sanctions.
(b) Preventing, if possible, the ethnic community from acquiring a territorial basis. This can involve legislation aimed at restricting the purchasing of land by members of certain ethnic groups, or other mechanisms designed to prevent or limit the settlement of a certain area.
(c) Attempts can also be made to establish an ethnic community as a political or administrative dependency. In this way, the development of a corporate organization can be closely controlled. The case of Indian reservations in Canada is a good example of such a mechanism.

The main point I wish to make here, however, does not concern specific mechanisms; rather, I wish to emphasize that when ethnic communities have some elements of an institutional system, the very conditions for the existence of such a system, let alone its expansion, are likely to become the object of a power confrontation between them. I would also hypothesize that the mutual concern for the relative strength of their institutional systems constitutes the source of the most intense conflicts between ethnic communities and the object of the most severe abuses of power.

Hypothesis 2   Closely related to the formation and maintenance of an institutional system in one or more domains of activity is the question of the sphere of jurisdiction. It can be hypothesized that the greater the degree of institutional parallelism, the more conflicts and exercise of power between the communities in contact will involve issues concerning the spheres of jurisdiction, that is the delineation of the respective domains of organizational activity. The domains can be defined in terms of activities or population areas. An ethnic community or a segment of it that has developed or is developing an organization in a particular field will want to be recognized as such by other communities. This follows from the very motivation to organize, especially on the part of elites. The process of becoming recognized involves the definition of the activities over which each will have jurisdiction and the definition of the population over which each will have authority, or that it will present. Moreover, the process can also involve the issue of whether the jurisdiction will be total or partial. Such issues can be raised by the ethnic local of a labour organization; by a political party in an ethnic area; by ethnic parishes as in the case of a number of so-called "national parishes" in Canada or the United States, and so on.

A basic condition for the sphere of jurisdiction to become an issue or a source of conflict is a "zero-sum" situation, that is, a situation where the expansion of the sphere of jurisdiction for one unit involves a corresponding reduction for the other unit. (I am, incidentally, making the assumption that, since the situation of organizational members, and especially of the elites, in terms of income, prestige, and power depends on the condition of their organization; they will not willingly accept a reduction in its sphere of jurisdiction. I am also assuming a relationship between the sphere of jurisdiction and the amount of awards available to its members. Not only will organizational members and leaders not accept a reduction, but it will frequently be in their interest to expand the sphere of jurisdiction either in terms of activities, of population, or both.)

To the extent, then, that ethnic communities have institutional systems, they will tend to experience conflict with each other over the domains of organizational jurisdiction. The conflicts will occur when the communities are involved in "zero-sum" situations; the issues raised will tend to be more numerous and, hence, the conflict more intense whenever one of the communities is attempting to expand its organizational domain and is perceived as sufficiently powerful to do so.

When members of an ethnic community have little or no institutional system, the relevant "sphere of jurisdiction" concerns individual activities and mobility (horizontal or vertical). That is, the issues that may arise in such situations concern existing limitations on individual actions or the protection of existing rights and prerogatives. Issues concerning discrimination in the labour market against individual members of an ethnic group constitute an example. In other words, when institutional parallelism is low, the issues that arise between ethnic communities tend to have to do with individual civil rights and with the set of opportunities available to individuals of different ethnic origins, and with the constraints they have to overcome in the pursuit of their life goals. In short, the issues have to do with the conditions necessary for full citizenship: for full participation of individuals in the institutional system of the society. On the other hand, if parallelism is high, the issues that tend to come up are those pertaining to what participants consider group rights, and with the resources necessary for institutional building, maintenance, and expansion.

Hypothesis 3   The greater the social and institutional ethnic parallelism in a society, the more the structures of the political system, especially the central one, become objects of controversy and power confrontations. In modern societies at least, the state apparatus is a critical instrument for institutional building, either in economic, educational, or cultural spheres. That is to say, it is the main organ for the mobilization of resources, material and social, for collective ventures. It is thus almost inevitable that an ethnic community with an institutional system will attempt to appropriate itself the state apparatus or some of its powers, and use it for its own institutional objectives. It is also equally inevitable that other organized ethnic communities will resist such attempts at self-appropriation. As a result, the structure of the state apparatus tends to be a regular object of conflict between organized ethnic communities. This is one reason why in societies with a high degree of parallelism, such matters as the constitution, the distribution of powers, the composition of the bureaucracy, and the selection of political party leaders tend to regularly become matters of interethnic controversy. Of course, the degree of tension depends on the extent of parallelism and on the degree to which one of the ethnic communities has already appropriated itself the state apparatus.

Modes of Incorporation in the Society

Another set of implications of the degree of parallelism pertains to the conditions and mechanisms of incorporation in the societal institutions, and of integration of the society itself. It follows from the previous discussion that, in one instance, we are dealing with processes whereby individuals become full-fledged members of the society. Obviously, the processes involved will tend to be different: incorporating, for example, the children of a cohort of immigrants in a school poses a different kind of demand on the educational institution than would the incorporation of an ethnic school. From one's experience in Canada, it is also easy to sense that the incorporation of cohorts of immigrants in the political parties, government agencies, and bureaucracies is not quite the same kind of phenomenon as the incorporation of an ethnic group that disposes of a formal political structure for corporate action. One situation involves cohorts of individuals, while the other involves organizational structures, and the adjustments that the political system has to make for their incorporation is quite different in each instance.

Threats to societal integration stem from difficulties in or the failure of incorporation. A cohort of disadvantaged individuals, whose aspirations for whatever life goals they happen to value are systematically thwarted, represents one type of frustration and one source of pressure for change, in the event it becomes mobilized. On the one hand, organizational elites, potential elites, and would-be entrepreneurs who see their organizations as being disadvantaged in the sense of having poor or no chance for growth, who experience limited access to capital and other necessary organizational resources, who feel the low status and power of their organizations, and who see limited possibilities of ameliorating the situation usually experience a different type of frustration and represent a source of pressure for a different kind of institutional change.

Generally, in one case, societal integration is fostered through structures and mechanisms facilitating the participation of individuals of different ethnic origins in societal institutions and the attainment of their personal goals; in the other case, it is fostered through structural accommodations and exchanges that facilitate the existence and growth of institutional structures with which members of ethnic communities are identified, and in which they try to attain their goals in particular spheres of activity.

CONCLUSION

In this essay, I have tried to show that the problems of ethnic stratification and of societal integration can be quite different under different degrees of parallelism. By way of conclusion, I would like to mention some other characteristics of ethnic communities that can interact with the degree of parallelism and as a result, tend to accentuate or modify the situations and processes discussed above. These characteristics are those that pertain to the group's capacity for concerted action. The problems of conflict, interorganizational bargaining, and definition of domains of jurisdiction are no doubt accentuated when the communities involved are well organized for socio-political action. The threat they represent to each other's traditional domains is more serious if the capacity for concerted action is high. On the other hand, the organization that this capacity represents may make it easier to engage in a bargaining process, resulting in new arrangements.

Under conditions of low parallelism, the sources of tensions between communities tend to be more situational, and tend to involve individuals – either individually or grouped in associations – rather than institutional systems. The capacity for concerted action in such instances tends to manifest itself in interest-group associations concerned with specific issues.

There are many factors that are related to the capacity for concerted action of ethnic communities. First, there is the type and amount of resources at their disposal. Resources refer to items such as demographic factors, material assets, solidarity, symbols of identification, and commitment to a cause.[9] Second, there are the factors pertaining to the social organization of the ethnic community. Among these, the most important appear to be the following:

1 The first mechanisms for collective action are required. These include: mechanisms for the collection and processing of information about the community, its population, its social, economic, and political situation, its resources; procedures for and the organizational channels through which issues can be raised and various points of view expressed; and procedures for reaching decisions and implementing them. It also involves an appropriate network of communication, especially between the leadership and the members of the community or segments of it. This can manifest itself in various ways, all the way from personal contacts to a complex organization with extensive grass roots.

2 The structure of authority is also important, that is, the set of roles vested with the authority required to make the above mechanisms operational.

3 A related feature is the presence or absence of an institutionally differentiated political function, that is, of specifically governmental organizations. In some ethnic communities, concerted action is organized through religious institutions; in others, cultural institutions (e.g., mass media, cultural associations) incorporate the collective decision-making function. But in still others, there are political and administrative structures. In some communities, there are various social elites playing a political role, but no political elite as such, while in others, both types of elites exist.

4 Another aspect of the capacity for concerted action concerns the ability to motivate and/or to constrain members of the community to participate and provide the necessary inputs of effort, time, and financial resources.

5 The degree of autonomy in the organization of action is also important. Communication networks may exist; mechanisms and procedures for collecting information and reaching decisions may be in place; means of social control may be available; but the use of these various elements of organization by the elite of a group may be subject to more or less extensive external controls. An ethnic organization may have a "client" relationship to another organization, depending on it for a significant part of its funds or of its technical expertise. The capacity for concerted action of such an organization is limited by whatever the interests of the "patron" organization happen to be.

6 Finally, a certain consensus among the segments of the community about what constitutes a matter for collective action, or about the definition and choice of alternatives as to what needs to be done is necessary. Differences of views and interest will usually exist among members of an ethnic community. These differences may stem from the adherence to somewhat different values, from differences in economic interests, or in

political ideologies. But whatever the source, the result is the presence of competing definitions of the situation, the problems, and their solutions. Mechanisms must exist for the formulation of super-ordinate goals if any concerted action is to occur.

It would be useful to explore further the impact of the capacity for concerted action on ethnic stratification and on the character and degree of societal integration, especially as variations in this capacity occur in conditions of high, in contrast to low, ethnic parallelism. It has been the objective of this essay to show that if the analysis of such phenomena as the degree of ethnic stratification and the degree and mode of incorporation of ethnic communities in the society takes account of the existing patterns of structural differentiation, it is likely to yield useful results, from both a theoretical and a policy perspective. Moreover, a greater understanding of the sociological features of different patterns of ethnic differentiation would be useful for a more fruitful analysis of the processes of conflict and change in interethnic relations.

CHAPTER THREE

Economic and Instrumental Aspects of Ethnic Inequality*[1]

An examination of the literature reveals that studies of ethnic stratification are carried out within the orientation of a particular theoretical perspective whether this is explicitly acknowledged or not. Moreover, three perspectives organize most of the existing research in the area of ethnic stratification: the individual competition approach, the class approach, and the conflict or social closure approach. These perspectives have oriented much of the study of stratification generally and of ethnic stratification in particular.[2] The first has received the most attention in the empirical literature, but the other two have been at the origin of models and hypotheses and some empirical research as well.

This paper attempts to describe the three perspectives and to examine their implications for ethnic stratification. Three dimensions of ethnic stratification and the ways they are dealt with in each approach are examined. First, the analysis considers the sources of ethnic inequality and the hypotheses to which each approach leads. Second, whether and to what extent each approach views ethnicity as an asset or a liability for various categories of social actors in the socioeconomic system is examined. This question is dealt with in relation to the orientations and strategies that people are likely to adopt with regard to their ethnic identity and background. Finally, what each approach identities as the main occasions of interethnic conflict is considered briefly.

---

* "Ethnic Stratification Viewed from Three Theoretical Perspectives," in *Social Stratification: Canada*, 2nd edition, edited by J.E. Curtis, and W.G. Scott (Toronto: Prentice-Hall, 1979), 270–94.

The analysis is limited to ethnic stratification in its socioeconomic or instrumental aspects. Status or symbolic stratification among ethnic groups will not be considered. Though the three aspects of ethnic stratification selected for analysis are interrelated, their inter-connections will not be analyzed systematically.

First, applying the three perspectives to the analysis of ethnic stratification, an attempt is made to show that each approach focuses on different features of the organization of work and of the related institutions – different structural conditions within which people work and pursue careers. Second, given differences in structural conditions, each points to different social organizational mechanisms by means of which people cope with these conditions. Third, the actors or decision-making units seen as critical in the stratification system differ from one perspective to the other. Finally, the processes that the actors must set in motion, the factors they must activate or manipulate in order to reach their career goals and certain income levels, are also different according to the approach adopted.

The next three sections of the essay take up each of the approaches consecutively. The fourth section deals briefly with changes in the structural conditions of work and how such changes can interact with particular configurations of ethnic diversity and affect the shape of ethnic stratification.[3]

Each approach captures different aspects of the social structure and different social processes.[4] The approaches should be seen as complementing rather than opposing each other: each has something significant to reveal about social reality.

It is important to emphasize that the analysis is not meant to apply to all types of ethnic diversity. The pertinent type of situation is that of "ethnic heterogeneity" as distinct from "ethnic segmentation."[5] The concern is with structures and processes in situations where the different ethnic groups participate in a common institutional system, especially those that have to do, directly or indirectly, with the organization of work. In plural situations where ethnic groups function in parallel institutional systems, and to the extent that they do so (since institutional parallelism is a matter of degree), somewhat different structures and processes are involved. It would be inappropriate to use the models and propositions presented here under each of the three approaches for an analysis of stratification in ethnically segmented societies.

INDIVIDUAL COMPETITION APPROACH

In this approach,[6] the organization of work is seen as consisting of a collection of interrelated occupations involving complex tasks and thus requiring different kinds and levels of skills. The result is an organization that is hierarchically shaped, largely as a result of technological and

administrative requirements. Another basic premise of this approach is
that those who are to occupy the positions in that structure differ in
motivation and/or ability to perform the tasks associated with the different
positions. The motivation and ability are determined by such factors in
the individual's biography as family influences, educational background,
and experience.

The processes whereby the supply of individuals with different kinds and
levels of skills are allocated among the positions in the occupational structure are embedded in labour market institutions. The main components
of these institutions are, of course, employers and potential employees,
and the mechanisms through which they relate to one another. The critical
function of these mechanisms is to permit the flow of information between
the two categories of individuals: information for potential employees as
to what jobs are available and what conditions are offered by various
employers; information that would reveal to employers what is likely to be
the true productivity of different individuals.[7] This flow of information is
the essential ingredient of the bargaining process; and it allows the necessary
comparisons among employers or among potential employees.

In this perspective, the distribution of earnings results from the interplay
among these three phenomena: an occupational structure, a supply of
individuals with characteristics relevant for the performance of occupational tasks, and institutionalized mechanisms that allocate the supply of
workers throughout the structure. A basic proposition in such a system is
that individuals are rewarded according to their productivity. This proposition is based on the assumption of a perfectly competitive labour market.
But it is also held to be applicable under conditions of imperfect competition due to factors such as incomplete information, the existence of
monopolies, or an individual's social attachments and loyalties. The propositions are still considered applicable, but the processes of allocation
operate inadequately and take much longer to have their effect than they
would if conditions of perfect competition prevailed.

The actor considered critical in this approach is the person acting as
an individual, autonomous agent. As someone selling his labour, the actor
is faced with the opportunities offered by the occupational structure, and
what he has to take advantage of are the processes leading to information
about it. This actor operates within a labour market in which employers
buy labour services: information about employers and the conditions they
offer is also important. Finally, the actor must engage in the more or less
explicit bargaining with possible employers. Once the actor is employed,
the factors that count are those related to job performance (with given
technology, materials, and organization).

The individual actor, then, faces an occupational structure, a labour
market, and a technological/organizational system. His eventual productivity

within those parameters is a function of three sets of factors. First, there are those related to finding the best possible niche in the occupational structure. They include access to information, opportunities to discover one's potential, and the resources for the geographical mobility that may be required. Second, there are factors related to the ability for "impression management," since one is involved in "judgmental competition."[8] Finally, there are those affecting one's proficiency in the performance of an occupational task. At the actor's disposal are personal resources: motivation, talent, physical energy, training, material resources, contacts,[9] and whatever other personal characteristics may be relevant.[10]

How is this approach applied to situations of ethnic heterogeneity? What sorts of hypotheses does it allow to be formulated concerning ethnic stratification? These questions will be examined in relation to three issues indicated earlier: the source of ethnic inequality; whether ethnicity is an asset or a liability and the related orientations that individuals are likely to adopt with regard to their ethnic origin; and the occasions of ethnic conflict.

Sources of Ethnic Inequality

If one observes occupational and income differences among people of different ethnic origins, they are due, according to this model, to the distribution of relevant personal attributes, across ethnic groups – attributes which affect the processes of allocation in the occupational structure and performance on the job. Two kinds of attributes have been given considerable attention in studies, and could be classified under this approach: personal resources and inter-ethnic attitudes and the accompanying discrimination. These attributes are in turn seen as the result of factors such as child rearing practices, religious values, achievement and present/future orientations and education.

Personal resources are important for three kinds of processes: gaining access to information, bargaining with employers and performing on the job. While some resources may be relevant to all three processes (e.g., motivation, education), some are more pertinent for some of these processes than for others. Networks of contacts appear as particularly relevant for access to information about jobs (Granovetter 1974). A network confined to an ethnic community will affect access to pertinent labour market information. Abilities for impression management and persuasive communication are important in the bargaining process. If cultural and linguistic differences exist between employer and potential employee, the latter's ethnic origin may be a liability compared to a competitor who shares the employer's cultural background and language. Finally, there are resources more directly related to the performance of occupational tasks such as specialized skills and experience, and achievement motivation.

The central point is that because of their cultural background and community attachments, members of different ethnic communities acquire and maintain personal attributes which affect their ability to function in the labour market, to find a niche in the occupational structure such that they can reach their optimal level of output. Thus, in a perfectly competitive system, if different ethnic groups are allocated differently, it is, in part, because they are unequal in their competitive ability either in teems of taking advantage of existing opportunities or in terms of performance on the job.

It is recognized, however, that there are imperfections in the labour market – imperfections stemming from such factors as the difficulties of moving people around, the costs of making information widely available, or the difficulties of making systematic comparisons either among employers or among potential recruits for a job. Insofar as there are such imperfections, ethnic inequalities can be the result of the interaction between them and certain ethnic characteristics. For example, social attachments increase the difficulties of moving people around; thus, differences among ethnic groups in the proportion of their members with strong ethnic ties would explain part of the variations in ethnic differences in income. Ethnicity accentuates certain rigidities in the functioning of labour markets or brings rigidities of its own.

Discrimination is also recognized as generating ethnic inequalities in this perspective. Discrimination derives from prejudice and stereotypes which, it must be underlined, are seen as characteristics of individuals. Whether they behave discriminatorily depends on their circumstances. As will be seen later, discrimination is approached differently in the other perspectives.

One effect of prejudice and stereotypes in this approach is to prevent individuals from either recognizing the right cues as to the true productivity of potential employees (if one is an employer) or from recognizing the best opportunities (if one is looking for a job). Another effect is to lead individuals to prefer certain types of people either as employers or as employees. Thus, the distribution of members of different ethnic groups in the occupational structure is affected by ethnic differences, blinding either employers or employees to what would be in their economic interests; or by ethnic identity being associated with patterns of positive and negative inter-ethnic attitudes.

In this approach, discrimination is considered possible only because there are imperfections in the market; that is, rigidities which make it impossible for the market to effect rapid adjustments by eliminating the factors that decrease productivity. For example, according to the purely competitive model, discriminating employers would eventually lose out to the non-discriminating ones, who hire the best workers at the lowest price, irrespective of ethnic origin. But because there are imperfections in the market, discriminating employers can frequently remain in the market.

Ethnicity as Asset or Liability, and Orientation toward One's Ethnic Identity

In the individual competition approach, then, ethnicity is either a determinant of personal resources or attitudes associated with job placement processes and productivity, or a factor bringing about or accentuating imperfections in the labour market. In this approach, the relevance of ethnicity stems from the fact that it determines individual characteristics. It provides the individual, whether buyer or seller of labour, with a package of traits and attitudes that may be useful or detrimental in relation to labour market processes.

The occupational structure and the labour market are ethnically neutral: in their ideal form, they are free of ethnicity or of any other phenomena such as sex or religious affiliation. In other words, the occupational structure and the labour market are seen as dissociated from other elements of the social organization of society. When factors such as ethnicity enter into the situation, it is as attributes of individuals who function in an ethnicity-free structure.

With this approach, and assuming no prejudice at all, we would hypothesize that individuals would adopt a personal strategy of selective acculturation: people would tend to retain those elements of their ethnic background and affiliation that help in acquiring information, in bargaining with employers, or in performing the job. A variation of this hypothesis is that members of some ethnic groups have a greater adaptive capacity,[11] possess cultural elements that are more suited to the requirements of a particular type of socioeconomic system than others, and therefore would tend to retain those elements. The proposition that ethnic cultures are slowly disappearing, giving way to a technological culture, is another variation of the selective acculturation hypothesis. Indeed, if each group retains from its culture only those elements that are useful in a particular technological/ economic environment, a cultural homogenization is inevitable.

Under conditions of prejudice and discrimination, the model predicts individuals will tend to adopt a personal strategy of complete assimilation, that is removal of all elements that serve as cues to one's ethnic origin; this would be one of the rational strategies to adopt. Underlying this hypothesis, however, is the assumption that ethnic traits are under one's control. To a considerable extent, this is the case. But what happens when a trait, such as colour, cannot be removed or kept in the private sphere of the person's life, or where it can be done, only with great difficulty, as with language?[12] In such instances, since individual strategies are not useful, there would be a tendency toward collective action.[13] To the extent that acculturation and individual integration are difficult or impossible, people will tend to revert to collective action in order to reduce or eliminate the discriminatory behaviour of employers or the institutional circumstances that lead the employers to discrimination. On the other hand, the more control individuals have over their ethnic traits, the more they will tend to adopt individual strategies of either selective or complete assimilation. This does not mean, of course, that they will not support actions aimed at reducing discrimination in the labour market. It is a matter of direction of the main propensity.

However, even in completely benign conditions, sheer ethnic differences may be a liability as well as an asset, depending on whether one belongs to a dominant or a subordinate group. This is particularly evident in the case of linguistic differences. For instance, linguistic and other cultural differences between employer and employee may reduce the latter's ability for impression management or for the manipulation of social networks to reach certain career goals. If the employee belongs to the same ethnic group as the employer, he will generally be in a position of relative advantage compared to one who is not. The model, then, leads to the hypothesis that members of the dominant ethnic group (the one to which most employers belong) would tend to make the most of that, while others would tend toward acculturation and structural assimilation – the adoption of the dominant culture and integration into networks connected with the dominant group. Such processes, however, would especially occur under conditions of prejudice and discrimination.

This approach leads to the proposition that ethnicity can be a liability in the labour market. Therefore, individuals who are not members of the dominant ethnic group tend to adopt a personal strategy of acculturation and integration. In some instances, certain elements of the ethnic background may be useful, leading to personal strategies of selective acculturation and integration. In either case, the result is a tendency toward cultural homogenization and the dissolution of ethnic boundaries.[14] However, if the ethnic characteristics are beyond the individual's control, there will be a tendency for collective strategies aimed at controlling the behaviour of employers. For members of the dominant ethnic group, however, ethnic identity and background tend to be an asset. They do not have to incur the social and psychic costs of acculturation for the pursuit of their careers.

Occasions of Inter-Ethnic Conflict

In this approach, intolerance is a matter of individual attitudes and behaviour that originate in early socialization, or in the psychological stress experienced in life situations. Accordingly, tolerance is increased through education, favourable intergroup contacts, and legal constraints. Whether practised by employers or employees, prejudice is a phenomenon that prevents the labour market from functioning well; it introduces imperfections, such as individuals not being allocated in the occupational structure according to potential or not being rewarded according to productivity. It is the failure (because of individual intolerance) to apply appropriate labour market or job performance criteria that occasions conflict. Typically, the issues involved fall under the category of "equality of opportunity for all." Discontent occurs when the actual operation of the labour market fails to approximate the ideal model; when facing an occupational structure and labour market mechanisms, some individuals, because of their ethnicity, are not able to operate as effectively as others.

CLASS APPROACH

The class approach[15] captures different features of the organization of work. The structural conditions that are considered important are those that derive from the social organization of production. The basic social phenomena are those of contract and property. In a class society, these phenomena become defined and institutionalized in certain ways. A contractual system defines the mutual obligations, prerogatives, and restrictions in specific types of social relations. Property, on the other hand, is a system of rights in relation to objects. The essential property rights "may be classified as those of use, of control (specifying who shall use and for what purposes) and of disposal" (Parsons 1960: 146). The content of contracts as well as the "legitimate and illegitimate means of securing the assent of the other party to a contract" (145) are usually defined within the perimeters of socially established rights.

In a class society, the crucial social relationships are those that pertain to the organization of production, and the definitions of property rights that are embedded in the institutionalized contract define the relationships of the groupings to the means of production. As stated by Giddens, the character of the property relations that constitute the basis of the class system is: "a minority of 'non-producers,' who control the means of production, are able to use this position of control to extract from the majority of 'producers' the surplus product which is the source of their livelihood" (1973: 28).

The basic social relations in a class system are those of conflict and mutual dependence. In the basic dichotomous system, classes are "placed in a situation of reciprocity such that neither class can escape from the relationship without thereby losing its identity as a distinct 'class.'" On the other hand, the interests of the classes are "at the same time mutually exclusive, and form the basis for the potential outbreak of open struggles" (Giddens 1973: 29). Classes are conflict groups who need each other, but whose interests are fundamentally opposed. This opposition does not necessarily involve class consciousness and mobilization; it is based on contradictory interests, a contradiction rooted in particular institutional forms of property and contract.

A class system usually involves more than the basic class dichotomy. There is considerable debate among class analysts as to the criteria that should be used to identify other classes accompanying the basic dichotomy and for defining their boundaries. This debate will not be reviewed here.[16] There are two critical points regarding the emergence of a more complex class system. First, classes or quasi-class groupings[17] emerge as a result of a further differentiation of the *social* organizations of production. Poulantzas, for instance, analyzes the differentiation that has emerged historically between "ownership," which refers to the "real economic control of the means of production to given uses ... to dispose of the products obtained," and "possession," which refers to "the actual control over the physical operation of production" (1975: 18). The relations of possession can become further differentiated between those having to do with the control of the physical means of production and those pertaining to the control over labour power (supervisory relations). In addition to the basic dichotomy, there may exist other classes, such as the petite bourgeoisie, or "contradictory class positions," such as with managers or semi-autonomous wage-earners (Wright 1976: 29–31). The role of such additional classes or quasi-class groupings cannot be understood outside the context of the basic class relations that provide the fundamental structure of the social organization of economic production in a society.

Classes themselves can be internally differentiated as well. Here, the distinction between the social and the technical division of labour is important. The class structure pertains to the social relations that surround the organization of economic production. But there is also a division of labour based on the differentiation of activities in relation to such factors as the nature of the task and the technology available for its performance. The technical division of labour exists both within and between classes. As a result the occupational structure tells a poor and perhaps misleading tale about the class structure, that is, the social relations of production. But it is relevant for the analysis of differentiations within classes, because these relate to mobilization for concerted action in the pursuit of class interests.

In an organization of production, the significant social relationships are not those between individuals or between coalitions of individuals whose interest in a particular segment of the occupational structure happen to coincide. Rather, the critical social units are classes which are groupings whose interests are defined in relation to the basic social organization of production. The distribution of income is determined by the character of the relationships between classes. The critical factor in that relationship is the relative power of the classes. The conflict may take the form of bargaining, or of a struggle in which the parties attempt to inflict losses on each other, to weaken or destroy their organizational apparatus. The conflict can be geared to two basic types of outcomes: obtaining as large a share as possible of the benefits of production – an outcome occurring within an existing class structure; or bringing about extensive structural modification of the class system itself.

The source of power that appears to be of greatest interest is the organization for collective action that exists within each class, and perhaps especially among those who sell labour. A critical area of concern, then, pertains to the conditions of class mobilization and of effective collective action.[18]

Sources of Ethnic Inequality

Since the critical social groupings are classes and since these are defined in terms of their relationship to the modes of production, there appears to be little room for ethnicity as a factor in the social organization of the system of work and of the critical relationships that it entails. In other words, ethnicity is not seen as a dynamic element of the social organization of a community that could impinge on the structuring of the class system. Rather, it is the system of production and the particular institutionalization of property relationships which are the determinant factors.

The ethnic differentiation of a community, however, may play a role in the historical formation of classes. Because of circumstances, individuals who are the active agents in the formation of a class, such as the bourgeoisie, may be of an ethnic origin different from those who end up in the class selling their labour. Through some sort of historical "accident," class cleavages would thus coincide with ethnic cleavages – a coincidence which would account for observed ethnic inequalities. The same argument could be true for the composition of other classes (petty bourgeoisie) or of "contradictory class locations"[19] (managers, small employers).

As long as the boundaries of social classes coincide with those of ethnic groupings, the class model is quite applicable to ethnic differentials in economic benefits. But in its classical form, the model has little to say about ethnic differentials occurring within classes. Ethnic cleavages are seen as having an impact on the dynamics of class relations (as will be seen later), but the approach did not go far in identifying processes through which ethnic stratification would emerge within classes.

To class analysts, ethnicity is an epiphenomenon: even if ethnic cleavages coincide with class cleavages, the true dynamic of the relationship stems from the class interests involved, not the ethnic differences. Generally, one could argue that pure class analysts see ethnicity as bringing about imperfections in class relations somewhat in the way that the individual competition analysts see ethnicity as bringing imperfections in the labour market.

Ethnicity *can be* a basis of social solidarity and social organization. Because of this, it can be seen as "competing" with class – not a very fruitful way of looking at the phenomenon, because it will tend to be seen as a source of embarrassment, of distraction from, or contamination of, the "true" social processes. Rather, ethnicity should be seen as interacting with class in the structuring of societal institutions and in generating inequality. This is the approach adopted by Bonacich (1972, 1976) in her split labour market theory.

According to Bonacich, "a split labour market refers to a difference in the price of labour between two or more groups of workers, holding constant their efficiency and productivity" (1976: 36). The labour market may be split along such lines as ethnicity, sex, and religion. Moreover, ethnic diversity in the labour force does not necessarily yield a split labour market. For a split condition to occur, the ethnic groups in the economic system must have such unequal resources and/or goals that their prices to employers are different. For instance, recruits from a poorer economy may offer their labour at a cheaper price; or they may sell it more cheaply out of ignorance of the unfamiliar economy; or they may be badly organized or without external protection and therefore more likely to strike a poor bargain (Bonacich 1972: 549–50).

Ethnic groups who compose the labour force may have such a different socioeconomic history and/or may exhibit such differences in their sociopolitical organization that, on the aggregate, the experience of their members as sellers of labour differs in some significant way. Bonacich's model recognizes a significant role to ethnicity (or other so-called ascriptive factors) in the social organization of the labour market. In class analysis terms, this means that ethnicity can be the basis for the formation of groups (sub-classes?) that have a different position in the basic social relation of production. The result of an ethnic differentiation of labour in terms of price to employers is a "conflict between three key classes: business, higher paid labour, and cheaper labour" (1972: 553), the last two corresponding to an ethnic cleavage.

These three classes have divergent interests which are at the basis of the dynamics of their conflict. For instance, employers have an interest in as cheap a labour price as possible, and because of this, they are always on the lookout for cheaper labour than that which they presently employ. The higher paid labour, on the other hand, is threatened by the possibility of, or the actual introduction of, cheaper labour, a phenomenon that would undermine its position. The class of cheaper labour wants to sell its labour, but because it is relatively weak (because of ignorance, poor organization, different goals), it is used by employers to undermine the position of the more expensive labour. Thus, as a result of the operation of another basis of social organization – ethnicity – the basic class dichotomy of the classical model is differentiated into a trichotomy involving more complex processes of conflict and interdependence.

At the beginning of this section, mention was made of the debate among class analysts over the delimitation of class boundaries. Wright's argument is that the class system can become differentiated as a result of the imperatives of "three central processes underlying the basic capital-labour relationship: control over the physical means of production; control over labour power; control over investments and resource allocation" (1976: 30). A possible result of this differentiation of the social organization of production is the emergence of "contradictory locations within class relations." The contradiction is due to an inconsistent position with respect to the three control processes. For example, some locations may involve control over labour power but none over the two other factors.[20]

In the classic class approach, economic relations of property determine class positions. Poulantzas, however, argues that political and ideological relations are also important in determining position within class relations (1975: 226–30). Wright attempts to specify Poulantzas' argument by suggesting that political and ideological factors are important in regard to contradictory class positions. For instance, many technicians are close to the working class because they have no control over labour power and over investments and resource allocation, but they are in a contradictory location because they have some control over their immediate labour process. This control not being very extensive, they remain close to the boundary of the working class as far as the organization of production is concerned. For them, however, the status division between mental and manual labour – an ideological factor – could be important and, if used, would tend to push them away from the working class (Wright 1976: 39–40).

Although Wright does not mention it, it is easy to hypothesize that a social factor such as ethnicity could also influence position in a system of class relations. If the incumbents of a particular contradictory location happen to be of the same ethnic origin as that of the members of the bourgeoisie, it may, in certain circumstances, bring them closer to the bourgeoisie through a process of social identification. Wright's argument about contradictory locations and the role of non-economic factors in determining their position in class relations appears to provide an interesting avenue for exploring ethnicity in class relations. If this were the case, class analysis could integrate ethnicity as a significant agent in the structuring of the class system and in the dynamics of class relations rather than treating it at best as a marginal phenomenon or at worst as an epiphenomenon. Indeed, the dynamics that are proper to ethnicity and its role in social organization would be seen as a factor in the determination of the position of some classes in the system of class relations.

Ethnicity as Asset or Liability, and Orientation toward One's Ethnic Identity

For the class of sellers of labour, this approach sees ethnicity as a definite liability. It is a factor of social differentiation that detracts from the critical conflict relevant for social stratification, namely class conflicts. Moreover, as a basis of social solidarity, ethnicity can weaken or prevent class solidarity, a fact that is detrimental to the pursuit of class interests. If the employers/sellers of labour cleavage correspond to an ethnic one, the ethnic difference tends to facilitate the exploitative process because the dominance of the class of employers can be buttressed by ideologies of racial, cultural, or social superiority. In the split labour market situation, the ethnic differentiation is a source of antagonisms within the class of sellers of labour (as well as between the sub-classes of sellers and the class of buyers of labour) and thus plays against the interests of the class as a whole. So under this perspective, the rational strategy to adopt is acculturation and assimilation as rapidly as possible.

For the class of employers, however, ethnic difference in the supply of labour can be an asset, either because it can be used to undermine the position of that segment of the labour force that has acquired a certain level of benefits from employers, or because, being a source of antagonism within the labour force, it can prevent or weaken employee organization, a fact that is in the interest of employers.

Occasions of Inter-Ethnic Conflict

In the class approach, there is little ethnic conflict, in that it has virtually no dynamism of its own independent of class conflicts. The antagonisms of class interests may be accentuated by ethnic differences, but the basic source of the conflict is found in class relations, not ethnic differences. There are no ethnic interests, only class interests. This is so in Bonacich's theory as well: "Ethnic antagonism is specifically produced by the competition that arises from a price differential" (1972: 554).

To the extent that there are "truly" ethnic conflicts, they are seen as vestiges of the past which will eventually disappear from the class-based social structure.[21] Or they are seen as artificially fomented by employers to weaken the capacity for concerted action by the sellers of labour.[22]

THE GROUP COMPETITION
OR "SOCIAL CLOSURE" APPROACH

A third approach[23] focuses on different aspects of the labour market and of the occupational structure and on different occupational attainment behaviours as relevant in determining the allocation of workers in the structure and the distribution of earnings. To a large extent, this approach focuses on what the two previous approaches consider as imperfections. These imperfections, it will be recalled, stem primarily from the fact that non-economic factors, which are seen as exogenous to the organization of economic activity, distort either market or power conflict processes. Both approaches view non-economic factors as preventing complete actualization of the true interests of the actors involved. While the first two approaches dissociate the economic and non-economic basis of social organization, the third approach sees them as inevitably intermeshed. The third approach systematizes, incorporates as an integral part of its framework what the other two consider as imperfections. This is reflected in the conceptualization of the organization of work, of the social unit that is seen as the critical actor, and of the dynamics through which the system functions.

To begin with, not all jobs are seen as disconnected from each other: some jobs are conditions for other jobs in a more or less rigid step-by-step system of advancement; other jobs are in relationships of functional interdependence with each other; others are not interdependent but are located in the same physical and social space. As a result of such interconnection, the labour market can be described as being organized into a series of occupational domains[24] with more or less clearly defined boundaries. These domains or sets of jobs are not purely physical or statistical groupings; rather, they become established through social and technical processes and constitute the structure of opportunities and constraints within which workers build careers.[25]

Moreover, the labour market institutions that link individuals to the occupational structure exhibit a corresponding pattern of segmentation. Certain channels of information and influence lead to certain sets of jobs or domains and not to others. These networks of job channels are also seen as socially organized and not simply as mechanisms for the diffusion of information.

Several features of these domains and labour market channels are seen as problematic: criteria for jobs to be included in a domain; criteria of eligibility to the various domains and jobs within the domains; rules through which mobility from one job to another is regulated; stratification among jobs within a domain; linkages among points in channels of information; and so on. These aspects of the organization of work or of particular domains are not taken as given, but as modifiable. They are not seen as emerging from purely technical imperatives, as if technology had a logic of its own, independent of the actors who have an interest in the organization of the work-setting. Rather, within certain technical and economic parameters, the organization of work itself, as well as the factors that determine one's place in that organization, are objects of individual and social action. In other words, the importance of the various aspects of the structure stems not from the fact that one's place in it and in the corresponding distribution of earnings is the result of "finding the best possible job," but of processes whereby the boundaries of occupational domains, their internal organization, and the rules governing behaviour within them are defined.

In a system of occupations and jobs organized into domains, taking advantage of opportunities takes a meaning quite different from the one it has in a system conceived as an array of individual positions. Rather than being a question of finding out about available positions and of bargaining over the conditions of employment, it is a matter of establishing control over a domain or a segment of it. Such control may be more or less extensive; but extending control over a domain, over its definition and internal organization, is an important mechanism for increasing one's access to economic rewards. And since to an occupational structure organized in domains there corresponds a segmented system of channels of access, taking advantage of opportunities also means controlling access to the channels of information and influence.

A critical issue, then, concerns the kind of social organization that will tend to emerge, especially among workers, in response to or in order to deal with conditions characterizing a system of work structured into domains. What will tend to be the distinguishing features of that social organization? Since the critical social process is the extension of control over a domain, the problem is to identify the features of the social organization stemming from the imperatives of control.

The Weberian notion of social closure. is basic in this connection: "The relationship will be known as 'closed' to those on the outside, so far as and to the extent that ... the participation of certain persons is excluded, limited, or subject to conditions" (1969: 97).[26] Weber identifies three main categories of motivations for restrictive social relationships: "the maintenance of quality and eventually that of prestige and the opportunity deriving from it to enjoy honor and possibly even profit;" "the scarcity of opportunities in relation to the needs of consumption"; and "the scarcity of opportunities for gaining a livelihood" (101–2). Because of this scarcity, an interest arises for restricting numbers relative to opportunities. This involves establishing monopoly over a set of given opportunities, a process which in turn entails social exclusion or regulated entry.[27]

Different elements of social organization can emerge for carrying out social closure; for instance, there is "gatekeeping." The gatekeeper is one who has access to information about jobs (and therefore controls who will obtain that information) and who may also have influence on the selection of persons to occupy various positions.[28] A related phenomenon is sponsorship. Defining the content of rules is another important mechanism for regulating participation. Of course, the rules defining the conditions of entry are critical here. But other kinds of rules can also be important. Language requirements affect the distribution of control of occupational domains: a given specification will be to the advantage of some and to the disadvantage of others. Because competence in the language used in an organization is necessary for job performance and success, the existing linguistic rules have an impact on career contours, access to jobs, and information about opportunities. These are matters of serious contention in the competition for ethnic control over domains.[29]

Seniority rules constitute another example. Sayles observed that "the rank and file find in the seniority provisions of the contract a fruitful means of obtaining new vested interests, not at the expense of management but rather at the expense of groups and individuals within the plant … Within the plant, the purposeful use of seniority as a means of gaining individual and group advantage is a recognized and tacitly accepted phenomenon" (1952: 56).

The social actors in this approach are not persons acting individually, but as members of a mobilized collectivity – mobilized for the pursuit of certain advantages. Becoming employed is not just a question of getting a job; it is also a matter of joining a group that has certain interests in a particular department, a particular organization, occupation, or an otherwise defined domain and that expects its members to at least protect if not actively pursue these interests. One's competitors for scarce opportunities are not simply other individuals; they are "outsiders," members of another collectivity.[30]

What counts in "taking advantage of opportunities," is not so much individual skills (either to obtain job information, for impression management, or for job performance)[31] as the effectiveness of the social organization for the control of domains and of access to them developed by the group with which one is affiliated. This effectiveness depends on gatekeeping and sponsorship mechanisms, on the applications of rules having a direct or indirect impact on access to the opportunities in the domain, and on the group's ability to pressure its own members to stay in line.

What is the pertinence of this approach for ethnic stratification? Does it lead to similar or different hypotheses as the previous ones? Its implications for ethnic stratification will be reviewed under the same three major headings.

Sources of Ethnic Inequality

In the first approach, observed income and occupational differentials between ethnic groups were thought to be the result of differences in personal resources of relevance for productivity or of imperfections in the labour market. With the present approach, such differentials are thought to be caused by differences in the group's ability to organize so as to either take or maintain control of a particular work domain. This involves as indicated above, ethnic control of gatekeeping positions, ethnic sponsorship, and struggles over rules and processes of selection that may directly or indirectly affect the ethnic distribution of advantages.

The resources that are critical in this regard are group resources, such as leadership, cohesive social networks,[32] mutual trust, means of communication. Personal resources are not irrelevant, but the important point is that the social organization of the group (cohesion, trust) must be such as to allow the sharing of these resources (information, techniques of job performance, etc.) (Coleman 1969). The critical factors in this approach are those that affect the group's capacity to organize occupational goals and to control certain domains and the channels leading to them.

A key question is why the social organization that emerges for the control of occupational domains (either within departments, firms, industries, or occupational specializations) is based on ethnicity, rather than on some other social factor? The social closure model predicts group formation for the monopolization of certain advantages. But on what basis will groups get formed? Theoretically, almost any factor of social differentiation can provide such a basis: age, sex, ethnicity, religion, political or social ideology, language, and so on. In fact, a systematic survey of work settings in a society like Canada would show that the basis of group formation varies considerably from one type of work setting to another. For instance, in organizations dealing with ideas, such as university departments and churches, school of thought and social ideology would be more likely to be the basis of group formation for occupational control than in organizations producing commodities.

But how can the issue of variations in the basis of group formation be approached? Mayhew, in his discussion of the continuing importance of ascription in modern societies, argues that "the staying power and functional capacity of ascription can be summed up in three words: it is cheap. Ascription involves using an existent, pre-established structure as a resource rather than creating a new specialized structure for the same purpose" (1968: 110). This principle can be applied to the formation of an organization for social closure: it will tend to occur on the basis of existent, pre-established structures of social relationships. Thus, if for historical, ecological, or other reasons, a community is structured along ethnic lines, that existing structure will tend to be reproduced in the organization of work and of labour market processes.

As was mentioned earlier, occupational domains are not purely physical or statistical groupings. Rather, they are socially organized in that their boundaries and their internal organization are socially, and not purely technically, determined. Mayhew's argument suggests that the social organization of occupational domains will reflect the social organization of the community in which they are located, simply because it is cheaper and more expedient to use existing structures than to build new ones. Because of this, it can be said that the social closure approach does not assume the occupational structure and the labour market institutions to be necessarily free of ethnicity or ethnically neutral; it is so only if the community is ethnically homogeneous or if ethnicity plays virtually no part in shaping its social structure.

Ethnicity as Asset or Liability and Orientation toward One's Ethnic Identity

While in the first approach, ethnicity was seen as an individual attribute, in this approach, it is seen primarily as a basis of social organization, as a basis for social mobilization and concerted action.[33] In such a perspective, it is an asset, to the extent that the ethnic collectivity has the resources to get organized for the control of occupational domains, and to the extent that its organization will be strong enough to obtain results. If there is a chance of success, a rational strategy is needed to mobilize the existing loyalty, cohesion, and other social assets in the ethnic group for increasing one's advantages in the labour market and/or to compete with other groups attempting to do so.

What is critical, then, is the distribution across ethnic collectivities of the resources and conditions necessary or useful for organization. Generally, there are two interrelated sets of factors that are relevant: those pertaining to the conditions internal to the ethnic collectivities, and those associated with the position that each collectivity occupies in the social, economic, and political structure of the society. A number of characteristics of ethnic collectivities, were already mentioned: level of resources, social cohesion and trust, channels of communication, leadership, and so on. Features of the social organization of an ethnic collectivity emerge, in part, from its own internal attributes and social dynamics, but they are also determined by the circumstances of its position in the social structure.

By looking at the position of the dominant ethnic collectivity, one can say that the institutional system of the society, in its overall dimension, constitutes the "domain" of the dominant ethnic collectivity. This is reflected in the fact that the cultural values of that collectivity are those that are embedded in the institutions of the society: the political, educational, religious, recreational, economic, and legal institutions incorporate features such as definitions of roles, rules for language use, knowledge considered valuable, criteria of evaluation and success, and mechanisms for occupying various positions, especially those of authority, that reflect the cultural system of the dominant group.[34]

As mentioned earlier, in this approach, the institutional system is not ethnicity-free; the dominant ethnic collectivity is the one that has historically succeeded in imposing its own ethnicity on the structure and functioning of the institutions of the society. Needless to say, members of the dominant ethnic group (and those who become integrated into it) have, as a result of this situation, tremendous advantage in the control of occupational domains.

The point illustrated by the case of the dominant ethnic collectivity, and to which this third approach draws our attention, is that a collectivity's capacity to organize for gaining occupational control is not only a function of its internal characteristics but also of the factors that are associated with its position in the social structure, a position that has political, legal, and symbolic, as well as economic components.

Thus, when a collectivity is strong in its capacity to organize, its members will tend to perceive their ethnicity as an asset; when it is weak, however, they will tend to perceive it as a liability. They will tend to show strong assimilationist tendencies, acculturating as rapidly as possible and doing their utmost to gain acceptance by one or another of the existing ethnically-controlled segments of the structure. Generally, the collectivity selected will tend to be the one that controls most, or the most interesting, segments of the occupational structure.

Occasions of Inter-Ethnic Conflict

The social closure approach points to three types of factors that may occasion conflict. Insofar as the organization of work is the result of technological and administrative factors, changes in these areas may well modify the boundaries and/or internal organization of work domains. If this occurs, it is likely to upset the existing distribution of ethnic control over the domains, a situation which can cause conflict.

The experience of discrimination is also an occasion of inter-ethnic conflict. However, the present approach does not see discrimination as an individual phenomenon, but as an institutional and a social one. Institutional discrimination stems directly from the fact that an ethnic collectivity has control over an area of institutional activity and has thus established structures, procedures and rules of behaviour that are in accordance with its own cultural imperatives and interests. Since institutions are not ethnicity-free, discrimination is the result of the very functioning of those institutions.

The unequal treatment that results may become an occasion of conflict between members of the collectivity victimized by the institutional practices and those that benefit by them. Whether such processes and their consequences are intentional or not, on the part of individuals, the effect is equally real and may lead the institutionally disadvantaged to challenge the group they see as responsible for the institutions and their functioning.

Social discrimination, on the other hand, occurs when the competition for the control of occupational domains takes place under norms considered illegitimate. If one of the parties in the competition engages in practices considered unacceptable (e.g., undercutting, strikebreaking, parachuting), it will be an occasion of interethnic conflict. The dynamics of such discriminatory practices are those of intense group competition rather than those of individual prejudice.

Conflict may also be occasioned when the strength and/or aspiration of an ethnic collectivity changes. This can result from immigration or internal migrations, changes in the level of personal resources within the collectivity as a consequence of a general increase in the standard of living, appearance of a new class of leaders in the community, the "demonstration effect" of the activities of other groups, and so on. An increase in the relative strength and/or aspiration of a collectivity could lead it to attempt to expand the size or number of occupational domains under its control – attempts which are likely to occasion conflict. Or it could lead it to attempt to change its social, legal, or political status, such as changing the legal status of its language. By affecting its relative position in the social structure, such changes could improve the collectivity's advantage in the competition over occupation (and other) domains. The changes are thus likely to be resisted by other collectivities who feel they would become relatively disadvantaged – another occasion of conflict.

VARIATIONS IN OCCUPATIONAL OR CLASS STRUCTURE AND ETHNIC DIVERSITY

Up to now, the occupational structure, labour market institutions, and class structure have been taken as given. But these structures and institutions can differ from one community or region to another, or change with time, variations which can be associated with certain patterns of ethnic stratification. The three approaches draw attention to different components of the structure that are important to consider.

With the individual competition approach, the focus is on the number of positions in the various occupational categories, on introduction of new occupations, or elimination of existing ones. A secondary focus is on the labour market mechanisms, such as those for the distribution of occupational information. The group competition or social closure approach is concerned with variations in the pattern of segmentation or discontinuities in occupational structure, and in networks of labour market channels and mechanisms. New patterns may emerge at the level of the economy as a whole, in particular industries, firms, or occupations. Organizational changes or differentiation can be at the origin of new domain boundaries. The emergence of specializations or sub-specializations may signal the appearance of new domains. Finally, what is important in the class model is the social organization of production and the particular structuring of property relationships that it entails. Important changes are those that pertain to the internal differentiation of classes, to differentiation of the class system through emergence of new classes, of contradictory class positions, or through the progressive disappearance of a class, and to the conditions of class conflict and its outcome.

Variations in the structural components can occur as a result of a multiplicity of factors. For instance, the functioning of the system itself can be at the origin of structural changes, as in the case of differentiation of control over the physical means of production from the control over labour power that came with expansion of the system. Technological changes, such as automation, and the implementation of new theories of management or of the organization of the work process can redefine work domains, create new positions, and eliminate some. Legislation concerning labour-management relationships, work practices, labour market processes, and so on, can also have an impact.

The interaction of a particular social and technical division of labour with the characteristics of different ethnic categories of participants in the economy may have an impact on the patterns of ethnic stratification. For instance, in their review of the literature on occupational concentration of immigrants, Yancey *et al.* point out that "to understand the occupational concentrations of immigrants, it is necessary to consider both the diverse educational and occupational skills which immigrants brought, as well as the specific work opportunities which were available at the time of their arrival" (1976: 392–3).

The interaction of the character of the economic structure with the characteristics of an ethnically differentiated labour force is also clear in Willhelm's argument that automation is eliminating jobs for which blacks are the primary suppliers of labour and, as a result, blacks will progressively become more and more marginal to the economy: the black worker is becoming "not so much economically exploited as he is irrelevant" (1970: 162). A number of years ago, Rayack presented evidence which "indicated that the relative rise in the position of the Negro was a product of the acute labour shortages which persisted throughout the war and post war period of 1940–48, shortages which opened up a wider range of job opportunities for Negroes" (1961: 214). In a similar vein, Tobin argues that "by

far the most powerful factor determining the economic status (both absolute and relative) of Negroes is the overall state of the US economy" (1965:
895). Katzman (1969) points out that ethnic groups are exposed to different sets of economic opportunities as a result of their differences in
regional location. He is referring to variations in factors, such as the
demand for labour at each skill level, the pattern of wages in different
jobs, and the level of unemployment. He shows that the economic performance of an ethnic group is "highly sensitive to the economic opportunities
of the metropolitan region in which it lives."

The structural conditions in particular occupations may be of relevance
as well. In some occupations, individual skills and talents may be more
important than in others; or performance may be more easily measured
and evaluated. Further, in some occupations there is no hierarchy of positions, or the job tenure is inherently insecure.[35] The number and distribution of such occupations in relation to the distribution of ethnic groups
at certain times and places may affect the pattern of ethnic stratification.

The basic point that the few studies cited are meant to illustrate is that
ethnic stratification may be the result not only of the characteristics and
behaviour of members of various ethnic groups and interethnic relationships, but of characteristics of the occupational and class structures as well,
and of their interaction with given ethnic configurations and patterns of
migration and settlement.

CONCLUSION

Three perspectives for approaching the study of stratification have been
described and applied to the question of ethnic stratification. The conception of ethnicity underlying the perspectives differs. One takes ethnicity
as an individual attribute, a set of characteristics – identity, cultural traits
– a person inherits at birth and through early socialization. The others see
ethnicity as a basis of group formation and social mobilization for action
that is cultivated whenever conditions are propitious. Moreover, ethnicity
is seen sometimes as an asset and sometimes as a liability for the individuals
involved. This varies with the different sets of circumstances identified by
each of the approaches. Under the individual competition approach, it
tends to be a liability and, to the extent that they have a choice, individuals
will tend toward acculturation or selective acculturation retaining the traits
that fit well in the prevailing system. In the class approach, it is an asset
for a class that is ethnically homogeneous and is in conflict with another
class of a different ethnic background. Ethnicity in such a case simply
reinforces class solidarity. Otherwise, it is a liability, because it weakens
class solidarity and thus acts against the fundamental interests of those
involved. Finally, in the social closure approach, ethnicity is an asset if the

group has sufficient mobilization potential and if groups can successfully assume control of an occupational domain. It is a liability for those who cannot do so.

If we assume that the different perspectives do capture different aspects of social reality, then whether ethnicity is an asset or a liability is a highly circumstantial phenomenon that depends on the social process selected for attention and the location of people with regard to those processes. It is not surprising, then, that we find considerable ambivalence in our society with regard to the desirability of ethnic retention. This ambivalence may exist within individuals, especially those with young children. It may exist within ethnic groups, some segments of it favouring retention, others favouring acculturation. Or it may exist in the society at large. The analysis presented here suggests that the issue cannot be resolved in a general way: it depends on the aspects of the social structure upon which one focuses.

CHAPTER FOUR

Symbolic Resources
and Status Inequality*[1]

In the social climate prevailing in a post-industrial, capitalist society like that of Canada, considerations of collective identity, symbolic interests and behaviour, and social status or honour appear to contribute little to the determination of social organization. The formation of groups, the structuring of their interrelationships, patterns of social inequality, and the functioning of societal institutions seem influenced primarily by material and utilitarian rather than ideal forces and interests. The central lines of conflict among groups and organizations would appear to revolve around the material basis of social life. The growth of that sphere and the distribution of the benefits generated from it seem the basis of the legitimacy of state institutions, and indeed of the entire social system.

Such an impression of society's driving forces can also be obtained from a rapid overview of sociological research in Canada. Indeed, this research seems to reflect how insignificant are matters pertaining to the symbolic-cultural order and the corresponding social agencies and resources.[2] The emphasis seems more on social classes than on status groups.[3] The utilitarian dimension of power relationships and inequalities – both economic and political – seem to receive more attention than its symbolic dimension. The prevailing theoretical approaches or those contending for intellectual dominance in the discipline seem to agree on the centrality of material interests: political economy, neo-Marxism, dependency theories,

---

* "The Production and Allocation of Symbolic Resources: An Analysis of the Linguistic and Ethnocultural Fields in Canada," *Review of Canadian Sociology and Anthropology* 21, 2 (1984): 123–44.

centre-periphery analysis, conflict theory,[4] and organizational or inter-organizational analysis.

This slant is also apparent in the recent preoccupation with the role of the state. Much attention is indeed given to the role that state institutions have and continue to play in relation to phenomena, such as the accumulation and investment of capital, science and technology, and human capital (including the changing place of women in the socioeconomic structure), and in relation to issues pertaining to the quality of life, but with a focus on its material dimensions – health, housing, and the environment.

Even the study of linguistic and cultural phenomena and especially of the relations among the groups involved has been affected by this "economisme,"[5] although the tendency is perhaps less pronounced in this than in other areas. In this article, I would like to argue that much of society's activities cannot be adequately understood if we over-emphasize the material dimension to the detriment of the symbolic dimension of social organization. This analysis will apply notions and propositions from Weber, analysts of symbolic behaviour, including symbolic interactionists, and from students of status behaviour and politics. First, some of the ways in which the symbolic order has changed will be examined, with a focus on the linguistic and ethnocultural fields. For this purpose, the distinction between the production of symbolic resources and their distribution will be used.[6] Initially, attention will be given to the processes involved in attempting to regenerate the cultural-symbolic capital of the society – to restructure the collective identity and the associated symbolic contents. However, the production of the symbolic order and its transformation entail, almost inevitably, an allocation or re-allocation of social status or recognition among various segments of the society. Accordingly, some of the processes involved in this redistribution and the resistance to it will also be considered.

Second, the role that the state[7] has assumed in these processes will be taken into account. As is well known, a vigorous debate has been going on about the linguistic and ethnocultural fields and government intervention in them. Up until recently, much of the controversy appears to have been over the content of these policies – what should or should not be done in relation to particular issues or problems. By and large, the debate seems to have occurred within a fairly wide consensus as to the necessity and perhaps even the desirability of state involvement in this domain.

Recently, however, a breach appears in that consensus: some critics begin to question or oppose the very idea of state intervention on matters of language and/or ethnicity (e.g., Brotz 1980; Peter 1981; Porter 1975; Roberts and Clifton 1982; Smiley 1980; Vano 1981). Implicitly, if not explicitly, these critics advocate a "laissez-faire" attitude on the part of state institutions in relation to the symbolic order.

This controversy is certainly worthwhile. The debate, however, would benefit considerably from more theory and research on the social forces leading the state to intervene in that field in the first place. Such an analysis, it would seem to me, should precede the formulation of models and hypotheses for the *evaluation* of government policies and programs and their impact. In the discussion that follows, the intention is not to argue whether or not the state should be involved in this area, but rather to consider some of the reasons for its intervention.

CONSTRUCTION OF THE SYMBOLIC ORDER

The formation of societies consists, at one level, in the construction of a symbolic order. This construction entails, first, the definition of a collective identity which, with time, becomes articulated in a system of ideas as to who we are as a people. This identity is represented in the multiplicity of symbols surrounding the rituals of public life, the functioning of institutions, and the public celebration of events, groups and individuals.

The identity component of the symbolic order is important for individual members of the society; it can mobilize their intellectual and emotional energies. This is so because it partly relates to the collective identity shaped by individuals on their own. As symbolic interactionists (e.g., Mead 1934; Blumer 1962; Turner 1968; Strauss 1959; Goffman 1959), social anthropologists (e.g., Cohen 1974b, 1977; Warner 1959), and other theorists (e.g., Duncan 1969; Berger and Luckman 1966; Gusfield 1981) have argued, there is an interdependence between the individual and collective processes of identity formation. Thus, individuals expect to recognize themselves in public institutions. They expect some consistency between their private identities and the symbolic contents upheld by public authorities, embedded in the societal institutions, and celebrated in public events. Otherwise, individuals feel like social strangers; they feel that the society is not *their* society.

The construction of a symbolic order also entails the shaping of cultural traditions: values and norms on the one hand; customs and ways of doing things on the other. Perhaps the most important component of this cultural way of life is that embedded in the forms and style of public institutions: the form of government and its institutionalized practices; the administration of justice; the school curriculum and the disciplinary methods; the organization of business activities; the conduct of labour-management relations; and so on. The forms and styles of the various institutions also become incorporated in systems of ideas that are symbolically reinforced in laws, official speeches and documents, constitutional provisions and their public discussion, advertisements, and other public relations behaviours.

As in the case of symbols of identity, individuals also expect to recognize themselves in the values and meanings incorporated in the culture of public institutions. They expect some concordance between their own and the public way of life or cultural styles. Gusfield has noted, for example, that law "provides a reassurance to some that the society is indeed *their* society, its meanings their meanings, and its morality their morality … The public order is capable of assuring those whose values it reflects that there is a society of consistent values in a culture of logical and morally satisfying meanings. It creates the illusion of cultural dominance" (1981: 182).

Finally, I wish to isolate language as a component of the symbolic order, because of its particular significance in multilingual societies. Language, of course, is a means of communication and as such is part of the instrumental culture. But it is also a critical component of the symbolic culture since it constitutes a basis for defining collective identities and life styles (Jackson 1977).

As in the case of identity and culture, members of the society tend to expect a certain degree of congruence between the public language and their own linguistic competence and style. Indeed, in a powerful way, the language used in public affairs and institutions signifies to individuals and groups "that the society is indeed *their* society," and the institutions, their institutions. Language is perhaps the most effective symbolic medium for assuring a mutual reflection of the public world of institutions and the private world of individuals.

These three components of the symbolic order – identity, way of life, and language – are, of course, closely interconnected. They usually reinforce each other. Even though it is possible to distinguish between them analytically, it is frequently impossible to disentangle them empirically. The distinction is nevertheless useful. Public policies, for instance, may address one or the other of these components. In addition, the components may not concord with each other, a situation of tension that may lead to institutional change.

Given the importance of the symbolic order, one can expect its transformation to be resisted in proportion to the magnitude of the perceived change. In fact, frequently such transformations will not be experienced as simple changes, but as disruptions of one's symbolic world of identity and meanings with a resulting sense of alienation. This concept is used here just as it was defined by Nettler: "The 'alienated person' is one who has been estranged from, made unfriendly toward his society and the culture it carries" (1957: 672). For many English-speaking Canadians, the recent changes have brought about a feeling of estrangement from the national society, as earlier changes had done for native peoples and French-speaking Canadians.

The resistance to change is thus quite understandable. And it can be quite intense. It could perhaps be argued that changes in the symbolic order are more strongly resisted than those in the material order, since the former involves identities and their social evaluation. This, of course, does not mean that the resistance is irrational. The defence of one's symbolic interests is just as rational as the pursuit and protection of one's material interests. In this connection, it is useful to note du Preez's remarks about the defence of ideologies or, we could say, of any significant element of the symbolic system. He notes that when individuals engage in such a defence "it is often because they believe that the alternative is chaos, an undoing of themselves as persons, an annihilation of their identity. They preserve the practices of their society because those preserve their identity. The argument that they can remain whatever they are even if society changes is nonsense because the participants see things in terms of their attachments to various institutions and practices" (du Preez 1980: 48).

Much of what has been going on in Canada during the recent decades can be profitably described and interpreted from this perspective. Indeed, much of the change has consisted in the restructuring of the symbolic order. These attempts have been varied in content and uneven in impact. They have been initiated by organizations in a variety of institutional sectors: churches, school boards, the media, labour unions, and various associations. Foremost among them were the institutions of the state. These have indeed led the way in this attempted reconstruction of the collective identity, of the system of ideas and symbols, and of the institutional practices that pertain to the linguistic and ethnocultural diversity of our society.

Clearly, the state is not only involved in the economy's management, the pursuit of growth, and the initiation or support of changes found necessary in that sphere. It is also engaged in managing the symbolic system, the protection of its integrity, its enrichment, and its adaptation to new circumstances. It is such a process of adaptive change that has been introduced in recent decades in order to better accommodate society's bi-national and multi-cultural composition. Warner (1959) argues that the periodic symbolic activities organized by state and other organizations serve to unify the community as a whole, and that they have an integrative function.[8] His analysis, however, assumes the existence of a symbolic system that expresses the common identity of all segments of society, though such segments may differ in other dimensions. Symbolic activities also serve to link present with past and assure the continuity of the community into the future. The situation in Canada, however, is somewhat different. It involves the creation of new symbolic elements and the transformation of the existing collective identity and its representation. To the extent that this is the case, recent events entail a break with the past and a partly new orientation for the future.

Historically, nation building in its symbolic-cultural dimension was oriented toward the construction of a British-type of society in Canada. This was to be reflected in the cultural character of the political, religious, educational, and other public institutions, in the language of society, in the customs, mores, and way of life, and in the symbols used to represent the society and its people. In that sense, English-Canadian nationalism was just as ethnic or cultural as French-Canadian nationalism, although both revealed considerable differences in content. The prevailing normative model called for the coincidence of nation and state.[9] It was unitarian and oriented toward cultural homogeneity. The attempts by other groups such as the Ukrainians and the French to maintain their own language and culture and to build their own sub-societies seemed to threaten the British model of cultural unity sought for in this country.

A tension between a latent unitarian model and the existing cultural diversity has persisted since the Conquest, as shown by numerous attempts to impose a common language and numerous conflicts over the control of cultural institutions, especially the educational system and the media, since these constitute the main agencies of symbolic control and socialization.[10]

The process of construction and the imposition of a British model of identity and a symbolic system was fairly successful in most parts of Canada. This success is well expressed by Grant:

Growing up in Ontario, the generation of the 1920s took it for granted that they belonged to a nation. The character of the country was self-evident. To say it was British was not to deny it was North American. To be a Canadian was to be a unique species of North American. Such an alternative as F.H. Underhill's – "Stop being British if you want to be a nationalist" – seemed obviously ridiculous. (Grant 1965: 3)

With some variations, the same feeling can be said to have existed among many Canadians growing up in other parts of Canada.

The success was also evident in the process of acculturation. The children and grandchildren of immigrants were being progressively incorporated into a collective identity and an institutional system whose symbolic character was fundamentally British, but regarded as Canadian.

Thus "being Canadian" was in the process of being defined as speaking English within a British-type institutional system. The legitimacy of this symbolic order was becoming established in most segments of the population.

There were, of course, exceptions, the case of the French being the most striking. With time, however, and with increasing cultural security, English-Canadian nationalism became somewhat more tolerant and open. As McNaught points out, what he calls the "racial component in the English-speaking view (of nationality) has steadily grown less significant" (1966: 63), and the notion of political nationality (as opposed to cultural nationality) has gained importance. In other words, once the symbolic order was fairly well defined and fairly securely established, cultural pluralism appeared less threatening.[11] The climate was ready for some recognition of that pluralism, except, perhaps, its French component.

Thus, confrontations over the symbolic order and over the means for the production and reproduction of that order became less frequent. Even the French community, at least for a while, seemed to have abandoned the fight at the level of public institutions after a number of defeats, particularly in the field of education. (A full analysis of this historical evolution would have to pay systematic attention to differences in the situation in the various parts of the country.)

In the years that followed World War II, numerous changes began – events that, in the 1960s and 1970s, were to challenge and often disrupt this on-its-way-to becoming consolidated symbolic order. As noted earlier, this consolidation allowed little for a French component. This was so in most parts of Canada and to a significant extent in Québec as well. It was also the case in the national institutions and in particular in the highly visible federal government which, in spite of its cohort of francophone members of Parliament and of cabinet ministers, was largely the government of English Canada, or at least was largely perceived as such by *both* French- and English-speaking Canadians. These perceptions were documented by the Royal Commission on Bilingualism and Biculturalism.

With the growing awareness of their own collective identity, Québec francophones began to express the fact that they did not recognize themselves in the central political institutions, and indeed in the evolving symbolic order of the entire society. Their intense feeling was that Canadian society was not their society, its institutions not their institutions, its meanings and symbols, not their meanings and symbols. They felt alien or strangers, and in increasing numbers, they wanted out.

Thus, a profound crisis of legitimacy emerged for society's institutions, especially for the state institutions. One of the ways in which institutional elites reacted to this crisis was to attempt to change the symbolic character of the institutions so that the French segment of the population could identify with them. Among the steps taken were: the establishment of the Royal Commission which, it is important to note in the present context, was to deal with *bi*lingualism and *bi*culturalism; the Official Languages Act in 1969; and the initiation of several programs designed to increase the francophone presence in various institutional domains, especially in the federal institutions. Numerous changes in the symbols themselves were also introduced: for instance a Canadian Flag was adopted in 1965; Trans-Canada Airlines became Air Canada; the Dominion Bureau of Statistics became Statistics Canada; "O Canada" was proclaimed as the national anthem; stamps were changed; the money was redesigned with more Canadian symbols; and the Constitution was patriated – a Constitution which was called, we must underline, the *British* North America Act. (One could perhaps add the introduction of the metric system as another illustration, since I suspect it was perceived by many as part of the same movement away from a British-modelled symbolic order.)

In short, the state intervened substantially to restructure and reorient the symbolic order, an intervention that has brought about various reactions. Some perceived the changes as a possible enrichment of society's symbolic system and, as a result, of their own symbolic universe. The changes were seen as an opportunity in terms of identity, life style, and cultural capital (Bourdieu and Passeron 1970; Bourdieu 1979). Others have been less positive in their reactions; however, after an initial opposition, have more or less reluctantly accepted change as necessary for national unity or some other such value. Still others have expressed negative reactions ranging from annoyance, resistance, all the way to outright opposition. In these cases, the interventions have been perceived and/or experienced as disruptions of their symbolic universe. They could not identify as easily as they used to with the new system of symbols; they did not feel at ease with the new culture of the public institutions; the new symbolic order was unfamiliar and a source of anxiety.

At the more extreme pole, we find those who saw the changes as an assault on their own identity, institutions, language, and way of life. They perceived the purpose of the interventions to be the dismantling of the institutional forms and customs and of the linguistic practices to which they had been accustomed and which, now, were being progressively replaced by another that was perceived not only as alien, but hostile as well.

For some, these changes no doubt presented a disruption of their career chances or a decreased access to governmental channels. I would argue however, that most Canadians have remained unaffected in their material interests. For them, the disruption was symbolic. First, as my late friend, John McDonald, pointed out at the time, the main significance of the separatist movement was that it challenged or disturbed the sense of benevolence of English Canadians: "Haven't we been fair in dealing with them?" "If it was not for us, their situation would be even worse." As Peterson Royce notes, "no one appreciates being put in the awkward position of being wrong or appearing to be a bigot" (1982: 200).

Second, it represented a transformation of the symbolic universe such that many could not recognize themselves in the societal institutions any more. Another group had taken over: "Bilingual Today, French Tomorrow," as Mr Andrew (1977) stated in his perhaps extreme attempt to express the new cultural-symbolic insecurity of his fellow Canadians. There was a sense of symbolic loss, indeed, a sense of usurpation of something very important to one's identity.[12]

Viewed from this perspective, many reactions become understandable – reactions which otherwise appear as irrational and purely emotional, if not simply ridiculous. For instance, the complaint that "French is being rammed down our throats" which appears completely misplaced in terms of an instrumental analysis of the Official Languages Act is understandable as a reaction to the symbolic component of the Act. Similarly, for some, French on cereal boxes and on other products is annoying, and even offensive, because it symbolizes the change of the collective identity and of the culture of public institutions. (I am not too sure why the cereal box has itself become a symbol of this transformation. It is perhaps in the morning that we are especially vulnerable to disruptions in our personal life style and that we are correspondingly loath to be reminded, by the innocuous cereal box, of changes taking place in the society-at-large.)

Finally, even among the sympathetic and responsive elements of the population, it generated some uncertainty and therefore cultural anxiety. Are these attempts going to succeed? How will they affect society's character? How can institutions be changed to effectively represent, culturally and symbolically, different collectivities?

The process of symbolic change is a conflictual one: "If culture is being shaped and society being formed as a public entity, then whose culture and whose society it is to be becomes an important counter in political act" (Gusfield 1981: 184). The conflict concerns institutional control of symbolic production and the resulting content of the symbolic-cultural character of the society.[13]

Thus, in attempting to deal with a legitimacy crisis, the institutional elites were running the risk of accentuating that very crisis or of generating another. Indeed, restructuring the symbolic order to make it easier for certain social segments to identify with its institutions could alienate and antagonize those accustomed to a sense of cultural dominance, and thus, it could put in motion an opposing set of forces that could destroy the new symbolic edifice.

THE SYMBOLIC ORDER AND ETHNIC STATUS INEQUALITY

There was, of course, much more going on in these transformations. In addition to their implications for restructuring the symbolic order, the institutional interventions also had consequences for the distribution of social status or honour among social groups.

Individuals seek a favourable self-image. This self-image is tied to their social identity, which "refers to the individual's knowledge that he belongs to certain social groups together with some emotional and value significance to him of this group membership" (Tajfel 1972: 292). Moreover, the process whereby individuals seek a positive social identity "is inextricably a matter of mutual comparisons between groups ... It could be said that there is a process of competition for positive identity, for each group's actions are attempts not at some absolute degree of value but a positively valued differentiation" (Turner 1974: 10).

The competition for a positive social identity occurs along socially defined attributes in a given society. Those attributes or criteria not only pertain to the class position of individuals and groups but also to their status situation. As Weber noted,

in contrast to the purely economically determined "class situation" we wish to designate as "status situation" every typical component of the life fate of men that is determined by specific, positive or negative, social estimation of *honor*. This honor may be connected with any quality shared by a plurality. (Gerth and Mills 1958: 186–7)

The status concerns of individuals will therefore bear not only on the actual position of the groups to which they belong relative to that of other groups but also to the community standards and the ways in which they are applied. They will be concerned with the status system and with the means of status attainment. Accordingly, they "will tend to reject as criteria of social status those characteristics not accessible to them and to support those that are."[14] This will be reflected in the reactions of individuals and groups to the institutional policies and practices – those of the state in particular – through which the criteria and standards of social status are established and applied.

Several institutional behaviours are manifestly symbolic: their main purpose is to bestow recognition and honour or to somehow change the existing distribution of social status. Relevant institutional behaviours, however, are not only those that are directly aimed at allocating social status. Some are manifestly instrumental, yet possess a significant impact on the distribution of social honour. Some authors have even argued that the manifest instrumental component is frequently quite secondary for most participants in socio-political and organizational processes and that the manifest content of the issues frequently weighs little in comparison with its implications for the distribution of prestige among participants. March and Olsen, for instance, claim that in organizations "most people ... are most of the time less concerned with the content of a decision than they are with eliciting acknowledgment of their importance in the community;

[that] participation in the process is a conspicuous certification of status" (March and Olsen 1976: 201). Although this may be an overstatement, it is, in my view, frequently applicable not only in organizations but also in the society-at-large.

Edelman (1964, 1971) also quite convincingly argued that much behaviour of public institutions and authorities and much of the reaction to that behaviour cannot adequately be understood unless attention is given to their implications for the allocation of social honour and recognition. Gusfield underlined the fact that public acts on the part of political groups and elites can be interpreted, at one level, as "ceremonial actions which affect the social status" of those on each side of the issue (1981: 21).

For instance, several institutional interventions mentioned earlier have implications beyond a restructuring of society's symbolic order; they also affect the distribution of social status among linguistic and ethno-cultural collectivities in the country. Sometimes this appears intentional; sometimes, however, it is unintended. Correspondingly, reactions to the institutional interventions in the ethnocultural field are, to a considerable extent, reactions to the changing status of one's group relative to other groups. Indeed, I would hypothesize that if we carried out a systematic content analysis of the public debate on issues related to bilingualism and multiculturalism, we would observe that many of its themes and key words concerned relative status, the possible loss of status in the society, the fear of definition as "second class citizens," the disapproval of recognition given to groups out of proportion with their perceived importance, and the perception that one's culture or language is being degraded.[15]

Doubtless the independentist movement in Québec and the nature of the official response to it were generating considerable anxiety among the non-British and non-French groups as to what their status in Canadian society would become. The name of the Royal Commission itself was a symbol generating status anxiety as were several other themes permeating the debate: founding peoples, charter groups, the two-nation society. What was happening was that a collectivity that hitherto had been considered as a minority was in the process of definition as part of the majority – a rather substantial change in the relative status of groups. British-origin Canadians were not assured of an unrivalled position of cultural dominance anymore, and members of other ethnic groups were becoming anxious about the possible accentuation of their minority status.

A re-ranking of status groups was being attempted and, as could be expected, these attempts were generating considerable anxiety and opposition. Status interests were at stake. A conflict existed between those who were attempting, with the assistance of the state, to increase the social valuation of their language and identity and those who were resisting a possible loss, relatively speaking, in official recognition for their own.

A feature of the situation that accentuated the conflict was what Hughes called a "contradiction in status." He suggested "that people carry in their minds a set of expectations concerning the auxiliary traits properly associated with many of the specific positions available in our society" (Hughes 1945: 354). Among these traits, some are "master status-determining" traits. In Canada, being British, French, or native, constitutes such "master" traits. Hughes also noted that in spite of the high degree of individual mobility and heterogeneity in American society, the "expected characteristic of many favored statuses and positions" remain white, Anglo-Saxon, male, and Protestant (ibid: 356).[16]

Events in Canada in the last few decades have been challenging those expectations concerning "the auxiliary traits properly associated" with certain public positions. More specifically, a situation was generated in which members of a collectivity considered historically to be of low social status, culturally, technologically, and economically inferior, and which, in most parts of the country was a small minority[17] were gaining some political power over members of the opposing collectivity. The position of various groups in the status order and the emerging distribution of political power was perceived as diverging, and thus the expectation that the higher status group should run the society was being disturbed.[18]

What complicated this process of change further was that it was taking place on two fronts simultaneously. The restructuring of the collective identity and the redistribution of social recognition were undertaken in Québec as well as on the national scene. The fact that the French-speaking community was split on a number of issues and that the proponents of various views and policies were political opponents is somewhat secondary in the present context. What is critical is that similar processes were going on in these two political arenas. (It should also be noted that the changes undertaken in Québec have, in many ways, been more substantial and have entailed a more dramatic state intervention than is necessary at the federal level.)

In Québec, the restructuring was based on the notion that the French collectivity was a majority. The collective self-conception changed from French Canadians – a minority situation – to Québécois. The state intervened to transform the public environment in terms of that new identity; virtually no public institutions not already conforming with that identity were left untouched.

It should perhaps be mentioned, parenthetically, that the direction of the evolution of this collective identity is far from being clear. Indeed, up until recently, there was close to a one-to-one correspondence between language and ethnicity in French Québec; those of French origin tended to speak French, while all others tended to speak English. To the extent that they are successful – as they seem to be to a significant degree – the new social and legal prescriptions will tend to dissociate language from ethnicity. The progressive absorption of people of non-French *origins* into the French-*speaking* community is likely to represent an increasingly serious challenge – a challenge to transform that community's symbolic system and re-define the social construct "Québécois" to be more culturally inclusive. In other words, one could hypothesize that Québec's ethnic nationalism is required to transform itself into a political and territorial nationalism, a transition bound to generate numerous social strains. This transformation of Québec's nationalism would parallel that which British Canadians have been undergoing for several decades.[19]

The changes taking place have also had implications for status distribution among linguistic and ethnocultural groups within Québec. For instance, the English language lost its official status. In the new dispensation, the historical importance of the anglophone community is still recognized, but its status is quite clearly reduced with its minority definition. It may not be regarded in the same light as other minorities, but it is nevertheless seen as a minority.

Of course, many of the specifications of Law 101 have implications for the material interests of the members of the various ethnocultural collectivities in Québec (and perhaps of a small proportion of other Canadians). To a large extent, however, its significance is symbolic. In fact, for most Canadians outside of Québec, it is almost exclusively symbolic. But even for those living in Québec, the symbolic component is considerable. The law, both in its totality and in the clauses that deal specifically with symbols (e.g., signs on commercial establishments), represents changes in the relative status of cultural groups. Its main thrust is to symbolically place one language and identity above the others, to change the ranks they had traditionally occupied.

Finally, it is also useful to consider the multiculturalism policy in this perspective.[20] The main significance of that policy derives from its integral contribution to the reconstruction of the symbolic system and to the redistribution of social status among linguistic and ethnocultural groups in Canadian society. Indeed, it soon became clear that re-shaping the social and institutional identity, customs, and symbols so that members of society's French segment might recognize themselves generated identification and status concerns not only among British-origin Canadians but among the non-British, non-French as well.

Thus, when the policy on multiculturalism was introduced, the non-British, non-French element was not primarily concerned with cultural maintenance. Rather, a status anxiety existed, fear of being defined as second-class citizens, marginal to the identity system, that was being established. The minority was resented for what seemed its special status. Thus, the policy responded to the status anxieties voiced with regard to themes like biculturalism, two-nation society, charter groups, and founding peoples. One of its objectives was to affirm symbolically that Canadian society is open to all cultural identities, indicating its recognition of them all, and the implications of cultural equality.

This is the profound meaning of the government statement concerning multiculturalism within a bilingual framework. The frequently quoted portion of the prime minister's statement to the House of Commons in 1971 concerns the implementation of this policy. This is indeed an important part of the statement. In my view, however, more attention should be given to that portion of the statement pertaining to policy objectives and its social context. I would like to quote a few paragraphs from that text:

A policy of multiculturalism within a bilingual framework commends itself to the government as the most suitable means of assuring the cultural freedom of Canadians. Such a policy should help to break down discriminatory attitudes and cultural jealousies. National unity if it is to mean anything in the deeply personal sense, must be found on confidence in one's own individual identity; out of this can grow respect for that of others and a willingness to share ideas, attitudes and assumptions. A vigorous policy of multiculturalism will help create this initial confidence. It can form the base of a society which is based on fair play for all ... The government will support and encourage the various cultures and ethnic groups that give structure and vitality to our society. They will be encouraged to share their cultural expression and values with other Canadians and so contribute to a richer life for us all. (House of Commons Debates 1971: 8545)

This document is a very interesting piece of data. It seems clear that a main concern of the government pertains to what I have called the cultural-symbolic order of the society. It speaks of "national unity," of "the various cultures and ethnic groups that give structure and vitality to our society," of "a richer life for us all." The image that emerges from the statement is more of cultural fusion than the perpetuation of a multiplicity of different cultures.

Another concern underlying the policy statement is with the status of the various cultural groups: "breaking down jealousies;" "fair play for all;" "respect for [the identity] of others." In fact, one paragraph deals quite explicitly with the proper recognition that the various cultural components of the society should receive:

In the past, substantial public support has been given largely to the arts and cultural institutions of English-speaking Canada. More recently and largely with the help of the royal commission's earlier recommendations in Volumes I to III, there has been a conscious effort on the government's part to correct any bias against the French language and culture. In the last few months the government has taken steps to provide funds to support cultural-educational centres for native people. The policy I am announcing today accepts the contention of the other cultural communities that they, too, are essential elements in Canada and deserve government assistance in order to contribute to regional and national life in ways that derive from their heritage yet are distinctively Canadian. (House of Commons Debates 1971: 8545–6)

The reader should note the government acceptance of "the contention of the other cultural communities that they, too, are essential elements ..." The second concern of the policy pertains to the recognition granted to the various ethnocultural collectivities.

I do not wish to deny that "cultural diversification" is part of the policy. But I would like to suggest that the policy is largely an instrument for restructuring society's identity system and for managing cultural tensions that arise in the process. By focusing too much on possible policy impact in maintaining (or not maintaining) ethnocultures, we have neglected an important if not central aspect of the policy and its role in transforming society's symbolic component.

This interpretation of multiculturalism's main thrust – both as a policy and a social movement – is consistent with the view that ethnicity in urban North America has taken a symbolic or regenerational character (Driedger 1977). As Gans points out, ethnicity now has "an expressive rather than an instrumental function in people's lives" (1979: 9). It is characterized by the fact that "people are less and less interested in their ethnic cultures and organizations – both sacred and secular – and are instead more concerned with maintaining their ethnic identity... and with finding ways of feeling and expressing that identity in suitable ways" (ibid: 7). Following this line of reasoning, I would argue that the search for institutional recognition and the competition for status are important means of ethnic expressions of identity – and not only, perhaps not primarily, through various forms of cultural expression.[21] "Groups want to be included in the official history of the society and its pantheon of heroes,"[22] something that in many ways would require a re-writing of Canadian history. They are also watchful of the institutional gestures vis-à-vis other groups and react accordingly (Schneider 1979: 6). "Pluralism involves a sort of jockeying for status and power. It involves a process of invidious comparisons."[23]

Recognition and status are sought in the following areas: from government in its legislation, programs, publications, and various symbolic gestures; from universities through special chairs, research centres, conferences, library collections, exhibits; from the public school system through language teaching or in courses and textbook content in areas such as literature and history; from media coverage of events that enhance the group's image or through special programs on aspects of the group's life or culture;

from churches through statements concerning the legitimacy of multiculturalism or through activities recognizing or celebrating the sacred and
secular dimensions of ethnic identities and cultures.

The pursuit of status also manifests itself in the search for a particular
group's participation in the historical formation and evolution of Canadian society or for identifiable contributions to the societal institutions
and culture. One increasingly hears, for instance, claims of a "founding
people status" on the part of people of different ethnic origins. The arguments presented revolve around the idea that one's group has played a
critical if not the main role in settling a particular region, province, or
community, and in building its institutions. The expectation is that this
role should be publicly recognized by society's status-giving institutions.

CONCLUSION

I have attempted to show that two sets of phenomena must be considered
to adequately understand Canada's linguistic and ethnocultural reality and
the activities and interventions in that field of various institutions, especially state institutions. These pertain to the structuring of the symbolic
component of the social order and to the distribution of social status and
recognition among ethnocultural groups.

Such processes can be quite conflictual and emotionally charged. Like
class politics, status politics constitute a struggle between contending groups
over the distribution of societal resources. In one case, the resources are
material; in the other, they are symbolic. Both are equally real. The struggle
involves the "certification of one's status" (March and Olsen 1976) as a
participant in the socio-political process or the relative decertification of
others. It consists of attempts by various groups to acquire "status rights"[24]
in particular domains or oppose the claims to such rights on the part of
other groups.

The political conflict may be limited to influencing the institutional
authorities. In some cases, however, it may concern the control of existing
structures and mechanisms for defining the collective identity and the distribution of status. In such instances, the conflict is likely to be more
intense. This appears to be central to French participation in the transformation of the symbolic order; it was perceived as overtaking institutional
apparatus rather than attempting to influence it.

The changes and attempted changes in the linguistic and ethnocultural
fields have involved a complex interaction between the material and symbolic orders – an interaction that could not be adequately considered in
this essay. Each sphere has its own relative autonomy, involving distinctive
kinds of resources and social processes which are interdependent in the

structuring, functioning, and evolution of social organization. Both operate simultaneously in the context of social action.

Several examples of the interdependence between the material and symbolic orders can be observed. For instance, symbolic resources can be used to achieve economic and other utilitarian objectives. They can be used by individuals and groups in competing for economic or political power. Conversely, economic resources can be used in the pursuit of prestige and in the competition that this pursuit entails (Coleman 1969). There are also situations in which the issues at hand involve mutually reinforcing class and status interests. They concord in the sense that the groups in competition or conflict stand to gain or lose on both at the same time. This appears to have been the case with regard to numerous aspects of the federal and Québec language policies. Such situations usually result in more intense conflict because the combination of the two types of interests brings more people into conflict – some primarily because the outcome may affect their businesses or careers, others primarily because the status of their culture or identity is at stake, still others because both sets of interests converge. However, there can also be situations of inconsistency, in which material advantage conflicts with symbolic interests. Minorities frequently face these kinds of situations: they pursue recognition and the development of their symbolic-cultural resources, frequently at the cost of considerable material sacrifices, either individually or collectively (see for example Vallee and Shulman 1969).

The pressure for change in the symbolic order and of resistance to attempted changes do not occur randomly; their sources can be located structurally. Specific groups on each side of the conflict could be identified by considering the fact that all segments of society are not equally advantaged (or disadvantaged) in pursuing a positive social identity according to existing institutional arrangements. As indicated, the dominant elements of identity and the prevailing criteria of social status will tend to be rejected by those finding it difficult to compete along those lines, but will be supported by those who are, or anticipate being, on the winning side. For instance, contribution to the construction of Canadian society as a criterion of official recognition and status favours certain groups to the detriment of others. The result is a conflict of status interest between those who feel they can claim a "founding people" status and those who have arrived or established themselves more recently in Canada – the former supporting and the latter rejecting this criterion of status.[25]

In this context, the intervention of the state derives some of its significance. Indeed, its intervention frequently modifies the system of opportunities and constraints within which individuals and groups attempt to construct a positive identity or certify their status. State policies can affect

– positively or negatively – the strategies and tactics available to members of various ethnocultural groups in their competition for social status (Peterson Royce 1982: 184–94; Lyman and Douglas 1973).

In Canada, the state has always participated in shaping the symbolic order and in managing the relationships among linguistic and cultural groups. This participation has changed over time under the influence of various forces, but it has seldom been absent.[26] Its participation in the symbolic order parallels its involvement in economic management and the relations among various organized or unorganized interests. It is interesting to note that the increasing support in recent times for the view that government should adopt a laissez-faire policy in the ethnocultural field seems to correspond to an increasing claim for less economic intervention.[27]

I would suggest that the argument for state withdrawal from the ethno-cultural field is as futile as is that for withdrawal from the economic sphere. Rather, an important task for social scientists is not so much to argue in favour of or against state intervention as it is to provide an explanation of current involvement. This would entail, for instance, an analysis of the factors that have been shaping state institutions and their relations not only to the economy but to the civil society as well. These include: the emergence of the welfare state;[28] the changing structures for the representation of interests, including the declining role of political parties;[29] the sectoral organization of government activity and decision making; and the changing conditions for maintaining state legitimacy. It would also require that the critical dimensions of the symbolic order be clarified along with the processes through which it is transformed as a system of collective meanings, the conditions under which the collective identity becomes meaningful for the different segments of the society, and the factors related to the degree of symbolic equality among them.

Another question could be raised about state intervention: what would be the probable consequences of leaving the ethnocultural field and the relations of groups within it open to the forces of the "market?" This kind of exercise would perhaps be largely speculative. Yet it would generate interesting hypotheses for analysing institutional intervention over the last decades, and the possibilities and limits of future interventions.

Finally, it should be noted that although the symbolic order and expressive stratification has been given special attention in this article, it does not imply that other dimensions of the social structure are considered secondary. The cultural-symbolic aspects of intergroup relations should be neither ignored nor presented in some intellectually imperialistic fashion as the most or the only important aspect of that reality. Rather, my argument is that without taking it into account, we will overlook an important dimension of the dynamics of language and ethnicity and of the related institutional policies and practices.

PART TWO

French-English Relations in Canada:
Ethnic Segmentation

CHAPTER FIVE

Social History of French-English Relations in Canada*

The history of English-French relations in Canada is one of competition between two collectivities engaged in constructing and maintaining a society. Long before the 1760 conquest, the two empires were attempting to establish and expand their commercial systems. Eventually, both groups established permanent communities, with their economic, political, and social institutions.

In pursuing commerce and society building, the English and French have regularly competed. Both have sought control over the resources necessary for their societal projects and, if possible, to monopolize them: to deny the other access to them; to displace the other if it was already occupying a particular resource domain; or to dominate it if this was not possible.[1]

Several categories of resources have been at stake: territory, material resources, population, political and military power, capital, access to markets, scientific and technological expertise, and alliances with surrounding collectivities. Cultural-symbolic resources are also required. Indeed, even though a society and its institutions have both an economic and technological base, they also have a symbolic dimension, a cultural character, and identity.

Competitive struggles and conflicts have been intermittent and limited to particular issues or institutional domains. The confrontations, sometimes coming close to civil war, have usually been resolved in some sort of accommodation (a treaty, a pact, a change in institutional structures or

---

* "French-English Relations," in *Understanding Canadian Society*, edited by
L. Tepperman and J. Curtis (Toronto: McGraw-Hill Ryerson, 1988), 557–86.

rules, an informal agreement). At times, these "accommodations" have been imposed by an external power, directly or indirectly.

This chapter reviews the history of English-French relations in Canada.[2] To facilitate the presentation, the history is divided into four phases: (1) pre-Conquest; (2) from Conquest to Confederation; (3) from Confederation to World War II; and (4) from World War II to the present. During each period, English and French have clashed in two or more of the following arenas: (a) North America as a whole; (b) Canada (defined differently depending on the historical period); (c) Quebec; (d) Acadia; (e) Ontario; and (f) the West.

This chapter is not an essay on Quebec (or French Canada) and English Canada. Rather, it deals with the *relationship* between the two collectivities. Of course, the analysis will consider certain aspects of their respective social structure and culture. The focus, however, will be on elements that affect their relationship. Given space limitations, the analysis will necessarily be selective.

THE PRE-CONQUEST PERIOD

There were two arenas of French-English relations during this early period: Acadia and Newfoundland on the one hand and eastern North America (most of the West had not yet been explored).

In the Atlantic region, the competition was for "territorial control ... and for domination of the valuable fisheries off its coasts" (*Canadian Encyclopedia* 1985: 1037); in the Saint Lawrence, Great Lakes, and Hudson Bay areas, the competition was for control of the fur trade. Dominating access to these resources was part of the mercantile interests of the metropolitan centres and was necessary for colonization and settlement.

The French colony in Acadia had barely begun when, in 1621, the Scots also claimed the territory. They named it Nova Scotia. After several military confrontations shifted control of the territory back and forth from French to English, it was captured for good by the English, although parts of it were retained by the French (Isle Royale, or Cape Breton; Isle Saint-Jean, or Prince Edward Island; and the area corresponding to contemporary New Brunswick). This was formally established by the Treaty of Utrecht in 1713.

When contact began in the rest of the continent, a French colony already existed, but it was small (about 2,000 people in 1660) and was primarily a fur trade centre. In 1670, the English established the Hudson's Bay Company. Since several important waterways flow northward into it, Hudson Bay was critical for the fur trade. Thus, the possibility that the trade could be diverted to English trading posts was soon perceived by the French as a serious threat to their trading system and to the colony that depended on it. In response, the Compagnie Française de la Baie d'Hudson (also called the Compagnie du Nord) was established "to challenge the Hudson's Bay Company on its own ground" (*Canadian Encyclopedia* 1985: 705). It established its own posts. Against the Hudson's Bay Company, it mounted a military offensive that failed. It went bankrupt in 1700.

In 1686, another French expedition led by Iberville occupied all the English trading posts. Not surprisingly, war soon followed. Here too, territorial control shifted back and forth between the two commercial empires. The confrontations ended with the Treaty of Utrecht (1713), whereby France ceded to England Hudson Bay and all the rivers flowing into it.

The Great Lakes and the Gulf of Mexico were other arenas of conflict. The French sought to contain the English colonies between the Allegheny Mountains and the Atlantic and established the colony of Louisiana, settlements in the Illinois country, and a garrison at Detroit. Had they succeeded, the English would have lost the fur trade in the Great Lakes region – an outcome they could not accept. Their response was to attack New France. The attack on Port-Royal was successful (1710), but the one on Quebec the following year was not.

There followed 30 years of peace during which each side consolidated their internal and external situation. The 1713 Treaty had been a disaster for the French in territorial control and access to resources. To help resist an increasingly powerful English empire, the French erected Louisbourg in 1714. They also worked to consolidate what remained of their access to the Great Lakes, strengthen the Louisiana colony, and extend their fur trade routes to the West. Several measures for internal economic development and population growth were adopted. The demographic imbalance, however, was already considerably in favour of the English: about 300,000 compared to about 20,000 in New France.

In 1744, new confrontations began in Acadia and Newfoundland. Both sides attempted to conquer and reconquer each other's colonies, and each established new settlements in the hope of containing the other's expansionary tendencies. In the middle of this conflict, the Acadians wanted to be neutral. But the English were suspicious: being French-speaking and Catholic, they were perceived as fundamentally untrustworthy. Major Lawrence's solution was twofold: first, deport them because they would always represent a threat and because they occupied valuable land that could be settled by English-speaking Protestants; second, implement a program of immigration of such settlers. Thus, between 1755 and 1763 over three-fourths of the Acadian population – some 10,000 – was deported.

A second area of confrontation was the Ohio River, an important trade route (which linked the Great Lakes and Louisiana), and Lake Ontario (which was an important link between the Saint Lawrence area and the Ohio Valley and Louisiana). A third area was Lake Champlain and the Saint Lawrence. From 1756 to 1760, the French colonies capitulated to

Figure 5.1
Treaty areas of Canada
Source: Reproduced by permission of *The Canadian Encyclopedia*.

the English: Louisbourg (in Acadia); Forts Frontenac, Dusquesne, and
Niagara in the Ohio-Lake Ontario area; Forts Carillon and Saint-Frederic
in the Lake Champlain area; Quebec and then Montreal in the Saint
Lawrence area.

In the first phase of French-English relations, then, the two groups tried
to gain control of a vast territory and its valuable resources. Given the
vastness of the territory, co-existence might have been possible. There were
indeed periods of accommodation during which claims to particular areas
were not challenged. But the expansion of settlement and the accompanying demand for new resources, the depletion of resources in a particular
area, and perhaps especially, the imperialistic propensities of both sides
led to repeated confrontations that ended only when one side conquered
the other.

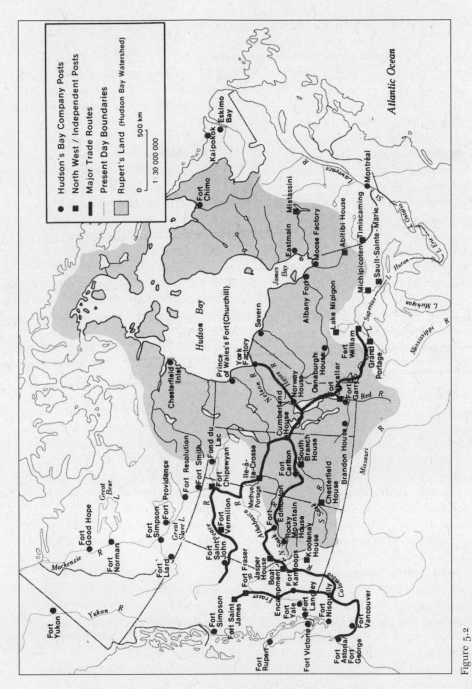

Figure 5.2

Fur trade after 1760

Source: Reproduced by permission of *The Canadian Encyclopedia*.

FROM THE CONQUEST TO CONFEDERATION

The conquest may have ended the conflict over territory, but the competition between the two groups continued. Instead of conflicts over geographic space, collisions occurred over the control of institutions. This was inevitable as the same societal framework was to be constructed by groups with different socioeconomic organization, organization, religion, and language, and a background of antagonism and war.

Both collectivities maintained their own institutions. Thus, a plural or segmented society was formed, that is "a social structure compartmentalized into analogous, parallel, noncomplementary sets of institutions" (van den Berghe 1969: 67) and to social networks largely enclosed within ethnolinguistic boundaries.[3] In addition, institutional arrangements for incorporating the two linguistic segments had to be forged. From the outset, each group was intensely preoccupied with the effectiveness and cultural character of its own institutions and with the possible impact of the common institutions on them.

Once the British had conquered New France, their first aspiration was to transform Quebec into a society with British institutions and an Anglo-Saxon majority. This was clearly the expectation of the Royal Proclamation in 1763. But things did not work out as planned. First, immigration was slow, so the French population remained significantly larger. Second, the French had established far-reaching connections for the fur trade, connections needed by the English-speaking merchants. Third, British administrators saw the feudal nature of the French social order as a source of support for their authority. Murray thought if the Canadians could be "indulged with a few privileges which the laws of England deny to Roman Catholics at home, [they] would soon ... become the most faithful and useful set of men in this American empire" (quoted by McInnis 1969: 156).

Fourth, although small, French Quebec was an established, ongoing society that had to be recognized for practical reasons and because of specifications in the 1763 treaty. Finally, Quebec had a strategic military importance in relation to the American colonies and to France. Their loyalty had, therefore, to be obtained.

Thus, partly because it was impossible to do otherwise and partly because it was to their advantage to do so, British administrators tried to accommodate the French community. The English-speaking colonists, however, also had to be accommodated, especially the mercantile class whose ambitions were enormous. They frequently viewed compromises with the French with suspicion if not outright hostility.

The Quebec Act of 1774 attempted to gain French support while satisfying, or at least not antagonizing, the English colonists and merchants. "The act was a final abandonment of the efforts at a uniform system of colonial government based on English institutions" (McInnis 1969: 160). It preserved several of them, but accepted French civil law; reaffirmed freedom of Catholic worship; and reinforced the Church and seigneurial system by extending their privileges.

With the Conquest, the French society had lost its political-administrative elite and its military officers. The transfer of the commercial dependence from Paris to London prompted many French merchants to leave. Some stayed and even gained by connecting themselves with the wider British mercantile system. The clergy and most seigneurs also stayed, and their positions were buttressed by the Act of 1774. Their position of social ascendancy was based, in both cases, on land ownership and on legally protected social and economic advantages (e.g., the legal right to collect tithes and rents), and on the dominance of their institutions.

This dominance was further reinforced by the virtual absence of competing elites, a phenomenon accentuated by the progressive relative decline of the French mercantile class. This decline was the result of factors opposite to those that favoured the English merchants. First, they were relatively poorly situated *vis-à-vis* the British market networks. Second, they were more inclined to accept the hierarchically ordered society to which they belonged by culture, language, and social ties. They responded to the opportunities it offered for social status and privileges: several used their gains from commerce to acquire seigneuries and thus gain social prominence.

The Quebec Act of 1774 rejected the idea of a "unitary" social and institutional structure and recognized that some institutional dualism was dictated by the circumstances. In its practical implementation, however, it accentuated some of the contradictions and related social tensions both within the English and French segments and between them. On the one hand, by instituting an authoritarian rule (a governor and an appointed council were to govern), it antagonized the English settlers, the merchants in particular. On the other hand, the authoritarian regime generated significant resentment in the French-speaking population – resentment against the increased power of the clergy and of the seigneurs.[4] The dualism and the feudal social structure that it strengthened was, in effect, a system of indirect rule. As the motivations of the British administrators mentioned above indicate, the idea was to obtain the support of a conquered population that had a different culture. Although a conqueror can impose its will, it is usually without moral authority. A system of indirect rule involves maintaining and even revitalizing native institutions and culture so as to be able to operate through them (Frazier 1957: 197). In the process, traditional authorities gain considerable power.

The critical precipitant of change in the institutional arrangements, however, was the arrival of the Loyalists after the American War of Independence (1775–83). Most of the about 10,000 who came settled in what

is now part of Ontario. They were followed by other migrants interested
in land. Most avoided the French-speaking region, primarily because of its
land holding system: "In the western country they held their farms as they
had in the old colonies. Besides. the language, customs, and religion of
Quebec were not theirs; and under the Quebec Act they did not find the
representative system of government they had always known" (Careless
1970: 114). To a significant degree, the Loyalists were the original
founders of English Canada:

The Loyalists began to build a Canada that was not predominantly French. Modern
English-speaking Canada really goes back to them, and to the Revolution that
drove them out. In a sense, the American Revolution itself really answered that
old problem of 1763 – of how to make Canada thoroughly a part of the British
Empire. (Careless 1970: 115)

The appearance of this new population with "hyperloyalism to Britain,
Crown, and Empire" (McRae 1964: 239) changed the pattern of political
demands and "rapports de force." The outcome was the division of the
old Province of Quebec into Upper and Lower Canada.

Cultural and linguistic diversity was largely managed by creating parallel
geographical, social, and institutional spaces for the two collectivities. But
"the merchants opposed a division of geographical area that was based on
purely cultural distinctions. They were sure that in doing this, England
was breaking the unity of the commercial empire of the St Lawrence Valley
to such an extent that it would become extremely difficult to work out
policies that would take into consideration the needs of the economy as
a whole" (Ouellet 1967: 167).

The tensions between the two collectivities were accentuated by the
progressive emergence of a new group on the sociopolitical scene: a
French-speaking professional class.[5] Earlier, the appearance of the Loyalists precipitated the collapse of the existing institutional arrangements.
Now, a new class emerging within the French collectivity set in motion a
new sequence of institutional change. The new class of professionals was
well educated but relatively poor and powerless. Politics was the channel
they chose to gain influence and social recognition. They organized the
Parti Canadien and the newspaper *Le Canadien.* Their mission was to promote the interest of the French-Canadian nation, strengthen the traditional society, and eventually attain political supremacy.

Such ambitions brought them into conflict with the merchants and cap-
italists who also used a political party and a newspaper to promote their
interests (the Breton Party and the *Quebec Mercury*). The professional class
perceived the merchants as determined to undermine French-Canadian
institutions and society. "The proposals to revamp the transportation system
were regarded as the logical concomitants of this general program: its only

possible objective was to flood Lower Canada with English immigrants in order to achieve union of the two Canadas, and thereby to drown the French Canadians in an Anglo-Saxon sea. The aggressive attitude of the more militant-minded British simply seemed to confirm them in their convictions" (Ouellet 1967:270). The merchant party, on its side, was attempting to counter the rising power of this group, since it opposed the realization of its economic ambitions. They were especially nervous about the Parti Canadien's demand to increase the role of the elected legislative assembly by introducing ministerial responsibility. This would make government officials accountable to a largely French legislative assembly. This organizational reform was an attempt by the new rising class to institutionalize its access to political power.

They also ran into conflict with the clergy. Their political liberalism clashed with the bishop's hierarchical conceptions of polity and society. This internal conflict is relevant, because on some issues the clergy sided with the government and the merchants' party and on others with the Parti Canadien. Their stand depended on their perceptions of how particular outcomes would support or upset the social order and the dominant position that they enjoyed in it.

The Parti Patriote's demands for reform were rejected by Parliament in London in 1837. This occurred at a time of severe economic difficulties. The high level of discontent in the population was articulated by various political organizations. The result was the Revolt of 1837, a revolt easily crushed by the government.

The rebellion in Lower Canada was part of a widespread movement in the British North American colonies. They all experienced, in varying degrees, "the rule of small, tightly knit colonial oligarchies, to which Canadian history has applied the vivid but somewhat misleading term Family Compacts" (McRae 1964: 240).[6] Papineau's rebellion was accompanied by Mackenzie's in Upper Canada, and by peaceful reform movements pressuring for responsible government in the Maritimes. Of course, in Lower Canada, the unrest over oligarchic government had an ethnolinguistic dimension, but the split was not complete: some French supported the British party (the name the Tories in Lower Canada used to refer to themselves), and some English-speaking reformers supported French-speaking reformers (Careless 1970: 175).

Lord Durham was immediately sent from England to examine the situation. His 1839 report contained four recommendations of importance here:

1 the establishment of responsible government;[7]
2 the reduction of the political power of the French Canadians by neutralizing the effect of their numerical majority in the political decision-making process – so they could not obstruct the development projects of the English-speaking business class;

3 the assimilation of French Canadians into the English culture because, left to itself, French-Canadian society would remain static and hopelessly inferior;
4 the union of Lower and Upper Canada as a step towards achieving these objectives.

The Act of Union of 1840 established "a single parliament with equal representation from each constituent section; consolidation of the debt;[8] ... banishment of the French language from official government use; and suspension of specific French-Canadian institutions relating to education and civil law" (*Canadian Encyclopedia* 1985: 7). This Act's intention was quite different from the previous position taken by the British governors and administrators; their policy had been to accommodate the two cultural groups in the institutional framework. The denial of that reality almost assured the new regime would not last.

Initially, its inherent problems were hidden, partly because much of the dualism remained due to the vast territory and differences in language, civil code, judicial system, and forms of land tenure (Ormsby 1974: 271). Another reason was the economic situation (e.g., chronic unemployment and the dependence of Lower on Upper Canada for wheat), which changed attitudes toward the canal system and economic development. The large emigration of French Canadians (primarily to the United States)[9] also preoccupied the elites, who saw it as detrimental to their institution-building efforts.

Finally, the political issue that dominated the period was responsible government. The new Act had not established it. This was the central issue in Nova Scotia, Prince Edward Island, and Newfoundland, as well as in the Provinces of Canada. Reformers in Canada's East and West formed a coalition that brought about the desired goal in 1848. This collaboration undoubtedly helped reduce the sting of the many negative features of the Act of Union.

But these remained and continued to erode that accommodation. Ormsby notes equal representation, as a critical aspect of the political decision-making system, contributed the most to its vulnerability:

There were occasions when measures affecting only one-half of the province were passed or rejected by a minority from that section with the aid of a majority from the other section ... For more than a quarter of a century, the union managed to function as a quasi-federal system, but eventually the forces of dualism came into direct conflict with the unitary character of the constitution. (Ormsby 1974: 272)

The English-speaking population grew considerably during this period: it "rose from 125,000 in 1820 to 450,000 in 1842 and then more than

doubled during the remainder of the 40s to reach 952,000 by 1851"
(Beaujot and McQuillan 1982: 21). This growth resulted in an increased
demand to abolish the provision for equal representation in the Act of
Union. Now that it was a majority, the English-speaking population wanted
"Representation by Population." But just as such a system was unacceptable
to Upper Canadians when they were less numerous, it was not acceptable
to Lower Canadians now that they were becoming the numerical minority.

These phenomena dictated a return to the federal idea that had been
incorporated in the 1791 arrangement, although not in that particular
institutional form. Several factors led to Confederation:

the threat of American imperialism, the fear of the westward expansion of the
United States, the necessity for improved railway communications [and] the political impasse in Canada ... But the fundamental problem which faced the delegates
who met at Charlottetown and at Quebec [was] that of reconciling the conflicting
interests of the two racial groups and of the conflicting principles of centralization
and provincial autonomy. (Stanley 1974: 276)

Federalism appeared to be the most appropriate for a situation of cultural
dualism. It involves different levels of government, each with particular
powers and functions. The 1867 arrangement

gave the central government control of all matters that did not divide the two
ethnic groups, on issues in which both shared a common interest. As a rule, the
central power took over general services, administrative, technical and military
activities ... Everything that dealt with social, civil, family, education, or municipal
organization was allocated to the provinces ... They also administered public lands
and forests, prisons, hospitals, and charitable institutions. The provincial jurisdiction covered municipal organization and the incorporation of companies for
provincial objectives. (Hamelin 1961: 264–5)

The negotiated arrangement permitted within the context of a common
framework, the realization of the societal ambitions of *both* groups, giving
each the means to construct institutions that would incorporate their own
culture, language, and sociopolitical philosophy (Silver 1982; Careless
1970; Berger 1970).

FROM CONFEDERATION TO WORLD WAR II

In the decades after 1867, institution-building competition in Canada was
particularly intense. The outcome largely favoured English Canada.

The 1880s witnessed the rise of Canadian imperialism, a movement for
the closer union of the British empire and for Canadian participation in

it (Berger 1970:3). This movement helped shape the Canadian collective identity and English-French relations. Cole points out that imperialists, as Canadians,

did not aim at the creation of a Canadian nation ... They could scarcely even have conceived of a Canadian nation ethnically differentiated from its Anglo-Saxon and British forebearers ... [They] did, however, possess a very deep ethnic sense, a very strong consciousness of nationality. Their ethnic identity was not Canadian, but emphatically and intensely British. (Cole 1971: 171)

The imperialist movement began to organize Canadian branches of the Imperial Federation League. Given their ethnocultural orientation and their conception of Canada as an extension of Britain, it is not surprising that they clashed with French-Canadian nationalists, whose ethnocultural commitments were equally strong, and in whose collective memory the Conquest was deeply etched. These conflicting orientations clashed frequently, especially when the Boer War began in 1899 and during the conscription crises of the two World Wars.

A second significant phenomenon for defining the collective identity and the character of societal institutions was the growth of Protestant churches as powerful religious denominations[10] (Clark 1962: 170–71). Accompanying this church building was the social promotion of Protestantism and anti-Catholicism. The Orange Order, the Protestant Protective Association, and the Ku Klux Klan all actively defined the society as Protestant.[11] Mann (1976) observes this was one factor behind the church union movement, that "Protestant interest in a national church was partly a reaction to the steady expansion of Roman Catholicism, especially that of French Canada. Eastern Protestants were very sensitive to Roman Catholic political power, and had organized before 1902 several specifically anti-Roman organizations which vigilantly scrutinized Roman Catholic actions and expansion" (Mann 1974: 396). In French Canada, the corresponding concern was with the Catholic character of the society. It was of special concern to the "Ultramontanes," who included the right wing of the Church, both clergy and laity. They believed in the primacy of church over state (Linteau *et al.* 1979: 314–21) and were anti-Protestant. As in English Canada, this period saw the institutional church grow enormously in people joining religious orders.[12] The Protestant and Catholic movements reacted to each other's ideologies and political activities. Although the linguistic and religious cleavages coincided significantly, religious issues predominated. "Linguistic issues might arise from time to time *within* the Catholic community, but the primary line of cleavage was religious during this important formative period" (McRae 1974: 243).

Third, the elites of the two collectivities were greatly concerned with population size – both absolute and relative: absolute because society-building and expansion requires population; relative, because political power depends partly on numbers. Immigration policy was the main demographic instrument used by English-Canadian elites (Richmond 1967); in French Canada, a natality policy was systematically pursued by the clerical elites (Henripin 1957). Both succeeded: the two linguistic groups grew at about the same rate, so that the French-origin population stayed at about 30 percent of the total population throughout the period.[13]

Fourth, although the French Canadians maintained their relative numerical strength, English Canada, already larger by 1867, continually expanded during this period with the development of the West. This made the competition for political power within the federal arrangement increasingly uneven, accentuating a tendency begun when the Compact took place. Even though the arrangement was fundamentally for the political accommodation of two cultural groups,

the meeting ... at Charlottetown and at Quebec introduced a new interpretation which has had a mighty impact upon the course of our later history, namely, the idea of a compact between the politico-geographic areas which go to make up Canada ... Once Canadians ... began to identify provinces with specific linguistic groups, the idea of a pact between races was transformed into the idea of a pact between provinces. (Stanley 1974: 280–81)

The addition of new provinces and their successful cultural and political appropriation by English Canadians compounded the ambiguity – an ambiguity substantially detrimental to the symbolic and political weight of the French component of Canada.

Fifth, in spite of the failure of the 1840 arrangement, a preference for a unitary system continued on the part of the English-speaking political elite. Strong centralist tendencies were manifest in the implementation of the British North America Act.[14] There was, of course, resistance – not only from Quebec but from other provinces as well, Ontario in particular. In fact, as Fox (1969) argues, there has been since Confederation a regular "oscillation in the assertion of political power between the federal government and the provinces."

Sixth, the French were underrepresented in the federal Cabinet during most of the period: French-speaking ministers held, on the average, 22 percent of the person-years in the different governments during the 1867–1966 period. Also, their representation differed by type of ministry: policy making, 15 percent; human capital, 9 percent; support, 34 percent; co-ordinative, 34 percent; and without portfolio, 14 percent (Breton and

Roseborough 1968). Francophones were also underrepresented in the federal bureaucracy:[15] from about 36 percent before Confederation (1863), their percentage fell to about 22 percent by 1918 and to about 13 percent by 1946.

Finally, at the economic level, a shift toward the centre of the country took place. In the pre-industrialization period, wood and grain were the two main articles of commerce and the main points of development (including ship building) were along the St Lawrence. (In the United States, they were along the Atlantic seaboard.) The substitution of steel for wood and the construction of the railroads moved the points of development to Southern Ontario in Canada, and the mid-West in the United States (Faucher and Lamontagne 1953). This shift also contributed to the decreasing weight of French Canada in the federation.

The founding of Assiniboia as part of present day Manitoba is primarily a history of commercial and military conflict between two trading companies: the Hudson's Bay Company and the Montreal-based Northwest Company. This conflict ended when Selkirk, a Hudson's Bay Company stockholder who wanted an area to settle surplus population from Scotland and Ireland, took control of the colony in 1816 to 1817.

The settlement process really began only after this initial conflict for commercial hegemony. Institutions were established by the British, French, and Métis (of Native and French or Scottish origin). Colony building was slow: by the middle of the 19th century, the community had about 5,000 people. But Easterners began showing an interest in the West. Businessmen saw its annexation as an opportunity for commercial expansion. Political groups, such as the Clear Grit Party of Upper Canada, saw it as additional land for settlement that would check emigration to the United States and permit more British immigration (McInnes 1969: 315). The ambition, however, was not simply colonization but to prevent the American annexation of the West and to preclude its appropriation by French speakers. Both were indeed showing an interest in making that part of the continent their own. It should be noted, however, that at that time the interested French speakers were only the Métis and those who had settled in the West. As Silver (1982) demonstrates quite convincingly, French Québécois did not see "the Northwest as a field of settlement for French Canadians." They "did not look on Rupert's Land as part of their country, [and] neither did they look on the French Catholic Métis as part of their own nationality ... Quebec alone was the French Canadian homeland" (Silver 1982: 74; see also Lalonde 1982). The elite seemed primarily interested in developing the West because of its possible economic benefits for Quebec. On the other hand, many feared its annexation to Canada would tip the balance of power still further in favour of English Canada.

Events changed drastically with the annexation of the West by the Canadian government, whose officials saw it "only in relation to the Hudson's Bay Company's control ... Not for a moment did Canada think of consulting the inhabitants of Assiniboia nor of guaranteeing them any specific rights." Surveyors began land division procedures without regard for the settlers already there (Hamelin 1961: 279–80; McInnes 1969: 364). The Métis resisted. In 1869, led by Louis Riel, a group of them "arrested the surveyors working on the registration of the Saint-Vital area, a region that the Métis considered a fief of their own" (Hamelin 1961: 281). Attempts to stop the usurpation were made. Later the same year, the Métis seized Fort Garry and established a provisional government. The planned counterattack at Forty Garry by the Canadian party led to the capture of several of its members by the Métis and to the eventual execution of Thomas Scott. In short, a serious confrontation was underway for the control of land and institutions between French-speaking Métis and English-speaking settlers and migrants from Ontario.

These events, and especially Riel's show of force, provoked a strong reaction in Ontario where the uprising was defined as a French-Catholic attempt to overthrow British institutions:

Ontarians were naturally struck by the prominent role which the French Catholic element played at Red River ... many [also] looked upon the opening of the North-West not only as a great opportunity for the establishment of their own people, but as a great work of national and human progress, which would build up the wealth and population of Canada, provide homes for great numbers of people and produce food for the world's hungry. Now that work of progress was being sabotaged ... many of them saw the uprising as a French-Canadian enterprise aimed at stopping what the *Globe* had called, in 1863, "the wheels of Anglo-Saxon progress toward the setting sun." (Silver 1982: 80)

Because of its lack of interest in the West as an area for French settlement, Quebec opinion defined the uprising as a part of a movement for self-determination. not a fight for French or Catholic rights. However, the definition of the situation in Ontario triggered a change in Quebec's perception of the events and of their own collective identity: the Métis came to be seen as their compatriots and the North-West as part of *their* social and geographical space. Because of Ontario's conduct – or at least Quebec's view of it – the North-West started to be seen as another French-Catholic province that could assist Quebec's struggles with English Canada (Silver 1982: 82–3).

The Manitoba Act of 1870 was the response to Riel's demands supported by Quebec's pressure on Ottawa. It incorporated most of the claims of

Riel's provisional government: provincial status, official bilingualism, denominational schools, and guaranteed property rights for the inhabitants. But the question of political, economic, and cultural control was not solved. The basic issue remained: "Would the institutions of French-speaking Roman Catholic Quebec or English-speaking Protestant Ontario prevail?" (Lupul 1970: 273). The ambitions of groups such as Canada First, the Orange Order, the Equal Rights Association, the Protestant Protective Association and the Canadian Imperialists were clear: it was to be British and Protestant. French-Canadian rights should be confined to Quebec. The French Catholics, on the other hand, were determined to maintain their identity and institutions. The determination of one side accentuated the resoluteness of the other.

The critical factor of control, however, was not the attitudes themselves, but the shift in the balance of political power that resulted from a drastic change in the composition of the population.[16] The emerging English-speaking majority had political power and used it to achieve its cultural and institutional goals. The process whereby the new majority imposed its identity and culture on the political and social (education in particular) institutions began soon after 1870 and lasted about 35 years (although the critical changes had been made by 1890). The use of legislative power and the resistance it generated intensified feelings and attitudes on both sides. It brought into the political conflict Ontario, Quebec, the federal government, the Supreme Court, the British Judicial Committee, and the Vatican. The intensity of the conflict was further accentuated by events such as the second Métis rebellion, Riel's trial and execution in 1885, and the Jesuit's Estates controversy (which lasted several years).[17]

In the end, the power distribution favoured British Protestants: in 1890 the Manitoba legislature abolished the official status of French and the dual church-controlled Board of Education. But the controversy continued. The next legislative step was the Laurier-Greenway compromise of 1896. The religious part of the agreement was accepted by the Catholic minority, following the advice of the 1897 papal encyclical. The language controversy was halted with the repeal of the bilingual clause in 1916. "The feeling against bilingualism was so strong that even the study of a second language was omitted" (Lupul 1970: 278). Similar developments took place in other parts of the West:

The Territories eliminated French as a language of instruction except in the primary grades in 1892, but restored it in the upper grades for one hour per day at the end of the school day in 1901. In 1918, Saskatchewan reduced the use of French to the first year of school only, though the optional hour at the end of the school day was retained. In 1931, after continuing debates about papal influence and foreign subversion, the government ... virtually eliminated French as a language of instruction in Saskatchewan schools. Alberta permitted only limited use of languages other than English after a crackdown on abuses of school regulations in 1913. (Friesen 1984: 260)

In New Brunswick,[18] the conflict over cultural dominance and institutional control also took place primarily in the field of education. The first move concerned religion, not language (in 1871, the Common Schools Act established a general public school system; public funds were provided to nonsectarian schools) (Lupul 1970:272). The conflict between Protestants and Catholics, however, evolved into one between English and French. After a long period of isolation, poverty, and low political organization brought about by the deportation, a renewed political consciousness and mobilization emerged among Acadians in the latter part of the nineteenth century. The level of education was increasing; an elite had emerged and was growing; there were several media of public communication within the community. They were geographically concentrated, and their numbers were increasing; within the Catholic component of the population, they became a majority. Thus, the Common Schools Act of 1871 occurred at a time when the Acadians' social and organizational capacity for political mobilization was increasing. In addition, the Act would, if implemented, have important consequences for the Acadians. Most of them were Catholic and poorer than the English-speaking population. They were thus strongly affected by a legislation that eliminated government subsidies to sectarian schools. Their strong protest included a riot in 1875 in which two people died.

Predictably, the opposition to the legislation, both peaceful and violent, attracted attention in Quebec. Initially, the Quebec press saw the Act as an attack on their "co-religionists." But by 1875, newspapers were referring primarily to the *French* population of New Brunswick. Also, not surprisingly, Quebec opinion associated the events there with those in Manitoba and began defining the situation as a conspiracy against the French in the Dominion (Silver 1982: 97–100). A compromise acceptable to the Catholic hierarchy was eventually worked out. But the English-French conflict continued within the Catholic institutional system.

The hierarchy of the Church was Irish and Scottish, so an institution important to the French-speaking Catholic Acadians was largely under the control of another cultural group. The issues were not doctrinal: the confrontation was over the identity of the institution and its control. Acadians saw the Irish hierarchy as determined to prevent their own institutional development within the Catholic system and to restrict them from the high levels of the hierarchy. Considerable evidence suggests that the English-speaking hierarchy was determined to maintain its ascendancy and to impose its language and culture in the institution (Spigelman

1975). It is with the Vatican's intervention that Acadian claims began to be recognized.

The field of education also witnessed a public conflict between the English and French in Ontario.[19] After Confederation, the existence of French schools was largely a matter of population. It is accordingly demographic changes that provoked conflicts, starting in the 1880s. First, the French-speaking population was increasing more rapidly than the English-speaking population. The French still represented only eight percent of the population in 1911 (compared to five percent in 1881), but their social visibility vas accentuated by their concentration in particular regions.

Also, a large Irish-Catholic population entered Canada during the second half of the 19th century, and those new arrivals, being Catholic, often found themselves combined with French Catholics in French and bilingual schools. The increasing English-Protestant population also often found themselves combined with francophones in traditionally French-language public schools. Objectively, those changes may not have been drastic. They were, however, perceived and interpreted in terms of the sociopolitical context of the period (described earlier) and of the societal aspirations of British-origin Ontarians. Many feared that French in the schools in Ontario would *undermine the Anglo-Saxon character* of the province (Barber 1969: 63, emphasis added).[20] The society's cultural character was not only a public issue: it was experienced daily by parents socializing their children.

The ethnocultural majority began exercising its political power to consolidate its threatened societal project. In 1885, the study of English was made compulsory. In 1890, it became the required language of instruction, except where impracticable. French was accepted as a temporary expedient (Barber 1969: 64). As in New Brunswick, these moves contributed to the politicization of the French community, prompting them to organize to maintain the institutional means they saw as necessary for achieving *their* cultural aspirations. Their increasing numbers, concentration, and cohesion based on the social organization of the traditional parish, was the basis for political mobilization. A further impetus came from the changes in collective identity in Quebec and from the emerging definition of the political situation (with regard to Confederation) associated with it. Indeed, the cause of the French minorities outside Quebec was becoming an integral part of Quebec's own societal ambitions, Quebec, however, was ambivalent. Even though a pan-Canadian collective identity was emerging, there was a lot of concern for provincial autonomy. Thus, Quebec could not pressure the federal government to intervene without risking the reduction of its own autonomy.

The controversy lasted for several years. New educational measures were introduced by the provincial government, each bringing serious reactions.

The political activity of the French in turn increased the resolve of English-speaking Protestants and the pressure they applied on the government. Ironically, English-speaking Catholics sided with groups such as the Orange Order on this issue, but for different reasons. First, they perceived an educational system differentiated on linguistic lines as a threat to their hope for a religiously-based separate school system[21] – a justified fear. Second, there was, as in New Brunswick, an internal conflict for the control of the Catholic Church, and the growing strength and politicization of the French was interpreted in that connection. The friction inherent in the school situation was aggravated by a perpetual church feud involving all levels of the Catholic clergy. Neither Irish nor French neglected any opportunity to strengthen their own position as they vied for control of the Catholic church in Canada. One prominent Irish Catholic of the time noted:

Now, no one wants to do the French Canadians an injustice. The British Crown has given them what is actually an empire in the Province of Quebec, but no right or claim have they on this account, or on any other, to all the Provinces of the Dominion. They have been, with difficulty, kept out of Church control completely, in Ontario and the Maritime provinces, with difficulty driven out of that control in British Columbia. They are still in control of the Church organization in Manitoba, Alberta, and Saskatchewan. In this struggle, French Catholics were steadily building up strengths against Irish Catholics in eastern Ontario. (quoted in Barber 1969: 69)

The French lost the first round: Regulation 17 in 1913 restricted French as a language of instruction to Form I (the first two years of school). But the struggle continued; in fact French resistance against Regulation 17 intensified on two fronts: political and ecclesiastical. It persisted until the Regulation was made harmless in 1927 by an arrangement allowing negotiations on a case-by-case basis (Choquette 1975: 173–220).[22] Choquette sums up the evolution of anglophones who became exhausted with the continual strife while eventually recognizing the need for an accommodation to assure the existence of the country. He also notes that an extensive change occurred among most concerned parties and, most important, the Unity League was established in Toronto. Also, organizations such as the Orange Order were in political decline.

One significant change in Quebec during this period was already discussed, namely, the political articulation of a bilingual conception of Confederation. It emerged progressively with the actions of English-Protestant groups outside Quebec:

In 1867, French Quebecers had seen their province alone as the home of the French-Canadian nationality, and looked to Confederation to separate it as much as possible from the others. But many were now coming to accept some notion of a Canadian nation based on equality between two races, each having guaranteed rights in *all* provinces. This view emerged from events in the intervening decades. It was only *after* French Quebecers had discovered and become concerned about French-Catholic minorities, only *after* they had tried to help the Métis, only *after* the Riel affair, the racial agitation of the late 1880s and the controversies of the 1890s – only *after* all this that the bilingual theory of Confederation could emerge (Silver 1982: 192, emphasis in original).

Another important development was the industrialization and urbanization of the province and the impact these had on its social structure, on its sociopolitical mobilization, and on its conceptions of its place in the Canadian social and political structure. Industrialization was introduced and controlled by English speakers – a phenomenon that an extremely powerful clergy was content to accept. By defining business and industry as English, the clergy maintained their social and cultural hegemony in the society. Thus, since English and French elites each had their own institutional domains, confrontations were reduced (or postponed). At least two other factors contributed to the absence of confrontations within Quebec (as opposed to the Canada-wide scene). First, the BNA Act guaranteed each group its educational system. Second, there was considerable emigration, primarily to the United States. The "exit" that over 800,000 people chose between 1840 and 1930 (Lavoie 1981) probably helped contain the tensions between English and French in Quebec. But the impact of the ongoing socioeconomic changes could not be curbed indefinitely.

FROM WORLD WAR II TO THE PRESENT

In the previous period, most of the pressure and organized actions to establish or transform institutional forms were initiated by English Canadians. To a considerable extent, they gained control over public institutions and established their cultural and linguistic ascendancy. French Canadians, as French, as Catholics, or both, offered considerable resistance, attempting to protect their own institutional domains. But by and large, they had to accommodate to the anglophone societal project. In the recent period, however, the pressures for change came from the French, primarily in Quebec. English speakers generally resisted their attempts to expand their economic, political, and cultural control, but some supported these changes.

As already indicated, the Quiet Revolution of the 1960s accelerated the processes of social and political changes that began much earlier (Guindon 1964, 1908; Behiels 1985). These broke down what remained of the traditional social structure. The percentage of the French origin population that was urban grew from 55 percent to 71 percent between 1941 and 1961, and the rural farm population declined from 41 percent to 13 percent. Between 1950 and 1960, school attendance "more than doubled in grades nine to twelve and increased beyond grade twelve by more than 50 percent" (Brazeau 1964: 325).

In many ways an increasingly new kind of population lived in Quebec. Its numerical expansion and power aspirations led to attempts to conquer or reconquer institutional spaces, generating confrontations with those who already controlled those spaces: the traditional French-Canadian elites, the clergy and the groups represented by the Duplessis regime; the English-speaking groups dominating the Quebec economy; the politico-bureaucratic groups controlling the federal government; and the "other ethnic groups" who had allied themselves with the Anglos and who, wittingly or not, supported their institutions.

The agenda of the new contending groups was to gain control of the means necessary for organization-building, particularly political power and capital; to displace, partly or completely, those occupying the coveted organizations and positions; to claim new ones that English speakers would, under the existing dispensation, have considered their own "turf;" and to redefine the collective identity in ways compatible with their societal aspirations. The resistance of English-speaking groups corresponded to these three lines of action: resistance to the redistribution of political and economic power; loss or potential loss of organizational domains; and transformation of the symbolic-cultural character of the Canadian society that they had struggled to establish.

Implementing this agenda led to confrontations in the Quebec, Canada-wide, and provincial arenas, although the specific claims at issue were frequently quite different from one to the other. Also, different groups of francophones pursued action in each arena. The differences – not to say contradictions – in their programs frequently brought them into conflict with one another.

In addition to a systematic change of French-Quebec society, the Quiet Revolution involved a nationalistic drive to transform its relationship with English-speaking Canada. This nationalism expressed itself in different ways, but the most important was the independentist movement. It generated an enormous pressure for change, both in Quebec and in Canada. Organizationally, the movement began in the mid-1950s with the formation of several organizations covering a wide ideological spectrum. They varied in terms of general sociopolitical philosophy; in their nationalist program; in the strategies advocated to reach independence (e.g., through democratic procedures versus violence).[23]

The most significant development, however, was the formation of the Parti Québécois, its initial electoral accomplishments (electing six members

to l'Assemblée nationale in 1970), and its victory as a majority government
in 1976. Terrorist activities, primarily by the FLQ, added enormously to
the pressure for change, culminating in 1970 with the kidnapping of James
Cross and Pierre Laporte, and with the latter's assassination. These events
provoked the proclamation of the War Measures Act, which affirmed the
power of the central state with the quasi-unanimous support of the federal
Parliament (Breton 1972)[24].

The independentist movement was a powerful force aimed at a drastic
redistribution of political power. At the cultural-symbolic level, it expressed
the alienation of Québécois who could not identify with the institutions
and milieu that British Canadians had created "in their own image" during
the previous historical period. It expressed a sense of powerlessness with
regard to institutions seen as anglophone-controlled: the sense of being
at the economic and political periphery. Complete political autonomy was
argued to be an essential condition for the economic and cultural vitality
of Québécois society.

Several interrelated lines of action were pursued. One of the most
important concerned the language of public institutions. The changes in
the linguistic rules of the game were part of the process whereby institutional control was sought. The use of state powers to impose the French
language was new in Quebec. In many ways, it corresponds to the earlier
use of state powers to impose English in other provinces.

As the history in English-speaking provinces shows, the process involves a
long political struggle, since the outcome sought is a new dispensation in
which one group assumes institutional dominance, defines the organizational rules and practices; and specifies the conditions of membership and
of access to rewards. Language is crucial for gaining organizational ascendancy: one's participation in the organizational system, the centrality of one's
position in it, and the rewards one can obtain depend upon one's competence in the language and linguistic practices of the controlling group.

The first comprehensive legislation "La loi sur la langue officielle" (Law
22) was adopted in 1974. It made French the official language of Quebec,
making that province officially unilingual like all other provinces except
New Brunswick (although its official unilingualism, like Manitoba's, is
restricted by the BNA Act). Law 22 contained a wide range of specifications
for the language of public administration and utilities, the professions,
places of work, business, and education. A few years later (1977), Quebec's
Assemblée nationale replaced that law with the "Charte de la langue
française" (Law 101). It reasserted many of the specifications of the previous
legislation, but went further by adding others, but especially by putting in
place increased legal and organizational means for their implementation.

Also, since the vitality of organizational systems, public or private,
depends in part on the size of the population, attempts were made to

direct immigrants into the French institutional system. This was especially necessary in view of the now very low birth rate among francophones. It required that control be gained over immigration (a federal prerogative), that the children of immigrants attend French schools, and that integration programs be created for immigrants. The compulsory elements of this strategy were strongly resisted by members of ethnic groups, who saw their chances of upward mobility potentially threatened by a reduced competence in the dominant language. It was also resisted by anglophone institutions, particularly the schools, which were about to experience a serious reduction in the size of their clientele and, consequently, in the opportunities offered by their institutions.

Both pieces of legislation were highly controversial. This was, in part, because they were redefining the cultural-symbolic character of Quebec society and changing the relative sociopolitical status of the two linguistic groups. They were also controversial because they were aiming toward an increase of francophone control of the Quebec economy, an objective explicitly stated.[25] The legislation tried to open avenues of social mobility to francophones in organizations in which the English language prevailed, and acted as a barrier for many upwardly mobile francophones.

Other lines of action were also pursued. For instance, the strategy of institutional development and control also involved taking over enterprises previously owned or controlled by anglophones: establishing state agencies for the accumulation of capital; and gaining control of existing sources of capital (such as the public Pension Fund).[26]

The overall objective was to create a society that would be predominantly if not exclusively French (just like the strategy in other parts of Canada was to create a British society.) It was a return to seeing Quebec as the homeland of the French in North America – a view that, as Silver (1982) notes, prevailed at the time of Confederation. The French community did not see itself as a minority in Canada, but as a majority in its own territory. They increasingly saw themselves as Québécois, not French Canadians. Correspondingly, British-origin Quebecers were being defined as a minority; they still had a special status, but they were nevertheless a minority.

It is not claimed that all components of the strategy were or will be successful. Gains appear to have been made, although a systematic and accurate assessment of these gains is very difficult.[27] It may even be premature to make such an assessment. Indeed, the legislation has been in place for a little over ten years only. This is a very short period of time for assessing trends and changes at the level of a society. But it seems that the legitimacy of French as the official and operative language in Quebec is increasing; that it is more used at work than before (Breton and Grant 1981); that immigrants are slowly being absorbed in the francophone social and institutional networks; and that more Quebec anglophones are bilingual.

Concurrent with the separatist movement was a movement to integrate Quebec in the Canadian sociopolitical and symbolic fabric. Those pursuing this objective – the federalists – struggled to increase the presence of francophones in the federal institutions, political and administrative. The aim was to raise the power of French Canadians in defining national goals and in allocating national resources. It was also to transform the cultural-symbolic character of federal institutions, so that French Canadians could identify with them and consider them their own (Breton 1984)[28]. This federalist component of French-Canadian nationalism, continuing with the nationalism that emerged during the previous historical period, defined Canada (and not only Quebec) as the homeland of French Canadians. Supported by many English-speaking Canadians, especially in the elite, French power increased in Ottawa: more francophones were appointed as cabinet ministers and to powerful ministries; important agencies were more likely to be led by francophones than was previously the case; the proportion of francophones in the civil service increased considerably (and rapidly); and the federal institutions began changing from a primarily unilingual to a bilingual system.

The two approaches are quite different. One tries to strengthen the boundary between the two communities. It assumes that Quebec is the homeland of the French in Canada; that francophone resources and energies should be used to develop that society. This "segmentalist" view states it is unrealistic to expect the French language and culture to survive and develop elsewhere in Canada (except, perhaps, in one or two regions). In the other "pan-Canadian" approach, the francophone and anglophone communities are seen to exist in all regions of the country. Thus, it is important that in all regions, whenever numbers warrant it, services be provided for the education of children in the language and culture of the family; that other cultural facilities, such as radio and television stations, be available, and that individuals be able to use, in their own language, the services of at least the federal government – but preferably those of the other levels of government as well.

The supporters of each approach tend to come from different social groups. Independence and sovereignty-association have been endorsed primarily by intellectuals,[29] other professionals, semi-professionals and technicians, and by clerical/sales workers. In the 1980 referendum, 67 percent of intellectuals, 61 percent of other semi-professionals and technicians, and 56 percent of those in liberal professions voted yes, in contrast to 38 percent of managers and proprietors, 39 percent of farmers, and 45 percent of workers.[30]

An intense opposition existed between the proponents of each of these approaches. The successes of one group were perceived as detrimental to the pursuits of the other. Some English-speaking Canadians supported the federalists because they agreed with them, although many did so because they saw them as the lesser of two evils. Many, however, did not see the opposition between the two political factions, and even sensed a sinister collusion between them to lower the status of English Canadians and erode their institutions and culture in Quebec, while taking control in the rest of the country.

Parallel changes occurred outside Quebec. Modernization created new elites and a renewed organizational capacity for political action. Changing attitudes among some English Canadians, government language policies, and the independentist threat contributed to a new sense of power among francophones outside Quebec. On the other hand, the Quebec-centredness of the independentist movement incited francophones outside Quebec to think of their communities not as extensions of Quebec but as distinct sociopolitical entities. In the process, regional identities were redefined, and the provinces were perceived as the significant political environments (Juteau-Lee and Lapointe 1979).

Thus, demands for change were also articulated in provincial arenas. There were, however, considerable variations in the results. The political difficulties in giving increased official recognition and institutional services to the francophones varied. In all provinces except Quebec and New Brunswick, francophones constitute a small percentage of the total population, frequently smaller than that of other ethnic groups. Many people do not see why the French should receive special treatment. Thus, institutional recognition and services are legitimated in reference to the larger pan-Canadian context, but not without meeting much resistance. Also, the high rate of assimilation of people of French origin (except perhaps in New Brunswick) weakens the political will of the provincial elites on these matters. This generates a downward spiral: the minority situation and the high rate of assimilation do not encourage governments to give recognition and services: this encourages assimilation which, in turn, reduces numerical and institutional strength.

CONCLUSION

Canada is a plural or segmented society, divided along linguistic lines into two parallel institutional systems. To a large extent, the material well-being of English- and French-speaking Canadians depends on the opportunities and services provided by their linguistic subsocieties. Their individual identities are largely constructed in relation to the cultural features of their respective institutions and nourished by their symbolic activities. Their self-esteem is determined by the societal status of the linguistic group with which they identify. Thus, members of each collectivity have an interest in the vitality and growth of their own subeconomies; in the cultural character of their own subsociety; and in its public status in relation to the other. They compare their societal condition with that of the other; they constantly "watch" how well the other group is doing in different areas compared to their own.

Accordingly, both seek institutional control for the realization of their material and symbolic-cultural interests. Both want their organizational domains to expand so as to provide more opportunities as their aspirations and/or population grow. Both want institutions that embody their culture and operate in their language. The historical overview presented here shows that the history of English-French relations in Canada is characterized by recurrent power struggles for the control of the means required for society building in its economic, cultural, and linguistic dimensions.

The existence of parallel institutional systems is not the only defining feature of a plural society. These systems operate and evolve within an overarching framework. There exist, so to speak, two interrelated levels of societal organization. What happens at one level can have momentous implications for the other. The policies of the federal government or of national corporations can affect the economic and cultural condition of each of the linguistic subsocieties. They can affect the linguistic groups *qua* linguistic groups or because of their geographical concentration (Nielsen 1985:143). Controlling the overarching structures of decision making and resource allocation is therefore critical. As we have seen, the English and French have competed for the control of these institutions since the Conquest.

On the other hand, what happens within each subsociety also has implications for the distribution of power at the level of the common institutions. Generally, the significant internal changes are those that have brought about new aspirations and, consequently, new demands for change, and those that have affected the relative power of the two linguistic collectivities. Three kinds of circumstantial changes that have triggered a new round of competition and conflict have been noted:

1 Changes in the extent to which one or both groups are politically mobilized either to take advantage of opportunities for further gains, or to resist or challenge the institutionalized system if they see themselves in a disadvantaged position.
2 Changes in the absolute and relative size of the two populations and the appearance on the sociopolitical scene of new categories of people or the growth of existing ones. Such changes have been the result of socioeconomic development: the rise in available resources, in education, and in organizational potential. They have accompanied the growth in state activity since World War II, especially in areas of provincial jurisdiction. Governmental expansion has meant the growth of a

professional-bureaucratic class. They have been brought about by external forces such as the American War of Independence and the massive American and Anglo-Canadian investments in Quebec after World War II.

3 Contradictions or problems unresolved by previous accommodations or caused by new arrangements. Such contradictions become progressively more apparent as the arrangements are put in practice.

The overview has shown that the outcome of the conflicts has depended on the distribution of power between the two collectivities: on the moderating impact of economic and other interdependencies: and occasionally, on the mediating influence of "third parties." The power inequality has varied from one historical period to another: the immediate post-Conquest period, the years of the American War of Independence, the second half of the 19th century, and the post-World War II decades have witnessed significant power shifts between French and English. Variations have also been noted between Canada-wide, Quebec, and other arenas of confrontation and accommodation (and these have differed over time as well). Given the regional character of Canadian society, and the differences in the situation of English and French in the different regions, it is misleading to speak of *the* relationship between English and French. The expression "English-French relations" refers to several relationships involving different distributions of demographic, economic, and political power. Nevertheless, there has been an underlying pattern of resource competition for societal construction and development; for the control of institutions, the opportunities they can provide, and the symbolic cultural features they embody.

CHAPTER SIX

From Ethnic to Civic Nationalism in English Canada and Quebec*

TYPES OF NATIONALISM: ETHNIC AND CIVIC

Nationalism is a component of the process whereby a particular kind of sociopolitical entity is constructed, maintained, expanded or otherwise transformed. The social construction process involves, on the one hand, the acquisition of control over resources – resources that tend to be territorially based. This is the instrumental or utilitarian dimension of society-building. The construction of a community or society also entails the definition of a collective identity, its content, and the forms through which it is represented. This is the cultural-symbolic dimension of social formations. These two components are closely interconnected: "The struggle to capture the core of personal identity mirrors more or less the struggle to control resources" (Westhues 1980: 353).

Nationalism is an ideology, a system of ideas that orients the social construction process and legitimizes its outcome. The ideological systems can be more or less theoretically elaborate, more or less grounded on historical evidence – real or fictitious – and more or less rich in symbolic and ritualistic expressions. But whatever their complexity, they tend to contain four basic elements:

a) Principles of inclusion and exclusion. Who is an insider and an outsider? Who has the "right stuff" to be considered a member and not an alien?

_____

* "From Ethnic to Civic Nationalism: English Canada and Quebec," *Ethnic and Racial Studies* 11, 1 (1988): 85–102.

Who can rightfully claim access to the resources controlled by the collectivity? Whose language and culture is to be embodied in the public institutions of the society? In addition, the ideology usually identifies who has the legitimate authority to define the "right stuff," to spell out the content of the collective identity or, at least, certify its sociocultural validity.

b) A conception of the "national interest." What does the collectivity need, and what problems does it face? What kinds of behaviours are particularly desirable to meet the needs or deal with the problems? This component of the ideology plays a special role in activating and sustaining the social mobilization process required for the construction of any social formation.

c) Comparisons with other groups. How is the group doing (politically, economically, demographically, and culturally) in comparison to others? What distinguishes it from other collectivities as far as history, values, and way of life are concerned? This dimension includes, implicitly or explicitly, a selection of the groups with whom comparison is appropriate (the "significant others"), and the criteria along which comparisons are to he made. For example, Quebec usually compares itself with Ontario, not France, the US, or Western Canada (although these may be selected as points of comparison in particular regards). French-Canadians compare themselves with "les Anglais," not with Americans. Ontarians, on the other hand, are more likely to compare themselves with Americans (e.g., "How different are we from them?"; "How does our standard of living compare to theirs?") than with other groups. Eastern Canadians rarely compare themselves to Western Canadians, unless the latter accuse Easterners of exploiting them, or otherwise draw their attention to their situation.

d) Views as to the ways in which the social environment can threaten or support the group. This includes the identification of the specific groups that can have an impact on one's condition, as well as theories concerning their motivations or interests, and their usual strategies.

Even though the social construction process and the related nationalistic ideologies usually entail both dimensions, the emphasis placed on the instrumental or on the cultural-symbolic can vary considerably. Some are based primarily, and even exclusively, on economic and political considerations; the content of others refers mainly to values, customs, and traditions. When this is the case, it is possible to analyse the evolution of collectivities in terms of two types of nationalism (Smith 1971; Cook 1977). As ideal types, they can be described as follows.

In one type of nationalism, the society and institutions that are constructed are seen as founded on cultural unity. The basis of inclusion and exclusion is ethnic (e.g., ancestry, language, religion, cultural distinctiveness of individuals to the collective entity is primarily symbolic and socio-emotional, rather than pragmatic or utilitarian. Hence, they are mobilizable for the pursuit of collective goals on the basis of loyalty to the collectivity, rather than of personal benefits they can derive from membership in it. They are less likely to leave the group when membership in another collectivity is perceived as providing a higher standard of living. A central preoccupation is with the cultural character of the community and its preservation. Accordingly, although the impact of other groups on one's material well-being is important, the main threats that the group and its elite focus upon are those that pertain to its cultural and linguistic integrity and maintenance.

In this type of nationalism, multilingual and multicultural states do not make much sense: they are perceived as awkward and unstable, as likely to entail discrimination and therefore internal conflict, and as a result they are seen as conducive to a lower quality of life. The ideal societies are those in which political and linguistic boundaries coincide. This type of nationalism has been labelled cultural, ethnic, or primary.

The other type emphasizes the instrumental dimension of societal institutions. Societies are constructed in order to acquire control over resources, to solve problems, and to defend members against enemies. Societies are seen as rational-legal entities. The preoccupation is with the domain or territory over which societal institutions have jurisdiction. The basis of inclusion or exclusion is civic: it is by birth or on the basis of legally-established criteria and procedures. Theoretically, anyone who meets the criteria can become a member. In addition, the criteria tend to pertain to the economic well-being or development of the society – not its cultural character. In this nationalism, the cultural is dissociated from the political.

The attachment of individuals to the social order is primarily utilitarian. The community is based on interest, not on symbolic identification. Comparison with other societies is in terms of the "national product," and other indicators of economic development and the standard of living. Culture is relatively easily sacrificed if a particular course of action is perceived as economically beneficial and if national sovereignty is preserved (so as to be able to make other advantageous moves in the future). This type of nationalism has been called political, civic, territorial, or secondary.

Since they are ideal types, few nationalisms correspond to these descriptions. There are few, if any, pure types in reality. The distinction is nevertheless useful. First, nationalistic ideologies and the accompanying definitions of collective identities do differ in the extent to which they emphasize one or the other orientation. Second, the existence of the distinction allows a comparison of situations where the distinction is irrelevant with those where it is. Third, nationalism can change in one or the other direction: from ethnic to civic or *vice versa*. Finally, there can be circumstances, such that one of the orientations and the course of action that it inspires is in contradiction with the other. For instance, the economic conditions in which a collectivity finds itself and/or its materialistic values can have policy implications in contradiction with its desire to maintain its cultural heritage and distinctiveness.

In particular, the distinction seems useful to understand the features of nationalism in English Canada and in Quebec, as well as its evolution over time. This is the object of this essay. After characterizing English-Canadian nationalism in its initial phase, the ways in which changing circumstances have impinged upon it will be considered. The transformations that it underwent will then be discussed, as well as the reactions – positive and negative – that this collective experience brought about. The same analysis will then be carried out with Quebec nationalism. Similarities and differences with the evolution of English-Canadian nationalism will be identified.

ENGLISH CANADA

In its early phase and, to a certain extent still today, the nationalism of English-speaking Canadians was ethnic. The society that this collectivity was attempting to construct was to be British:

the only phenomenon in anglophone Canada that can qualify as nationalism is precisely the Britannic or Anglo-Saxon ideology which identified Canadians with their anglophone partners within the Empire or elsewhere … Its nationalists are, quite confusedly, called imperialists, but its adherents had far more in common with German, pan-slav, Italian (or French-Canadian) nationalism than with anything that should be termed Canadian nationalism. (Cole 1980: 1–2)[1]

The ideal envisaged was the coincidence of cultural with political boundaries in Canada. It is not an accident that the document that became the country's constitution was called the *British* North America Act.

Ethnic minorities were to be assimilated. The prevailing ideology was "Anglo-conformity" (Palmer 1976a). The hope was that the conquered French would eventually accept and internalize the values and way of life of the British civilization. Immigrants were also expected to adopt the culture of the Anglo-Saxon group. When seen as necessary, cultural conformity was to be enforced as much as possible. British institutions were favoured. This was perhaps especially striking with regard to language: the teaching of languages other than English was made increasingly difficult, when not entirely forbidden.

These cultural expectations, and the related imposition of the English language and of British institutions, were based on a sense of cultural

superiority. Anglo-Saxon values, religious and secular, and the corresponding way of life were considered superior. Hofstadter's analysis of American
thought in this regard appears to be applicable to British-Canadians: "The
Darwinian mood sustained the belief in Anglo-Saxon racial superiority
which obsessed many American thinkers in the latter half of the 19th
century. The measure of world domination already achieved by the 'race'
seemed to prove it the fittest" (Hofstadter 1944:172–3).

On the other hand, the French and other ethnic minorities were seen
as a threat, or at least as a major challenge, to the cultural future of the
society under construction. In the case of non-British immigrants, it is true,
as Palmer points out, that they were associated in people's minds with
slums, radicalism, intemperance, and criminality, but "the most pervasive
fear of opinion leaders was that southern and eastern Europeans would
wash away Anglo-Saxon traditions of self-government in a sea of illiteracy
and inexperience with 'free' institutions" (Palmer 1976a: 494). Thus,
members of ethnic minorities were not to be "allowed to speak their own
language, to be led by priests of their own faith or to read newspapers in
their own language" (Rea 1977: 6).

Protestant churches and especially the schools were seen as the main
agencies of assimilation. In this connection, Rea notes that:

Any rough survey of educational materials used in the Manitoba schools from 1910
through the 1920s reveals that the values being emphasized were British-Canadian
nationalism, individualism, the Protestant work ethic, materialism, and so on. It is
a truism, of course, to state that a public school system reflects the values of those
who control it. In Manitoba's case, after 1916 those who devised curricula, selected
textbooks and directed patriotic observances were committed to the use of the
schools as an assimilative agent. (Rea 1977: 9–10)

In short, the basis of inclusion in Canada was Britishness by birth or by
assimilation into it (Anglo-conformity). The "national interest" was largely
defined in terms of preserving and buttressing the cultural character of
the society and its institutions. Social comparisons processes focused on
other cultural groups, the neighbouring French Catholic community
being one of the most important at the time; and the comparisons were
occasions to reaffirm the superiority of British culture, language, and institutions, religion being central at the time. The main threats perceived
were cultural; they were posed by groups whose cultures were deemed to
be either inferior to or incompatible with the values and ways of life of
the ethnic group attempting to establish its cultural ascendancy.

With time, several problems and obstacles to the construction of an
ethnically British society were encountered. There was, in particular, a
growing tension between that conception of the cultural character of the

society and the composition of the population.[2] First, the "French fact" was not disappearing, and in all likelihood, would not do so in the foreseeable future. To a considerable extent, the presence of this linguistic group had been accommodated with the adoption of a federal political system. But a new phenomenon began to take place toward the latter part of the 19th century, namely a significant change in French-Canadian nationalism. At the time of Confederation, the French-Canadian elite saw Quebec as the homeland of the French in North America. They generally favoured the confederative arrangement because they thought that it would give them enough independence to assure the maintenance of their culture and institutions. They had little or no interest in the rest of Canada, except for its potential economic and political impact on their own society.

But incidents, such as the Riel rebellion in Manitoba, the school question in New Brunswick, Manitoba, and Ontario, and the reaction to those events in English Canada, especially in Ontario, gave rise to a pan-Canadian nationalism among the French. Progressively, the collectivity that mattered was extended to all Canada. It was not restricted to Quebec any more. Accordingly, the French began to demand the institutional means necessary to preserve the French language and culture throughout the country (Silver 1982). That is to say, the attempts to impose Anglo-conformity on the French outside of Quebec, although successful to a considerable extent, generated a strong opposition that reinforced the French-Canadian determination to survive as a distinct cultural group.

Second, the demographic and economic components of nation-building produced results that hindered the entrenchment of a British ethnic nationalism. The pragmatic, utilitarian dimension of nation produced policies that were to eventually endanger the cultural project of British Canadians. A social contradiction was to emerge between the politico-economic and the ethnocultural orientations of their nationalism.

The desire to settle the West, for instance, led to the recruitment of a large number of non-British immigrants. The increase of this immigration began in the early part of the century and, although slowed down considerably during the Great Depression and the Second World War, continued to the late 1970s. Although seen as necessary for the development of the country, the newcomers nevertheless represented a major cultural challenge: what does it mean to have an ethnically British society when an increasingly larger proportion of the population have other ethnic origins?

Finally, the challenge faced by English-Canadian nationalism was also the result of its success in the imposition of Anglo-conformity, at least in its linguistic dimension. Indeed, most immigrants and their descendants willingly or reluctantly adopted the English language and internalized the conception of Canada as an English-speaking country.

These changes had several consequences, or more precisely, they set in motion a number of social and political processes, the effects of which progressively manifested themselves over time. The following are among the most important in the present context.

First, the linguistic assimilation of minorities dissociated ethnicity from language. Being English-speaking did not reveal one's ethnic origin. One was part of the linguistic but not of the ethnocultural collectivity. This dissociation meant that the English language was increasingly reduced to being a means of communication; it was losing its significance as a vehicle of culture and a symbol of group membership.[3] It also meant that the definition of the English-Canadian collective identity became quite confused. Indeed, who is an English-Canadian in such circumstances? How is that identity to be defined? What are to be the principles of inclusion and exclusion? The ambiguity of terms such as "anglophone" and "francophone" is very revealing in this regard. It is also significant that these terms are now widely used: they almost have to be, as there does not seem to be any other that would denote more accurately the existing collective identities – identities that are themselves in the process of being defined (or redefined).

Also, ethnicity became progressively dissociated from religion. During the early decades of the century, ethnic and denominational affiliations coincided to a considerable extent: a large proportion of British-origin persons belonged to British-heritage denominations. In situations where ethnicity and religion are superimposed, as was the situation in much of Canada in the 19th and early 20th centuries, "it was easy for cultural attachments to mask themselves as theological principles" (Grant [1972], quoted by Cheal 1981: 45). However, with the demographic changes due to immigration, the coincidence of ethnic and religious boundaries became increasingly blurred. Ethnicity and religious identification became more differentiated: "By the end of the 1960s it must have been increasingly difficult for British-Canadian cultural attachments to mask themselves as theological principles" (Cheal 1981: 45). The trend toward secularization no doubt facilitated this change by decreasing the importance of religious boundaries.

In addition, the basis of membership in the collectivity could be less and less defined in ethnocultural terms. Full membership and the accompanying rights had to be defined "irrespective of national origin, race, religion, ethnic origin." The growth in the number of those of the second and third generation among members of ethnic minorities was an important factor in bringing about this transformation. Indeed, these people were definitely Canadians and could therefore not be defined as "strangers" or aliens in any legal sense. They may have continued to be considered as less than completely Canadian by some segments of the "host" society; as possessing only part of the "right stuff" to be full members, either at the symbolic-cultural or at the instrumental level. But they were there. And they thought of themselves as Canadians. They saw themselves as citizens "à part entière," even though they were not members of the anglo collectivity.

Finally, the changing circumstances undermined the historical basis of the collective identity that had been articulated in the nationalistic ideology of British-Canadians. Indeed, it became increasingly difficult to maintain the view that "Canada's destiny would be played out in and through the British Empire ... By the time WWI ended, a different kind of Canadian national feeling was increasingly shouldering aside the old, traditional, imperialist, British-oriented type of nationalism" (Vipond 1982: 82). In other words, the link with a particular history became more and more irrelevant, as the composition of the linguistic collectivity changed. This process was accentuated by the progressive decline of the British Empire.

These are some of the processes involved in the transformation of English-Canadian nationalism from an ethnic to a civic orientation. The emerging collective identity is partly based on the notion of cultural pluralism. That is to say, the circumstances are forcing the collectivity to a new conception of itself – that of a collectivity that fully incorporates as citizens, people of different ethnic origins.

This does not mean that the transition was welcomed, that the project of an ethnically-British society was rapidly abandoned. On the contrary, resistance to the anticipated changes increased on several fronts. Nevertheless, a number of opinion leaders began to see that their conception of Canadian society would have to be modified. First, English-Canadian collective conception began to change in the face of the failure to assimilate French-Canadians, a failure that "aborted the entrenchment of a British sense of identity, or of a British pan-nationalism, in Canada" (Nock 1981: 92). Recurrent linguistic confrontations and their impact on national unity also contributed to a change in collective identity. For some time, anglophone historians (and in all likelihood, other members of the cultural elite) had accepted the idea that the British constituted a race, a people who were descended from a common stock. Their discourse was cast in terms of "blood," "hereditary mental traits," and "instincts" – this last being one of the favourite words (Levitt 1981: 2–3).

The weight given to heredity progressively decreased, because the cultural and institutional clashes between English and French represented a serious obstacle to the integration of Canadian society:

Glorifying the Anglo-Saxon race made good nationalist sense because it increased pride in the British heritage and made it possible to envisage a greater Canadian role in world politics as a "linchpin" connecting the British and the Americans. But such an outlook threatened national unity by disparaging French-Canadians ... If French-Canadian nationalism was indeed anchored in the "blood," then no

amount of persuasion would induce its proponents to shift their attitudes. Moreover, harping on racial differences would raise the inevitable question of why a
Canada should exist at all, if the most numerous ethnic group in Canada belonged
to the same race as the majority of Americans. (Levitt 1981: 4–5)

Thus, the racial thinking was tempered by the belief that mental traits
could be modified, in the long run, by culture and geography.

Second, English Canada slowly moved, more or less willingly, toward a
multicultural conception of its society, that is toward a greater acceptance
of ethnic diversity within its social boundaries. For a long time, the presence of a variety of ethnic groups was accepted, to the extent that their
members exhibited "Anglo-conformity" in their behaviour and their attitudes. Their presence was also used as an argument against further recognition of the "French fact" in Canada: "if special recognition and status is
given to the French language and culture, the same will have to be done
for the other ethnic minorities and, as a result, the country will be unmanageable." But this set of attitudes has changed in recent decades. The federal and provincial policies of multiculturalism can be taken as an indicator
of such a change. Public opinion surveys also show a greater acceptance
of cultural pluralism (Berry 1976). In other words, a shift from an ethnic
to a civic nationalism can be observed; a shift from a culturally-exclusive
to an inclusive conception of the collectivity is slowly taking place.[4]

It should be emphasized that the process of transformation is still under
way: a number of sub-groups in English Canada still attempt to promote,
or at least maintain, the British character of Canadian society. But British-
oriented nationalism is becoming a minority group phenomenon. It
expresses itself primarily as a reaction to events, to actions of other groups,
or to government policies and their application. Those who aspire to such
a nationalism were dominant at one time, but have progressively been
displaced from the centre to the periphery of the nation-building process.
They re-emerge on the public scene from time to time, whenever they and
their leaders perceive opportunities for the promotion of their conception
of what Canada should be (and of their related economic or political
interests). This negative stance is largely the result of the fact that building
a British-type of society is not a legitimate agenda any more. What the
orientation of the collective agenda should be, however, is far from clear;
what cultural pluralism means in terms of institutional arrangements and
practices remains largely undefined (Harney 1987); what has emerged is
mostly a view of what it should *not* be.

FRENCH CANADA AND QUEBEC

French-Canadian, like the initial British-Canadian nationalism, is based on
an ethnic conception of society. Ethnocultural criteria serve to determine

membership in the collectivity. Of course, the nationalism of French Canada did not include a sense of empire, of being a participant in a grandiose civilizational enterprise. It did, however, contain an element of "messianism," a sense of being a chosen people with a mission in the world. The conquest – military at first, political and economic subsequently – made it a minority and largely cut its ties with France. Its ethnic nationalism was primarily defensive (*la "Survivance"*) and oriented to the past, in contrast to the British-Canadian sense of participation in the present and continuing success of an empire.[5] Its concern was the preservation against external threats of a culturally defined type of society – a preservation sought through isolation from other collectivities. In spite of important differences, the nationalisms of British- and French-Canadians resembled each other, in that both aspired to the construction of an ethnoculturally defined society. They differed primarily in the means at their disposal for the pursuit of their nationalistic ambitions.

Also like in English Canada, a number of phenomena have progressively transformed French-Canadian society. It changed as a result of phenomena, such as industrialization, urbanization, the diffusion of American culture, the Black awakening in the United States, and the movement toward self-determination in the "Third World." It is now a population with higher levels of education and economic and political expectations; it is considerably secularized; its attitude toward the state is that of an instrument for collective advancement.

Many of these changes began relatively early in the century, but culminated in what came to be known as the "Quiet Revolution" in the 1960s. As the term "revolution" implies, the changes experienced by this traditional society were profound, and involved almost all sectors of social life. A few of these transformations are particularly relevant for the present analysis.

Perhaps the most significant was the fact that the community underwent a shift from a minority to a majority conception of itself. This change is reflected, for instance, in the substitution of Québécois for "French-Canadian" as the acceptable self-denotation. Related to this is a shift from a pan-Canadian to a Quebec definition of the boundaries of the collectivity – a second reversal, so to speak: that is, a reversal to the view that prevailed at the time of Confederation. It should be pointed out, however, that these shifts are not general throughout the entire collectivity. Indeed, there is considerable debate over the definition of the collective identity and over whom the community includes or should include, as the confrontations between independentists and federalists clearly show.

Second, Quebec nationalism[6] has lost much of its defensive, past-oriented, and *"Survivance"* character, to become assertive and oriented to development. Its aim is to acquire control of the structures and processes that can have an impact on its political, economic, and cultural well-being.

It also seeks to gain increasing control over its external relations with other collectivities (Juteau-Lee 1979: 61).

Third, partly because of the new aspiration to control events rather than to protect itself through isolation, and partly because of the secularization trend, State (rather than Church) institutions have come to be seen as the critical instrument for the realization of collective ambitions. With a majority group self-conception and the aspiration to establish one's group as such, "province-building" under the leadership of State authorities has a tenor in Quebec that is somewhat different from the one it has in other provinces.

Finally, the fertility rate has declined considerably (as it has done in other Western societies). The traditional means used to maintain the numerical strength of the collectivity and the vitality of institutions, that depends, in part, on numbers has been abandoned. On the one hand, the Church is now unable to implement its natality policy, as it did in the past. State authorities, on the other hand, although equally preoccupied with the matter as were ecclesiastical authorities, have so far found it almost impossible to develop an alternative policy that would be moderately successful. It is in this context that the integration of immigrants within the French-speaking collectivity has become an important political issue.

As a result of these changes (and certainly of others), attitudes toward other groups changed, whether they were of British or of other origins. First, just like British-Canadian nationalists were confronted with a French population that would not assimilate, Québécois nationalists, with their majority group identity, have to deal with an anglophone population that will not go away either, at least not entirely. In this connection, I would venture to hypothesize that ultra-nationalists in Quebec are far from displeased, and may even rejoice, with the statistics showing an exodus of anglophones from Quebec. Similarly, there is informal evidence[7] that ultra-nationalists in English Canada are quite pleased with the low level of fertility among French-origin Canadians.

Second, the presence of non-British, non-French groups – a presence that increased with the post-war immigration – also generated cultural anxiety among the Québécois as it did (and still does) among British-origin Canadians. As noted earlier, the concern is with the possible undermining of the cultural character of the society and with the possible erosion of the public predominance of the language. However, the "problem" that the non-British, non-French immigrants and ethnic groups poses for the French Québécois is not that same as the one noted earlier in the case of British-origin Canadians. In Quebec, members of ethnic minorities have traditionally opted to join the English-speaking, not the French-speaking collectivity. They therefore did not threaten the French collectivity directly, but indirectly, by increasing anglophone numbers and by reinforcing their institutions.

A study was carried out in the early 1970s, in which francophones and immigrants in Quebec participated in group discussions about issues involved in the 1968–69 St Leonard school crisis. It was observed that relatively few of the statements of either francophone or immigrant participants made reference to the direct relationship between their respective ethnic groups. Over 75 percent of the statements made by francophones "referred either to the dominance of the anglophone upper class or to an alliance of Anglophones and immigrants against francophones … Severe inter-ethnic conflict between francophones and immigrants therefore had no independent existence, but depended upon the relationship of each group to the anglophone dominant class" (Cappon 1978: 331). The prevailing view was that something should be done to constrain immigrants to speak French:

Cultural nationalists tended invariably to take a hard line on the school question, demanding that immigrants forgo their material interests by sending their children to French schools. For them, the cultural growth of the French-Canadian nation depends not upon socio-economic transformation but rather upon constraining New Canadians to speak French. (Cappon 1978)[8]

Thus, the French began to react to ethnic minorities the way British-origin Canadians had reacted in an earlier period. The expectation is that minorities should adopt the language and way of life of the majority, and if they do not move spontaneously in that direction, they should be compelled to do so. Thus, the traditional opposition to immigrants is slowly being transformed into an expectation of "Franco-conformity."

The St Leonard school crisis that the above study dealt with was the beginning of the long process whereby French was legally imposed as the official language of Quebec and as the language to be operative in its public institutions. The Québécois did what British Canadians had done earlier in response to a similar cultural threat. The specific nature of the threat was defined somewhat differently by the French in Quebec than it was decades ago by British-Canadian cultural nationalists. In addition, because of differences in the political, economic, and demographic context (e.g., the predominance of English in North America), the means available to each group to deal effectively with the threat are quite different. Nevertheless, the character of the perceived threat in relation to their ethnic nationalism is fundamentally the same.[9]

At the moment, the non-British, non-French population is not growing rapidly in Quebec. Significant economic development, however, would, in all likelihood, accelerate immigration. If immigrants were to continue to integrate primarily into the English-speaking community, the situation that existed prior to the Quiet Revolution would continue, namely that of a national minority facing the possibility of further minoritization by the growth of the linguistic group that is a majority everywhere else in the country (and the continent). Such a situation could reinforce the defensive ethnic nationalism that has existed up to now and that remains latent. It could also give an impetus to separatist tendencies. Indeed, political independence would, in all likelihood, be perceived by some groups as the only effective way of dealing with such a demographic threat.

On the other hand, immigrants could become part of the French-speaking majority. The extent to which this is likely to take place depends on several factors and circumstances. Among those is the degree of success of the linguistic policies and programs of the Quebec government. Even though the legislation is fairly recent, there is evidence that it is affecting to some degree the direction of the integration of members of ethnic minorities. For instance, in 1985–86, 59.6 percent of students whose mother tongue is neither French nor English were pursuing their primary and secondary education in French; only 23 percent did so in 1976–77. Also, the percentage of those of non-English and non-French mother tongues who did not speak French decreased from 52.8 to 37.7 between 1971 and 1981. The corresponding percentages among those of English mother tongues are 63.3 and 44.9 (Paillé 1986: 36–7).[10]

The integration of ethnic minorities in French Quebec will also depend on the extent to which any economic expansion is under the control of a French-speaking economic elite. This is important, since those who define the rules of access to jobs control much of the system of incentives that determine the direction of linguistic assimilation. Needless to say, the extent to which the English-speaking economic gatekeepers will apply the regulations of "La Charte de la Langue française" is also of critical importance in this regard. Indeed, they still control a large part of the Quebec economy and are likely to continue to do so in the future.

Finally,[11] it will also depend on the absence of ethnic discrimination, that is on the possibility for members of ethnic minorities to be upwardly mobile in the French-controlled part of the economy. As long as a minority self-conception existed, a common attitude among francophones was that opportunities for themselves were limited, sometimes severely so, and that they could therefore not be expected to "give any of them away" to members of other groups. But the situation is different for people who think of themselves as constituting a majority group. To the extent that members of their group actually control significant resources, they are confronted with a new set of normative expectations with regard to their accessibility to minorities.

To the extent that immigrants adopt French in their private as well as their public lives, the collectivity will experience variants of the same social processes as did British-origin Canadians. They will be variants, because the demographic, political, and socioeconomic circumstances are some-what different from those prevailing four or five decades ago. One of the processes will be the progressive dissociation of language from ethnicity, as more and more people of different ethnic origins adopt the French language. The imposition of "franco-conformity" will progressively yield the same results with regard to French as those brought about by the imposition of "Anglo-conformity" with regard to English. In fact, to a considerable extent, a "francophone" is already socially defined as some-one who speaks French, not as someone who belongs to an ethnocultural group. In other words, French will become less and less the distinctive *cultural* attribute of an ethnic community, and more and more the *means* of communication of an economic and political collectivity.[12]

Religion will also become progressively dissociated from the ethnic culture. Traditionally, Catholic culture in French Quebec had a strong ethnic ele-ment; although part of the larger Church, it was very much an ethnic religion playing a critical role in *"La Survivance"* of the collectivity. But if the new trend continues, there will be an increasing number of French-speakers who will be Catholic, but of different ethnic origins. Also, there will be Protestant, Jewish, and Moslem French-speakers. As in the case of British Canada, the religious content of cultural attachments will decrease in importance, as it will have little meaning for the members of "other" ethnic origins. It will be difficult for French ethnicity to be defined by a religion embedded in the symbolism and values of its own culture.

Also, now that a "Québécois" identity is established, that a *"projet de société"* is ambitioned, and that the State is seen as the means to pursue it, membership cannot be defined in terms of ethnic attributes, but in terms of citizenship. As in English Canada, the collective identity has to be redefined in such a way as to incorporate the people of non-French origins who are legally members of the polity. As long as the French collectivity saw itself as a minority, as long as it was in a defensive position, it made sociopolitical sense that the ideological basis of its nationalism be ethnoc-ultural. It was perhaps the most effective means of social and political mobilization. But to the extent that it effectively becomes a majority – in self-conception and in control of institutions – it will run into serious problems of legitimacy and loyalty unless it permits and supports full participation of minorities in its economy and polity and does not make them feel alien, as not having the "right stuff," as being second class citizens. In other words, the political values and norms that prevail in Western societies, in Canada, and in Quebec (as witnessed by the existing Charters of Rights) will exert pressure toward the full inclusion of minorities in public institutions.

Finally, to the extent that people of other ethnic origins are absorbed into the collectivity, the latter will find it increasingly difficult to conceive of its destiny in terms of its traditional historical experience (as British-Canadian nationalists had to abandon the idea that the destiny of the society they were building would be "played out in and through the Empire"). Its past will have little significance, if any, for the new members. It will have to "rewrite" its history in ways that make sense to them. The social construction of a new historical community in Quebec may be facilitated by the fact that the "sense of history" has already begun to decline among the younger generation of French-Québécois. *"Notre maitre le passé"* is a symbolic statement that is losing much of its meaning. The modernization trend and the spread of a present and future-oriented business culture seem to have decreased the importance of the past in the collective consciousness. This change is also apparent in the relative political decline of cultural elites (e.g., clergy, intellectuals of education and of the media), and the ascendancy of economic elites within the French collectivity. The utilitarian dimension of its nationalism is gaining importance and may well come into conflict with its cultural aspirations. This is likely to generate a certain amount of cultural anxiety and resistance (as it did among British-origin Canadians). Indeed, this is already taking place in connection with the perceived "demographic crisis," and with what should he done to avoid what some anticipate will be a "demographic catastrophe" (Dansereau 1987).

The low fertility rate is the object of a debate "that looks increasingly like the next 'national question' the real 'to be or not to be' of the Québécois" (Bissonnette 1987). This debate seems to include three central preoccupations. The first is that, in spite of the linguistic successes indicated earlier, people of non-French origins will in large proportions turn out be anglophones in the sense that even though they will *know* French, they will habitually *use* English. In addition, their commitment to the maintenance of the French language is likely to be weak. Thus, although their inclusion is seen as essential, they cannot replace French-speakers of French origin.

A second issue is whether the French "ethnic" will disappear in Quebec. Demographer Henripin has been quoted as saying that "if the birthrate stays the same, and if massive immigration makes up the difference ... by 2080 only 12 to 15 percent of Quebecers will be able to trace their ancestry to today's population" (Bissonnette 1987). The following are expressions of the anxiety generated:

Mais quand un éditorialiste, un pasteur, un député ou un ministre proclame que la "rédemption" du Québec depend de l'immigration, je m'inscris, en faux – et vous devriez faire de même. Cette idée est une tromperie. Elle implique que l'ethnie canadienne-francaise ait renoncé à exister. De fait, un peuple qui se fie sur l'étranger pour garantir un niveau de ressources humaines sur son territoire a déja abdiqué devant la vie. (Gendron 1987)

Le Québec s'achemine inexorablement vers une configuration multi-ethnique et multi-culturelle. La population est-elle prête à prendre ce visage? Que devons-nous faire pour integrer les immigrants sans les assimiler mais sans nous perdre? (Pagé de l'Alliance des professeurs de Montréal, quoted by Dansereau 1987)

A third concern is that Quebec will not only become multi-ethnic but multi-racial as well, and that it will also include non-Christian groups. That is to say, it will contain groups perceived as very difficult to assimilate. The cultural anxiety that this anticipation generates is largely as intense in Quebec as it in the rest of Canada.[13] An important difference, however, is that English Canada had several decades of experience with "white ethnics" before having to deal with the integration of non-white minorities. French Quebec has to cope with both simultaneously. In other words, it will have to undergo a more substantial change in a smaller period of time.

CONCLUSION

It seems fairly clear that the French community of Quebec is now going through the sociocultural transition that British-Canadians began earlier in the century. Its nationalism, its cultural identity, its ideology concerning other groups and their position in Quebec society is in the process of transformation. The prevailing social definition of who "really" belongs is in the process of changing; what constitutes the "national interest" has become very ambiguous in this regard; the importance of *"les Anglais"* as a comparison group and as a threat to the survival of the collectivity is diminishing, while that of other groups, such as the immigrants, ethnic minorities, and non-white and non-Christian groups, is increasing. If the history of the evolution of English Canada can be any guide as to what we can expect in Quebec in this connection, a long and stressful process is to be anticipated. In fact, in English Canada, the transformation from an ethnic to a civic nationalism is not complete even though it has been under way for more than 50 years.

CHAPTER SEVEN

The Independentist Movement and Terrorism in Quebec in the 1970s*[1]

This paper is an attempt to examine the events of October 1970 in the light of certain characteristics of the sociopolitical context, of the groups present in the sociopolitical arena, and of the relationship among these groups. A basic postulate is that the dynamics of the events cannot be understood without locating them in the general sociopolitical context of society.

Much of the sociopolitical change, and attempted change, that has taken place in Canada, and particularly in Quebec, in the last decade or so, involved the redistribution of power and influence among various groups and organizations in the society. In this process several groups have confronted one another with different models for the reorganization of a particular institutional domain, or of the society as a whole, and with plans as to the way in which power and influence should be allocated. Problems of power and influence always involve issues concerning the nature of the decisions to be made and the people who will be empowered to make these decisions.

I will first argue that the redistribution of power and influence has been a quasi-general phenomenon in Quebec during the last decade, that there is hardly a single institutional sphere that has remained unaffected. I will then examine some of the factors that have brought about this redistribution and attempt at redistribution. These considerations will provide the background for the discussion[2] of three questions pertaining to the October events: (a) What are some of the factors related to the occurrence of

* "The Sociopolitical Dynamics of the October Events," *Canadian Review of Sociology and Anthropology* 9 (1972) : 33–60.

Front de Libération du Québec (FLQ) violence in Quebec since 1963? (b) Why did the kidnappings of the British diplomat James Cross and the Quebec Labour Minister Pierre Laporte, which were, of course, extraordinary happenings in themselves, become a major political event? (c) What were some of the problems associated with the exercise of authority in the circumstances?

WIDESPREAD CONFRONTATIONS OVER THE DISTRIBUTION OF POWER AND INFLUENCE

There are many ways in which social change can involve the redistribution of power and influence: the centralization or decentralization of decision-making within certain institutional spheres, the appearance of new groups seeking to influence or take over the centres of decision-making, the removal of certain groups or their retreat from positions of power, the transformation of institutional structures and the ensuing reallocation of authority, and the creation of new domains of activity in society as a result of social or technological innovations.

Each of these processes involves groups in conflict with one another over the allocation of influence. That is, each involves the confrontation of groups with different interests and values, and hence different ideas as to the kinds of decisions that should be taken and/or as to the way in which the institution should be rearranged. Groups in confrontations differ considerably from one another in terms of their present position in the sociopolitical structure, in terms of their objectives or the model they propose, and in terms of the means they use to reach their objectives.

Whenever confrontations become intense and widespread, in the sense that many social groups, and/or in the sense that several institutional spheres, are involved, instability results in the social system. The instability stems from the fact that power is being redistributed, and/or from the disagreements over the values and norms that should constitute the basis of the ensuing dispensation. The redistribution and the accompanying anomie are, of course, a matter of degree. Here, I would like to show that a widespread confrontation among groups over the distribution of power and influence is what characterizes Quebec's last decade. I do not wish to argue that such confrontations are peculiar to Quebec, although they may be more widespread and intense there than in the rest of Canada. Moreover, the ones mentioned are not the only ones that have been or are now taking place.

Education

Perhaps the most extensive institutional transformation has taken place in the field of education.[3] This transformation includes the virtually complete transfer of power and influence from the Church to lay teachers and administrators, and to the government bureaucracy, a considerable removal of authority from the local level, and an extensive concentration of power in the hands of the provincial bureaucracy. The transformation can be observed at all levels of the educational system. Of course, this redistribution of power has not taken place without considerable tension and conflict, usually between the provincial bureaucracy where the power was being concentrated and the local elites; between the bureaucracy, and teachers and their associations; and between the bureaucracy and particular schools. The transformations also generated diffuse apprehension in the public at large.[4]

Health and Welfare

Health and welfare is another institutional sphere where extensive transformations have taken place, particularly with the considerable withdrawal of the Church from this domain, and with the introduction of provincial plans of hospital and medical insurance, and old age pensions. These transformations have also occasioned conflicts between the provincial bureaucracy and hospital administrations, professional groups and the federal government. Again, most of the redistribution of power has been from the latter groups to the provincial bureaucracy.

Federal Provincial Relations

Another important arena of conflict has been the federal-provincial network of relationships. The arena is complex, being defined by a centre and sub-centres, and including policy-making bodies, bureaucracies, political parties, and groups of citizens. Traditionally, the distribution of power has followed linguistic lines quite closely, the centre being largely under the control of English-speaking groups, and the Quebec sub-centre under the control of French-speaking groups.[5]

Generally, redistribution of power can take place between centre and sub-centre (without modification of their traditional linguistic composition) or between the two linguistic groups, within the institutions of the centre and the sub-centre. Both types of change seem to have taken place to a certain extent. On the one hand, Quebec has made considerable gains in the federal-provincial distribution of power; on the other, a number of French-speaking groups have gained power and increased their influence within federal institutions.[6]

These changes have had a significant impact on federal-provincial relationships. The usual tensions and confrontations inherent in the relation between two levels of government, remain, and so do many of the tensions and confrontations along the linguistic cleavage. But now, there is the added tension and confrontation between groups within the French-speaking community, between various shades of federalists and various shades of provincial autonomists, and between separatists and anti-separatists. Ten years ago, the opposition among these groups was weak, compared to what it has become, and compared to what it seems likely to become.

What has changed is that some groups of French-Canadians have made some gains in power and influence at the federal level. Both federalists and provincial autonomists have a power base to defend. The confrontation is intensifying, as more French-Canadians have a vested interest in the centre as well as the sub-centre of political power.[7] Of course, the eventual outcome of this confrontation depends to a large extent on the development of the power base at the federal level, and in the federal bureaucracy in particular, where much of the power is located. If the top levels of the bureaucracy do not open up significantly to French-speaking persons, then it is quite easy to predict who will win in the confrontation. Conversely, groups of French-speaking Canadians will support and defend a confederated state to the extent that they have power at stake in it. The last few years have seen the beginning of the development of such a power base.

In this connection, it is important to realize that French-speaking people in Québec are developing a new "Québécois" identity, as opposed to a "French-Canadian" identity. Each subgroup will develop attitudes vis-à-vis each other. The "Québécois" may think of the others as less "genuine" or as being assimilated, hence "lost;" the other French-Canadians, on the other hand, are likely to resent these exclusionist attitudes and to think of the "Québécois" as aiming for a closed society. The nature of these attitudes is of less concern here than the fact that a cleavage is shaping up within the French-speaking community which appears to parallel the evolving dispensation of power and influence. It should be noted, for instance, that a large proportion of French-speaking Canadians in the federal bureaucracy come from outside of Quebec. Finally, in addition to the groups on each side of the confrontation, there are the groups who derive advantages from both sides. For instance, it is better for businessmen to have allies at both the provincial and the federal levels than at only one level. I would hypothesize that there are more and more groups in Quebec who are gaining influence at both levels of government.

Labour Relations

Confrontations and tensions accompanying the redistribution of power have also occurred within work organizations. Significant events have occurred within unions, between unions, and between unions and management (Crispo and Arthurs 1968; Jamieson 1970). The last decade has witnessed a significant increase in the incidence of wildcat strikes. One of the characteristics of these strikes is that they represent a form of protest by workers against the leadership of their union (Flood 1968). The refusal of union members to ratify the agreements negotiated by their leaders is another manifestation of intra-union tension (Simkin 1968).

Another change has occurred within unions during the last decade. According to Dion, "on a vu apparaître dans le syndicalisme la presence d'une nouvelle intelligentsia qui, en certains endroits, a plus ou moins réussi à établir un pouvoir par parallèle et à orienter l'action syndicale vers des prises de position et des aventures susceptibles de mettre en danger la cohésion indispensable à tout groupement" (Dion 1969: 335). Moreover, Dion points out that since 1960, the leadership of the unions (CSN, FTQ, CEQ) has been replaced with new personnel. Given these changes, and given the increase in membership, "le syndicalisme au Québec apparait actuellement en pleine crise de croissance et d'orientation. Il est en lutte à une contestation interne et externe" (Dion 1969: 335). The same point is made by Crispo and Arthurs (1968: 243).

During the last decade there was also a significant increase in inter-union conflicts. Dion (1967) and Roberge (1969) carried out an analysis of raiding and rivalry among Quebec unions which shows the period 1964–67 to be a peak period of union feuds in Quebec. Not only have there been tensions and confrontations within unions, but also between unions that find themselves in competition with each other for power and influence in the field of labour relations.

Jamieson (1970) points out that between 1900 and 1967, there have been at least 250 labour disputes in Canada, in which violence, illegality, and the use of force by the police occurred, and that of these, about 90 (about 36 percent) occurred during the period 1957–66.

Another development in the field of labour relations relates to the expansion of the provincial bureaucracy. It was partly brought about by the transformation of the educational system, by the partial take-over of the field of health and the expansion of the public sector into certain segments of industrial activity, by the formation of Hydro-Québec, and by the increase in size of the traditional civil service. The result of this expansion has been that almost 40 percent of unionized workers are in the public sector and negotiate directly or indirectly with the government or with public administrations, mostly at the provincial level (Dion 1969: 334).

Citizen Groups

Parallel with the tension between union members and their leaders, we can observe an increase in tension between various citizen groups and their governments, municipal (for example, Front d'Action politique,

FRAP) as well as provincial and federal, between citizen groups and the establishment (the FLQ seems to fall in this category), between students, and the faculties and administrations of their institutions. A common theme in these confrontations is demand for the reallocation of authority, of decision-making power. Whether the slogans are formulated in terms of autonomy, authoritarianism, some say in the decisions affecting one's life, participation, or whatever, the common denominator is more influence and/or power in the decision-making process.

Ethnic Relations and Demography

Another area of increased tension pertains to the relations between French-Canadians and the other ethnic and linguistic groups in Canada. Whether we take the distribution of the population by ethnic origin, mother tongue, or official language, it seems that a certain balance between the French and non-French population has maintained itself over the years. Among the factors that have affected this balance are the birth-rate of the two linguistic groups, immigration policy, linguistic assimilation of immigrants, the shift of members of the native population from one linguistic group to another, and policies relative to the use, transmission, and diffusion of the two official languages.

All these factors are among the most serious political and social issues of Canadian society, the reason being that the linguistic distribution of the population is closely tied to the distribution of power in our society. High natality and programmes to prevent assimilation into the English group have been the main sociopolitical weapons used by the French in the demographic struggle. Immigration (its size and ethnic composition) and various types of restrictions relative to the use and diffusion of the French language have been the main political weapons used by the English group.

One factor which has operated and still operates in favour of the English language, and which requires virtually no intervention, is the adoption of English rather than French by most immigrants to Canada. The sheer demographic and economic weight of the English language in North America is sufficient to achieve this purpose (Dion 1971; Joy 1967; Royal Commission on Bilingualism and Biculturalism 1967, 1969).

A most significant demographic trend in relation to this question is the declining birthrate among the French population of Quebec, and perhaps in the other provinces as well. Indeed, official statistics show that the birthrate in Quebec is the second lowest in the country, having dropped from 30.0 per thousand during the 1950–55 period to 16.3 per thousand in 1968. On the other hand, the linguistic characteristics of immigrants have not changed drastically for several decades, as far as French language is concerned. The proportion of all immigrants speaking French has increased only a little since 1950 (from 1.1 percent to 3.0 percent), while the proportion speaking either French only or English and French has remained about the same. It is the proportion of immigrants speaking English only which has been decreasing, particularly during the 1951–61 period, with a corresponding increase in the proportion speaking languages other than English and French.

Given that most immigrants go to provinces other than Quebec,[8] and that most immigrants adopt English as their language, even in Quebec, and that the birthrate among the French has declined sharply (and assuming the continuation of these trends), one would hypothesize the distribution of power in the society to be demographically threatened, and the threat to be perceived by the elites of the two linguistic groups, but primarily the French.

Given these conditions, one would predict an increasing concern with natality on the part of the sociopolitical leaders and more attempts at formulating policies and implementing programmes to increase the birthrate. The possibilities in this direction, however, seem limited at the moment, largely because of the increasing secularization of life and the corresponding difficulty of using a powerful religious ideology in order to promote certain natality objectives.[9] One would also predict a greater emphasis than in the past on measures related to immigration, linguistic assimilation of immigrants, and the use of the two languages, particularly in the fields of education and work. Finally, one would also predict an increasing suspicion of and opposition to any attempt at promoting multiculturalism on the part of the federal government. This occurs at a time when the rising power and influence of some ethnic groups makes it impossible for the government not to respond with some sort of multicultural policy. In one respect, the situation is almost ironical, in that the rising of cultural expectations and claims seems to have been triggered by the initial awakening of the French-Canadians themselves.[10]

It is possible that the demographic trends described above could be checked and the present linguistic balance maintained, through the implementation of certain programmes. But it is also possible that the trends are too strong and/or that the policies arrived at will be too weak, and that as a result, the French group will start decreasing as a proportion of the total Canadian population. If this occurs, or if the fears that it will occur increase seriously (it seems that such fears are increasing), then the pressures toward a different distribution of powers or a complete separation of powers between the two groups are likely to increase. This is likely to occur because, as mentioned earlier, the demographic condition is closely related to the relative power of the two groups. We are here, of course, assuming that no one gives up some of his power without proportionate resistance.

Mass Media

An important development with respect to the mass media consists of increasing concentration of ownership and control. Data to this effect have been published showing that in the past few years, two organizations have acquired ownership and control of a large proportion of radio and television stations, and newspapers (Guay 1969; Maistre 1971). With the government, they now constitute the three centres of control of the mass media.

Influences on Attitudes

The source of influence on mores, social attitudes, and political orientations has also changed in recent years. The Church, as a source of such influence, has been, to a considerable degree, replaced by various intellectual and social leaders, particularly those with access to the mass media. The influence of the Church has been replaced, not only in regard to nonreligious matters, but in regard to questions traditionally seen as falling in the domain of its authority. This development is important, not only because it involves redistribution of influence, but also because of the people that it affects, namely an important segment of Quebec's cultural and intellectual elite, writers, journalists, and artists – an elite that has gained considerable importance in Quebec society. It is probably not accidental that this particular concentration of ownership and control has been attacked in a number of publications.[11]

The Separatist Movement

Finally, the separatist movement has also witnessed intense tension within its own boundaries. Since the movement gained momentum in the early 1960s, a number of potential leaders have emerged, attempting to rally people under particular sociopolitical orientations, solutions, and programmes. More than a dozen organizations or political parties have been formed (Hagy 1969), either as new groups, splits from existing ones, or mergers of two or more existing associations.

There are two dimensions to the tension between groups in any organization. There is conflict over the allocation of power, and tension between those whose commitment to the goals of the organization or association (for example, independence) overrides everything else and those who are prepared to accept certain expedient compromises in order to facilitate goal attainment. As Hammond and Mitchell point out, one group tries to "maximize goal commitment at the expense of adaptation," while the other tends to "adapt at the expense of goals" (1965: 134). The two types of conflict may involve the same groups; that is, the purists or radicals may be the group claiming a greater share of the leadership, while the compromisers or moderates may make a similar claim on the grounds that they are largely responsible for the success of the organization up to that point. Although all organizations tend to be exposed to such tensions, they are not all equally so. For instance, new organizations[12] and normative organizations are probably more likely to experience them than other types of organizations, such as utilitarian or coercive organizations.[13]

The multiplication of associations during the first six to eight years of the separatist movement is indirect evidence of internal tensions – especially in that most separatist associations quite clearly identified themselves in terms of a leftist, centrist, or rightist orientation, the FLQ being the most extreme case. There is also evidence of tension of the type discussed here within the Parti Québécois, tension between the leadership (the executive of the party) and the membership, and between the centre and the radical wing.[14] Of course, as we shall discuss later, the "events" accentuated the internal tensions.

SOME FACTORS TRIGGERING THE REDISTRIBUTION OF POWER

It appears then, that one of the significant dimensions of the sociopolitical context in which the October events took place is a quasi-generalized redistribution, and attempts at redistribution of power in Canadian society, and in Quebec in particular. The reallocation of power and influence, or the attempts at such reallocation, did not occur in one direction only; it involved the centralization or concentration of power, as well as the allocation of influence to groups away from the traditional centre of decision-making.

It should be emphasized at this point that the FLQ is very much part of this over-all phenomenon. It is one of the groups contending for influence and power. It is one of the groups attempting to change the social system in accordance with its values. From this point of view (gaining power and influence for the realization of specific goals), it does not differ from any of the other groups involved. It can be singled out as special, however, in terms of the means it uses to achieve those aims. This will be discussed further, in the third section of the essay.

It is beyond the scope of this essay to go into an analysis of the factors that have triggered the processes of reallocation of control and influence over decision-making in the various institutional spheres of the society. However, a line of investigation is suggested by the preceding description, namely, that we should be looking for factors that in one way or another upset the existing traditional distribution of power and influence. At least five broad sets of such factors can be identified:

(a) The change in the level of opportunities for control and influence resulting from the expansion or contraction of certain institutional spheres, as for instance the expansion of activities in the field of education, health and welfare, and those made possible by technological innovations. It is through such expansions that Quebec society has witnessed, mostly during the last decade, the emergence of a new elite of public administrators, of labour leaders, of journalists, of film and television producers and artists, and of writers. And, as a result of the emergence of these new elites, the distribution of power is undergoing important modifications.

(b) The Church has withdrawn from a number of fields of organizational activity, such as education, health, and welfare, creating a vacuum of power, and encouraging the appearance of groups competing to take over control of these organizations. The withdrawal has also been accompanied by a weakening of the Church as a system of values, legitimating institutions, and behaviour, and also creating an ideological vacuum demanding to be filled. This vacuum has become an opportunity for various cultural elites (intellectuals and mass media people) to attempt to shape public attitudes and values in certain directions. This, in turn, has resulted in a large number of ideological confrontations.

(c) A transformation of social identities has occurred in such a way that people are no longer content to remain at the periphery of institutional decision-making. This is a result of the rise in level of education, the activities of its new elites, the increasing level of group conflicts in the society, the circulation of social and political ideas that accompany these conflicts, and taking sides in these conflicts by being drawn into them at least psychologically. The changes occur along many dimensions, but there are two interrelated areas that are of interest here: the conception of one's sociopolitical ability or competence to deal with life problems, and one's conception of oneself as an autonomous unit, both of these being enhanced. Such changes in self-conceptions, if they extend over large numbers of people, create a massive pressure for control and influence.[15] There seems to be little doubt that such a phenomenon is occurring in Quebec, an important one to be examined empirically.

(d) There are expansionist tendencies in the organizational centres of power, originating from processes internal to the organizations themselves. As long as no effective opposition makes itself felt, there seems to be no reason why the elites manning particular bureaucracies should not expand their domain of influence as much as they can. The occurrence of such processes is, of course, not peculiar to Quebec; similarly, it is difficult to argue that Quebec bureaucracies would be exempt from them.

(e) Demographic changes have affected the relative sizes of various social groups and the territorial distribution of the population. The demographic changes of interest here are those that impinge on the existing balance of power. For instance, rural-urban migrations are not relevant in the present context, because they uproot people, disrupt their traditional social relationships, or disturb their traditional values. Urbanization is relevant because it may disturb the balance of power; the groups and elites whose power derives from the importance of small communities and rural areas may be threatened by urbanization; or the groups and elites in control of urban institutions may be threatened by the newcomers. Other demographic factors related to the allocation of control and influence are the birth-rate, patterns of immigration and emigration, and the patterns and rates of ethnic and linguistic assimilation.

THE USE OF VIOLENT MEANS IN A CONFRONTATION

It was indicated earlier that the FLQ is only one of the many groups involved in the redistribution of power and influence, but that it has distinguished itself by the tactics, especially the recourse to violence, used to affect political decision-making. It is one thing to explain the origin of the confrontation, and another to account for the character of the tactics used in it. As Dahrendorf points out, "the violence of conflict relates rather to its manifestations than to its causes; it is a matter of the weapons that are chosen by conflict groups to express their hostilities" (1959: 212). The present section deals with this choice, by attempting to identify some of the factors affecting the propensity to use violent means in one's struggle.

The distinction is not only an analytical one, for it also pertains to social perceptions of reality. For example, I have heard or read in newspapers of a number of people saying that the violence of the FLQ was inexcusable, since there were legitimate ways of protesting and bringing about change in our society, or that the use of violence would only be defensible in a dictatorial regime.

Uncertainties as to the Legitimacy of the Separatist Option

There are three institutional elements that a "conflict group" can challenge: the decisions made and enforced, the personal or social qualities of the decision-makers (such as their fairness or representativeness), or institutional arrangements themselves (the structure, rules, and procedures under which decisions are made). As one can easily surmise, each type of challenge will raise its special brand of problems for the groups concerned.

The separatist movement questions the adequacy and legitimacy of Canadian political institutions. It constitutes a rejection of Confederation, thus the basis of the Canadian political community. The very nature of such dissent makes it difficult for the political authorities to cope with it in a positive way, difficult in a social sense although not necessarily in the legal sense. It is relatively easy to pressure a government to modify one of its decisions; it is more difficult to bring about changes in the social composition of those who hold positions of authority; but it is still more difficult to bring a political community and its authorities to accept its own dismemberment.

Separatists, by the very nature of their option, can easily be put out and/ or place themselves out of the social bargaining process (Nieburg 1969). This can be achieved in different ways. For instance, no systematic attempt is made to occupy key positions in the federal decision-making bodies (policymaking, bureaucratic, legislative); doing this would tend to weaken their basic political option. At the same time, great care is taken by the federalists who now occupy these positions to keep the separatists away from them. These are two mutually reinforcing processes. Attempts are made to reach potential separatists to integrate them into the existing political structure, thus increasing their commitment to it, but it is difficult to assess the success of those attempts.

There is a "dialogue de sourds" going on. On the one hand, a number of federal bureaucrats and politicians are complaining that "these people won't even talk with us." On the other hand, the separatists point to the fuss that is made in the English language press over the idea of recruiting 250 francophones (out of 1250) into good jobs in the civil service, a recommendation of the federal Civil Service Commission.

There are also processes of symbolic exclusion – that the federalists have sold out, that the anti-separatists reject their own origins, that they do not understand the deep aspirations of their own people, that they are out of touch with the dynamics of present cultural evolution, and hence, that they are not the proper authorities. Reciprocally, the separatists are said to be only a minority, that they are out of touch with what the majority of the population wants, that some of the most important separatist agitators are outsiders (like de Gaulle), that they cannot agree with each other, that they are only a bunch of radical idealists, and hence, that they do not constitute proper political opposition.

To the separatists, the federal authorities are not really legitimate; to the federalists the separatists are not part of the legitimate opposition. The dilemma is a serious one. Federal authorities cannot deal with the separatists on the latter's terms, for doing so would be to question the very basis of their own authority. On the other hand, if political authorities are to be responsive to dissent in certain segments of the community, they must consider such dissent as legitimate, that is, an indication that some need is not being properly met.

The dilemma also manifests itself in the debates and lack of consensus over the issue of Quebec's right to separate. An April Gallup poll posed the following question: "Do you accept the principle that Quebec should have the right to separate from Canada, if the majority of its people want to, or do you think that Quebec should be held in confederation by force, if necessary?" *(Toronto Star,* 17 April 1971). Nationally, 40 percent said that Quebec should have the right to separate; 46 percent said that it should not be permitted to; and 14 percent were undecided. Implicitly, and almost explicitly, the question raises the issue of the right of one province to secede as against the right of the political community as a whole to fight to maintain its integrity.

Difficulties Encountered by Separatist Associations in Integrating their Radicals

As mentioned earlier, most organizations have their radicals and, therefore, face the problem of integrating them in some way. "The viable organization finds room for its radicals ... thereby minimizing disruption that radicals might create without sacrificing their potential insights by excluding them altogether" (Hammond and Mitchell 1965: 134). The same is true for social movements, which need groups of highly committed individuals, but must integrate them within their boundaries in such a way that they do not prevent the growth of the movement, destroy its image in the community at large, or disrupt the orderly functioning of its activities.

From the point of view of a social movement or a social group, radicals are both a potential source of dynamism and ideas, and a potential source of disruption. From the point of view of the community at large and its authorities, they are primarily a potential source of disruption. A social movement, however, has an interest in controlling the behaviour of its radicals, as does the community, although for different reasons.

It can be hypothesized that the probability of disruptive and violent behaviour is partly related to the inability of a particular association or group of associations to integrate and thus control its radicals.[16] Little evidence is available for testing this hypothesis. However, Morf (1970), in his study of Quebec terrorism, mentions that a number of terrorists had at one time been members of a separatist association, but had quit, dissatisfied with its slow success and the gradualism of its approach. However, Morf's biographies of the terrorists are not systematic; it is therefore impossible to know how general an experience this is among the members of the FLQ.

There are, of course, many reasons why radicals have not been integrated into the associations and parties of the movement. For instance, the notion of integration assumes the existence of some sort of a structure with an ideological as well as a social centre. It assumes the existence of a mainstream, indicating the direction of the movement. But in the early phase of the separatist movement, or of any movement, for that matter, it is doubtful whether such a centre or mainstream exists. The very fluidity of the situation gives rise to various groups attempting to define the situation, shape the structure, and give it an orientation according to their particular set of values and preferences. In the initial phases, a social movement has few structural means to cope with potentially disruptive elements.

Once associations are formed with an identifiable leadership and programme, other factors become important. For example, if the association is clearly identified with one person or a small group of persons, it will be more difficult for people with different views to gain influence on leaders, or themselves to become leaders. In such cases, splitting away and forming separate associations is highly probable.

Another difficulty stems from the fact that an organization readily becomes too structured and rigidly controlled from the top. This is particularly crucial with normative associations, such as sociopolitical groupings. Whether this was the case with many separatist associations and parties is difficult to tell. It seems to be one of the problems of the Parti Québécois, if we judge from the articles and letters to the editor in a number of publications.[17]

Still another difficulty may arise from the diversification of the membership that frequently accompanies the growth of an association. It seems, for example, that initially middle-class (normative) organizations are somewhat subject to difficulties in integrating members of working-class origin. The latter's feeling of being left out may simply come from differences in the level of education and in the modes and styles of communication; in some cases, it may come from the fact of being kept out of the positions of importance in a more or less deliberate fashion.

Difficulties may also arise from social class differences in preferred political strategies and tactics. It is noteworthy that 10 of the 12 FLQ members discussed by Morf, on whom there were class data, were of lower- or working-class origin. Several of these people started, but did not complete, a university education. It is possible, then, that the radicalism of some individuals is a response of upwardly mobile people trying to make it in organizations dominated by people of middle-class origin.

Internal Group Processes

Once radical elements have formed groupings of their own, their ideology or sociopolitical orientation develops according to its own logic. The group is now removed from a number of possible checks and restrictions on the development of its orientation and activities. Contacts are established with other radical groups. Thus a subculture develops, and reference groups are acquired that approve radical approaches to social change, including the use of violence.

Radical groupings eventually come to face recruitment problems. Probably the more extremist the group, the more serious the difficulty of recruitment and allegiance maintenance will be. The need for new recruits, and ideological developments tend to lead the group to expand their targets and escalate their tactics. As indicated, a reason for the formation of groups like the FLQ is the slowness of progress of the non-radical groups. It is therefore important that the radical group soon be able to show significant results, if it is to maintain the appropriate level of commitment. In other words, the group needs a system of reward that will recruit new members and sustain their commitment, and that is consistent with its ideology.

This seems to be what happened in the case of the FLQ. From 1963 to 1969, there was a progressive generalization of targets. An examination of the FLQ activities reported by Morf reveals that in the first wave,[18] the attacks were restricted, almost exclusively, to British and federal institutions and symbols (Wolfe and Queen Victoria monuments, military buildings, mailboxes, the RCMP building). The second and third waves involved a change in both tactics and targets. Instead of exploding bombs at various points, attempts were made to organize a revolutionary army. The second wave ended with the arrest of six persons calling themselves the Armée de Libération du Québec, and the third wave consisted of the formation of a military training camp for the Armée Révolutionnaire du Québec. According to Morf, such camps were to be established all across the province.

The violence of the second and third waves does not seem to have been terrorist in nature. Rather, it seems to have been the by-product of attempts to acquire (through robberies) the necessary funds, radios, equipment, and armaments for military operations. Not surprisingly, these two waves involved military depots, banks, a firearms store, and a radio station. An interesting development, however, is that a number of French Canadian establishments were robbed (a Caisse populaire, and branches of the Banque canadienne nationale and the Banque provinciale).

The fourth wave included a number of robberies for equipment but, importantly, also explosions at companies with workers on strike. The same is true of the fifth wave, with further new targets – provincial government buildings, provincial political parties (explosions at the clubs of the Liberal and Union nationale parties), municipal institutions (the Montreal City Hall), and even a labour organization with more moderate views. This last wave (before the kidnappings) seems to have been the most intense, both in the number of explosions (or attempted explosions) and in the diversity of targets.

Whether or not these developments were planned is difficult to tell with the evidence available. As Torelli (1971: 20) has pointed out, there is a revolutionary literature describing various strategies, and it is possible that such a literature was used to formulate an over-all plan. It is also possible, however, that the developments were mainly the results of unplanned group processes, the more likely explanation, in my view. More evidence, not only of the type that the police collects, would be necessary before any conclusion could reasonably be reached.

Choice of Tactics: A Matter of Differential Access

Neiberg states that "the choice of tactics for bargaining and influence is largely a matter of differential access. When influence upon government is sought, there is little difference between the soft word spoken to the President on the golf course by his industrialist friend, and the harsh words echoing shrilly from a demonstration by poor people" (1969: 64).

However, the fact that the institutional structure of the political community itself is questioned renders more difficult the use of normal channels of access. One of the bases of the legitimacy of political authority and opposition is weakened. The process of exclusion from channels of influence is already in motion. Moreover, if certain subgroups are not, for one reason or another, properly integrated within the opposition or the social segment seeking change, these subgroups are still further away from the accepted channels of access. Thus, the necessity for certain groups to develop extraordinary means of gaining power in the sociopolitical system arises.

The Response of the Authorities and the Public

Finally, another reason for escalation in tactics may perhaps have been the failure of each of the previous phases of activity. The FLQ was not really getting anywhere. The political authorities defined the terrorists as ordinary criminals, people to be dealt with by the police. The authorities did not, or could not, recognize them politically, although this is not to say the authorities were not worried by them.

The public's initial reaction seems to have been quite negative, but people learned to live with the annoyance of occasional explosions. In other words, the public's reaction was very similar to that of the authorities: members of the FLQ were seen as crackpots and criminals to be dealt with by the police.

Being ignored or treated as an insignificant entity is a very humiliating experience. It generates anger and can easily bring about extreme reactions. On this basis, I would hypothesize that the progressively weaker, even negative response, to the activities of the FLQ spurred the expansion of targets and the escalation of tactics.

Reform and protest groups were also negative towards the FLQ, at least in later phases, because the FLQ was providing political ammunition to the establishment – that is, to the groups they were opposing. Those opposition groups did accord a political significance to the terrorists, but with time, it became less and less clear whose interest their activities were serving. These responses pushed the FLQ still further away from integration into the legitimate opposition and, at the same time, accelerated the evolution of their radicalism.

THE "EVENTS": AN ARENA FOR GROUP CONFRONTATIONS

When the next wave of FLQ activities began, involving new tactics that clearly meant a further escalation, the currently accepted definition of the situation prevailed. Of course, the confrontation between the FLQ and the authorities was much more intense than it had ever been. But the situation was still basically defined as one that should be dealt with by the police. Since the life of Mr Cross was involved, and since he was a representative of another country, a number of complications arose which concerned the government directly. Yet it was only in that sense that the situation was defined as political and not in the sense of confrontation for power. Mr Bourassa's trip to the United States is an indication of how secure he felt in his position of authority.

The situation soon changed, taking the dimension of a major political event. Yet the event was not a riot, nor a revolution, nor an uprising or social disorder. It was a kidnapping. It was an act of political violence, but not one of a collective nature. The reaction to it was certainly collective, but the act itself cannot be put in the same category as riots or other manifestations of collective violence.

The FLQ wanted desperately to be defined as political enemies of the established powers, something they failed to do since 1963. They wanted to be a power taken into account in the social bargaining equation, but even after the kidnapping of Mr Cross, the political authorities did not change their definition of the situation. According to some newspaper reports, there was apparently some disagreement among subgroups of the FLQ as to whether the kidnapping of a person like Mr Cross would be sufficient to force the government to negotiate seriously with them. Newspaper accounts also suggest that the kidnapping of Mr Laporte was a further attempt to force the government to bargain. My view is that the kidnappings should be interpreted as a more or less desperate attempt of the FLQ to affect the distribution of power. By this time, they had become virtually complete outsiders to the power structure. The significance of their act was that it was a last desperate attempt to enter the political arena and be considered an element to be contended with.

Another very important process was triggered by the first kidnapping. Extraordinary events, by definition, bring about a situation that is unstructured. This sets in motion a definition of situation process, whereby "certain external factors are selectively reorganized and given subjective significance. They are construed as means, obstacles, conditions and limitations, with reference to the attainment of the dominant desires or value" (MacIver 1964: 256).

Undefined situations do not remain so for very long, for at least two reasons. First, they are laden with uncertainties and therefore anxiety-creating and uncomfortable. Second, and more important for the present analysis, they provide an opportunity for interested groups to structure them to their advantage. Moreover, the groups who see the situation as an opportunity to further their cause are also most likely to realize that their political opponents may avail themselves of the opportunity if they do not do so first. Finally, the groups who are the most likely to take advantage of an undefined situation and/or the most likely to be suspected of doing so, are those that have recently made or tried to make their appearance on the sociopolitical scene. In other words, people react to undefined situations in terms of their own sociopolitical goals and interests.

The kidnappings developed into a major political event, because the circumstances they created provided an arena for a number of the group confrontations described in the first part of this essay. The events could serve the advantages of the municipal politicians or of the groups of citizens who oppose them, the goals of the police or of the groups opposing the expansion of police powers; the goals of the federalists or of the provincial autonomists, of the separatists or of the anti-separatists (French or English); they could enhance the influence of the intellectuals, of the mass media, of the political left, right, or centre.

In a number of instances, the attempt to take advantage of the situation for one's purposes seems to have been deliberate, like Mayor Drapeau making statements against his political opponents in the municipal election campaign. In other cases, the action taken may not have been intended for such purposes, but was clearly so interpreted. The "provisional government" incident and the proclamation of the War Measures Act seem to qualify here. In such circumstances, the interpretations given by individuals and groups to the behaviour of others is as important, or perhaps even more important in determining the course of events than is the objective content of the actions themselves. In talking to people connected with different groups, other than the FLQ, and in reading their statements in the press, I formed the impression that after the heat of the events, some people felt as if they had "lost," while others felt as if they had "won" in the course of the events.

In short, the kidnappings became a major political event, in part because of and in terms of, the sociopolitical context described in the first part of this essay. They created circumstances which provided an arena and a set of opportunities to various groups involved in the redistribution of power and influence in the society.

PROBLEMS IN THE EXERCISE OF AUTHORITY

The redistribution of power and influence, especially if it is widespread, is potentially disruptive of the functioning of the sociopolitical system. This is because such redistribution entails institutional dislocations, the emergence of new elites and groups, the relative withdrawal of old elites and groups, and the more or less intense confrontations of ideologies and groups. It is always possible that these processes will prevent almost all decision-making, or will prevent role incumbents from pursuing their activities. Various organizations or social institutions may be seriously jeopardized in the performance of their functions. Because of this, the occurrence of the processes associated with the redistribution of power and influence tend to trigger the operation of social control processes. The possibility of, or actual social disruption, raises problems of authority; latent or manifest social confrontations raise the problem of their regulation.

Different problems are raised by the kind of sociopolitical context described at the beginning of this essay. There is the problem of integrating the new groups (and their elites) into the structure of power and into the networks of sociopolitical influence. As long as they are left out, the danger of social disruption will remain high. This implies that effective social bargaining must occur for orderly social change to take place. Certain types of issues, however, tend to take an all-or-none character, and, hence, do not lend themselves very easily to any bargaining. They rather assume the character of wars of religion, in which the opponent is not accorded any legitimacy and, indeed, is defined as evil.

There is also the possibility that the conflict will become violent, that is excessively damaging to the persons directly concerned and/or to the community. And there is, whenever group confrontations are occurring in most of the institutional domains of the society, always the possibility that a given overt confrontation will provide a climate and an opportunity for many latent conflicts to manifest themselves. The generalization of the conflict situation may also result from the fact act that certain cleavages in society are such that a systematic alignment of groups can crystallize itself and thus bring about a rather massive confrontation. Moreover, if the systematic cleavage concerns people's basic social identities, the confrontation is likely to be not only general, but also quite intense. Whenever basic social identities are involved, most people in the community take sides; few remain aloof or psychologically removed from the conflict. In such instances, it takes relatively little for them to get drawn into an actual confrontation (Coleman 1957).

A widespread redistribution of institutional and social power also raises the level of mistrust in society. The number of groups and ideological conflicts generates a considerable amount of uncertainty in the community as to who is right, who is simply an opportunist, and whom one can trust. In that sense, authority in society is weakened. People who hold positions of authority are suspect in the eyes of at least certain segments of the population.

Finally, there is a high level of discontent and sense of inequity in segments of Quebec society, a discontent that, presumably, could be mobilized for either constructive or destructive collective action. Moreover, the discontent is not only high, but also cuts across several institutional domains and strata of the society. Indeed, it is associated with the widespread redistribution of power, influence, and access to resources described earlier.[19]

The argument presented here is that, given the sociopolitical conditions in Quebec on the eve of the October events, there was a problem of potential social disruption, of potentially uncontrolled social confrontations. Moreover, to the extent that the kidnappings brought about a special set of opportunities for several of the groups in conflict, the possibility of uncontrolled confrontations became still greater.[20] In other words, there was a problem of social control, of social regulation. There was a problem of authority before the October events, and this problem was accentuated by these events.[21]

There were also problems associated with the exercise of authority, for people in positions of authority can either weaken or strengthen their own authority in the process of using it. Authority will be weakened if some of the basic values of the community are seriously offended by the measures used. (The police waking people up in the middle of the night or keeping them in jail for some time without any shoes is not likely to weaken authority, but systematic police brutality is quite likely to.) A measure which results in a high proportion of useless arrests of innocent victims is likely to generate a lot of mistrust, as will a measure with a diffuse rather than a specific target. A measure which is clearly disproportionate to the severity of the danger will, at least as an after-effect, throw doubt on the trustworthiness of the authorities. The application of the War Measures Act appears to have involved useless arrests, a diffuse target, and to be somewhat disproportionate.[22] It should be added, however, that by their very nature, terrorist organizations do not provide an easily identifiable target. By design, these organizations disperse themselves throughout the population and form loose networks that are difficult to map out.

What leads authorities to overreact is partly related to the crisis situation itself and partly to conditions brought about by the redistribution of power in society. By definition, extraordinary situations take people by surprise. Reliable information is scarce; reliable channels for communication are primitive or non-existent. The usual premises for decision-making have to be discarded. As Pye (1969:167–73) points out, the initial decisions of authorities, which are crucial, must be taken in a vacuum. Moreover, it is not only the number of unknowns that can lead to panic, but also the lack of experience and the scarcity of institutionalized mechanisms to cope with such situations.

In addition to the characteristics of the crisis situation, there is also the fact that the legitimacy of those occupying positions of power and/or of the regime itself is questioned by main groups when attempts at redistribution of power are widespread in society. This weakening of legitimacy is likely to make authorities insecure and highly sensitive to any possibility of social disruption.

A second condition which can be detrimental to the exercise of authority is that a given measure of social control may favour certain groups over others, which is particularly serious when there are widespread group confrontations. If some groups feel that the measure applied by those in authority gives an advantage to their opponents, they will resent the actions taken by the authorities. If they suspect that this was done intentionally, they will resent the authorities themselves. The measure may then make uncontrolled group confrontations more likely. On the other hand, some measures would have just the opposite effect. For instance, the postponement of the municipal election in Montreal would have done more to control one possible source of disruption, without increasing the level of mistrust, than the War Measures Act.

Another factor which raises problems of the exercise of authority is that people in positions of authority are frequently partisans in social confrontations as well; they are themselves affected by the redistribution of power and influence, the very process they are responsible for regulating. Similarly, those who are assuming a social leadership role, but are not in positions of political authority (for example, those concerned with civil liberties) are frequently partisans also in social confrontations. As Nieburg points out, "the two primary issues of politics – who shall apportion values (authority issues), and how they shall be apportioned (policy issues) – are inextricably involved in all questions of political relationships and can be separated only theoretically" (1969: 111).

This particular condition, I would argue, was one of the main characteristics of the October events and those of the following weeks. Earlier, it was indicated that during the events, various groups of people were seeing each other as taking advantage of the situation in terms of their own struggle for power, imputing certain kinds of motives to each other. One of the roots of this is that the actors in the events were simultaneously social leaders or political authorities and partisans in the conflict, hence the very high degree of suspicion on both sides. The statement on the part of the authorities that public order was threatened was received by some opposition groups as an argument to cover up their underlying intentions. Similarly, the avowed concern of a number of social leaders that decisions be to the advantage of the community as a whole, and that civil liberties be protected were also received with suspicion by the political authorities.

Is it possible to create conditions for the exercise of authority that would not be subject to such dilemmas? The optimism now fairly well rooted in our political culture would lead one to believe that it is possible. If institutional solutions can be formulated, however, I suspect they will involve in one way or another the role of a third party. Indeed, conflict regulation almost invariably involves the intervention of a third party (Dahrendorf 1959: 229, 230).[23] Whatever the merit of this idea, the whole area of institutional mechanisms for assessing the danger of social confrontations getting out of control, and for coping with such dangers, is in great need of research and critical analysis.

Finally, the management of a crisis can strengthen the political authority rather than weaken it. One of the basic socio-psychological reasons for this is that crises generate uncertainty and considerably raise the level of anxiety in the population. Ordinary citizens do not have the means to cope with a crisis, and their powerlessness in the situation raises their level of anxiety still more. As a result, any authority that copes effectively with the crisis will gain in the confidence of the population.

Such a socio-psychological climate brings about two kinds of dangers for the authorities. There is a temptation to take unfair advantage of the public's anxieties to introduce or prepare the ground for certain measures (for example, identity cards, investigation of course content in schools, legislation to facilitate police searches).[24] Because of the violence and the sense of crisis, the public may feel that such measures are necessary. In this sense, a crisis may facilitate strengthening in the exercise of authority. This is especially the case if the political authorities take the opportunity to institutionalize certain practices rather than keeping to temporary measures.

The second danger for authorities in a crisis and the accompanying socio-psychological climate concerns the possible consequences of failing to act. In a confrontation, the behaviour of one of the parties involved is a very important determinant of the response of the other. In this sense, the failure to act is a very important behaviour, which is likely to encourage the other party in certain directions. Moreover, given the socio-psychological climate, and given that the crisis becomes an arena of confrontation for various groups in conflict, it is possible that the situation will get out of control. The failure to act or to act in time may thus weaken authority considerably. Until methods for rapid assessment of the dangers of a crisis situation are developed, if this is at all possible, political authorities will have to rely on their judgment as to whether there are more dangers in introducing special measures or in not doing so. The point made here is that both alternatives entail considerable danger.

CHAPTER EIGHT

Relation between Linguistic and Regional Cleavages in Canada*

(with Albert Breton)

Though its relief as a "media-problem" rises and falls with the vagaries of events and the caprices of the media themselves, national unity, or more exactly national disunity, is very much a contemporary Canadian problem; and it remains, even after the discussions and debates of recent years, a badly understood problem. The diagnosis that we make in the following pages is not a complete and final one, but something like it has been so conspicuously absent from ongoing discussions that one could be forgiven for believing that accepted views serve as much to obscure reality as to enlighten it.

In this first chapter, we seek to accomplish two tasks. First, we compare, in broad terms, the hypothesis underlying our analysis with the dominant views of what constitute the roots of Canadian disunity; and we try to show how these various views and our own are interrelated. Second, in developing the first point, we summarize our own diagnosis of the problem, leaving to the following chapters a more detailed discussion of the major building blocks of that analysis.

* "A New Perspective on National Disunity," Chapter One, in *Why Disunity? An Analysis of Linguistic and Regional Cleavages in Canada*, Albert Breton and Raymond Breton (Montreal: Institute for Research on Public Policy, 1980), 1–10. The book is based on lectures initially presented in 1978 as the "Dal Grauer Lectures" at the University of British Columbia.

COMPETING ALTERNATIVE HYPOTHESES

What constitutes the problem of national disunity in Canada? At heart, it is a struggle between certain groups over the distribution of what we have chosen to call organizational power. That it is a struggle, sometimes fairly open, at other times more covert, no one appears to disagree. But that is about as far as the agreement goes.

The groups involved in that struggle are language and regional ones and no other; the struggle is over the distribution of organizational power, not of wealth, income, equalization payments, or other; the roots of national disunity are not to be found in the struggle over the sharing of constitutional powers between the levels of government that make up the Canadian federation; a link possibly exists between the struggle over the distribution of organizational power and the distribution of constitutional power.

To be specific, the francophones and the anglophones make up the language groups; the regions are the West, mostly British Columbia and Alberta, and the East, more often being Ontario alone, but sometimes including Quebec.

No one should quarrel with our choice of labels; we use them to expedite matters. Not all Canadians can be classified as francophones or anglophones, but since these labels refer to the general usage of the French and English languages, most Canadians fall into one group or the other. What is more important, the struggle does not involve all francophones nor all anglophones. Most Canadians are more or less passive in that struggle, having not much more than sympathies for one group or the other. So references to francophones and anglophones, or in brief to language groups struggling over the distribution of organizational power, are primarily references to the organizational elite in these two groups and to those who aspire to become members of these elite.

This point needs emphasis. The struggle over organizational power is one between the elite of the organizations located in the two language groups and not between the "ordinary" men and women in these groups. This fact of itself helps to explain why national unity has such wide variation as a captivating public issue. Indeed, only if a major event takes place – such as the 1970 kidnappings in Montreal or the November 1976 election of the Parti québécois – will the media, which is inevitably attracted to mass sensationalism by its mode of financing, raise the relief of the issues; in "ordinary time," it recedes from those who are not directly involved because it cannot, as a rule, be sensationalized. The elitist character of the national unity issue also helps to explain why in "ordinary times," the polls report that the "public" does not believe it to be a problem.

What we have said about the language groups holds, with appropriate adjustments, for the country's regional groups. This part of the struggle over the distribution of organizational power is between the elites of Western and Eastern Canada, not between all the people in these regions. Indeed, in this particular case, what in Western Canada is called the "East," and what we, children of the "West," have adopted as our label, never includes the Atlantic provinces; so it is an even less precise label than the ones we have affixed to the language groups. But it will do.

Given these definitions and clarifications, we note that the national unity question in Canada has two dimensions: one linguistic, the other regional; and that although related, they are two separate, distinct, and important aspects of that question. These two dimensions are so closely related that those involved in the struggle over the distribution of organizational power have a vested interest in confusing the issue and in playing one dimension against the other.

The interrelatedness of the two dimensions also explains the pivotal role of Ontario (and, to some more limited extent, of Quebec) in the national unity debate. Whether one looks at the anglophone-francophone or at the East-West dimensions, the elite of Ontario (and of Quebec) enter on one side of the struggle. A redistribution of organizational power towards the francophones, towards the West, or towards both always harms the Ontario elite (but not always the francophone one). It is not an accident, therefore, that national unity is more of an issue in Ontario (and Quebec), as the polls confirm, and that the strongest resentment against separatist forces, be they those of Quebec or of Alberta, is to be found in Ontario.

Our argument so far is based on the supposition that the roots of national disunity are a two-dimensional struggle over the distribution of organizational power and not over the distribution of income, wealth, or constitutional powers. We will address that question in more detail.

Assuming that the parties to whatever struggle is going on are the elite in each of the groups involved, it is easy to show that the struggle is over the distribution of organizational power and not over something else: non-elite, that is, "ordinary" men and women, do not struggle over power; only those who have power, or aspire to it, play that game; these are the elite.

We can do better than that, but we need a more elaborate definition of *organizational power* and a more precise meaning of the word *organization*.

Organizations are the many hierarchical bodies set up to carry out one or a number of well-defined activities; they include political and public bodies, such as governments, Crown corporations and agencies, and school, liquor control, and public utility boards; business and financial bodies, such as corporations, partnerships, and proprietorships, and a large number of smaller businesses and farms large enough to have a hierarchical structure; educational institutions, such as universities, colleges, and schools, whether primary, secondary, professional, or technical; labour unions and trade associations; charitable and eleemosynary institutions;

health care organizations, such as hospitals and clinics, orphanages and convalescent homes; ecclesiastical bodies, such as parishes, churches, councils, and assemblies of various sorts.

It should be clear that the term "organization" comprehends a very large number of bodies of all kinds: the above list only serves as an illustration, though it probably includes the most important types of organizations to be found in any society.

Organizational power is the control that some individuals in organizations possess, not only over the decisions, policies, and orientations of those organizations, but also over the decisions, policies, and orientations of *other* organizations, through the vast system of interlocking ties that join organizations. Organizational power can be found at two places in an organization: in its formal and informal structures of command. We look at both of these only briefly here, since the next two chapters are devoted to the examination.

Organizations are always hierarchical; true, the degree of hierarchy varies, but all of them do have a formal hierarchical structure. It is with this formal structure that one associates the position as well as the formal role and functions of an individual in an organization; and these, in turn, confer on the same individual the formal discretion, authority, and control over some of the material resources of the organization, as well as impose restrictions and responsibilities in the use of that discretion and authority.

In other words, if one occupies an important position in the hierarchy of an organization, one possesses some amount or organizational power from that fact alone, because one is able to influence the policies of the organization and the decisions related to those policies.

The second focus is to be found in the informal structure, which we associate with the notion of networks. These are the informal contacts, connections, and relationships that bring members of the organizations informally together for the purpose, at least in the minds of those who control the networks, of influencing the decisions and policies of the organization. These networks, which are based on trust and understanding between the members, make it possible to offer rewards or payments to all who contribute to the policies and decisions.

It is not necessary to insist that the two loci of power within an organization are related to one another. What must be emphasized is that some organizations are larger and more important than others; so that it is possible to say that there exists a *de facto* hierarchy of organizations. The more important an organization in the hierarchy, the more power those who are in that organization are likely to be given by both the formal and informal structures of the organization.

The foregoing analysis gives substance to the simple proposition that individuals can accumulate power by using some of their time, energy, and money (1) to climb in the hierarchy of their organization; (2) to move to another organization; (3) to build networks; (4) to promote the growth of their own organization in the spectrum of all organizations; or (5) some combination of these when the alternatives are not incompatible. All of these different ways of investing resources will give more power to those who use them.

Individuals in a society are often forbidden access to some of the alternatives listed in the previous paragraphs. Indeed, as is argued in some detail in chapter four, barriers always appear, along the dominant lines of differentiation – colour, religion, language, region, social class, depending on factors peculiar to each society – which prevent some individuals from acquiring as much power as they would like, given their resources, skills, education, and other capabilities. In Canada, these dominant lines of differentiation are language and region.

National disunity is rooted in a struggle over the distribution of organizational power and not over the distribution of income, wealth, employment, equalization payments, or other economic indices. Put another way, the struggle is over the distribution of *the means* to acquire income, wealth, and employment, rather than over these magnitudes themselves. If the struggle were over the product of economic and social activity and not over the means – organizational power – to acquire that product, the struggle would not involve the elite and those who seek to join them; it would not involve, as initiators in the struggle, those among the francophones and Westerners who feel that they now have the skills and resources necessary to further their own interests, in opposition to the anglophones and Easterners, who have historically made the policies and the decisions about the policies of a large part of Canada's organizations.

Since these are the groups involved, the struggle between francophone and anglophone, and Western and Eastern elite is over the distribution of organizational power, and not over the consequences of possessing power.

Further evidence that the dominant lines of differentiation in Canadian society are language and region, and therefore that the struggle over the distribution of power takes place along these lines, is that all cleavages and lines of demarcation that affect the distribution of the means to socioeconomic betterment in a society provide social and political entrepreneurs with the opportunity to exploit the frustrations resulting from the cleavages. This is a simple notion. Since lines of differentiation act as barriers to the accumulation of organizational power, those who are forbidden access to that power will be frustrated, unhappy, and usually in a state of mind to do something about it. Such a situation is an opportunity for some individuals to mobilize that unrest by seeking to deliver the social and political changes the frustrated individuals desire.

The profile of the various political and social entrepreneurs exploiting the opportunities offered by the multifarious cleavages that exist in a society does change with events. But the notorious lack of success of the entrepreneurs in Canada, who have sought to exploit the opportunities offered by the cultural, racial, and class cleavages, among others, compared to those who have placed themselves along the language and regional cleavages, is an indication of the saliency of the latter.

THE CONSTITUTION

Some individuals implicitly have accepted the view that the roots of Canadian disunity are not to be found in a struggle over the distribution of income, wealth, and employment, but seem to argue that the roots of disunity can be found in the struggle over the distribution of constitutional powers between the federal and provincial levels of government in Canada. These individuals seem to say that if the constitutional powers were reassigned from the federal to the provincial level, the tensions and uneasiness that mark Canadian life would disappear.

This is a more subtle argument than the one that identifies the roots of disunity with a struggle over the distribution of one or more economic magnitudes, because it places the issue at the proper level of analysis. To be specific, it puts the issue at the level of the means or capabilities for achieving socioeconomic betterment; it also defines the struggle, albeit implicitly, as one involving the elite and those who aspire to join their ranks. If one chooses to disagree with such a diagnosis of Canada's predicaments, disagreement cannot be at that level of analysis.

As the analysis outlined in the preceding, and continued in the following pages indicates, Canada's problems do not lie in the Constitution, nor would a change to the present Constitution do much to resolve the pending issues; although such a change could partially allay the national disunity problem, it could just as well worsen the current malaise for the reasons that follow.

Constitutional change involves only one type of organizations in society, namely governmental ones, and only a limited dimension of such organizations at that. One could possibly argue that other organizations that are closely linked to governments would be affected, but such effects would be indirect, should they exist. The entire spectrum of other organizations, from business corporations, law firms, the media, and labour unions, to educational and other non-profit bodies would not be affected by constitutional change. This is a very important point for at least two reasons.

First, suppose that a new constitution did reassign powers between governments in the best possible way; so that the new constitution could not be seen and used as a barrier to the accumulation of organizational power by any of those who wished to dispose of the resources at their command in this way. (The reader should not interpret the foregoing sentence to mean that we believe that the existing Constitution is such a barrier: we do not think that it is; we are simply placing ourselves on the ground of those who seem to believe that the Constitution is currently such a barrier.) Such a change would not remove the barriers that exist in the other organizations of Canadian society. Because these barriers are the real obstacles to the accumulation of organizational power, we cannot accept that constitutional change would much alleviate Canada's problems.

The second reason, which is closely related to the first, is simply that constitutional change may provide the best, that is, the most legitimate, way of *not* attacking the real problems. One can make this point more strongly. All those who stand to lose – anglophones and Easterners – from a reduction in the significance of language and regional cleavages as barriers to the accumulation of organizational power have a vested interest in channelling the social energies aimed at changes towards the kind that would affect them least. The incentive to do so is even stronger if the barriers to be removed by a long process of problem solving are not the true barriers. When those who are frustrated by the real barriers discover that not much was achieved by constitutional change, they will not be very happy, to put it mildly. This is the reason why constitutional change could exacerbate national disunity as much as help to reduce it.

Could it really help to reduce it? In trying to answer this question, we must note that a constitution is a formal structure, just as the codified hierarchy in organizations is a formal structure. Similarly, as there is an informal structure in organizations – we have called it networks – there exists an informal structure of relationships that partly governs the real assignment of powers between governmental levels. It was asserted earlier that these two structures were interrelated, without stating which one governed the other.

It seems very difficult, given our present knowledge, to be specific about whether the influence of the formal structure on the value of the informal is greater than the influence of the latter on the former. Those who seem to be saying that constitutional change would help to dampen the divisions in Canadian society are implicitly saying that a change in the formal structure that would reduce language and regional barriers would also, in time, reduce the barriers that exist as a result of the structure of social networks at the informal level. That may be so, but we do not know and would hate to commit ourselves to that view.

CONCLUSION

In this chapter, we set out the main lines of our hypothesis as to the roots of Canadian disunity and argued that alternative views are difficult to accept. We trust we have been successful in demonstrating the internal consistency of our own analysis and in showing its consistency with the facts. The elaborations of the next chapters will, we hope, convince those readers who are still skeptical.

CHAPTER NINE

Symbolism and Constitutional Change: The Meech Lake Confrontation*

Almost any object, statement, document, historical fact, or monument can become a symbol for a group or society. It can come to represent something beyond its immediate reality or its practical use. Symbols are conveyors of meanings. They serve as vehicles for concepts, ideals, worldviews, and collective identities,[1] and as such, can become sources of conflict. At the heart of the conflict is not the object or document itself, but the concepts or ideals that it represents. Such a conflict may be over competing views of the sociopolitical order in a society, the relations among groups in that order, the proper role of particular institutions in society, and so on. In short, symbolic conflicts are struggles over different theories of society.

The context of a symbolic project, the way symbolic change is managed, and the symbolic content itself are all potentially controversial. The drafting of a constitution is full of potential for symbolic gain and loss – that is, gain and loss with regard to whose social theory should prevail in the structure of society.

But before we examine the element of symbolic conflict in the Meech Lake controversy, it is worthwhile to look briefly at the distinction between the symbolic and the legal-instrumental elements of constitutions, and of public policies more generally.[2]

---

* "Symbols in Constitutional Change," Chapter 1, in *Why Meech Failed: Lessons for Canadian Constitution-making* (Toronto: CD Howe Institute, 1992), 1–25.

POLICY AS INSTRUMENTAL AND SYMBOLIC

Constitutions – and all policies, for that matter – usually contain a mixture of instrumental and symbolic elements, although the mix can vary considerably. Policy may deal with the structure of government, its administrative apparatus, the division of powers, the management of the economy, and the maintenance of order in society. The debate surrounding these matters tends to focus on practical implementation and on issues of effectiveness and efficiency. Institutional arrangements lend themselves well to negotiations: they can be broken down into separate, practical elements over which the give-and-take of bargaining can occur.

But these arrangements always incorporate some of the basic principles and values of a society. As such, they have a symbolic dimension: they represent the philosophy on which the social order is based, and may even be accompanied by statements to that effect. For example, policies dealing with privatization may refer to values regarded as important in a free enterprise society. Policies on the redistribution of wealth may evoke principles of justice and compassion. These references to basic principles will be convincing only if people can see the connection between the values evoked and the policy proposal, and if they do not see the proposal as contradicting other important values.

Some components of a constitution or a policy are primarily symbolic and cultural, such as those dealing with identity, religion, ethics, and culture. Although they may have the practical purpose of regulating behavior or allocating resources, they are primarily affirmations of particular values in society. They signify principles of social and political organization and cultural identity, and refer to the history and projected future of the collectivity.

The underlying logic behind statements about the character of society and its values is primarily sociocultural, rather than a logic of means and ends.[3] Bargaining is thus problematic, as values and principles of social order cannot easily be divided into exchangeable elements.

A policy or constitutional statement may be seen as symbolically appropriate if, for example, it expresses the society's unity, or if it conforms with certain moral values. Such a statement can affirm the importance of institutions for the maintenance of the moral order and the containment of crime, or proclaim the right to a minimum of well-being, protection against physical attack, and assistance in the event of a personal calamity.[4]

Policy and constitutional statements may also symbolically affirm the principles that ought to prevail in relations among groups in society or between groups and particular institutions – especially institutions of the state. Finally, they may give recognition to particular groups on the basis of their historical importance, their culture, or their special need for protection.

Policy and constitutional statements may also be found lacking in one or more of these respects. They can, implicitly or explicitly, rank social groups or communities by assigning to each a different status in society's central institutions. Differential allocation of status or recognition among groups may be perceived as violating basic values or as diminishing the social importance and historical role of some groups compared with others.

Questions of this sort are particularly important in a highly differentiated society such as Canada's, one that places a high premium on the equal treatment of all individuals and categories of citizens. Ideally, the symbolic statements considered legitimate in our society are those that affirm the equality of all groups or social categories.

In Canada, equality is generally recognized at the level of three social entities: equality of individuals, equality of provinces, and equality of the two major linguistic communities.[5] The demand of native peoples for equal status – as nations or as a province – is also rapidly gaining recognition.[6]

Words or statements that become symbols of high or low status for a province, a linguistic, ethnic, or racial group, a gender, or a religious group are likely to be resented by those who see themselves as symbolically diminished, treated as unequal, or not given due recognition. For example, the expression "founding peoples" can be very offensive to people who feel that it ignores or minimizes their own contribution to the construction of the country or who, through historical accident, are necessarily disadvantaged by this kind of distinction. Our language still contains expressions that symbolize the inferior status of women. Another example is "Parisian French," a term that symbolizes the high status of that kind of French and hence of those speaking it and the correspondingly low status of other forms of French. "Ethnic group" or "ethnics," "immigrant group" – referring to groups that have been in Canada for three or more generations – "Negro" and "Indian" are other examples of terms that symbolize an unequal status and are felt as socially denigrating by many of those so labelled.

In short, people are likely to assess not only the pragmatic instrumental dimension but also the symbolic appropriateness of policy and constitutional statements. In fact, people may react primarily to the symbolic component of a policy or a constitution and entirely ignore its legal-instrumental dimension. Thus, there may be a strong response to a policy even if people know little about its specific technical, legal, and administrative content. Such reactions are emotional, but emotions are involved even in hard-headed economic transactions. They are rational reactions to what the symbolic statements appear to imply for their society, and for their place in it.

Policymakers can emphasize either the instrumental or the symbolic dimension of a policy. They can decide to play down its symbolic aspects and define the task as primarily technical. Or they can decide to include in their proposals significant symbolic statements that refer to what the basic character of society is or should be. They may evoke principles of relationship among groups in society. Even if such statements are not accompanied by the specifics of implementation, they may still have long-term implications for society's organization and for the place of different groups in it.

SYMBOLIC CONFLICTS

Symbolic statements are not necessarily controversial. But by their very nature, symbols assume meanings beyond their manifest content. Symbols may evoke different, even contradictory, interpretations – and corresponding emotions – from different groups.

Consequently, the use of symbols, like the use of other kinds of resources, entails risk. The nature of the risk varies according to the resource used. But whatever the resource involved – financial, technological, natural, human, or symbolic – the way it is invested and managed can yield either positive or negative results. It may not only fail to bring about the desired outcome but actually bring about the opposite of what is sought.

Several factors affect the degree to which the use of symbols can provoke social conflict. Three are considered here: the degree of ambiguity wittingly or unwittingly built into the proposals, the collective memories they bring to the fore, and the occurrence of climate-creating events. When all three factors combine, symbolic conflict is bound to occur.

The Ambiguity of Symbolic Statements

Ambiguity can be introduced into a constitution or policy to lay the foundation for particular model of society, in the hope that it can be progressively institutionalized, and it can thus pave the way for future symbolic gains. It also makes policymakers highly vulnerable, however, since ambiguity can represent an opportunity for opponents or those with a different social agenda.

Ambiguity also augments the symbolic potential of an object or statement.[7] When a statement is not given a clear, specific referent, a variety of meanings can be infused into it. Its immediate, literal meaning is likely to lose relevance, as attention focuses on the ideas and values that lie behind it. Moreover, unless the statement is accompanied by a clear interpretive framework, people are likely to give it meaning in relation to their own situation, experience, and ideology, or that of the groups to which they belong, rather than in relation to the intended goals of the policy.

One ambiguous element of symbolic statements is that for some people, they may affirm the values and character of society, while for others, they reflect a different kind of society than the one they believe exists or should exist. People in the latter category will read the statement as a threat, as it seems to propose a transformation of society and its institutions.

By augmenting the symbolic potential of a statement, ambiguity also increases the weight of the symbolic baggage it is likely to carry. For those who value what it refers to, the symbol will become increasingly important, even if it had not previously been part of the symbolic repertoire of collective self-definition. Abandoning it becomes tantamount to a surrender of identity and self-respect. But for those who fear it, it comes to symbolize what is wrong with society and the way it is governed.

The Role of Collective Memories

Individuals and groups have a history. Relations among groups also have a background that may include positive experiences but may involve tensions and conflicts as well. Accommodations among groups may have been worked out in the midst of intense controversies and accepted reluctantly by the various groups concerned.

The relationship between Quebec and the rest of Canada, and between English- and French-speaking Canadians, has a long history characterized by intermittent conflict over a variety of issues. Some of these have had to do with the cultural-symbolic definition of society and its institutions. Several measures have been adopted to affirm the French character of Quebec society and institutions. Other measures have attempted to transform the cultural-symbolic character of federal institutions in such a way that French-Canadians can identify with them and consider them as their own and not exclusively those of another cultural group. Underlying these changes has been the principle of Canada as a bilingual society.

The cultural features of institutions and their symbolic activities influence the shaping and nourishing of people's identities. The social status of their linguistic group affects their self-esteem. Members of each collectivity will therefore take a legitimate interest in the cultural character of their institutions. They will compare the treatment that their own language and culture receives with the way other groups are treated and pay regular attention to how well "they" are doing compared with "us." Each group seeks institutional control to advance its symbolic-cultural interests.

It was in this context that the Meech Lake Accord was introduced onto Canada's political agenda and that Canadians interpreted the proposed changes. Canadians saw these changes in the light of the recent history of institutional evolution and interpreted them as further symbolic gains or losses.

Climate-Creating Events

After 1987, several events contributed to creating a climate unfavourable to a reasoned debate on the complex constitutional issues involved in the Meech Lake Accord. Various groups interpreted these events as demonstrating the shortcomings or downright unfairness of the Accord. Some of the attempts to prevent the success of the Accord were, of course, deliberate. But other events had a sabotaging effect that was largely inadvertent.

As mentioned earlier, the significant decline in support for the Accord took place in the last six months of 1988: from 52 percent in June 1988, support fell to 31 percent by January 1989. There was also a considerable increase in the proportion of people registering no opinion. Several events during those six months may account for this shift – events that influenced the way people were interpreting the Accord.

One was the bill amending the Official Languages Act to expand bilingual services in the federal government. This bill was passed into law in July 1988 after considerable opposition, particularly from the Western provinces. It accentuated the feeling that francophones – together with other segments of Central Canada – had disproportionate power in Ottawa and that the views of Western Canadians were not being taken into account. The reaction was a mixture of anti-French feeling, a sense of the preferential treatment of the French in Ottawa, and a genuine concern about the policy of bilingualism. All these were compounded by the overall sense of Western alienation.[8]

Another set of events had to do with Quebec's Bill 178, on the language of commercial signs.[9] The legislation was intensely debated, as it did not conform to the Canadian Charter of Rights and Freedoms – or to Quebec's own Charter of Rights. Other elements in the controversy included the use of the "notwithstanding" clause to allow its adoption and the resignation of three Quebec ministers over the bill. Coming at that particular time, there is little doubt that Bill 178 coloured people's view of the Accord. There was extensive opposition to the bill: 76 percent of Canadians opposed it and most believed it would complicate passage of the Meech Lake Accord.[10] The Quebec government did not even receive full support from its own electorate. A December 1988 poll in that province showed that 67 percent did not agree with the government's approach to the language question.

This law gave a particular meaning to the notion of "distinct society." It was generally perceived as unfair: bilingualism was imposed in the rest of Canada while unilingualism was imposed in Quebec. The prime minister declared: "I neither approve nor do I believe it meets the tests of fairness set by the Supreme Court of Canada."[11] This message was confirmed by Manitoba's decision not to ratify the Accord unless Quebec changed its policies and gave public assurances that it would not use the Accord to suppress minority rights. Some people hailed the premier of Manitoba as a hero for this decision.

Another influential event was the coming into effect of Bill 8 in Ontario, which increased local services for francophones. This legislation had worried people in several municipalities, partly because it was to the advantage of a particular ethnic minority, partly because that minority was French, and partly because it was seen as imposing additional financial burdens on municipalities. It contributed to the wave of declarations of unilingualism in several Ontario municipalities during the fall of 1988.

Implementing these provincial laws would probably have been controversial whatever the national circumstances. But with a major national controversy in full swing, they gained significance beyond their provincial boundaries. In English-speaking Canada, Bill 178 added momentum to the protest against the distinct society clause and special measures for francophones. In Quebec, the Ontario unilingualism movement fuelled the feeling of humiliation and rejection.

Another climate-creating event was the federal proposal for a free trade agreement with the United States, a major issue in the federal election in the fall of 1988. The idea of greater continental economic integration, and its possible impact on the political autonomy and cultural integrity of the country, raised considerable anxiety in English-speaking Canada. Some Canadians were even concerned for the country's survival. They saw the Meech Lake Accord as emphasizing the provincial or regional dimension of Canada, while the free trade agreement promoted continental linkages and corresponding cross-border institutions. Each neglected Canada itself as a distinct entity whose cohesion needed support. A number of English-Canadian nationalists saw free trade supporters in Quebec as lacking sensitivity to their English-Canadian compatriots' cultural anxieties and problems of cultural and political survival.

In short, events of the second half of 1988 turned many people who had been supporters of Meech Lake, or at least undecided, against the Accord. Other events continued to add new meaning to the Accord in 1989 and 1990. The resignation of a federal cabinet minister and the subsequent formation of the Bloc Québécois constituted another climate-creating event. It confirmed the presence of pro-independence forces – of people who were working toward the break-up of the country – in the federal government. It was the symbol of an inimical force at work at the very centre of power. Furthermore, events that had taken place before the Accord was even negotiated, such as past measures to accommodate linguistic and ethnic groups, were reinterpreted in the context of the current debate.

MEECH LAKE AND SYMBOLIC CONFLICT

The Meech Lake proposal for constitutional change included ambiguous statements – in particular, the distinct society concept. No coherent explanation of this concept was provided, even though it was the one most subject to discussion and controversy. The Quebec government was adamant in refusing to define it. The explanations supplied by first ministers were vague and, in a number of instances, contradictory. One premier even said that he was not quite sure what the concept meant and that its meaning would eventually have to be spelled out by the courts. Little attention was given to the process of legitimation. No systematic framework was presented to explain the changes and to justify them in relation to a public philosophy. Why?

The authorities seemed to be confident either that there would be little dissent, or that if aspects of the proposal were questioned a consensus would soon spontaneously emerge. Perhaps they believed they could manage the process so that the Accord would eventually be ratified. Perhaps they were at a loss as to how to legitimate the scheme, or perhaps they simply did not think about this aspect of the situation.

The distinct society clause was seen as having implications for the structuring of institutions and the division of powers. But since no framework was presented to explain what the changes would mean and why they were necessary, questions and criticisms were inevitable.

Largely because of its ambiguity, the Accord raised several questions. The most important one was this: was the Accord simply an official recognition of Quebec's cultural distinctiveness, or was it a mechanism for redistributing power?

The Pursuit of Power

In English-speaking Canada, the central issue raised by the Accord was one of power and, by and large, the opposition to it was based on arguments related to power. Thus, it was argued, the socioeconomic condition of francophones had improved considerably during the past 30 years or so, and they had made power gains both in Quebec and across the country.

Several opponents also considered that the federal distribution of power was now somewhat unbalanced in favour of Quebec and of francophones generally. They perceived Quebec as having a decisive influence over national issues and over who is elected at the federal level. For them, the Accord would simply accentuate that influence and, by the same token, their own relative lack of influence. They accordingly opposed it.

This view was particularly prevalent in Western Canada – symbolized by the federal government's 1986 decision to award the maintenance contract for the Canadian Forces' CF-18 jet fighter to a Montreal company, when a Winnipeg firm had submitted a lower bid. It was also present in parts of Ontario and the Atlantic provinces; its most potent symbol in Newfoundland, for example, was the unfavourable terms under which the province sells electric power from Churchill Falls to Quebec.

Of course, not all English-speaking Canadians shared that diagnosis of the situation. Many, while acknowledging that francophones had made power gains, did not consider that these gains favoured francophones unfairly. Judging from the results of polls on attitudes toward official bilingualism, the changes were supported by a majority of English-speaking Canadians.[12] However, even those who did not perceive an unbalance found it difficult to justify further changes – or at least the changes proposed by the Accord. While many social and intellectual leaders in English-speaking Canada came forward to defend controversial institutional changes in the 1960s and 1970s, fewer were prepared to support the Accord.

This reticence may have been due to recent changes in the main orientation of English-French bargaining and accommodation. A few decades ago, there was a consensus that the grievances voiced by francophones – particularly by those in Quebec – were legitimate and that something had to be done about them. But many of those who had acknowledged such grievances now appeared to believe the changes made during the past 30 years had rectified the situation. For example, a 1991 Environics survey showed that 49 percent of a Canada-wide sample thought that, compared with other parts of the country, Quebec was better off. Among Quebecers, the corresponding percentage was almost the same, at 47 percent.[13]

People thus found it difficult to interpret the Accord as a further rectification of grievances. It was easier to assess it in terms of claims for power, as expansionist rather than corrective. Some believed the political power of francophones had become disproportionate to their population, and that the French language was becoming too predominant. It was now the turn of other groups to have their grievances addressed.

The main language provided by our political culture to justify the acquisition of power is that of the rectification of socioeconomic or political inequities. For instance, it was suggested that the Accord was necessary, because in 1982, an injustice had been inflicted on Quebec "for which it was necessary to obtain forgiveness." Thus, the Accord was "the price of Quebec's forgiveness."

But the language of grievance was not enough to convince most English-speaking Canadians, as the nature of the injustice involved was not specified. Did it refer to the process of patriation, or to the fact that existing institutional arrangements were unjust for Quebec? Or both? Many English-speaking Canadians did not see the 1982 constitutional patriation and change as an injustice toward Quebec; more pertinent to them was the fact that the negotiations were carried out on Quebec's behalf by a government dedicated to Quebec's political independence.

If the language of grievance cannot be applied, change must be justified in reference to valued objectives: that it will improve an already acceptable situation, that it represents a move toward some social or moral ideal, or that it is in line with what people understand their society to be and thus confirms elements that are already part of people's identity.

But proponents of the Accord were unable to justify it in terms of a positive overall conception of Canadian society. Rather, they justified it in terms of the urgency of having it passed. The need for Quebec to be able to sign the Constitution "with honour and enthusiasm" was stressed. The importance of bringing Quebec back into the Canadian family was emphasized. These were positive justifications for ratification, but they did not begin to deal with the particular changes introduced by the Accord.

Proponents also stressed the consequences of failing to ratify the Accord. Such failure, they argued, would mean that, as the prime minister put it, "Quebec's isolation would become a fact of constitutional life … slowly creating two Canadas in respect to the country's basic law."[14] It was also suggested that the Accord would increase the legitimacy of federal institutions in Quebec. But the reasons the changes were necessary were not spelled out, except that they were the minimum conditions set by Quebec. In short, justification was only negative: failing to ratify the Accord would have detrimental consequences.

Another dimension of the power issue was increased autonomy for Quebec. This dimension was central to the political discourse in Quebec: not more power in Ottawa, but more power in Quebec City, justified in terms of francophone Quebecers' distinctiveness and special needs as a linguistic minority in North America.

One result of the Quiet Revolution is that state institutions have replaced the Roman Catholic Church as the embodiment and locus of Quebec's identity and culture. More political autonomy is, accordingly, seen as the natural evolution of its *projet de société*, its cultural self-realization.

The reaction of English-speaking Canadians to Quebec's demands for increased autonomy was ambivalent. On the one hand, they generally recognized and accepted Quebec's distinctiveness. On the other hand, they questioned whether its locus should be the Quebec government rather than Quebec society. They also questioned the underlying intentions of the quest for autonomy. Did Quebec really need more powers to protect francophones' language and culture? Or was it a disguised pursuit of sovereignty-association, through which Quebec could reap the advantages of federalism, while bearing as little of the cost as possible? Quebec would then have increased its powers at the provincial level while retaining its considerable influence in federal decisions and in the allocation of national resources.

Some English-Canadians suspected that the distinct society clause was a symbolic instrument introduced in the Constitution to be used later in the pursuit of more powers, and that the Accord was another step in a process with no foreseeable end. Further claims would surely be forthcoming if Meech were to be ratified.

Political authorities and analysts were not able to convince the suspicious that this was not the case – that some additional autonomy was necessary, but sovereignty was not the *de facto* outcome. On the contrary, some Quebec government officials suggested that the Accord was just the beginning of a substantial transfer of powers, and that the distinct society clause was to be used for this purpose in subsequent negotiations. Its significance would be interpreted by the courts in the light of the new needs of Quebec society. The terms of reference of the Allaire Committee, set up about four months *before* the Meech Lake deadline, also clearly stated that the Accord was only a step in preparation for subsequent negotiations. It recommended a massive transfer of powers to the province.[15]

Finally, the more cynical saw the disproportionate importance given to the public desecration of the Quebec flag in Brockville, Ontario,[16] and more generally, the emphasis that Quebec politicians and opinion makers placed on the themes of rejection and humiliation as ways of concealing the real nature of the clause – the creation of a constitutional instrument for the pursuit of power.

Recognition and Status

While in English-speaking Canada, the Accord was perceived as dealing with power, in French-speaking Quebec, the central notions were recognition and status.[17] The questions and opposition expressed by English-Canadians were perceived as a refusal to recognize Quebec's distinctiveness, both cultural and historical. They were also considered a withdrawal of historically-acquired status in the federation.[18] Losing something is probably always more painful than failing to acquire it.

One of the anxieties of francophone Quebecers is the fear of being reduced to the status of other ethnic groups. Because of this, they regard the federal policy of multiculturalism with suspicion – even though the Quebec government has adopted essentially the same policy, albeit with another name. This status anxiety is also at the root of Quebec's resistance to the notion of the equality of the provinces.

A Quebec minister said in late 1991 that "Quebec will never accept to be treated at the same level ... because we are distinct first, but also because of our population, and because of our status in the federation."[19] Treatment at the same level would be a withdrawal of that status.

The vocabulary used to denounce opposition to the Accord and to the distinct society clause included terms such as humiliation, rejection, isolation, and being put in one's place. Such perceptions were cast in the context of the history of English-French relations in Canada. For instance, a number of francophone Quebecers believed nothing had been done to recognize the distinctiveness of Quebec and to accommodate its cultural and linguistic character during the past 30 years. The considerable institutional changes that had taken place, as well as the changes in attitudes and behaviour in a large segment of the anglophone population, were either not known, considered irrelevant for the current debate, or dismissed as too little, too late.

Another view was that francophones could not rely on anglophones for their cultural survival and vitality: they had to assume the entire responsibility themselves. In fact, a common view was that English Canada had not only not helped in this regard but had offered resistance all along. For English-Canadians, this view held, the experience of institutional change meant having had French "rammed down their throats."

From this perspective, English Canada's refusal to accept the distinct society clause was yet another instance of resistance to Quebec's cultural aspirations. It was an attempt to weaken or abolish existing institutional measures to protect and enhance the cultural and linguistic character of Quebec and the francophone presence in national institutions, and to forestall any additional ones. The insistence in English Canada on the Charter of Rights and Freedoms was simply a way of disguising the opposition to those measures. The emphasis on individual rights was thus a device to oppose the collective rights of francophones; indeed, to reject the very idea that there are such things as collective rights.

Just as some francophone Quebecers made statements that confirmed the pursuit-of-power diagnosis that was widespread in English Canada, so too there were expressions of rejection and humiliation – such as the desecration of the Quebec flag and statements by leaders of extremist groups – that confirmed the rejection and humiliation diagnosis that came to prevail in Quebec. The repeated showing of the Brockville flag incident on Quebec television was widely interpreted as a systematic attempt to portray English Canadians as vicious and to arouse feelings against them.

These diagnoses – a question of power on the one hand, a question of acceptance and respect on the other – came to dominate the interpretive schemes on each side of the linguistic divide. It was increasingly difficult for English-Canadians to see that Quebec faced cultural problems that were quite different from those of the rest of the country, and to consider that perhaps some special measures were needed to cope with them. It also became very difficult for francophone Quebecers to recognize the considerable goodwill among anglophones and to acknowledge the magnitude of the changes that had already taken place. They found it impossible to believe that the grievances and frustrations of people in certain parts of English Canada over the distribution of power in federal decision-making and over the power wielded by Quebec – and, one might add, by Ontario and Toronto – perhaps had some validity and were not simply expressions of anti-Quebec feelings.

CONCLUSION

This analysis of the symbolic dynamic of the Meech Lake controversy leads to suggestions for dealing with the symbolic component of the Constitution and for finding a framework that validates institutional change.

Dealing with the Symbolic Component of Constitutions

Constitutional documents usually have instrumental rather than symbolic value. This was the case, for example, with Canada's original constitution, the British North America Act of 1867.[20]

But since the 1982 patriation, the Constitution has acquired considerable symbolic value, particularly because of its Charter of Rights and Freedoms. For many Canadians, it does more than specify their rights as members of society. It is a statement about the character of Canada and something with which people identify. With the distinct society clause, a statement that was almost exclusively symbolic, the Meech Lake Accord enlarged the symbolic component of the Constitution, although, as discussed earlier, it was also thought to be an instrument for subsequent power gains.

All societies – indeed, all groups and organizations – have a symbolic repertoire through which they represent who they are as collective entities and through which they affirm and celebrate their character and values. The repertoire may include a name, a costume, a flag, a founding myth, monuments, rituals, and ceremonies whereby special historical events and heroes are celebrated. For Canada, this repertoire has come to include the Constitution.

As we have seen, symbolic policy statements are risky: their ambiguity may have a divisive rather than an integrating effect. Several statements of the "Canada Clause" included in the current constitutional proposals seem to be safe in this regard.[21] They refer to basic values over which there is a widespread consensus. In that regard, the clause might therefore have an integrating effect. On the other hand, it also contains controversial statements that may neutralize that positive effect. It is not the positive elements that will "sanctify" the controversial ones; rather, it is the controversial ones that are likely to contaminate the overall symbolic affirmation.

Symbols that allocate group status in society may generate envy and tension among those groups, particularly if there is a history of competition for prestige and official status among linguistic, ethnic, or regional groups.[22]

This does not mean that status symbols should be avoided in constitutional documents. It means that if the symbols allocate status or recognition, the distribution must be balanced among the major territories or population segments in society. The forms of recognition need not be the same for all groups or social categories, but they need to be balanced or they are likely to have a divisive impact.[23] Commonness and interdependence should also be symbolically emphasized. A statement that suggests special status based on anything other than achievement is likely to be rejected, unless it is legitimated in reference to stated and accepted values.[24]

In a highly differentiated society, such as Canada, any symbol embedded in the Constitution that underscores ethnic, linguistic, or regional differences raises the social and political awareness of these differences and is fraught with risks for the cohesion of society. Again, this does not mean that such symbols should not be used, but they should be based on widespread consensus about the contexts in which such differences should be acknowledged.

If the use of symbols is unmanageable for historical or sociopolitical reasons, it is best to avoid them altogether, however meaningful they may be for a particular group. Recognition may be achieved through other symbolic, as well as practical means.

Given the "unbalanced" nature of the distinct society statement and the negative connotations it acquired, it seems obvious that for the sake of social cohesion, it would be best to drop it from the Constitution. But dropping the clause now would create still more tension because of the greater significance it has acquired in Quebec since the confrontation. However, as the central objection to the distinct society clause did not relate to a rejection of the distinctive character of Quebec, but rather to its ambiguous implications for the distribution of power, the constitutional statement needs to clarify this question. Legal opinions on whether the clause gives more power to Quebec may not be sufficient, and anyway, there is no legal consensus on the matter.

An additional statement must make it clear that recognition as a distinct society does not imply more powers for Quebec, that it would not be used in the future to obtain more powers, and that Quebec's distinctiveness would simply be recognized within existing constitutional arrangements. This may be unacceptable to Quebec, given statements by Quebec officials during the course of the controversy. However, a senior Quebec cabinet minister said in 1991 that "if Quebec wants to be recognized as distinct, it's not because we want more powers or to be considered as superior. We don't want to be better, but we do want to be legally recognized as being different."[25] If this could be taken as an official position, the proposed clarification would be acceptable to Quebec.

As noted elsewhere in this book, however, other statements by Quebec officials have indicated that power was one of the intentions behind the distinct society clause. The existence of different interpretations of the clause and the fact that contradictory statements were made are additional reasons for a clarification in the Constitution itself.

The underlying ideas are, first, that the vitality of a community's culture depends on the vitality of its institutions and, second, that special measures may be required to protect and strengthen these institutions, particularly in view of the predicament of a francophone minority in anglophone North America. Once the reality of this situation is recognized, several issues need to be considered.

First, what powers are needed to maintain the vitality of the cultural community? Some argue that the state must be active in all institutional spheres: political, economic, cultural, and social (this is the position of the Allaire report); others maintain that the powers involved are those concerning language and culture.

Second, to what extent is the state the main agent of cultural maintenance and development? Should there not be more reliance on civil society? In contemporary Quebec political culture, the state is paramount; civil society is assigned a relatively small role. It should be noted that this is a relatively new phenomenon: the transformation and revitalization of Quebec society in the course of the Quiet Revolution was primarily a civil society phenomenon. The state became active in it, but its involvement was largely the result of a social movement. Now, change is much more under the direction and management of the state.

But the limits of government in preserving culture need to be recognized. Modern communication technologies have a way of bypassing government policies, as Canada and several other countries are finding out. The massive influence of the United States cannot be stopped at the border by a law. English as the *lingua franca* of international relations in commerce, diplomacy, and science is a reality beyond the scope of Canadian legislation. The cultural impact of economic and political transactions with the rest of Canada and with the United States cannot be removed by legal specifications or transfers of powers. Cultural maintenance and development relies heavily on civil society.

Third, what level of government should assume the responsibility of the institutional and cultural vitality of the francophone population of Quebec? This is perhaps the most important issue underlying the distinct society proposal. Generally, the view in English-speaking Canada as well as in Quebec is that this responsibility belongs to Quebec. Some, however, feel that the federal government also has a role to play in this regard and that, in fact, it is already assuming such a responsibility. It has contributed significantly to the Quebec economy, to its educational, health, and social welfare institutions, to its research capability, and even to its cultural development.[26]

The ways in which this issue is dealt with can profoundly affect the evolution of Canadian society. The more the protection and vitality of Quebec as a distinct society is defined as belonging to Quebec, the less the federal government would have a meaningful role in that province and the less would be its linkages with Quebec residents. Instead, its relationships would be with the Quebec government, not with its citizens either directly or through a variety of institutions. As a result, Quebecers' already weak identification with the federal government would become even weaker. Ottawa would be defined as a tax collector and a manager of distant functions, such as defence.

The alternative would be to define the vitality of Quebec as a distinct society as a responsibility of both levels of governments – a view that is not new in Canadian federalism, but that would need to be rejuvenated. Of course, moving in that direction would be difficult at the moment. Indeed, Quebec's political and bureaucratic elites and intelligentsia largely reject such a view: as noted, this appears to be the force behind the constitutionalization of the notion of distinct society.

In addition, English-speaking Canada would need to accept such a responsibility. In other words, a significant way of recognizing Quebec's distinctiveness would be to accept a role in maintaining it. At the moment, this acceptance does not appear to have taken hold. A 1990 public opinion poll showed that 57 percent of English-speaking Canadians did not agree with the proposition that "in view of the dominance of English in North America, the French language needs special protection in Quebec to ensure its survival."[27] By contrast, 94 percent of francophones agreed with the statement. However, as anglophones probably interpreted the statement in the context of Bill 178 and of other recent tensions over language legislation, support might have been higher – 35 percent disagreed and 22 percent strongly disagreed – if the special measures had been seen to entail positive programs rather than restrictive laws.

The Need to Legitimate Institutional Change

In order for institutional change to take place and to be considered legitimate, it is not enough to simply pass it through all the legally required steps and procedures.[28] The legitimacy of a constitution depends on the extent to which people accept its basic ideas. A legitimating framework must help people make sense of the innovations by explaining the proposals, and it must justify them by showing that the values embedded in the policy are congruent with widely acceptable cultural values.

When this is the case, the statements reinforce the values and worldviews of citizens by making them explicit. The constitution becomes a monument celebrating what people consider the underpinnings of their social and political world. But if no such scheme is provided, if the link between the proposed change and an accepted system of ideas and values is not made explicit, citizens may not regard the proposed change as valid.

The absence of a compelling explanation and justification for the Meech Lake proposals generated considerable suspicion and anxiety: was the basic character of Canadian society being changed by that proposal? If so, how? This vacuum also opened the stage to active competition among different conceptions or theories of Canadian society and of its political organization. And once the competition was in full swing, articulating a legitimating framework became an almost impossible task, as arguments put forward to justify (or oppose) the proposal were perceived as self-serving.

Once the controversy was under way, the political authorities were confronted with a serious dilemma. On the one hand, what was the point of formally adopting the changes when they were not widely considered legitimate? (For those who demand social as well as legal validation of institutional change, the failure of the Accord can be seen as a success.) On the other hand, once a high level of emotional and ideological fervour had been reached, it became almost impossible to withdraw the proposal without making matters even worse. A postponement of the deadline (as some were requesting) would probably have been the best course of action, since it would have made it easier to make explicit the theory of Canada underlying the proposal and to explain and justify it to the people of Canada.

PART THREE

Immigrant Communities in Canada: Ethnic Heterogeneity

CHAPTER TEN

The Institutional Completeness of Immigrant Ethnic Communities*[1]

Many researchers, in attempting to explain the integration of immigrants, have stressed the factors pertaining to the social background, the motivation, and the primary group affiliations of the immigrant (see, for example, Mills *et al.* 1950; Warner 1945; Eisenstadt 1954; Reepolds 1935). In the present study, the view was adopted that some of the most crucial factors bearing on the absorption of immigrants would be found in the social organization of the communities which the immigrant contacts in the receiving country. There are three communities which are relevant: the community of his ethnicity, the native (i.e., receiving) community, and the other ethnic communities.

It was also felt that the integration of the immigrant should not be seen from a purely assimilationist point of view, in which integration is said to have taken place when the immigrant is absorbed in the receiving society. Integration was rather conceived of as taking place in any one of the communities mentioned above, or in two or three directions at the same time. That is, an immigrant can establish a network of social affiliations extending beyond the boundaries of any one community. Finally, it is also possible for the immigrant to be unintegrated.

It is argued that the direction of the immigrant's integration will, to a large extent, result from the forces of attraction (positive or negative) stemming from the various communities. These forces are generated by the social organization of the communities. In the present paper the

* "The Institutional Completeness of Ethnic Communities and the Personal Relations of Immigrants," *American Journal of Sociology* 70 (1964): 193–205.

influence of the institutional completeness of the immigrant's own ethnic community on the direction of his social integration is examined. In other words, I will examine the extent to which the institutional completeness of the ethnic community is related to its capacity to attract the immigrant within its social boundaries.

Ethnic communities can vary enormously in their social organization. At one extreme, there is the community which consists essentially in a network of interpersonal relations: members of a certain ethnic group seek each other's companionship; friendship groups and cliques are formed. But beyond this informal network, no formal organization may exist. The immigrant who is a member of such a group will establish all his institutional affiliations in the native community, since his ethnic group has little or no organization of its own.

Most ethnic groups probably were at one time – and some still are – of this informal type. Many, however, have developed a more formal structure and contain organizations of various sorts: religious, educational, political, recreational, national, and even professional. Some have organized welfare and mutual aid societies. Some operate their own radio station or publish their own newspapers and periodicals. The community may also sustain a number of commercial and service organizations. Finally, it may have its own churches and sometimes its own schools. Between the two extremes, much variation can be observed in the amount and complexity of community organizations; the degree of institutional completeness, in fact, shows variations from one ethnic group to another.

Institutional completeness would be at its extreme whenever the ethnic community could perform all the services required by its members. Members would never have to make use of native institutions for the satisfaction of any of their needs, such as education, work, food and clothing, medical care, or social assistance. Of course, in contemporary North American cities, very few, if any, ethnic communities showing full institutional completeness can be found.

When the immigrant is transplanted from one country to another, he has to reconstruct his interpersonal "field." He will rebuild in a new community a network of personal affiliations (Eisenstadt 1952). Such a reconstruction is accomplished through his activities to satisfy his immediate needs: making a living, learning the new language, participating in social life, going to church. To satisfy these needs, he will use a certain institutional setup; he will introduce himself into a social group. Which one? The native community? His own ethnic community? Another immigrant community of an ethnicity different from his own? Will he integrate himself primarily in one of these communities, or will he split his affiliations among them?

In the present paper, two questions will be discussed: (1) Does the interpersonal integration of the immigrant in fact take place in different directions? In other words, to what extent are immigrants integrated in the native, their own, or another immigrant community? (2) To what extent does the institutional completeness of the ethnic community determine the direction of the interpersonal integration of the immigrant?

DATA AND METHODS

The analysis of the effect of the community characteristics on the direction of integration was carried out through a comparison of the personal relations of immigrants from 30 different ethnic groups. The findings are based on data from interviews with 230 male immigrants in Montreal, Canada, 163 of whom were re-interviewed 14 months later.[2] In drawing the sample, no restriction was put either on the length of residence in Canada or on the ethnicity of the immigrant.

The sample was drawn in two stages. The first stage was an area sample, in which 13 census tracts were randomly selected. The census tracts in which the number of immigrants was extremely small had first been eliminated. Of the 18,415 households in the 13 census tracts, 75 percent were visited in order to enumerate their foreign-born population. From this enumeration was drawn a list of 1,689 male immigrants 18 years of age or older, who had been at least 15 years of age when they came to Canada. In the second stage, a sample of 350 was drawn at random from the list.

Questionnaires were then administered in personal interviews. Approximately 14 percent refused to be interviewed; others were not interviewed because they were "never at home," because no one was found to conduct the interview in their own language, or because they had moved during the four to five months between the enumeration and the interviewing. Losses in this last category probably constitute the most serious bias in the sample. Finally, some of the returns of those interviewed had to be rejected because of their poor quality.

The measure used to rate the ethnic communities according to their degree of institutional completeness is constructed from information on the number of churches, welfare organizations, newspapers, and periodicals in each ethnic community. Because all spheres of social activity are not covered, it is possible only to approximate the level of institutional completeness of each ethnic group. However, the error is probably consistent for all ethnic groups, and consequently does not affect their ranking along that dimension, particularly in view of the fact that the ranking is a very gross one: "Low" or "High."[3]

The direction of the affiliations of the immigrant was determined by the ethnic character of the persons with whom he was in contact. The respondent was first asked whether during the week preceding the interview he had visited any people in their homes or had received any visitor

Table 10.1
Ethnic composition of interpersonal relations for total sample and by length of residence
in receiving country

		Years of residence		
Interpersonal relations	Total (N= 173)*	0–6 (N=73)	7–12 (N= 57)	13+ (N= 48)
PROPORTION WITH MAJORITY OF THEIR PERSONAL RELATIONS				
In own ethnic group	0.59	0.70	0.58	0.42
In another ethnic group	.14	.15	.07	.21
With members of native group	.19	.10	.25	.28
In none of the above groups	0.08	0.05	0.10	0.09

* Respondents with no personal relations and those who did not give the necessary information are
  excluded.

himself. He was also asked whether he went to the movies, theatre, night
clubs, dance halls, taverns, bowling alleys, or other similar places; whether
he attended concerts, sporting events, or other entertainments of some
sort; and if he did, whether he went alone or with other people. Finally,
he was asked if he met socially some of his co-workers, if he had any.
Information was obtained on the national origin and birthplace of each
person met (identified by first name or some other symbol). Then the
respondents were classified, according to the proportion of the people
met who were from each group, as having a *majority* or a *minority* of their
personal relations in their own ethnic group, among other immigrants, or
among members of the receiving community.[4]

ATTACHMENTS TO NATIVE
AND TO ETHNIC COMMUNITIES

Most immigrants become absorbed into the new social system in the sense
that they establish some personal attachment to it. But in which direction?
Table 10.1 presents data bearing on the extent to which immigrants are
interpersonally integrated inside or outside their own ethnic community.

The relations of the immigrants with their ethnic group seem quite
strong as far as social ties are concerned. Indeed, nearly 60 percent have
a majority of their personal ties with members of that group, and compar-
atively few – approximately 20 percent – have most of their relations with
members of the native community.

If we examine the changes that take place as the immigrant spends more
time in his new society, we find that the idea of the immigrant segregated
from the native community fits more closely, although far from perfectly,
the situation of the recent immigrant. But this situation changes more and

Table 10.2
Institutional completeness and in group relations

	Degree of institutional completeness of ethnic group		
	Low	Medium	High
A. Proportion of *individuals* with majority of relations within ethnic group	0.21	0.54	0.89
Number of individuals	(62)	(28)	(83)
B. No. of *ethnic groups* with majority of all relations within group	5 out of 21	4 out of 5	4 out of 4

more as the number of years spent in the receiving society increases. It is partly true that at one time, the immigrant is drawn into the ethnic sub-system, but it does not take too long before he begins to break these ties and to form new attachments outside his ethnic community. Indeed, it is after six years in the host country that the ties with the native community show a substantial increase.

INSTITUTIONAL COMPLETENESS OF THE ETHNIC COMMUNITY

The presence of formal organizations in the ethnic community sets out forces that have the effect of keeping the social relations of the immigrants within its boundaries. It tends to minimize out-group contacts. This is what Table 10.2 shows. The communities showing the highest degree of institutional completeness have a much greater proportion of their members with most of their personal relations within the ethnic group: 89 percent of the members of highly institutionalized communities, as compared with 21 percent of those from ethnic groups with few or no formal organizations. The relationship between institutional completeness and in-group relations is about the same when the groups themselves, rather than the individual immigrants, are classified on these dimensions (Part B of Table 10.2).[5]

The institutions of an ethnic community are the origin of much social life in which the people of that community get involved, and as a consequence, become tied together in a cohesive interpersonal network. We may note, incidentally, that the same result would be obtained in the case of ethnic organizations whose stated purpose is to help the immigrant to "adjust" to the conditions of life and cultural habits in the country of adoption. Through such organizations, immigrants may become partly acculturated; but at the same time they would become more strongly integrated into an interpersonal network of their own group. In other

Table 10.3
In-group relations, by number of churches in ethnic community and church attendance*

		No. of churches in community			
		1 or 2		3 or more	
	None	Non-national attendance	National attendance	Non-national attendance	National attendance
Proportion of respondents with majority of relations within ethnic group	0.12	0.62	0.85	0.82	0.98
$N^\dagger$					

* a (effect of number of churches) = 0.16, $P(a \le 0) < 0.05$; b (effect of attendance at a national church) = 0.19, $P(b \le 0) < 0.02$.

† Respondents from communities without churches are not considered in the calculation of the index. This measure of the effect of an independent attribute X on a dichotomized dependent attribute Y is the mean of the percentage difference in each pair of comparisons when controlling for other independent attributes. The sampling variance of this statistic is obtained by summing the variances of each percentage difference and dividing by the square of the number of paired comparisons through which these differences were obtained. This estimate of the variance and a table of the standardized cumulative normal distribution are used to find the level of significance. For the basis of this statistic see Coleman (1964).

words, the existence of an institution in the group would tend to have the observed effect on the cohesiveness of the ethnic group, irrespective of its orientation toward the native and its own national culture.

SOCIAL ORGANIZATION OR INDIVIDUAL PARTICIPATION?

Do the institutions of an ethnic community affect the social relations only of those who use them, or do they generate a social life that extends beyond the realm of the participants? Table 10.3 shows that the presence of churches in a community is related to more in-group relations, even among those who do not attend the ethnic church.

The number of ethnic publications also affects the composition of interpersonal networks, but only among non-readers (Table 10.4). The non-readers are much more likely to associate within their ethnic group if the latter has several publications rather than a single one ($d = 0.31$), but the difference in the case of readers is not only much weaker, but in the opposite direction ($d = -0.09$). This is perhaps due to the difference in the distribution of the members of each category of ethnic groups in terms of education, language read, or other relevant attributes. The size of the sample, however, does not allow a more detailed analysis.

Table 10.4
In-group relations, by number of publications in community and reading of publications*

| | No. of publications in community | | | | |
| | 1 only | | | 2 or more | |
	None	Not read every month	Read at least every month	Not read every month	Read at least every month
Proportion of respondents with majority of relations within ethnic group	0.35	0.43	0.91	0.74	0.82
$N^\dagger$					

* a (effect of number of publications) = 0.11, $P(a \leq 0)$ = 0.27; b (effect of attendance of publications) = 0.28, $P(b \leq 0) < 0.01$.

† Respondents from communities with no newspapers and periodicals are not considered in the calculation of the index.

There is further evidence in Table 10.4 concerning the effect of publications in the ethnic community on in-group relations. This is found by comparing the difference between readers and non-readers of ethnic publications in communities having only one publication, with the corresponding difference for communities having more than one publication. These differences are .48 and .08, respectively. If the immigrant is a member of a community with many publications, it does not seem to make much difference whether he reads them himself or not. If, on the other hand, there is only one publication, then it seems important that he be directly exposed to its influence if it is to affect the composition of his personal relations. We may note that the respondents from communities with no publications at all are the most likely to associate outside their ethnic group.

Through what processes does the institutional completeness of the community affect the composition of the interpersonal networks of the members of an ethnic group? There are at least four such processes about which we can speculate:

1 *Substitution.* The ethnic group succeeds in holding its members' allegiance by preventing their contact with the native community. This is achieved by a process of substitution, whereby ethnic institutions rather than those of the native community take hold in the immigrant's social life. Immigrants have to find jobs; if they belong to a religion, they will want to go to church; being members of an occupational group, they may wish to join a work association; like other members of a modern society, they will read newspapers, listen to the radio, and watch television; they will send their children to school, etc. The immigrant and his family

establish a wide range of institutional attachments, inevitably or nearly so, through the performance of their work. If these attachments are established within the native community, they will constitute channels for the formation of personal relationships with the members of that community.

If, however, the ethnic group develops its own institutions and forms its own associations, it will, in this way, control to a large extent the interpersonal integration of at least those of its members who become participants in the ethnic, instead of the native organization.

Indeed, the findings presented in Table 10.3 show that, to the extent that there is actual substitution, that is to say, to the extent that individual immigrants attend ethnic religious institutions instead of others, the expected effect on the composition of interpersonal ties is observed. But this effect through the process of substitution is fairly weak. In fact, if we take as a measure of this substitution effect, the average difference between those who attend a national church and the others (the value of b in Table 10.3), we find that it accounts for less than one-fifth of the total variation in the composition of personal ties. If there is at least one church in the community, a large proportion of the immigrant's personal relations are contained within the social boundaries of the community. The increment in that proportion stemming from the individual's actual attendance at the ethnic church is not very large.

2 *Extension within the community of the personal networks of the participants in institutions.* The immigrants who belong to ethnic organizations value highly their nationality, and as we have seen, form associations within it. The organizations sustain and perhaps increase this group of "attached" individuals, who, in turn, nourish the national sentiments of non-participants and include them among their associates. Since we do not know if the non-members have among their personal relations other individuals who are members, we can only suggest that this may be one of the processes taking place.

3 *Organizations and associations in a community also raise new issues or activate old ones for public debate.* The arousal of public interest in the life of the group probably results in greater cohesiveness of the group. For instance, the group may become united in some action against outside elements, such as over an immigration bill which would be detrimental to this particular group, or the expropriation of houses which would force a large number of families of that ethnic group to move away, or again the attempts of a non-national parish to have the national church closed down in order to increase its own membership. Of course, issues which divide subgroups within the ethnic community will also have the effect of keeping the personal relations within the ethnic boundaries. The attachments of the members of each subgroup will be strengthened. To the extent that they become polarized on the issues facing their group, association with individuals who are not members of the ethnic group will be less appealing,

unless they could become allies in the conflict. An important controversy among Italians, for example, will make Italians associate among themselves in cliques fighting each other.[6]

4 *Leaders of organizations actively attempt to maintain or enlarge the clientele.* This is particularly true if the rate of immigration is decreasing, and because of this, the survival of some of the organizations comes to be in danger. An illustration of this is found, for example, in Wittke's history of the German press in America. He notes that "at various times efforts were made to organize German press clubs on a local, state, or national basis." He reports that in 1863,

a number of German publishers and editors met at Reading, Pennsylvania, to work out plans to solve the problem of the rising cost of paper during the Civil War. The agenda was expanded to include a discussion of ways and means to keep the German press alive by supporting German Sunday Schools, reading clubs, and libraries, and by insisting that German be taught in the schools. From this meeting stemmed an organization. (Wittke 1957: 215–16)

After about 25 years, the organization died.

This example suggests that some ethnic organizations are dependent on other ethnic organizations for their survival and expansion. In the case quoted above, there was even a direct attempt to create new organizations in the ethnic community for the purpose of keeping alive a particular one. Such direct attempts, however, may occur only when the leaders (in this case the publishers) have some personal interest in the survival of the organization. But this is perhaps only a question of degree, in the sense that leaders always have some personal interest in the survival of the organizations for which they are responsible.

TYPE AND NUMBER OF INSTITUTIONS

Effect of Different Types of Institutions

Of the three types of institutions included in the index of institutional completeness – churches, welfare organizations, and newspapers and periodicals – religious institutions have the greatest effect in keeping the immigrant's personal associations within the boundaries of the ethnic community. This is shown in Table 10.5, where the effect of the other types of institutions is controlled. In both cases, the presence and number of religious institutions explain about the same proportion of the variation in the dependent phenomenon (40 percent and 45 percent).[7]

The weight of the religious institutions can be attributed to the dominant role they hold in the community. Churches are very frequently the centre

Table 10.5
Churches, welfare organizations, publications, and extent of in-group relations

	No. of churches in community							
	2 or less		3 or more		2 or less		3 or more	
	Welfare organizations				Publications			
	None	Some	None	Some	None	Some	None	Some
Proportion of individuals with majority of relations within ethnic group	0.26	0.54	0.75	0.95	0.23	0.67	0.73	0.98
N	(61)	(48)	(4)	(60)	(70)	(39)	(11)	(53)

Note: a (effect of welfare organizations on in-group relations) = 0.24, $P(a \leq 0) \simeq 0.05$;
b_1 (effect of churches holding welfare organizations constant) = 0.45, $P(b_1 \leq 0) < 0.01$;
b_2 (effect of churches holding publications constant) = 0.40, $P(b_2 \leq 0) < 0.01$;
c (effect of publications) = 0.35, $P(c \leq 0) < 0.01$.

of a number of activities; associations are formed, and collective activities are organized under their influence and support. Also, the national sentiments of the immigrant find support in having experiences in church very similar to those in the country of origin – the language is the same; the images used in preaching are the same; the saints worshipped are also those the immigrant has known from early childhood. Moreover, religious leaders frequently become advocates and preachers of a national ideology, providing a *raison d'être* for the ethnic community and a motivation for identification with it.

Publications have the second most important effect on the immigrant's interpersonal network. The presence of publications in the ethnic community explains 35 percent of the variation in the proportion of in-group relations.[8]

Newspapers have a role in promoting the national ideology and keeping alive the national symbols and values, national heroes, and their historical achievements. Moreover, they interpret many of the events occurring in the country of adoption in terms of the survival or interests of the ethnic community. It is the very business of the national periodical or newspaper to be concerned with the events and personalities of the ethnic group.

Finally, the presence of welfare organizations has the least effect It explains only 24 percent of the variation. This, we presume, is due to the fact that these organizations are not concerned with the national interests of the community. They deal with people in need of food, shelter, clothing, or medical attention. They have to support "human" feelings rather than "national" feelings; nevertheless, the existence of such organizations points to the presence of an active elite in the community which perhaps has its

Table 10.6
Various community organizations and extent of in-group relations

| Community organization | Proportion of individuals and no. of ethnic groups with majority of in-group relations | | | | |
| | Individual | | | Group | |
	Proportion	$d*$	N	No.	Total
NUMBER OF CHURCHES					
2 or more	.80	.13	(108)	7	8
1 only	.67	.55†	(15)	4	6
None	.12		(50)	2	16
NUMBER OF WELFARE ORGANIZATIONS					
2 or more	.58	$-.28^\dagger$	(36)	3	4
1 only	.86	$-.57^\dagger$	(72)	3	5
None	.29		(65)	7	21
NUMBER OF NEWSPAPERS AND PERIODICALS					
2 or more	.93	.26†	(62)	3	3
1 only	.67	.37†	(30)	3	5
None	.30		(81)	7	22

* Difference between the proportion in the first column and the proportion immediately below it in the same column. The variance of the differences was estimated by using the method suggested by Goodman (1961).
† This difference is significant at least at the .01 level.

influence on the community's cohesiveness through channels other than the welfare organizations themselves. Also, their existence has a negative effect on contact with the host community: immigrants in need, who address themselves to ethnic organizations, miss a chance of contact with the "native" community.

Variation with Increasing Number of Formal Organizations

What most differentiates one community from another in its capacity to control the social integration of its members is not so much its having many formal organizations as having some, as opposed to none at all. This is shown in Table 10.6, where the extent of in-group relations is presented for immigrants whose group has no organization of a certain type, for those whose group has one organization of that type, and finally, for those who belong to groups with two or more such organizations.

All comparisons show that it is the existence of the first organization which makes the greatest difference. Second, third, or further additions have an effect on the extent of in-group relations, but much smaller than the effect of the first organization, or in the opposite direction. A drastic expansion occurs in the ethnic interpersonal network when the ethnic community ceases to be an informal system and acquires some first elements of a formal structure. This expansion continues as the formal structure develops but in increments smaller than the initial one.

CHANGE IN COMPOSITION OF INTERPERSONAL NETWORKS

If the ethnic community to which he belongs determines to a certain degree the composition of an immigrant's interpersonal network, it should also show some effect on the rate at which the immigrant changes his personal associates, as well as on the kind of people he includes among, and abandons from, his personal relations.

Changes took place in both directions: some immigrants associated more within their ethnic group, some less. Of those who were not members of an ethnic interpersonal network at the time of the first interview, 22 percent were included in one a year after; on the other hand, 17 percent of those who associated mostly in their ethnic group had become interpersonally integrated in the native group.[9]

The changes in the composition of the immigrants' personal relations were then approximately as likely to be in the direction of the ethnic community as in that of the native community. This fact is of crucial importance for this study; indeed, it serves to validate the scheme used in the analysis. It supports the idea that the integration of immigrants cannot really be studied without taking into account the fact that it can be achieved in at least two directions, that is, within the native or within the ethnic community; and that the integration can take place as frequently in the one as in the other direction. Integration within the ethnic community cannot be ignored under the assumption that it is relatively unimportant or that it occurs relatively infrequently.[10]

The degree of institutional completeness of an immigrant's ethnic community is one of the main factors determining the direction of the change in the composition of his personal relations. As Table 10.7 shows, the immigrant who is a member of an institutionalized ethnic community is more likely to have shifted to a high proportion of in-group relations than the one who belongs to a less institutionalized one (29 percent as compared to 18 percent).

Also, Table 10.7 shows that the immigrants who had no personal relations at the time of the first interview and acquired some between the interviews acquired different kinds of associates, depending on the degree of institutional completeness of their ethnic group. If the immigrant is a member of a group with organizations of its own, he is three times more likely to have acquired associates within his own group than if he is a part of a group with a more informal social organization (62 percent as against 20 percent).

Table 10.7
Institutional completeness and change in ethnic composition of personal relations

Proportion of relations within ethnic group	High degree of institutional completeness			Low degree of institutional completeness		
	Wave II			Wave II		
	Minority	Majority	N	Minority	Majority	N
WAVE I						
Minority	0.71	0.29	17	0.82	0.18	34
Majority	.15	.85	60	.14	.86	7
No personal relations	0.38	0.62*	13	0.80	0.20*	10

* $d(0.62 - 0.20) = 0.42$ is significant at the .03 level.

The degree of institutional completeness and the magnitude of the ethnic interpersonal network are interdependent phenomena. It can be argued that the existence of an informal structure in an ethnic community is a prerequisite for the appearance of formal organizations. But it is also true that once a formal structure has developed, it has the effect of reinforcing the cohesiveness of already existing networks and of expanding these networks. This expansion is achieved mostly by attracting the new immigrants within the ethnic community. A community with a high degree of institutional completeness has a greater absorbing capacity than those with a more informal social organization. The present findings on the changes in the composition of personal relations show the difference between the two types of ethnic communities in their ability to exert influence on the direction of the interpersonal integration of the immigrant.

On the other hand, the ethnic community does not seem to have much effect in preventing some of its members from establishing relations outside its boundaries. The proportion who had most of their relations within their own ethnic group and who now have most of them outside of it is the same for members of communities with either formal or informal social organization. The proportions, however, are based on a very small number of cases.

CONCLUSION

Having found that the institutional completeness of the ethnic community is an important factor in the direction of the social integration of immigrants, it is interesting to speculate about the determinants of this property of an ethnic community. There seem to be at least three sets of factors related to the formation of a public for ethnic organizations.

First, the ethnic group may possess some differentiating social or cultural attribute which can set it apart from the native community. Language,

colour, and religion are prominent among these features; but other traits
and customs of a group can bring about the same result. The more different the people of a certain ethnicity are from the members of the native
community, the easier it will be for them to develop their own institutions
to satisfy their needs.

In the present study, it was found that a difference in language was
associated with a high degree of institutional completeness. It was also
found among ethnic groups with a different language that the higher the
proportion in the ethnic group who are ignorant of the native languages
(French and English), the higher the degree of institutional completeness
of the group.[11]

The differentiating characteristics of an ethnic group constitute the
basis for the formation of a clientele or a public for ethnic organizations.
The mobility potential of the immigrant is reduced by such factors; he is
more confined to his ethnic group. This is particularly true – or perhaps
only true – when the differentiating features are negatively evaluated by
the native community.

The second set of factors related to the degree of institutional completeness
has to do with the level of resources among the members of the ethnic
group. If a large proportion of the members of an ethnic group have few
resources of their own, as indicated, for instance, in rural origin and lack
of occupational skills, then there is, in this ethnic group, an important
"clientele" to support welfare and mutual benefit organizations. Such a situation is likely to incite a "social entrepreneur" within the ethnic group to
try to organize something for the new immigrants in need, seeing there an
interesting opportunity for himself. His rewards would be either monetary
profit, prestige in the community, more members for his church, or more
buyers for his newspaper. In the present study, a strong positive relationship
was, in fact, found between the proportion of manual workers in an ethnic
group and the degree of institutional completeness of that group.[12]

A third set of factors relates to the pattern of migration. The number
of immigrants of a given ethnicity and the rate at which they arrive are
relevant factors in the formation of an ethnic public. Perhaps a more
important factor is whether the migration is an individual or a group
phenomenon. Immigration during certain periods of time or for a given
ethnic group can be the result of discrete decisions by individuals experiencing similar conditions in their country of origin; but it can also be a
more or less organized group response, ranging from the migration of a
group (such as a sect) under a leader, to the pattern in which a migratory
chain is established over a few years within a kinship network or a village,
with funds being collected in the new country to pay the passage of others
from the native village or city.[13] Such factors provide very different sets of
conditions for the development of ethnic institutions.

Ethnic communities are formed, grow, and disappear; they go through a lifecycle.[14] They probably begin as simple aggregates of individuals, as amorphous informal groups, or as fairly well structured informal groups. This group can constitute a public for ethnic organizations, a set of opportunities for social entrepreneurs. The organizations established by these entrepreneurs will maintain themselves as long as a public exists to use their services, or as long as the ethnic identity of the organization is important for the members of the ethnic group. The very existence of such organizations, as the findings of this paper show, act to strengthen this identity. But other mechanisms also operate, such as the fact that the leaders of the organizations have a vested interest in these organizations and will attempt in various ways to strengthen the ethnic identity so as to keep their public as large as possible.

If the rate of migration is low or nil, the ethnic public will progressively decrease, because even a high degree of institutional completeness will not prevent some integration into the native community. With time – and it may well be quite long – the ethnic organizations will themselves disappear or lose their ethnic identity, completing the life-cycle of the community.

CHAPTER ELEVEN

Immigrant Ethnic Groups and Social Incorporation*

(with W.W. Isajiw, W.E. Kalbach, and J.G. Reitz)

This study addresses three major issues – issues that have been central in the work of students of ethnicity.

The first issue concerns the persistence of ethnicity over time and through generations. What is the extent of persistence? How does ethnicity change as a basis of identity and social organization? How is its content transformed? What are the social conditions associated with diverse patterns of evolution within or between ethnic collectivities?

The second issue concerns the incorporation of members of ethnic collectivities in society as a whole. How successfully are they incorporated in social, economic, and political structures? What is the degree and nature of their participation in the institutions of the society? What forms of equality or inequality arise? What social conditions facilitate or hinder their full incorporation in the social fabric?

These two issues have a long history of research and debate. Traditionally, they have been seen, implicitly or explicitly, almost as opposites. They have seemed to be two dimensions of reality varying together, but in opposite directions. As one increased, the other decreased. Thus, successful incorporation into society was taken to be more or less automatically associated

---

* "Introduction" and "Conclusion," in *Ethnic Identity and Equality: Varieties of Experience in a Canadian City*, by Raymond Breton, Wsevolod W. Isajiw, Warren E. Kalbach, and Jeffrey G. Reitz (Toronto: University of Toronto Press, 1990), 1–13, 256–64.

with loss of ethnic, social, and cultural attachments. In recent years, however, this automatic negative association between persistence and incorporation began to be questioned.

Thus, a third issue concerns the dynamic interaction of ethnic persistence and incorporation in society. Is ethnic social organization always a liability with regard to incorporation? Which aspects may be compatible with social incorporation? Under what conditions can ethnicity act as a facilitator rather than as an obstacle? In short, is the loss of ethnicity necessary for full social incorporation, or can ethnicity persist in certain social forms, and even be a positive factor in bringing about full incorporation?

This book attempts to provide answers to these questions for the case of one major multi-ethnic urban centre: Toronto. The book is based on a study of a number of different ethnic and racial minority groups, as well as the dominant or "majority" group (which, depending upon the precise definition, is no longer actually a numerical majority). Each of the groups has been surveyed to permit an analysis of ethnic social formations, ethnic group incorporation into society, and the relation between the two. Because of the inclusion of a variety of groups, the study permits an examination of ways in which the answers to our questions may very from one ethnic group to another.

Our results should be of interest to students of ethnicity, and also to policy makers dealing with ethnic minorities. The study is research-oriented, and is addressed primarily to readers concerned with research results, such as professional researchers, graduate students, and senior undergraduates. However, the issues have serious policy implications as well, and the results should be of interest to those who are mainly preoccupied with public policy, whether they are in government or in ethnic or other civic organizations.

In the first part of this chapter, the broad issues of concern are specified in somewhat greater detail. The concluding part of the chapter brings together the main findings,[1] and indicates the conclusion we have reached regarding our basic questions of ethnicity and social incorporation.

RESEARCH ISSUES: ETHNICITY AND SOCIAL INCORPORATION

Ethnic social formations, and the incorporation of ethnic group members in the larger society, are concepts that must be made more specific for any detailed study. As well, the interrelation between the two has several distinct aspects in the various domains of social life. Some further points are needed to indicate how these ideas will be used as a framework for this study.

Ethnicity as a Basis of Social Organization

An important line of variation to be considered in the study of ethnicity and ethnic groups is the extent to which ethnic ancestry and culture play a role in the way people think of themselves and in the choices they make concerning such matters as work, residence, sociocultural activities, and political behaviour. To what extent do people retain their ethnic heritage and use it, individually or collectively, as "cultural capital" in coping with problems of identity and of social and economic well-being?

There are many areas of life in which ethnicity can be an active force. At a fundamental level, it can shape identities by determining who provide social roots and a sense of belonging, of not being lost in the multitude. As Isaacs (1975: 35) put it: "An individual belongs to his basic group in the deepest and most literal sense that he is not alone, which is what all but a very few human beings most fear to be. He is not only not alone, but here, as long as he chooses to remain in and of it, he cannot be denied or rejected. It is an identity that no one can take away from him." Ethnicity can be the basis of such a social identity (Dashefsky 1972, 1975; Deshen 1974; Driedger 1975, 1977).

Ethnicity can also be the basis for the construction of neighbourhoods. The psychological sense of belonging, of having a home, can be supported or reinforced by a geographical or social belonging (Driedger and Church 1974; Driedger 1978). Thus, ethnicity not only affects the daily lives and social relations of urban dwellers; it also contributes to the structure of the physical and social configuration of the urban environment (Lieberson1961a; Glazer and Moynihan 1963; Fischer 1975; Taylor 1979; Darroch and Marston 1984). At one level, the map of the city is based on an ethnic code.

The market for jobs and the social relations at work can also be structured along ethnic lines. It is as if family, kinship, and neighbourhood ties were transposed into the work domain. Ethnic solidarity is extended beyond the private to the public sphere of economic activity. In other words, economic action is embedded in structures of social relations (Granovetter 1985), and some of these relations are based on ethnicity (Hughes and Hughes 1952); Lieberson 1963; Hannerz 1974; Hechter 1978).

Finally, ethnic solidarity can be mobilized for collective action. Such action can be for the construction or expansion of community institutions; for the performance of community functions; for the shaping of electoral outcomes; and for protection against external expressions of hostility. In short, ethnic solidarity can have a political dimension (Glazer and Moynihan 1963; Cohen 1974a; D. Bell 1975; Dahlie and Fernando 1982). In other words, political action, like economic and cultural activities, is embedded in structures of social relations, some of which are ethnic.

Ethnicity, however, can also become progressively insignificant in these same areas. Sometimes, and in several respects, the identity of individuals is not based on their ethnic origin. Many persons have few, if any, social relations with others of the same origin. They have forgotten the language, history, and traditions of their group and find little meaning in its customs, even if they occasionally practise them. They do not participate in ethnic associations and activities. They are unconcerned with the possibility that their children might marry outside the ethnic collectivity. To the extent that this is true, ethnicity has lost its importance as a factor in individual lives and as a basis of social, economic, and political organization (M. Gordon 1964; Borhek 1970; Greeley 1974; Reitz 1980b). Ethnic solidarity is weak or absent; ethnic cultures are phenomena of the past. People may retain some sense of their ethnic identity, but may be less interested in the cultural and organizational expressions of this identity (Gans 1979).

Clearly, the impact of ethnicity in shaping identities and social organization is a variable. It may vary in degree and in the ways in which it operates. Ethnicity can be critical, totally insignificant, or have a whole range of effects in between. It can affect several, a few, or no areas of individual and collective life. As Yancey *et al.* have said, it does not make sense to think of ethnicity as merely "a constant ascribed trait that is inherited from the past ... The assumption of a common heritage as the essential aspect of ethnicity is erroneous. Ethnicity may have relatively little to do with Europe, Asia, or Africa, but much more to do with the exigencies of survival and the structure of opportunity in this country" (1976: 400). Ethnicity is also a reflection of the present and the anticipated future. The impact of ethnicity varies depending upon current conditions and the experiences of individuals and groups in relation to the members and institutions of the larger society.

The Incorporation of Ethnic Group Members into Society

One important respect in which ethnicity is not simply "a constant ascribed trait that is inherited from the past" is that ethnic heritages tend to be transformed through the group's interaction with other groups in their environment, especially the dominant group. As Glazer and Moynihan note, "the ethnic group in American society became not a survival from the age of mass immigration but a new social form. One could not predict from its first arrival what it might become or, indeed, whom it might contain" (1963: 16). The organization and culture of ethnic groups is not simply brought from the society of origin and preserved in the new social environment. Much of it is a new creation in a context that is itself in evolution (Thomas and Znaniecki 1927; Cohen 1974a; Yancey *et al.* 1976; Isajiw 1977; Reitz 1980b). It is through the process of becoming members and participants in the society that the ethnicity of groups is selectively retained, transformed, reconstructed, or disappears. As a result, the ethnicity of destination, if one exists at all, can be significantly different from the ethnicity of origin.

Thus, another line of variation that needs to be considered in the study of ethnic groups is the extent to which and the ways in which they become incorporated in the structure of the society. Incorporation can occur at several levels. The economic sector is one of the most basic, and a considerable amount of attention has been devoted to it by researchers and policy makers. Identity and culture, residence, and politics are also important domains of incorporation (Richmond 1964, 1967; Blishen 1970; Darroch 1979; Lieberson 1980; Richmond and Kalbach 1980). Each of these is considered in this study.

Incorporation in the larger society entails involvement in institutions, the construction of social ties, participation in sociocultural activities, and, most important, equal access to the rewards that the economic and political systems generate and distribute. Incorporation is a matter of degree. It usually occurs over a fairly long period of time and frequently over generations.

Ethnic Social Formations: Assets or Liabilities in Social Incorporation?

Incorporation entails two sets of processes: one on the side of members of ethnic groups; another on the part of individuals and institutions of the larger society. Gordon (1964: 71) has included the two dimensions in his typology of assimilation, the second part of which referred to the "reception" by the larger society in different areas of activity ("attitude receptional assimilation," or absence of prejudice, and "behaviour receptional assimilation," or absence of discrimination).

In other words, incorporation is the result of factors and processes internal and external to the ethnic group, or internal or external to the larger society. Two sets of ethnic boundaries are involved: those of the established groups in the society and those of the groups seeking full membership and equal participation in it. That is to say, incorporation involves ethnic boundaries, both of the dominant and of the minority groups (Isajiw 1974).

Ethnic social formation, and the boundaries they imply, can be obstacles or barriers to incorporation for individual minority-group members (and hence for entire groups). They may prevent or make difficult the development of more encompassing levels of solidarity and integration. They can be the basis of inequality and inequity in the functioning of economic and political institutions. They can be used for the maintenance of inequalities in social status and separateness in social relations and neighbourhoods.

For instance, particular ethnic identities may not be as respected and accepted as others. They may be considered less worthy or inferior; they may be seen as alien, less Canadian than that of the dominant group. Also, just as ethnic identities can find a social and psychological space in a neighbourhood, the assignment of a low status to them may result in the refusal to accept those with the stigmatized identity as neighbours.

The control of job networks and career lines provides advantages to some that may be used to the detriment of others. The solidarity that includes some may exclude others – a line of differentiation that tends to follow the dominant-majority axis. In addition, members of various ethnic groups can bring different skills, values, and attitudes to the job market, the workplace, and other institutions. These may be associated with factors such as cultural background, past advantages or discrimination, and conditions at the time of immigration. But whatever their sources, these differences can reinforce ethnic barriers and generate sep- arateness and inequalities among groups. On the side of the ethnic minor- ity, they can do so by creating and maintaining "mobility traps" (Wiley 1967b). On the side of the dominant groups, they can do so by facilitating the control of positions of advantage and the exclusion of minorities (Porter 1972, 1975).

Ethnic social formations may facilitate, as well as hinder, the process of becoming part of the larger society. They may provide the resources nec- essary to overcome the obstacles or barriers to participation in the society's institutions. Indeed, social networks and collective action can be oriented to making gains for group members; to combating discrimination; to over- coming the disadvantages generated by the policies and practices of indi- viduals and of organizations, whether public or private. In short, the cultural, social, economic, and political resources of ethnic groups can be used to challenge entrenched systems of privileges, to open up the insti- tutions of the larger society, and facilitate full participation in them on the part of minorities.

Thus, there are two related but distinct lines of variation in the situation of ethnic groups: in the extent to which the ethnic heritage constitutes a basis of individual life and social organization, and in the degree of incor- poration in the larger society. When we say that they constitute two distinct lines of variation, we are asserting strongly that one cannot be taken as the obverse of the other. Incorporation does not necessarily mean that ethnicity is disappearing as a basis of social organization and individual identity. The existence of a vibrant ethnic community does not imply that incorporation is failing to occur. The variations in the two phenomena may be correlated: but they are not the same.

A central hypothesis is that the two dimensions can be put together to constitute a conceptual space in which ethnic groups can be located

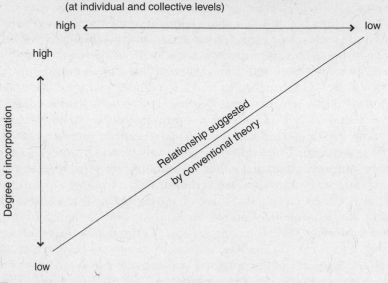

Figure 11.1
Possible relations between significance of ethnicity and degree of incorporation

depending on their position in each of them. This space can be visualized as in Figure 11.1 above. If incorporation necessarily entailed the disappearance of ethnicity as an operative social factor, than all groups would fall along the diagonal from the lower left to the upper right segments of the diagram. If no single necessary relationship is assumed between the two dimensions, groups could be located in other portions of the two-dimensional space (as well as along that diagonal).

OBJECTIVES OF THE STUDY, AND FOUR RESEARCH FOCI

There are, then, four major objectives pursued in the analysis that follows. They are to describe and analyse

1 the variations among several ethnic groups in the degree and pattern of incorporation in the larger society;
2 the variations among groups in the ways in which ethnicity shapes their identity, social relationships, and activities;
3 variations across groups in the impacts (positive and negative) on incorporation in the larger society of ethnicity and of social relations based on ethnicity; and

4 variations over time, specifically across generations, in the role of ethnicity for members of different ethnic groups, and in the degree of their incorporation.

The study deals with these issues in four areas: ethnic identity, residential segregation, participation in the socioeconomic opportunity structure, and sociopolitical organization.

Ethnic Identity and Retention

Ethnicity consists of at least one, or a combination, of six components: (a) distinct overt and covert cultural behaviour patters; (b) personal ties, such as family, community, and friendship networks; (c) organizations, such as schools, churches, enterprises, media; (d) associations, such as clubs, "societies," youth organizations; (e) functions, sponsored by ethnic organizations, such as picnics, concerts, teas, rallies; and (f) identity as a social psychological phenomenon.

Ethnic identity is conceived as a specific phenomenon rather than as an omnibus combination of all the components. Thus, ethnic identity is defined as *one* aspect of the way in which individuals conceive of their location within and their relationship to the social system at large and to others in it. Ethnic identity can have a variety of contents or forms: not all persons who locate themselves in the group of their ancestors do so in the same way. One may perceive oneself as inferior or superior in relation to others. One may identify with an ethnic group by feeling an obligation to attend as many functions sponsored by ethnic organizations as possible, or one may feel no such obligation at all, yet identify with the group in terms of other obligations or on some other basis. One may simply choose to live in an ethnic neighbourhood as an expression of ethnic identity.

This part of the research (Chapter 2 in Breton *et al.* 1990) analyses the retention of ethnicity by focusing primarily on retention of ethnic identity and analysing the other components in relation to it. Its objective is to study which aspect of ethnicity in general and which forms and intensities of ethnic identities in particular are retained from generation to generation.

Ethnic Residential Segregation

The growth of urban communities is usually accompanied by increased specialization and differentiation of economic activity, which, in turn, is reflected in the spatial distribution of these activities and of residential neighbourhoods according to the socioeconomic and cultural characteristics of their inhabitants. The traditional model of urban growth relates the expansion of the central business district to the expansion of middle- and upper-class residential areas into suburban areas at the expense of deteri-orating neighbourhoods in the inner core. Residential mobility becomes a vehicle for social mobility, and the move to better housing and better neigh-bourhoods commensurate with improved economic status and changing housing needs reflects both upward-mobility aspirations and achievement.

In the classical model of urban growth, the areas of transition, between the expanding business district and the retreating middle- and upper-class residential areas, provide housing opportunities for the relatively unskilled workers, including native-born internal migrants, as well as immigrants from abroad. Ethnic and racial enclaves develop and serve as general recep-tion areas to assist the new arrivals in getting established. Subsequent moves from these initial areas of settlement, either by the original migrants or their children, are possible as the individuals manage to acquire the nec-essary skills and economic means to improve their position in the economic and social system. It has been generally assumed that those who remain in the original reception areas do so because they have not acquired the nec-essary skills to improve their economic status, because they have experi-enced racial or ethnic prejudice, or because of their own preferences. In any event, the patterns of residential distribution exhibited or perceived by various ethnic and racial groups would tend to reflect the extent of their adaptation to the social and economic system of the community as a whole.

This part of the research (Chapter 3 in *Breton et al.* 1990) addresses some of these issues. Specifically, it seeks (a) to establish the extent and pattern of ethnic residential segregation by generation; (b) to determine the significance of ethnic origin relative to other social and economic characteristics and with respect to existing patterns of segregation; and (c) to analyse the relationship between various indicators of segregation and ethnic identity, participation, and networks.

Ethnicity and Labour Markets

Occupational opportunities and rewards available in labour markets are frequently unequally allocated among individuals of different ethnic ori-gins. The rewards associated with occupation include status or prestige and income. The allocation of job rewards is, in part, affected by the qualifications of incumbents. Job qualifications include years and type of education, years of work experience, and knowledge of English. Ethnic inequalities are partly due to such qualifications, but inequalities can remain after these qualifications have been taken into account.

How do ethnic formations, or ethnic concentrations in labour markets, alter the allocation of job rewards? Several theories suggest ways in which ethnic concentration in occupations or work groups may reinforce existing inequalities. When this happens, then ethnic economic formations represent obstacles to social incorporation. However, such negative effects may apply only in extreme cases. Or they may depend upon the type of labour-market concentrations. Sometimes ethnic businesses may provide a basis for altering the distribution of occupational rewards, generating resources and reallocating them within the ethnic group.

Three forms of ethnic concentration in labour markets will be considered: concentrations in occupational categories (such as Italians in construction trades, or Chinese in certain service occupations), in minority businesses as entrepreneurs and as employees, and in work groups within organizations.

This part of the research (Chapter 4 in Breton *et al.* 1990) describes ethnic inequalities of occupational opportunities and rewards, and examines ways in which ethnic concentrations in labour markets influence those inequalities. The analysis will examine the extent to which the allocation of rewards depends on factors other than qualifications, and the extent to which these are reduced or enhanced by ethnic concentrations for each ethnic group.

Ethnicity and Collective Political Action

Collective action can be organized in order to take advantage of opportunities, to pursue commonly agreed upon goals, or to deal with problems experienced by members of the community. In other words, members of ethnic groups can have interests that they can, if the necessary conditions are met, pursue through collective action.

The organization of such action involves at least three broad categories of processes: the identification of matters as requiring concerted action; the mobilization of commitment and participation, including material support; and the organization of the action itself to deal with the problems or objectives identified. These processes require leadership, a decision-making structure, conflict-resolution mechanisms, and means of communication and co-ordination. The existence of material resources in the ethnic population and a degree of social cohesion are important resources in this regard. So are attitudes favourable to collective action, perceptions of its possible effectiveness, and the perceived legitimacy of the leadership and organizations in the community.

This part of the research (Chapter 5 in Breton *et al.* 1990, and excerpted in Chapter 13 of this volume) deals with the latter elements, namely with the perceptions and attitudes of member of ethnic groups with regard to the problems faced by their group, to the type of action that could be effective in dealing with them, and to the existing leadership and decision-making in the community. In other words, the analysis examines the public opinion in different ethnic groups with regard to matters of importance for concerted action.

FINDINGS[2] AND CONCLUSIONS

In Breton *et al.* (1990: Chapters 2–5), several findings have shown both a significant degree of incorporation in Canadian society and the continuing role of ethnicity for individuals and groups. It was seen that, in many ways, members of ethnic minorities are becoming part of the culture and structure of the larger society. It was also seen, however, that such a trend does not necessarily mean that ethnic identities disappear, that cultural heritages are abandoned, or that social relationships and group formation are not based on ethnicity. In addition, it was observed that although ethnicity appears to impede incorporation in the larger society, it sometimes provides the social resources that can facilitate it.

The results, however, vary considerably depending on the ethnic group and the dimension considered. These can be summarized along the major lines of variation that were, as indicated above, the focus of the analysis: variations among ethnic groups in the pattern of incorporation and in the ways in which ethnicity constitutes a basis of identity and group formation; variations in the effects (positive and negative) of retention on different aspects of incorporation; and variations across generations in the pattern of incorporation and of ethnic retention or reconstruction.

Incorporation in Canadian Society

Several more or less direct measures of incorporation were considered in the study: access to economic rewards; perceived job discrimination; perceived disadvantage if ethnic culture is retained; acceptance as neighbours and relatives; perceived acceptance by the society as reflected in immigration legislation; residential dispersion; and the sense of political efficacy, that is, of having an influence on the political institutions of the society.

The German and Ukrainian respondents showed a consistently high degree of incorporation on all these dimensions. They have equal access to economic rewards. They feel accepted socially and politically in the society. Both groups tend to be, and to perceive themselves as being, equal and full participants in Canadian society. As will be seen in more detail later, the two groups differ in the way they combine incorporation in the larger society and the retention of their ethnic culture and social organization – a difference suggested by the higher percentage of Germans than of Ukrainians who feel that members of ethnic minorities should blend into Canadian society, and by a residential dispersion much more similar to that of the majority Canadian population than that exhibited by the Ukrainians.

The Jewish respondents, by contrast, do not show a consistent pattern of incorporation: they are high on the economic and political, but not on the social dimension. They have been fairly successful in becoming part of the economic structure, although a significant proportion perceive problems of job discrimination. They also show a fairly high degree of political efficacy. They are, however, the most highly segregated residentially, the second most likely to perceive problems of acceptance as neighbours (after West Indians), and the most likely to feel not easily accepted as relatives. They are also the least likely to favour a pluralistic model for Canadian society.

The Chinese and West Indians are the two groups who encounter the most problems of incorporation, whether economic, social, or political. Members of these two groups, especially the West Indians, are the least likely to have rewards in line with their qualifications. They experience problems of discrimination and social acceptance, and they are the least likely to feel that they are taken seriously by the political authorities. Members of these groups show a strong tendency to favour blending into the larger society, which may be reflected in their somewhat unique patterns of residential dispersion, characterized by several scattered areas of concentration.

The Italians and Portuguese occupy an intermediate position. Generally, they have rewards appropriate for their position, but a certain proportion report problems of job discrimination and social acceptance. Italians, however, are more likely than Portuguese to express a sense of political efficacy, and thus, the capacity to deal with problems. Both groups are strongly in favour of blending into the larger society. Yet the Italians show a greater tendency towards residential dispersion in later generations than is evident for those of Portuguese origin.

Ethnicity as a Basis of Identity and of Social Organization

As already indicated above, incorporation in the larger society does not necessarily imply that ethnicity disappears, that it ceases to be an organizing force in the personal and social life of individuals. In the process of becoming participants in Canadian society, many individuals abandon elements of their culture; but not always all of them. Several establish ties beyond the social boundaries of their own group, but many ethnic ties are preserved. The organizations of the larger society tend to absorb the members of ethnic minorities, but elements of ethnic social organization are maintained.

There are many ways in which ethnicity can manifest itself: personal identities; knowledge and use of language; the retention of traditions and customs; participation in ethnic activities; occupational and residential concentrations; social relationships at work or elsewhere; and in sociopolitical organization.

For the Jewish, cultural background is the most important element in shaping their individual and collective behaviour, for all the dimensions considered: identity; economic relationships; cultural practices; and sociopolitical organization. Ukrainians follow fairly closely, although in their case, ethnicity does not seem to have much of an impact in the economic domain. But it does have a significant role in the other areas.

The Germans, by contrast, show the lowest degree of retention in virtually all dimensions. It is not that it is absent; but it is very low compared to the other groups. In the case of the four other groups, ethnicity appears significant in some but less in other dimensions. For instance, Italians, Chinese, and Portuguese are highly concentrated in occupations. Residential segregation increases across generations for the last two (Chinese and Portuguese) as well as for the West Indians. At the same time, the three groups tend to occupy a somewhat lower position on the indicators of sociopolitical organization.

The Relationship of Retention with Incorporation

The above findings indicate that incorporation does not necessarily mean the loss of ethnicity. In other words, incorporation in the larger society can be associated with either high or low ethnic salience. The Jewish are quite clearly found in the first category and the Germans in the second. Ukrainians and Italians tend to be closer to the "high" end of the continuum, while the Portuguese appear to be somewhat closer to the "low" pole.

But there are also indications that a relatively low degree of incorporation can be accompanied with either high or low ethnic salience. The West Indians and Chinese seem to follow the second pattern. They do not appear to lean strongly in the direction of ethnic retention or reconstruction: indeed, they show a strong aspiration to blend into Canadian society and a low degree of occupational concentration and of sociopolitical cohesion. Yet they are the least incorporated of the groups considered.

The pattern followed by Italians and Portuguese is more ambiguous. Both are on the way to full incorporation in Canadian society. Whether ethnicity will continue to provide a basis of social organization for these two groups is more problematic. It seems plausible to hypothesize that, for them, incorporation will tend to be accompanied by the declining significance of the ethnic background.

Different elements of identity and culture appear to be retained as incorporation in the larger society proceeds, as happens with concrete objects such as food and artistic articles that act as symbols of the cultural background. Although less so, the same retention also occurs with social ties (friendship and marriage). Thus, these are the three items the most retained by the Germans, who, it was seen, are the most incorporated. By contrast, some cultural elements seem to be less likely to be retained: language; the practice of customs, community participation, and the sense of obligation *vis-à-vis* the group.

In the case of residence, the best example of the classic pattern of declining segregation with subsequent generations is the population of German origin. The Ukrainians and Italians exhibit considerably higher initial levels of residential segregation, that drop significantly for the second generation, but remain relatively constant thereafter at intermediate levels. In the case of the other minority groups, incorporation does not seem to be associated with an increase in residential dispersion. For some groups, the visible minorities in particular, their patterns of segregation may be a partial indicator of a lack of social acceptance by the larger society.

Ethnic concentrations in labour markets have varying effects on incorporation – defined in terms of equality. Sometimes they are obstacles, but not always so. The effects actually depend on the type of concentration, the particular ethnic group, and the level of incorporation being considered. Ethnic occupations have certain discriminatory effects on Chinese and West Indians, and the Portuguese are also concentrated in very low-level occupations. However, in some of the more established groups, labour-market concentration seems to have little if any effect. The Germans, Ukrainians, and Jewish are all fairly well incorporated. Germans and Ukrainians have very low labour-market concentration. The Jewish are highly concentrated, more so than any predominantly immigrant group. Thus, a high degree of occupational concentration is possible, whether levels of ethnic concentration are high or low. Italian men represent an intermediate case. For them, extensive labour-market concentration has led to partial incorporation. Italians have established ethnic businesses enabling Italian men (but not women) to achieve income mobility, while remaining, however, in low-status occupations. Later generations may be abandoning ethnic concentrations to achieve more complete incorporation. Some types of ethnic concentration, such as work groups in mainstream organizations, have little effect in any group.

Finally, the degree of sociopolitical organization appears to be positively related to incorporation in the society, since such organization is an instrument with which to deal with the problems encountered. Two of the well-incorporated groups – Ukrainians and Jews – perceive their group as having a high degree of political cohesion, a capacity to act in a concerted way to cope with problems. The two least incorporated groups – Chinese and West Indians – are also low on most indicators of sociopolitical organization, as perceived by their members. The Italians and Portuguese are intermediate on both dimensions. The Germans show a different pattern: they are high on incorporation but low on sociopolitical cohesion.

In short, the results suggest not only that incorporation does not necessarily imply the declining salience of ethnicity, but also that ethnic identity and social organization can have an effect on the degree of

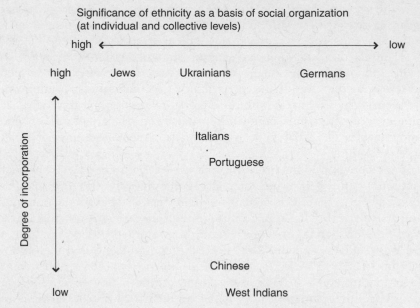

Figure 11.2
Findings by group on relation between significance of ethnicity and degree of incorporation

incorporation in the larger society and that this impact can be either positive or negative.

In the introduction, it was mentioned that the two dimensions – incorporation and ethnicity as a basis of social organization – constitute a conceptual space in which different ethnic groups can be located. The findings of the study suggest that the position of the groups included in this study is approximately as shown in Figure 11.2.

INCORPORATION AND RETENTION ACROSS GENERATIONS

For Germans, Italians, Jews, and Ukrainians, generational changes were examined. The four groups do not exhibit the same pattern. It has already been observed that the Germans are the least likely to retain their culture, social ties, and elements of ethnic social organization. This pattern holds across generations, as well as for the group as a whole.

The Jewish and Ukrainians were described as relatively well-incorporated "high retainers." Even though this description is accurate, the two groups show a different pattern across generations, although there are a few similarities. Jews are the most likely to retain the ability to read, write, and speak their language across generations. Ukrainians, by contrast, not only show a lower propensity for language retention, but the retention among them tends to be restricted to the ability to speak, not to read or write, the language. A similar pattern is revealed among Italians.

The retention of other elements (customs, artistic articles, food, social ties, and social participation) is also the highest among the Jewish. In fact, the retention increases slightly over generations, suggesting a pattern of reinforcement of ethnic identity among later Jewish generations. Among Italians and Ukrainians, cultural and social retention is not only lower than among the Jewish, it also decreases with successive generations.

Occupational concentration decreases over generations for Ukrainians and Italians (it is consistently low in the case of Germans). In addition, it seems to play for them a decreasing role for access to economic rewards. Among the Jewish, however, it increases with the generations, and it involves, in the third generation, the establishment of concentrations in additional high-status occupations.

Finally, residential segregation, as already indicated, decreases with subsequent generations, primarily among the Germans. The decrease is less pronounced among Ukrainians and Italians. The opposite trend is seen among the Portuguese, Chinese, and West Indians: it increases with the generations. Among the Jewish, it remains high for all generations.

SOME GENERAL RESULTS

In short, the study provides evidence in regard to seven propositions. First, it shows that, to a considerable degree, members of certain ethnic minorities become full participants in the social fabric of Canadian society: that they become incorporated in its social and institutional life.

But second, it also shows that some groups or categories within groups encounter serious barriers or obstacles to their full economic and/or social incorporation. Such obstacles are most prevalent for recent immigrants. But clearly, there is also a racial factor involved. Difficulties of incorporation are especially significant for the two non-white groups included in the sample, the Chinese and West Indians. The Jewish also experience barriers to social acceptance, even though they are well incorporated economically. Thus, being non-white, a new immigrant, or Jewish continues to involve disadvantages for full and equal participation in Canadian society. In addition, it was found that a number who do not aspire to the retention of their culture and community – that is, who want to blend into Canadian society – were experiencing problems of incorporation.

Third, even if there is a significant incorporation into the larger society, a substantial degree of ethnic retention can be observed even among individuals who can, by most indicators, be considered integrated in the larger society. Thus, although their members are individually incorporated, some groups seem to retain collective goals for which they mobilize at least some degree of participation. Nevertheless, substantial loss also takes place, whether it be in terms of language, participation in activities, customs and traditions, or social ties.

A conceptual implication of these results is that the incorporation of members of ethnic minorities in a society cannot be regarded as the simple opposite of cultural retention. The definition of one is not the negative side of the other. A single concept such as integration is not sufficient, since we are dealing with two distinct phenomena. They are interrelated, as we have seen, but not in such a way that if one increases, the other necessarily decreases. In other words, it is not necessarily true that if members of a group are fully incorporated in Canadian society, they have abandoned all elements of their ethnic identity and background. Similarly, if members of a group show a low degree of ethnic retention, it does not necessarily follow that they are highly incorporated in the social fabric of the society.

In fact, in addition to underlining the fact that ethnic retention and societal incorporation are distinct phenomena, the study shows, fourth, that retention can have an effect on the degree and pattern of incorporation in the larger society. That is to say, it was observed, as in other studies, that the incorporation of individuals and groups in the larger society depends-on a wide range of factors. The foregoing analysis, however, emphasizes the role of ethnic retention as a factor in the incorporation of minorities in the larger society. That is to say, cultural retention and the maintenance of ethnic organizations have implications for the degree and patterns of social incorporation – implications that can be positive as well as negative. Cultural retention does not necessarily retard or impede incorporation: it may facilitate it.

The study has recognized that both retention and incorporation are multidimensional realities. Both have structural, cultural, and identificational dimensions that can manifest themselves in several domains of activities and relationships: economic, political, residential, and sociocultural. Since the study included several of these dimensions, its comparative nature has yielded a fifth important result: different groups do not exhibit the same pattern of retention and incorporation. General propositions about the evolution of ethnic minorities have a very limited validity, if any. Propositions must be conditional on the situation of the groups considered. Although not the only significant one, the distinction between groups of European origin and visible minorities was found to be particularly important with regard to the rate of incorporation in society.

The sixth result is that the effect of retention on societal incorporation is not the same for all groups. It can be positive, negative, or nil, depending on the specific internal conditions and external circumstances in which a group finds itself. Ethnic culture and organization can help in gaining access to economic resources, in gaining the attention of political authorities, and generally, in coping with problems encountered.

But ethnic culture and organization can also be a liability. Again, visibility or race seems to be a particularly important differentiating factor in this connection. A comparison of the experience of the Jewish and Ukrainians, on the one hand, with that of the Chinese and West Indians, on the other, suggests that whether ethnicity is an asset or a liability depends on both internal and external factors. The behaviour of individuals and institutions in the larger society is clearly important; but so are the internal factors related to the capacity of the group to organize itself.

The seventh and last overall result is that incorporation and retention do not evolve in the same way across generations for all the ethnic groups considered. The results support the view that rather than being simply "a *constant* trait that is inherited from the past, ethnicity is the result of a process that *continues to unfold*" (Yancey *et al.* 1976: 400; emphasis added). And because of internal and external circumstances, the process of evolution is different from one group to another. It may be that the past has a different relevance for some groups than for others, but the current situation is clearly of great significance in explaining inter-group variations in this regard.

CHAPTER TWELVE

The Ethnic Community as a Polity*

The ethnic community is a multidimensional phenomenon. It can be viewed as a network of interpersonal relations and of mutual assistance; as a set of institutions to meet the various needs of group members; as a system of social classes; as a micro-economy with enterprises, a labour market, a clientele for commodities and services, and sources of capital. It can also be approached as a cultural entity that provides a framework for individual identities, means for cultural expression and development, and mechanisms for the transmission of the group's cultural heritage.

In this book [i.e. *The Governance of Ethnic Communities*], the ethnic community is seen as a political entity: how ethnic communities govern themselves is the basic question that it addresses. A central dimension of "community" is the existence of a public life beyond the private lives of the individuals, families, and small groups that conduct their public affairs through more or less institutionalized structures, mechanisms, and practices. These constitute their "government" or system of governance.

An understanding of ethnic communities is virtually impossible, or will be very limited if adequate consideration is not given to the political dimension. Of course, this is not an entirely new perspective on ethnic communities, but it is one that is relatively underdeveloped. As will be seen throughout the analysis, several studies on particular political institutions, mechanisms, or relationships in ethnic communities can be found in the literature. The most systematic treatment of ethnic communities as

---

* "The Ethnic Community as a Polity," Introduction to *The Governance of Ethnic Communities* (New York: Greenwood Press, 1991), 1–14.

polities is perhaps Elazar's (1976) study of American Jewish communities. The political structures and processes of ethnic communities have not, however, received the attention they deserve.

A concern with the political functioning of ethnic communities is important not only for the understanding of these communities as important social realities in themselves (Breton 1983). It is also particularly critical given the political importance placed on ethnic communities in recent years by government policies and programs and, as a result, by other societal institutions, such as the schools and the media (Rothschild 1981). Of course, ethnic communities have always had significance in the institutional arenas of the larger society; today, however, their existence and role in society are becoming increasingly institutionalized. Ethnic communities are becoming explicitly incorporated as such into the institutional fabric of society (Stasiulis 1980; Jenkins 1988). This may not generally be the case, but it seems to be happening in Canadian society.

The following analysis is not intended to apply to "territorial minorities," especially if the minority constitutes a political majority in a region of a country, and as a result, is incorporated in the constitutionally established state institutions of the society. Thus, it is not meant to apply to, for example, the French community of Quebec, which, because it controls the provincial government of the province, has an officially recognized government. It is restricted to ethnic groups with "unofficial governments."

THE ETHNIC COMMUNITY AS
A POLITICAL COMMUNITY

In his analysis of North American Chinatowns, Lyman (1968: 53) observes that the elites of the community organizations "conduct an unofficial government, legislating, executing, and adjudicating matters for their constituents." Thus, what has been said about urban neighbourhoods is largely applicable to ethnic communities: that they are "in origin and continuity a political unit" (Kotler 1969: 8). "Like the communities that Tocqueville observed, today's urban neighbourhoods frequently have their own unofficial arrangements for performing certain essential functions – a capacity to form and express a collective interest, the executive power to produce collective or public goods. What is usually missing is the distinctively political means for conducting this political business – legitimate physical force" (Crenson 1983: 12).

The public affairs of a community involve such phenomena as collective decisions, community events and activities, public ceremonies and rituals, debates and controversies over issues, fund-raising for community projects, the selection of community leaders, and the exercise of influence and power. The political process involves action and events pertaining to "the determination and implementation of public goals and/or the differential distribution and use of power within the group or groups concerned with the goals being considered" (Swartz 1968: 1).

Thus, to ask how ethnic communities govern themselves is to enquire about the processes of collective decision-making, the ways in which participation and resources are mobilized for collective projects, the relationship between elites and members, the differences of interests and ideologies, the management of conflicts, and the exercise of power in the management of community affairs. It is also to enquire about the network of organizations through which community governance takes place. Indeed, political processes occur through relationships among individuals, groups, and organizations that may be more or less structured and that may involve more or less formally defined roles. That is, the structural forms in which politics occur can vary considerably, and as Swartz points out, policies or political action should not be associated with a particular form as a matter of determination.

In particular, politics and government should not be tied exclusively with the state and its various institutions. There are stateless polities that govern themselves. This is the case with ethnic communities. They have no *state* institutions, but they have *public* ones. Physical force cannot be used legitimately (which, of course, does not mean that no coercive practices can be observed in ethnic communities), but the exercise of power and influence is common in the conduct of their public affairs. No community can operate without politics, but communities can operate politically without a state apparatus. "Western contact with African and Asian cultures as well as the surviving tribal cultures of the Americas has brought a renewed cognizance of the existence of polities that are not states" (Elazar 1976: 5)[1] "There is rough parallel, in fact, between the task of finding the political system in an urban neighbourhood and the business of discovering politics in a tribal society that has no distinct government or formally designated rulers.[2] In both settings, one is likely to encounter examples of 'diffused government'" (Crenson 1983: 11).

Ethnic politics, however, are "encapsulated political systems" (Bailey 1970). They are embedded in a larger sociopolitical framework that includes state and other public institutions. Accordingly, their public affairs include relationships with their social and institutional environments. Thus, like regional and national entities, ethnic political communities have "external" as well as "domestic" affairs.

Internally, their public affairs and institutions pertain to matters such as aid to new immigrants, welfare services, facilities for the aged, cultural maintenance and development, education, the celebration of heroes and historical events, recreational activities, and the dissemination of news and opinions. Externally, the matters requiring action can be the experience of prejudice and discrimination, immigration legislation and its implementation, the organization or content of public education, civil rights legislation and the activities of related agencies, relations with the country of origin and its representatives, multiculturalism policies and programs, and relations with various institutions of the larger society (e.g., media, government, police, schools, employers, labour unions).

Ethnic communities are socially differentiated or segmented in terms of factors such as social class, age, gender, income, education, religion, generation, political ideology, and regional identification (Boissevain 1970; Nagata 1979; Jansen 1981). Thus, within each domain of domestic or external activity, many interests and point of view can interact and come into cooperation or conflict with each other. Given the multiplicity of fields of political action and of interest groups, it is inappropriate to define an ethnic community as an interest group. It is more accurate to refer to it as a polity. It is, of course, possible that in certain circumstances, an ethnic community will act in relation to a governmental body or agency as a single interest group. However, frequently, it is a particular interest group within the ethnic polity that relates to the external agency for its own particular purposes, one of which can be to frustrate or overcome its rivals within the ethnic community.

Political action involves two types of relationships: competitive or conflictual, on the one hand, and concerted or cooperative, on the other. To the extent that participants in the public affairs of the community have different interests and ideologies, they will promote or support more or less contradictory policies and programs. Accordingly, they are likely to compete for the acquisition of power and for the control of community resources so as to assure that their own material, ideological, or symbolic interests prevail. Viewed from this angle, the ethnic community is an arena in which rival groups may confront each other over economic interests, political philosophy, organizational prerogatives, social status, and whatever resources the collectivity has to offer or that can be generated through it.

This view, it should be emphasized, is radically opposed to the idea that "community" necessarily involves cohesion or unity; it is in contradiction with what is essentially an apolitical conception of community. Instead of adopting the notion that as long as there are divisions and conflict, there is really no community, the view adopted here is that community necessarily involves social and economic differentiation, and consequently, different and more or less divergent interests. When there are no controversies and debates over the state of affairs and possible courses of action, that is, when there are no public issues, little is happening in the community. The community does not have much of a public life; in effect, there is not much of a community. What exists, rather, is a collectivity sharing a "symbolic ethnicity" (Gans 1979), or simply an aggregate of people of a particular ethnic origin.

Social cleavages and opposition, instead of being considered obstacles to or destroyers of community, should be regarded as essential ingredients of the public affairs of any community. It is the ways in which people deal with contradictory interests or their failure to deal with these interests that can be destructive of social cohesion, not the interests' existence as such. "Ironically," writes O'Brien (1975: 83–4), "it is the apolitical orientation of community development which is so instrumental in promoting rancorous conflicts," since it is an orientation that ignores the "possibility of creating organizational structures and strategies which might institutionalize the conflict."

It is misleading to think in terms of a single community interest, either in the community at large or in a particular domain of activity, and when failing to find it, to conclude that the community is weak or lacks cohesiveness. It may be that, in certain circumstances, a consensus does emerge with regard to a particular problem or condition. Such an occurrence, however, should not detract attention from the process, frequently conflictual, through which that consensus came about. Indeed, even when there is a clearly identifiable external threat or internal problem, there usually is some disagreement among individuals and subgroups about the cause of the problem and/or about the best way to cope with it.

As Warren (1974) has argued, and as will be examined in more detail later, the "single community interest" is frequently a political assumption made by those who claim to represent the community and who claim that there are no competing groups or organizations with different views in the community. Promoting the idea of a single community interest can also be an ideological or tactical tool used by officials of mainstream organizations for the purpose of strengthening particular organizations in the ethnic community, by arguing that they are more representative of the community than other organizations.

THE COMPONENTS OF POLITIES SELECTED FOR ANALYSIS

This book [of which the present chapter is the Introduction] is about the organization and functioning of ethnic communities as polities. It is about the structures and processes through which they conduct their variations in the organization and functioning of ethnic communities. Indeed, ethnic collectivities may not show equal levels of political organization; their governance may be more or less formally organized as an institutionally distinct function; and their governance organizations may vary considerably in form or structure.

Political systems include a large number of components, all of which could be analyzed. Some components pertain to the structure of the system: the organizational apparatus through which political action takes place, and features such as the system's size, form, differentiation, and complexity. Other components have to do with governance processes, for instance, the exercise of leadership, power, and authority and political participation.

Clearly, not all aspects of ethnic politics can be considered in a single work. The analysis must inevitably be selective and focus on variations of dimensions of governance that are arguably central in the functioning of an ethnic political community. Thus, the following have been selected as the major components of the study: the organization of governance; two sets of processes that governance entails, namely the exercise of leadership or power and policy-making (or the definition of collective goals); and two dimensions of the construction and maintenance of the community – participation in the public affairs of the community, and the definition, maintenance, and transformation of the collective identity.

The Organization of Governance

At one extreme, the organization through which a community governs itself can simply consist of a network of interpersonal relationships; at the other, governance may take place through a complex, formally-structured system of organizations. Considerable variation can exist between the two extremes. In addition, variation can be observed among the collectivities in which some sort of formally organized system has been established. That is to say, the type of organizational arrangement may not be the same across communities with the same level of organization.

The Exercise of Leadership, Power, and Authority

Leadership, power, and authority are essential ingredients in the functioning of any political system. Several questions can be raised in connection with this dimension of politics. What is the distribution of power among the various segments of the community? Who becomes a leader in the community, and who fails to do so? How can the existing distribution of power and leadership be accounted for? What strategies are used to gain power and to hold on to positions of power?

Policy-Making, or the Definition of Collective Goals

This work is concerned not with the substance of issues that constitute the public affairs of ethnic communities, but rather, with the processes involved in policy-making in ethnic communities.

Participation in the Political Process

The ethnic political community can include a more or less important fraction of the collectivity. Some of the potential participants may remain permanently at the margin of its public affairs. For them, their ethnicity is entirely private, or leads them exclusively toward cultural activities. Other people may get involved, but only in certain domains of activity and the issues that emerge in those domains. Thus, they participate when, for example, questions of immigration arise, but remain indifferent with regard to other matters. In short, as far as involvement in public affairs is concerned, the ethnic community does not differ from other types of political communities: participation varies widely in degree, depending on the position of individuals in the social structure and on the domain of activity.

The Definition and Maintenance of the Collective Identity

The analysis of the ethnic polity cannot assume the existence of an ethnic community. Indeed, the community is itself a sociopolitical construction. The political process entails the creation of an ethnic consciousness among individuals belonging to an ethnic category (McKay and Lewins 1978). Creating an ethnic consciousness is one of the basic tasks to be accomplished if an ethnic polity is to be established and maintained, let alone function effectively. The boundaries of ethnic communities are not defined legally or territorially. The definition of the collective identity, of the social and symbolic boundaries of the community, is, accordingly, a central dimension of the formation and functioning of the ethnic polity (Barth 1969; Kallen 1977; Cohen 1985). Moreover, this identity is not formed once and for all: its formation is continuous.

THE FRAMEWORK OF ANALYSIS

Ethnic communities have been described and analyzed from a number of perspectives. Two of these stand out, at least as far as the purposes of the present work are concerned. The following brief description presents these perspectives as distinct approaches. The work of researchers, however, usually draws from both perspectives, although not necessarily to the same extent. In one perspective, community organization is basically seen as a response to expressed needs on the part of members of a collectivity – needs experienced in the process of coping with their social environment. In the other perspective, community organization is the outcome of entrepreneurial activity on the part of individuals who have access to the resources required for "community building."

In the "social demand' approach, the ethnic collectivity, or some of its fragments, is organized in order to meet a demand for commodities, services, social support, protection, or cultural expression. That is to say, the demand can be for instrumental needs, such as housing, jobs, and language training; for expressive purposes, such as cultural activities or the transmission of values and ways of life to the next generation; for solidarity needs; or for defence against discrimination and hostility.

Thus, the degree and type of community organization that emerges is a function of the characteristics of the members (that is, of the potential clientele and their expressed needs) and of the features of the social environment with which the collectivity has to cope. In this approach, communities would differ in their sociopolitical organization, or a given community would change over time because of differences or changes in social composition, and accordingly, in needs and interests. These differences or changes can pertain to factors such as the community's size, the class composition of the collectivity, the relative size of the generations that constitute it, and the age structure of the membership. Accordingly, the demand for services will differ across communities or will change over time, variations that will tend to be reflected in the community organization.

The level and content of sociopolitical demand may also be determined by environmental circumstances and their transformations. In other words, problems and the corresponding needs they generate can have causes outside of the community. For instance, discrimination is generally recognized as one of the main reasons organization is a response to a need, namely the need to combat hostility, and resist oppression and discrimination (Baureiss 1982).

In addition to discrimination, government policies and programs, as well as significant events on the international scene, can have a critical impact on the demand for community organization among members of an ethnic minority. Features of the contemporary bureaucratic and technological society have also been hypothesized as being an impetus for ethnic community organization. Isajiw (1977) suggests that because of the isolation, anomie, and meaninglessness that many individuals experience in such environments, they feel the need to rediscover their sociocultural roots, to establish or consolidate a basis of social integration, and, in the process, to anchor their own personal identity in a community that has meaning in their personal history. Thus, they constitute a potential clientele for various kinds of ethnic organizations, particularly organizations with a significant social and cultural component.

Figure 12.1 illustrates basic propositions of the social demand approach.

In the second approach, the "social supply" approach, the ethnic collectivity is conceived of as an arena of entrepreneurial activity. The basic idea is that ethnic collectivities become organized to the extent that they

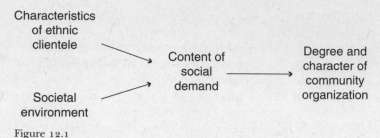

Figure 12.1
Community organization as a function of social demand

provide possibilities of action and gain to potential entrepreneurs. The opportunities they afford can be in fields of economic, political, or cultural activity (or any combination of these). In this approach, community organization does not depend primarily on the expressed needs of members, but rather, on the range of opportunities available for entrepreneurial activity, and on the fields in which they occur, whether or not these are related to needs or problems experienced by members of the collectivity.

The resources and related interests of potential organizers play a central role in this perspective. They constitute the driving force underlying organizational formation and activity in the community. That is to say, the aspirations and decisions of entrepreneurs, actual or aspiring, are a function of the resources at their disposal. These resources can be economic or material (real estate, land) or "human capital," such as experience, managerial skills, and connections with important mainstream individuals. They can also be organizational, a type of resource that can be particularly important in mobilizing, and combining "the factors of material, symbolic or socio-emotional production" (Collins 1975: 56–61)

In this approach, community formation and functioning is examined from the perspective of individuals who see opportunities for their own gain in terms of power, prestige, income, or ideological commitments. What is perceived as an opportunity is, in turn, a function of the particular assets that entrepreneurs control. For instance, people in religious roles control symbolic and socio-emotional resources. They will, accordingly, attempt to build organizations and pursue activities that involve that type of resources. Those with legal skills will focus on matters that can be dealt with through litigation or legislative changes, those with political skills will address issues that can be politicized, and so on (Brettel 1980; Lavigne 1980: Rothschild 1981). Figure 12.2 summarizes the basic proposition of this approach.

It can be noted, parenthetically, that debates over government intervention in the ethnocultural field (e.g., the multiculturalism policy of the Canadian government) consist, to a significant extent, in two approaches just discussed.

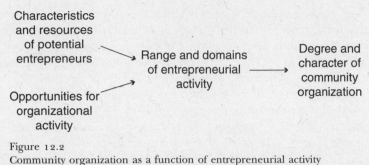

Figure 12.2
Community organization as a function of entrepreneurial activity

Essentially, critics of such intervention argue that by institutionalizing ethnicity, governments produce a set of opportunities for potential entrepreneurs, that they increase the profitability of social and political action on an ethnic basis rather than through mainstream channels. It is suggested that such policies either artificially create circumstances for ethnic organizational activities or detract attention from the "true" needs and problems of the community. The impetus for action comes from above, so to speak, rather than from the grassroots of the community.

Those in favour of government intervention and support argue, in contrast, that ethnic leaders and their organizations are attempting to deal with real community needs and problems. They view the leaders as genuine representatives of the community, who are aware of its needs and problems and are the most able to deal with them. Accordingly, government programs are needed to assist in the formation and maintenance of organizations that can carry out activities in relation to the needs and problems of ethnic collectivities.

An important difference between the two approaches pertains to conflict. In the social demand approach, conflict is a problem: it is a phenomenon that prevents groups from dealing effectively with the issues that confront them. The focus, then, is on strategies to prevent the emergence of conflict and, if it does occur, to limit its impact. Embedded in this approach is the apolitical view of community previously mentioned: that if there is division and conflict, there is no community.

In the social supply approach, conflict, or at least competition, is expected and almost inevitable. If community life is such that it offers a wide range of opportunities for action, several entrepreneurs are likely to appear on the scene. There will be competition among them and their supporters for the control of community organizations or of the resources necessary to pursue particular types of activities. They are likely to oppose each other over the allocation of community resources. They will tend to use different ideologies to justify their plans of action. In this approach, the absence of competition means that there is not much going on in the community. In fact, while in the first approach, conflict means the absence of community, in this one, it is the absence of opposition that signifies that a community has ceased to exist, since there is nothing left that is worthwhile fighting about, or over which to compete.

The two approaches can be used as a basis for the analysis of the political dimension of community organization and functioning, since they both deal with the exercise of power. Indeed, the social demand approach corresponds largely (although not exactly) to what Gamson (1968) has referred to as the "social control" perspective on the exercise of power. In this perspective, the focus is on the power of the collectivity as an organized system – its power to mobilize and use resources to deal with collective problems or to attain collective goals. The accumulation of power is a collective phenomenon; power is accumulated for the entire collectivity in order to enable it to cope with its external environment and with internal needs and issues.

In contrast, the social supply approach tends to fit Garrison's "influence" perspective on the use of power. This perspective focuses on the individuals and groups in the system, on their interests, and on the strategies they deploy to win in the competition against each other. In this perspective, the community consists of a multiplicity of actors (entrepreneurs and groups) with competing interests. Power is accumulated for individual or sectarian purposes; each subgroup and its leaders attempt to acquire as much power as possible in order to bolster or improve their position in the community or to attain specific objectives.

The temptation can be strong to label either the social control/demand or the influence/entrepreneurial approach as the best. It would be possible to argue for a long time over the merits and shortcomings of each, labelling the first as "functionalist," and the other as based on a "conflict" view of the sociopolitical order. This would be a futile and even misleading exercise for the reason that both set of processes occur in all communities. They may not occur to the same extent and in all circumstances, but both can be observed in organized collectivities. The two sets of processes identified by Garrison correspond to two aspects of the exercise of power and thus, to two basic dimensions of the political functioning of communities.

Thus, to analyze how ethnic communities govern themselves is to inquire about these two sets of processes within ethnic communities. Organizational structures can be established and sociopolitical processes set in motion in order to cope with problems experienced by members of the collectivity. But this does not imply that individuals and groups are not in competition with each other for access to, and control of, the resources that the community has to offer. The two sets of processes are far from being mutually exclusive. In other words, community politics involve both concerted action and competition for resources and power among subgroups with divergent interests and ideologies.

In addition, since the ethnic polity is encapsulated within a larger political structure, the possible impact of external interventions needs to be considered. Indeed, the initiative to deal with issues and problems can come either from within or from outside of the ethnic collectivity. That is, the needs and problems of a community may be perceived as requiring intervention by individuals in the larger society, as well as in the ethnic collectivity itself. The leadership of the early phase of the civil rights movement in the United States and the "red power" movement among native people in Canada was at least partly external. Several whites helped activities within the black and the native communities in order to bring about reforms that would be beneficial for the minority.

Individuals in the larger society can also act as entrepreneurs in ethnic communities for themselves and their organizations. For example, church leaders compete to reach ethnic clientele. Some have occasionally succeeded in recruiting members or in establishing some control over ethnic religious organizations, even though they are not themselves members of the community. Mainstream labour leaders and politicians have also attempted to, and sometimes succeeded in, playing entrepreneurial roles within ethnic communities.

The framework for the analysis of the organization of governance, leadership, policy-making, political participation, and the definition of collective identity is designed in terms of concepts drawn from the social demand and social supply perspectives, taking into account the encapsulated condition of the ethnic polity. Specifically, the five components are examined as the result of two broad classes of forces: those stemming from the sociopolitical environment, and those deriving from political competition among subgroups within the ethnic collectivity.

Environmental Circumstances and External Interventions

Ethnic communities experience events and circumstances that occur either within or outside of their boundaries. These can be perceived as beneficial, harmful, or neutral. The term *governance* refers to the capacity to cope with these environmental problems and opportunities.[3] *Political action* refers to the determination and implementation of public goals in relation to environmental conditions. Insofar as the community responds to its environment, the environment is a factor in shaping the community's structures and practices.

The sociopolitical environment, however, should not be seen exclusively as a set of possible problems and opportunities. It also includes organizations whose agents may have an interest in the public affairs of the ethnic polity, and as a result, intervene in these affairs, directly or indirectly. What happens in the ethnic polity may be perceived by authorities of societal institutions as of some significance for their own political interests and objectives. This may lead them to intervene directly in the affairs of the ethnic polity, either to shape its political structures, to affect the relative power of its subgroups, or to orient its political action (Stasiulis 1980; Savas 1987; Breton 1988b).

On the other hand, organizations and groups in government, business, labour unions, churches, and political parties may adopt policies and carry out activities that have implications for ethnic groups and their members. Such policies and programs provide some of the parameters within which members of ethnic groups function (Stasiulis 1980). As a result, these external bodies indirectly shape structures and processes in ethnic polities.

Political Competition

The ethnic community is socially differentiated, and as a result, is likely to include groups with more or less contradictory interests and/or ideologies with regard to particular events, circumstances, and courses of action. Because policies and their implementation can affect subgroups positively or negatively, subgroups will use the resources at their disposal to orient action in their favour. Governance, in this context, has to do with the differential use of power by the groups potentially affected by the outcome of public decisions. Competition and conflict are the dynamic forces in the political arena, and they help to shape the governance structures and practices.

A critical factor in the evolution of the competitive process is the distribution of power resources among the subgroups in the ethnic polity. If the distribution is fairly even, the main questions concern the conditions under which an accommodation among competing groups is likely to be worked out, and its modalities. However, if power is distributed unequally among competing subgroups, the main questions concern the processes whereby political ascendancy is established and maintained by one group, and the implications of this ascendancy for the functioning of the system of governance.

CHAPTER THIRTEEN

Ethnic Organizations and Political Action: An Analysis of Public Opinion*

In the course of their experience in the larger society, members of ethnic groups pursue certain values and encounter problems and opportunities. The combination of aspirations, problems, and opportunities constitutes the basis of the group's system of interests in relation to the rest of the society.[1] These can be collective phenomena, because they are or could be part of the experience of a significant number of members of the group. There could be a common experience, for example, around employment aspirations, problems, and opportunities. If they are sufficiently frequent, if they have a symbolic value for the group, or if the situation of individuals depends to a significant extent on their group membership, individual problems and opportunities can become collective problems. However, groups can also face circumstances that affect them as a group, such as immigration laws, anti-discrimination programs, cultural policies, or job specifications. To a considerable degree, these are "collective goods" (or "bads"), which, if they exist, affect all members of the community. They are largely indivisible (Olson 1965).

In order to assist their members in connection with their goals, problems, and opportunities, or in order to pursue collective objectives, a more or

---

* Abridged from "The Ethnic Group as a Political Resource in Relation to Problems of Incorporation: Perceptions and Attitudes," Chapter 5, in *Ethnic Identity and Equality: Varieties of Experience in a Canadian City,* by Raymond Breton, Wsevolod Isajiw, Warren Kalbach, and Jeffrey G. Reitz (Toronto: University of Toronto Press, 1990), 196–255.

less elaborate sociopolitical organization may progressively be established in the collectivity.[2] Such an organization involves ideologies, structures, and mechanisms for the pursuit of concerted action. At least three basic processes are involved: the identification of matters as being of collective interest and the articulation of related issues; the mobilization of commitment and participation, including the investment of resources; and the organization of the action itself to deal with problems identified or objectives formulated.

The components of social organization required for such processes include leadership, a decision-making apparatus, communication channels, social-control structures, and conflict-resolution and coordination mechanisms. In addition, the mobilization of participation and the organization of action do not depend solely on appropriate organizational structures; they also require the availability of material resources, a degree of social cohesion, an ideology, and a system of social norms. The latter give legitimacy to the social definitions of aspirations, problems, and opportunities that come to prevail in the group, to the type of action undertaken, and to the organizational system established in the community.

The results presented in this chapter deal with the latter elements, namely with some of the perceptions, ideas, and attitudes of members of ethnic groups with regard to the problems faced by their group and its members, to the type of action that could be effective in dealing with some of these problems, and to aspects of their community, its leaders, and organizations. In other words, the analysis deals with features of the public opinion that exists in various ethnic groups with regard to a number of elements deemed important for concerted action.

This chapter limits itself to a few aspects of ethnic public opinion. The first part deals with what are perceived as problems by the members of the ethnic groups included in the study. Findings on the types of action considered more or less effective to get things done or obtain results are the object of the second part. More specifically, data on the attitudes towards the use of community organizational resources in connection with certain issues or problems are presented. The third part examines the relationship between the propensity to favour the use of ethnic organizational resources to deal with problems, and the respondents' involvement in community affairs and their relationship with community leaders. The fourth and last part relates the attitudes towards ethnic organizational action to the perception of various features of the sociopolitical organization of the ethnic group: the decision-making structure, the efficacy of the community leadership and their relationship with societal institutions, and the factors that divide the group.

PERCEPTION OF INDIVIDUAL
AND COMMUNITY PROBLEMS

Generally, ethnic groups and their members can face two broad types of problems. They can, on the one hand, encounter difficulties in becoming fully incorporated in the society and, on the other, experience problems of cultural loss. This section examines the extent to which problems are perceived in these areas. As far as incorporation is concerned, the perception of problems with regard to social acceptance and discrimination will be described. This discussion will be followed by a presentation of results on the perception of problems with regard to the maintenance of traditions and customs, and to the use of the group's language.

Perception of Problems of Social Incorporation

The incorporation of individuals and groups in a community and the social equality that full incorporation implies have an instrumental and an expressive dimension. They involve both matters pertaining to the position one occupies in the social structure with its associated benefits, and matters related to the acceptance, respect, and status one receives from others. Thus, in attempting to improve their condition, ethnic groups and their members will seek social acceptance and will attempt to avoid discrimination. Deprivations of either type are an indication that human and civil rights are not fully enjoyed. What are the perceptions and opinions on these two components of incorporation?

1 *Social Acceptance:* Two sets of indicators are used to explore possible problems of social acceptance; one concerns interpersonal relations, and the other pertains to acceptance expressed by the larger society through its immigration legislation.

Respondents were asked "how easily the Majority Canadian group" accepts them as neighbours and as "close relatives by marriage." In addition, Majority Canadian respondents were asked if they would have someone from each of a number of groups as a next-door neighbour or as a close relative. The results for both sets of questions are presented in Table 13.1 for each of the groups.

The upper panel (A1) of the table on acceptance as neighbours reveals considerable variations, but primarily in the *degree* of easiness with which people perceive the Majority Canadian group as accepting them. That is to say, the percentages who feel they are accepted very easily vary between 19 and 66, with the West Indians, Jews, and Chinese showing the lowest percentages, and the Germans and Ukrainians the highest. If, however, we combine the "very" and "somewhat easily" categories, variations are

Table 13.1
Acceptance of minority groups as neighbours and as relatives (percentages)

	Chinese	German	Italian	Jewish	Portuguese	Ukrainian	West Indian
A1. PERCEPTION OF ACCEPTANCE AS NEIGHBOURS							
Very easily	31	66	48	22	54	61	19
Somewhat easily	54	28	41	56	34	33	39
Not easily	6	3	8	16	7	2	33
Don't know	9	4	3	5	5	4	4
N – weighted*	(56)	(178)	(431)	(168)	(66)	(89)	(118)
Number of interviews*	(152)	(321)	(351)	(348)	(161)	(353)	(150)
A2. ACCEPTANCE AS NEIGHBOURS BY							
Majority Canadians**	83	92	85	89	84	91	67
Others***	85	85	83	86	84	88	68
N – weighted	(1,393)	(1,278)	(1,058)	(1,299)	(1,375)	(1,345)	(1,334)
Number of interviews	(1,861)	(1,706)	(1,696)	(1,698)	(1,844)	(1,643)	(1,862)
B1. PERCEPTION OF ACCEPTANCE AS RELATIVES****							
Very easily	10	59	42	8	44	54	10
Somewhat easily	47	32	45	34	34	32	25
Not easily	23	2	7	45	7	5	43
Don't know	20	8	6	13	16	8	22
B2. ACCEPTANCE AS RELATIVES BY							
Majority Canadians**	65	87	84	77	68	87	49
Others***	52	72	70	68	66	75	39

*[For information on the Toronto survey sample and weighting, see Breton *et al.* (1990, 20-33)]

**The weighted N for Majority Canadians varies between 767 and 784; the number of interviews between 224 and 229. ["Majority Canadians" include persons of English, Irish, and Scotish origin whose families have been in Canada three or more generations; see Breton (1990, 21)]

***"Others" include all non-majority Canadians, except respondents for the group concerned.

****See under Section A1 for the N's and number of interviews.

considerably reduced: a strong majority in most groups feel that they would be accepted as neighbours by the Majority Canadian group. For West Indians, the size of the majority is significantly smaller: 58 percent.

Panel A2 of the table shows the degree of acceptance of the different groups by Majority Canadians and by the minority groups combined. (Unfortunately, the distinction of degree, namely "very" and "somewhat easily," is not available; the percentages refer to overall acceptance.) It can be noted that, as far as acceptance as neighbours is concerned, the expressed attitudes of the Majority Canadians are not very different from what members of the groups themselves perceive. Two discrepancies, however, are worth noting. Jewish and West Indian respondents are less likely to feel accepted than what the Majority Canadians declare: a 12 percent and 9 percent difference in the case of Jews and West Indians respectively. The level of acceptance as neighbours by the other ethnic minorities (combined) is about the same as by the Majority Canadian group.

The level of acceptance as close relatives is presented in Panel B of Table 13.1. Generally, the level of acceptance as relatives tends to be lower than as neighbours. Ever since Bogardus's work (1928), this result was to be expected. The differences in these two areas of social acceptance, however, are not the same for all groups. The greater perceived acceptance as neighbour than as relative is as follows (Column A):

	A	B
Chinese	21 percent	11 percent
German	7 percent	4 percent
Italian	6 percent	3 percent
Jewish	14 percent	8 percent
Portuguese	10 percent	11 percent
Ukrainian	7 percent	4 percent
West Indian	9 percent	13 percent

It should also be noted that the difference in the percentage of those who declare not to know the attitudes of the Majority Canadian group for each type of relationship also varies among groups. This fact is shown in Column B above, the positive differences meaning greater uncertainty about acceptance as relatives than as neighbours, in three of the groups in particular. A "don't know" in this context could mean that the respondents lack the experience required to form an opinion on the matter, that they have a doubt as to whether acceptance would occur if the circumstances required it, or that they do not want to tell. The first of these possibilities is unlikely, and the other two (uncertainty and willingness to tell) contain an element of hesitation that suggests a feeling of less than full acceptance.[3]

Whether the "don't knows" are considered as negative or not, the Chinese, Jewish, and West Indian respondents are significantly less likely than the other groups to feel accepted as relatives. In addition, the Majority Canadian respondents also show less acceptance of these than of the other four groups. There is, however, a discrepancy: the Majority Canadian respondents declare a higher degree of openness than what is perceived by the members of the three minority groups concerned. The Portuguese, by contrast, perceive a level of acceptance as relatives higher than what Majority Canadian respondents show.

Finally, the ethnic minorities are somewhat less likely than Majority Canadians to accept as relatives individuals of other ethnic minorities. This finding is true for all groups, except the Portuguese. As noted earlier, this tendency of minorities to be non-accepting was not observed with regard to acceptance as neighbours.

The immigration legislation also reflects the degree to which various groups are accepted in a society. Such legislation embodies the official attitudes of a country *vis-à-vis* immigration generally and the immigration of particular groups. Because of this relation, the legislation will usually be a matter of some concern to members of ethnic minorities and of the majority group. The reason is that it affects their relative sizes and thus, their relative importance in society, and that it may have an impact on the allocation of scarce resources and social status among them. There are, of course, other reasons why people may be concerned with immigration, such as the possibility of having relatives, friends, or simply people of one's own cultural background come to Canada.

An attempt was therefore made to find out whether or not respondents see the legislation as presenting a problem for their group. Specifically, they were asked if present immigration laws make it too difficult for persons of their own origin and too easy for those of other origins to come to Canada.[4] The results appear in Table 13.2 for each ethnic category.

Given the previous results, it is to be expected that West Indians and Chinese respondents will be among those who are the most likely to feel that present laws make it too difficult for people from their home country to come to Canada. This feeling is indeed what we observe, although this view is even more frequent among the Portuguese. In these three groups, the percentages of people who think that the laws are too restrictive (for their group) vary between 49 and 70. Other groups show significantly lower percentages (Table 13.2, Panel A).

Panel B of the table presents the percentages of those who feel that it is too easy for certain groups to come to Canada: in all except one of the ethnic categories, at least 45 percent think so (the Portuguese being the exception, with only 35 percent).

Table 13.2
Views about immigration policies and changes in relative size of groups, by ethnic group (percentages)

	Chinese	German	Italian	Jewish	Portuguese	Ukrainian	West Indian	Majority Canadian	English 1st & 2nd gen.
A. PRESENT LAWS MAKE IT TOO DIFFICULT FOR GROUP TO COME TO CANADA									
Agree	49	8	40	13	70	22	61	8	24
Disagree	34	79	47	69	20	58	28	74	64
Don't know	5	12	11	14	9	18	7	17	11
B. PRESENT LAWS MAKE IT TOO EAST FOR CERTAIN GROUPS TO COME TO CANADA									
Agree	52	59	47	49	35	64	45	63	58
Disagree	19	30	37	39	31	25	34	28	29
Don't know	19	8	14	11	31	9	14	9	10
N – weighted	(57)	(178)	(431)	(168)	(67)	(88)	(118)	(787)	(415)
Number of interviews	(152)	(321)	(351)	(348)	(161)	(353)	(150)	(226)	(264)

Note: The "neutral" response and the non-responses are not included, however, for the calculation of the percentages.

2 *Discrimination:* Job discrimination is among the serious problems that members of an ethnic group may face. It is an important aspect of the instrumental incorporation of persons in a society. It may be experienced by individuals, or one may perceive it as a problem without having personally experienced it. Both types of questions were addressed to the respondents.

Discrimination is a phenomenon with many facets. Its complexity cannot be adequately dealt with in this context. However, this complexity is recognized in the fact that several questions were asked about the experience of discrimination or its perception. At a general level, respondents were asked if "discrimination against members of their group as far as jobs, pay, or other working conditions are concerned" is a problem in Toronto. The percentages of those who feel that it is for their group appear in Table 13.3 (Panel A).

The West Indian group is the most likely to report discrimination: a majority of them (57 percent) think that it is either a very serious or a somewhat serious problem. The next most likely to say that discrimination is a problem are the Chinese (37 percent) – the other non-European group – and the Portuguese (33 percent). Italians and Jews follow with 20 and 15 percent respectively. The percentages for the remaining groups are quite small (between 3 and 8 percent). It should be noted, however, that aside from the Majority Canadians and the "English, first and second generation," it is only among Germans and Ukrainians that a majority declare that job discrimination is not a problem at all (75 and 58 percent respectively).

These findings are consistent with the results of the analysis presented in the previous chapter (Breton *et al.* 1990: Chapter 4) on the differential allocation of job status. Indeed, it was found that for West Indians, the discrepancy between actual job rewards and those expected on the basis of job qualifications was the greatest. Discrimination may well be a factor in their case, and in the case of the Chinese, as well. For other groups, such as Jews and Italians, there may be discrimination in the majority-controlled sectors of the labour market, but it may be counterbalanced by a relative autonomy in other sectors (see Chapter 4 in Breton *et al.* 1990).

Respondents were also asked if various groups are treated fairly by employers, or if they experience discrimination.[5] From the distribution of responses in Table 13.3 (Panel B), it can be noted, first, that the rank order of groups along the percentage perceiving some or a lot of discrimination by employers is about the same as the one obtained with the previous question. Another observation to be made from the table is that, with one exception, the Majority Canadian group appears to agree with each group's perception of its treatment by employers. In the case of Italians, Portuguese, and West Indians, a slightly greater percentage of the

Table 13.3
Perception and experience of discrimination by members of minority groups (percentages)

	Chinese	German	Italian	Jewish	Portuguese	Ukrainian	West Indian
A. DISCRIMINATION RE: JOB, PAY, AND WORK CONDITIONS							
A very and somewhat serious problem	37	3	20	15	33	8	57
Not too serious	42	17	37	46	26	30	23
Not a problem	17	75	41	35	33	58	14
Don't know	3	4	2	4	8	3	6
N – weighted*	(57)	(178)	(429)	(168)	(67)	(89)	(118)
B. EMPLOYERS PERCEIVED AS DISCRIMINATING A LOT OR SOMEWHAT							
By group itself	53	18	30	40	30	24	66
By Majority Canadians**	47	17	38	39	49	16	76
By minority groups**	37	18	32	28	37	16	61
C. HAVE EXPERIENCED DISCRIMINATION							
WHEN TRYING TO FIND A JOB	17	5	7	12	5	10	22

*The Ns are the same for sections A and C of the table.
**The weighted N for Majority Canadians is 787. For the minority groups combined, the N varies between 1,097 and 1,107.

Majority Canadian group perceives discrimination than of the groups themselves. In the case of the Chinese and Ukrainians, it is slightly smaller.

The Portuguese constitute an exception: a greater percentage of the Majority Canadian group (49 percent) than of the Portuguese themselves (30 percent) perceives discrimination by employers. One possible explanation could be that they are more likely than other groups to work for employers of their own ethnic origin. Thus, they would not perceive ethnic discrimination. Majority Canadians would, at the same time, respond to the question in terms of "Majority Canadian" employers. The Portuguese, however, are unlikely to work in a business or company managed by people of their own group. Only 5 percent do so, in contrast to 38 percent among Jews and 23 percent among Italians – the two groups for which within-group employment is the most frequent.

Minority groups who perceive discrimination by employers, and as seen earlier, who perceive problems of social acceptance, do not appear to be under the influence of a persecution complex: generally, Majority Canadians and members of other minority groups tend to agree with them. Moreover, it would seem quite doubtful that those in the majority and minority groups who declare that there are problems of discrimination and of social acceptance are all under some sort of delusion. There clearly are problems to be dealt with, especially in the case of certain minority groups. The findings presented earlier with regard to the restrictiveness of immigration laws also show that the problems perceived by members of minorities are not the result of paranoia.

Another interesting finding is that in a number of cases, the other minority groups are less likely to perceive discrimination on the part of employers than is the Majority Canadian group (and sometimes, than is the group concerned, itself). This phenomenon can be seen for Chinese, Jews, Portuguese, and West Indians in Table 13.3 (Part B). The differences between majority and minority Canadians in this perception vary between 10 percent and 15 percent, depending on the group they are asked about. In other words, there appears to be a greater sensitivity to the existence of employer discrimination against those four groups on the part of Majority Canadians than on the part of minority-group members.

The above questions deal with perceptions of the experience of entire groups. Information was also obtained on the respondents' own experience: they were asked if they had "ever been discriminated against in Canada because of [their] ethnic or cultural background." The percentages of those who say they have been subjected to job discrimination appear in Table 13.3 (Part C) by ethnic origin. It can be seen that the rank ordering of the groups on this question tends to be similar to the ones obtained earlier: job discrimination is more frequently reported by Chinese and West Indians, followed by Jews and Ukrainians. Very few

Italians, Portuguese, Germans, Majority Canadians, and "English – first and second generation" report any experience of job discrimination.

Although the rank order is about the same, the percentages on experienced discrimination are significantly lower than those for the perception of discrimination by employers. This difference is not surprising; it only indicates that in the latter case, people are referring to cases they have witnessed or have heard about in addition to their own experiences. It could also reflect the influence of the media, which, to a degree, shape popular perceptions on this, as on other matters.

The experience of discrimination tends to vary by generation, but not in the same way for all groups. For three of the groups for whom generational data are available (Italian, Jewish, and Ukrainian), the experience of discrimination is reported more frequently by the second than by either the first or the third-or-more generation respondents. Among Germans, the percentage declaring they have experienced discrimination decreases significantly from the first- to later-generation respondents (table not presented).

The perception of job discrimination as a group problem, however, decreases significantly with each generation: from 29 percent in the first, to 12 percent in the second, and 6 percent in the third-or-more generation respondents. This phenomenon really applies for only two of the groups (Jews and Italians), as there are no generational differences for Germans and Ukrainians.

Problems of Cultural Maintenance

As a result of their minority situation, members of ethnic groups usually experience the loss of at least some elements of their culture. The loss of language, traditions, and customs may be more or less extensive. Moreover, such loss may or may not be perceived as a problem, either because it is limited, because it is expected as a normal phenomenon within the Canadian context, or even because it is felt that one's cultural background should be replaced by Canadian cultural traits. The latter view may be held because it is felt as necessary to avoid discrimination or to facilitate one's acceptance by other groups, especially by Majority Canadians. Data presented in the previous section suggest that this view may well exist and may even be fairly widespread within certain minority groups.

Conversely, the maintenance of at least some cultural elements may be valued, and their loss perceived as a problem. Finally, individuals may be ambivalent with regard to their cultural heritage. They may see it as a liability in the Canadian context, as indicated above; and at the same time, they may value their culture, not only in itself, but also because it is an integral part of their personality.

In order to explore this matter, respondents were asked whether or not they perceive the loss of their group's traditions and customs and the decreasing use of their language as a problem, and, if so, how serious a problem. The results are presented in Table 13.4. First, it is only among Jews that a majority see the loss of traditions and customs as a "very or somewhat serious" problem. About a fourth of Chinese, Italian, and Ukrainian respondents think so, as do a fifth of Germans, and 15 percent of West Indians and Portuguese. Second, it is only among the Portuguese that the majority (55 percent) do not see the loss of traditions and customs as a problem at all. It is seen as a problem by a majority of the other groups, although few appear to find that it is a serious problem.

There does not seem to be much of a relationship between the perception of and the actual loss of traditions and customs. For instance, although the majority of Jews see cultural loss as a problem, it is in this group that it declines the least over generations (a decrease that varies from 1 to 7 percent, depending on the item considered). In the other three groups for whom generational data are available (that is, Germans, Italians, and Ukrainians), the generational decreases are much larger, except in the case of food. These groups, however, do not seem to be very likely to see the loss of traditions as a problem.

With few exceptions, the results are similar when the decreasing use of the group language is considered: the majority of all groups feel it is a problem, but relatively few consider it a very serious one (the question is not relevant for West Indians).[6] It is also among the Jews and the Ukrainians that it is most frequently considered a "very or somewhat serious" problem (50 and 41 percent respectively).

The use of one's ethnic language does decrease considerably in all four groups for which generational data are available. By the third generation, 98 percent of Germans, 89 percent of Italians, 78 percent of Jews, and 86 percent of Ukrainians use their ethnic language "rarely or never." Yet this situation is more likely to be seen as a serious problem by Jews and Ukrainians than by the other two groups.

A better understanding of this distribution of responses can perhaps be obtained by examining the attitudes on the desirability of forming ethnic communities. Respondents were asked if members of their group "should try as much as possible to blend into Canadian society and not form ethnic communities."[7] The majority of respondents agree with this proposition, and close to one-fourth of all respondents "strongly agree" with it. Moreover, the majority are of this opinion in all groups, except among Jews. In their case, a majority (50 percent) disagree with the view that members of their group should blend and not form communities. It will be recalled that the Jews are also those who are the most concerned with cultural loss (traditions, customs, and language).

Table 13.4
Loss of traditions and customs and decreasing use of ethnic language as a group problem in Toronto, by ethnic group (percentages)

	Chinese	German	Italian	Jewish	Portuguese	Ukrainian	West Indian
A. LOSS OF TRADITIONS AND CUSTOMS							
Very or somewhat serious problem	24	19	26	51	15	26	15
Not too serious	31	32	30	24	23	28	35
Not a problem	40	44	41	23	55	43	44
Don't know	5	5	3	2	8	3	6
B. DECREASING USE OF GROUP LANGUAGE							
Very or somewhat serious problem	24	26	30	50	22	41	–
Not too serious	30	26	23	21	32	23	24
Not a problem	42	43	46	27	44	33	76
Don't know	4	5	1	2	3	3	–
C. EITHER LOSS OF TRADITIONS AND CUSTOMS AND/OR DECREASING USE OF LANGUAGE A VERY OR SOMEWHAT SERIOUS PROBLEM	33	31	38	64	25	46	15
N – weighted	(56)	(177)	(430)	(167)	(67)	(89)	(117)

These two sets of data may appear contradictory: on the one hand, a majority of most groups think that the loss of traditions, customs, or language is a problem, and on the other, a majority also feel that they should blend into Canadian society. In addition, if the two questions are cross-tabulated, we observe a relationship in the expected direction: the percentage who feels that the loss of tradition and language use is a serious problem is higher (37 percent) among those who disagree with the view that immigrant groups should blend into Canadian society than among those who agree (24 percent). But this pattern does not hold for all groups. It is the reverse in the case of the Chinese. There is no difference among Italians, Ukrainians, and West Indians. In short, the expected relationship is observed only among the Germans, Jews, and Portuguese.

In order to explore this question, respondents were classified in terms of their responses to both questions. The first category constitutes those who feel that minorities should blend into Canadian society, and who do not see the cultural loss as a problem.[8] These respondents do not appear to favour the maintenance of distinct ethnic identities. They could be called "assimilationists." The second group consists of those who feel that minorities should not blend into Canadian society: they are "cultural pluralists." This category consists of two subgroups, depending on whether or not they are concerned with the loss of customs and traditions, and with the decreasing use of the language. Finally, there is a category of respondents who favour blending into Canadian society, but nevertheless see cultural loss as a problem. They will be referred to as "integrationists."

Jews show the highest percentage of "pluralists" (53 percent). The next highest percentages are observed among Ukrainians (38 percent) and Chinese (25 percent). It should be noted, however, that the Jews constitute the only group of "pluralists" concerned with cultural loss: 33 percent of them do not favour blending *and* perceive a problem of cultural loss. In the other groups, most pluralists do not see cultural loss as a problem.

Four groups show a pronounced "assimilationist" tendency: the Portuguese (75 percent), West Indians (67 percent), Germans (64 percent), and Italians (60 percent). This orientation is also quite frequent among Chinese (55 percent) and Ukrainians (46 percent). The Jews represent the only group in which it is weak: 28 percent.

"Integrationists" think that minorities should blend into Canadian society, yet perceive cultural loss as a problem. There is a larger percentage of "integrationists" than of "concerned pluralists" (except among Jews), but they are proportionately less numerous than the "assimilationists." This combination of responses indicates that group maintenance is not seen as being opposed to incorporation in the larger society. It may even be valued as a means towards incorporation. It could be that these respondents see their community as a locus of social integration and activity, but also as a source of support and protection. Such an interpretation would lead one to expect that this last pattern of response would be more frequent among those, for instance, who perceive discrimination and social acceptance as problems than among those who do not. This is indeed what we find. The perception of problems of discrimination or of social acceptance is associated with cultural orientation: "pluralists" are more likely to be found among those who perceive certain problems, while "assimilationists" are somewhat more frequently found among those who do not. It would seem, then, that a number of respondents favour ethnic-community formation for protective reasons, that is, to cope with problems of incorporation in the society.

Finally, some respondents may be ambivalent with regard to these matters. This conclusion is suggested by the fact that the respondents referred to as "integrationists" (that is, those who favour blending, while seeing cultural loss as a problem) are more frequently observed among those who "feel that it is difficult (or a problem)" to be both an ethnic and a Canadian at the same time (28 percent) than among those who do not feel such a difficulty (16 percent).[9]

THE ETHNIC COMMUNITY AS A RESOURCE: TYPES OF ACTION FAVOURED

There are a number of ways in which a community can be a resource for its members.[10] It can be a source of relationships for the satisfaction of one's socio-emotional needs; of assistance in dealing with matters related to job and housing; of services performed in the context of a familiar cultural context. It can be a milieu in which one finds social acceptance and is given respect and recognition, especially if such advantages are not forthcoming from the larger society; a milieu in which individuals can find support in correcting situations that harm them. As an organized social unit, it can also provide leadership, and promote action to combat discrimination and pursue objectives with regard to culture maintenance and immigration policies. In short, it can be a resource in relation to individual and community needs or problems, such as those discussed above.

This section examines some of the ways in which the ethnic (and the larger) community is seen as a potential resource in relation to some of the problems faced by ethnic groups. This end is achieved by focusing on the channels that respondents think would be effective in dealing with certain matters. Two problem areas have been selected: job discrimination, and immigration laws and procedures. The question is what actions, and by implication, what types of resources the respondent favours in terms of getting results with regard to cases of discrimination or to changes in immigration laws and procedures.

In Relation to Instances of Discrimination

There are various ways of dealing with problems encountered or of seeking certain objectives. In order to explore the views of the respondents in this area, they were asked about various courses of action in relation to a case of discrimination at work, and to a desired change in immigration laws or procedures. The question dealt with the perceived effectiveness of these actions, that is, the likelihood that they would get results.[11] In the instance of job discrimination, the possible actions presented to the respondent can be grouped under three headings:

1 Individual action:
   Complain directly to the boss or personnel manager;
   Say nothing, but work harder than the others so as to impress the boss.
2 Activation of social networks:
   Get together with co-workers to complain to the boss;
   Deal with the situation by contacting a friend one happens to have in the company.
3 Use of organizational resources:
   Take the case to the union or employee association, if there is one in the company;
   Take the case to an organization of the ethnic community;
   Take the case to a community agency like the Ontario Human Rights Commission, whose purpose is to handle cases of discrimination.

The distribution of responses appears in Table 13.5 for each of the ethnic groups.

Taking one's case to a "community agency like the Ontario Human Rights Commission, whose purpose is to handle cases of discrimination" is the action that, in most groups, is the most frequently seen as most likely to give results (74 percent). Also, with few exceptions, taking one's case to the union comes as a close second-most-favoured action (71 percent). Generally, then, the use of the organizational resources of the larger society appears to be the most favoured option. This is the preferred action among the Majority Canadians, among the ethnic minorities, and the "first- and second-generation English."

An important observation, however, is that the organizational resources favoured appear to be those of the community-at-large, not of the ethnic community: 39 percent for the latter, in comparison with over 70 percent for the other two types of organizations. Ethnic organizations are not the least favoured of all types of action, but they are thought, on the average, as significantly less efficacious than organizations of the society-at-large. They are the least favoured in two of the groups whose members are the

Table 13:5

Actions with regard to a case of discrimination perceived as very or somewhat helpful to change the situation (percentages)

	Chinese	German	Italian	Jewish	Portuguese	Ukrainian	West Indian	Majority Canadian	English 1st & 2nd gen.	Total
A. INDIVIDUAL										
Complain directly to the boss	38	52	53	38	39	50	33	46	48	46
Work harder to impress the boss	36	47	41	35	27	39	30	45	47	42
B. SOCIAL NETWORKS										
Get together with co-workers to complain to the boss	43	50	49	40	37	43	25	45	35	43
Deal with situation through a friend in the company	28	36	35	29	23	33	20	32	25	31
C. ORGANIZATIONAL										
Take case to union or employee association	57	72	69	66	52	72	59	76	71	71
Take case to an organization of the ethnic community	27	35	43	44	24	30	19	44	38	39
Take case to an agency that handles such cases	56	73	69	72	70	69	73	80	73	74
N – weighted	(56)	(178)	(429)	(168)	(67)	(89)	(118)	(787)	(413)	(2,307)

most likely to be victims of discrimination, as we have seen earlier: only 27 percent of the Chinese and 19 percent of the West Indians think taking the case to an ethnic organization would help very much or somewhat to change the situation. However, the percentage for this type of action is high among Jewish respondents (44 percent), who are also, as seen above, among the most likely to experience problems of social rejection and discrimination.

Some of the reasons for these patterns of response will be explored later in the chapter. At this point, it is worth mentioning what much of the literature on collective action suggests, namely, the importance of organization in translating discontent, grievances, or aspirations into collective action. In social-psychological terms, this means that individuals will favour the type of action that they perceive as having the best organizational apparatus and support system for its execution. This may be the reason why societal institutions like the Human Rights Commission are the most favoured. This may also be why Jewish respondents are more likely to favour action through their own organizations than are members of other minorities: indeed, Jewish communities tend to be among the better organized for a variety of purposes, including combating anti-Semitism.

Dealing with the case of discrimination through a friend in the company is generally the least frequently selected course of action, although in some groups it is at par with or close to other actions. Among Ukrainians and Germans, for example, it is almost equally less favoured as taking the case to an ethnic organization. Among Portuguese and Italians, it is at par with working harder to impress the boss. Among Chinese respondents, however, it is favoured even more than the use of an ethnic organization.

In Relation to a Change in Immigration Laws or Procedures

A similar classification can be made of actions oriented to a change in immigration laws or procedures:

1 Individual action:
  Write to a member of parliament or to government officials;
  Write letters to the editors of newspapers.
2 Mobilization of social networks:
  Get as many of one's friends and neighbours as possible to write or talk to the member of parliament or to government officials;
  Organize support for or opposition to certain candidates at election time.
3 Use of organizational resources:
  Work through one of the political parties to get something done;
  Work through an organization in the community to get something done.

As can be seen from Table 13.6, the distribution of responses by ethnic groups does not reveal as clear a pattern as in the case of discrimination: the range of percentages favouring each type of action is not as wide, and some of the different types of action are equally favoured. A reason for this distribution may be simply that the possibilities presented to the respondents can easily overlap. For example, writing to a member of parliament or to government officials can be seen as an individual action or as part of a campaign launched by an organization. Similarly, the organization of support for or opposition to a political candidate can involve one's personal networks, but it can also extend to action through organizations. However, even though patterns are less pronounced, they are not absent.

First, it appears that the mobilization of social networks is perceived as the action most likely to help in bringing about a change in immigration laws or procedures (54 and 48 percent). The individual action items, by contrast, seem to reap the lowest percentages (31 and 35 percent). The use of organizational resources falls in between (44 percent).

It should be noted that in the case of immigration laws and procedures, community organizations are not more favoured than the political parties. Unfortunately, a difficulty with this result is that the item does not specify "ethnic community." Thus, some respondents may have taken it to refer to organizations of the larger community and others of the ethnic community. The impact of this ambiguity cannot be assessed.

INVOLVEMENT WITH ETHNIC-COMMUNITY AFFAIRS AND RELATIONSHIPS WITH LEADERS

The attitude towards the use of ethnic organizational resources may be associated with the extent of involvement in ethnic community affairs. It is reasonable to expect that the most active and well-connected within their community will also be the most likely to favour the use of community organizational resources. It therefore seems appropriate to examine a few dimensions of the relationship that respondents have with their ethnic community.

Two sets of measures of participation in the ethnic community will be used. First, there are items dealing with involvement in organizations and in community activities; second, there are some pertaining to the relationships of community members with community leaders.

Ethnic-Community Organizations and Activities

An essential component of involvement is a person's knowledge of any organizations or associations in the ethnic community. Another is actual membership in community organizations or associations, and the extent to which one is active in them. A third aspect considered is the distance

Table 13.6
Actions perceived as very or somewhat helpful to change immigration laws or procedures (percentages)

	Chinese	German	Italian	Jewish	Portuguese	Ukrainian	West Indian	Majority Canadian	English 1st & 2nd gen.	Total
A. INDIVIDUAL										
Write to a member of parliament or government official	53	38	38	32	33	41	29	30	38	35
Write letters to the editors of newspapers	30	34	30	27	12	30	25	32	34	31
B. SOCIAL NETWORKS										
Get as many friends and neighbours as possible to write to MPs or government official	36	54	53	49	40	56	32	61	54	54
Organize support for or opposition to certain election candidates	32	53	45	46	28	45	38	56	46	48
C. ORGANIZATIONAL										
Work through an organization in the community	28	44	45	43	27	50	30	46	45	44
Work through a political party	45	44	44	42	23	48	31	45	49	44
N – weighted	(57)	(178)	(431)	(168)	(67)	(88)	(117)	(787)	(415)	(2,309)

from the centre of community activities, as perceived by the respondent. A last indicator used is the frequency at which respondents "express their views about important community affairs, either in meetings, in letters to the editor, or directly to community leaders." After a brief examination of the extent of involvement in community affairs on the basis of these indicators, its relationship to the propensity to favour the use of community organizational resources will be considered.

There are considerable variations in the degree of involvement among the ethnic groups. For most items, it is among Jewish respondents that the percentages of participation in community affairs are the highest. The level of participation is next highest among Ukrainians. These two groups show the highest percentages on three of the four items: knowing and being a member of community organizations, and expressing their views on community affairs. The exception is the item pertaining to the closeness to the "centre of activities" in the community: they occupy an intermediate position on this item. Involvement is the lowest among Germans, Chinese, and West Indians. It is slightly higher among Portuguese respondents. Italians occupy an intermediate position.

The relationship of participation with the attitude towards organizational action is limited to two items: membership in associations, and the expression of views about community affairs (Table 13.7). Overall, there is no relationship between participation and the propensity to favour ethnic organizational action to deal with a case of job discrimination. In the case of memberships in associations, the relationship is in the expected direction in three of the seven groups: Chinese, Portuguese, and Ukrainians. There is no relationship in the case of the Jews and the West Indians, and a negative relationship for the Germans and Italians (that is, those without memberships are somewhat more likely to favour ethnic organizational action than are members).

The other item attempts to identify individuals who are likely to bring issues to the attention of community organizations. The question, indeed, refers to the expression of views about important community affairs, either at meetings, in letters to the editor, or directly to community leaders. One would have expected that those who express their views would be more likely to favour ethnic organizational action than those who do not. But this expectation is not met.

For the sample as a whole, the relationship is in the expected direction, but it is weak: 43 percent of those who express their views, compared to 38 percent of those who do not, favour ethnic organizational action. When groups are considered individually, a relationship in the expected direction is observed only among Italians and Ukrainians.

In short, the propensity to favour ethnic channels to deal with cases of discrimination is not in any important way a function of the involvement

Table 13.7
Percent favouring ethnic organizational action and participation in community affairs, by ethnic group

| | Membership in ethnic associations | | Expressed views about community affairs | |
	Yes	No	Yes	No
TOTAL	40	40	43	38
	(269/536)	(740/1164*)	(283/511)	(727/1167)
Chinese	36	29	30	30
	(6/21)	(44/111)	(13/29)	(37/101)
German	27	39	20	40
	(16/26)	(149/273)	(16/31)	(150/256)
Italian	38	50	53	46
	(80/56)	(303/267)	(114/91)	(269/229)
Jewish	47	46	46	47
	(100/209)	(60/121)	(71/150)	(89/180)
Portuguese	34	25	14	29
	(9/25)	(52/125)	(11/30)	(50/120)
Ukrainian	39	24	40	26
	(43/180)	(39/147)	(36/148)	(47/175)
West Indian	21	20	23	20
	(14/19)	(94/120)	(23/32)	(86/106)

* The first number is the weighted N; the second refers to the number of interviews.

of individuals in their ethnic community. They are almost as likely as not to favour such channels, whether they are active participants or not. The Ukrainian is the only group in which a positive relationship is observed for both indicators of participation.

Relationship with Ethnic Leaders

The relationship with leaders is another aspect of incorporation in the community as a sociopolitical system. Are leaders known to the community members? Are there personal contacts between leaders and members? Are members informed of the activities of the leaders? And is the extent of contact with leaders related to the attitude towards the use of community organizational resources to deal with perceived problems? Before presenting the results, it should be noted that the notion of "leader" was not defined for the respondents. They responded to the questions with their own idea of who constitutes the leadership of the community.

As with involvement in community affairs, considerable variations exist among ethnic groups in the extent of relationships with leaders. It is in the Jewish, followed by the Ukrainian and Italian groups, that leaders are the most frequently known personally by members, and that there is the greatest familiarity with their activities. Next come the Portuguese, followed by the Chinese and West Indians. Finally, among the Germans leader-member relationships are the least frequent.

As with the participation items, the relationship between knowing leaders and the attitude towards organizational action is weak and inconsistent. In the sample as a whole, there is a positive but very small relationship (41 percent versus 38 percent). The relationship is in the expected direction only among Ukrainians. In the other groups, it is nil or negative. In short, knowing leaders does not appear to make one more likely to favour ethnic organizational action, except among Ukrainians.

Generally, there is a weak and inconsistent relationship between personal involvement in the ethnic community (as reflected in measures of participation and of relationships with leaders) and the propensity to favour the use of the community's organizational resources to deal with problems of discrimination. In spite of this fact, however, there is a certain pattern when groups are examined separately on the three items. First, Ukrainians show a consistent positive relationship between the three community-involvement items and the propensity to favour ethnic organizational action. For them, participation affects their views on the matter. Jews and West Indians also show a consistent pattern: they show no relationship between ethnic organizational action and the three indicators of participation. Their likelihood of favouring ethnic organizational action is unaffected by the degree of involvement. There is also consistency among German respondents. In their case, there is a negative relationship on all three items. Those uninvolved are somewhat more likely to favour ethnic channels than those who are involved. Finally, there is no consistency across items among Chinese, Italian, and Portuguese respondents.

PERCEIVED SOCIOPOLITICAL FEATURES OF ETHNIC COMMUNITIES

The propensity to favour the use of ethnic organizational resources to deal with problems may be related to the perceived possibility of effective concerted action in the community. In other words, as a sociopolitical entity, the community may or may not be perceived as having the social and organizational characteristics required to undertake actions that would bring about results. Three sets of characteristics pertaining to the community as a sociopolitical entity are considered: (a) the decision-making structure; (b) the efficacy of the community leadership; and (c) the social cleavages within the community.

These variables are taken as indicators of the community's capacity for concerted action. The way decisions are made in the community, the ability of leaders to obtain results in various domains of activity, and the social cohesion of the community are among the important components of community organization for sociopolitical action. The present analysis deals with people's perception of these components of social organization, not with their direct measurement.

Perception of Community Decision-Making

Three items pertaining to decision-making in the community appear in Table 13.8. They deal with the perception of who makes the decisions and of the character of decision-making in the community. A first observation to be made from this table is that, as for the items presented in the previous sections, there is considerable variation among groups in the perception of how decisions are made in the community. The percentages who agree that "the ordinary member does not have much to say about how things are run" vary between 21 percent (Germans) and 62 percent (West Indians) – a 41 percent difference (Table 13.8, Panel A). The perception that leaders are very much or somewhat concerned with community problems and interests is shared by 80 percent in the Jewish group and by 45 percent of the Portuguese – a 35 percent difference (Panel B). Finally, 66 percent of Jewish respondents consider that their leaders devote a lot or some effort to get community approval, in contrast with 32 percent of the Chinese – a 34 percent difference.

A second observation is that there is a certain consistency in the ranking of the groups on the three items. That is to say, the Chinese respondents tend to show a pattern of response indicating a distance between leaders and members, whether it be in terms of members not having "a chance to say much about how things are run in the community;" of decision-makers making little or no effort "to get approval from the members of their organizations or from the community;" and of leaders being little or not at all concerned "with the problems and interests of the ordinary members of the community." West Indians and Germans also tend to show a relatively low degree of integration of members and of their concerns in the decision-making process, as perceived by members.

By contrast, Jewish respondents tend to express a high degree of closeness between leaders and members in the running of community affairs. This perception holds for the three items. It is also worthwhile noting that Jewish respondents are the least likely to declare that they "don't know" on all three items. This response suggests an awareness of the leaders and of their activities, and as such, could be taken as another indication of closeness between community members and leaders. Ukrainians are fairly close to the Jews in their perception of the leaders' relationship with members in the management of community affairs, as shown by their responses to the three items. Ukrainians are followed by the Italians, and then by the Portuguese.

Table 13.8
Perceptions of different aspects of decision making in one's ethnic community* (percentages)

	Chinese	German	Italian	Jewish	Portuguese	Ukrainian	West Indian	Total
A. ORDINARY MEMBER DOES NOT HAVE MUCH TO SAY ABOUT HOW THINGS ARE RUN								
Agree	48	21	31	31	38	27	62	34
Disagree	15	57	54	60	36	58	19	49
Don't know	24	19	10	6	18	8	16	13
B. LEADERS ARE CONCERNED WITH COMMUNITY PROBLEMS AND INTERESTS								
Very much and somewhat	48	49	67	80	45	72	60	64
Little or not at all	33	23	25	13	41	18	19	23
Don't know	19	28	9	6	14	10	22	14
C. EFFORT BY LEADERS TO GET COMMUNITY APPROVAL								
A lot or some	32	36	50	66	43	58	42	49
Little or none	41	13	25	17	32	21	25	23
Don't know	27	51	25	17	26	21	33	29
N – weighted	(57)	(173)	(431)	(165)	(66)	(88)	(118)	(1,099)

*The "neutral" and non-responses are not included in the table, but they were included for the calculation of the percentages.

Table 13.9
Per cent favouring ethnic organizational action by perception of community decision making, total and by ethnic group

	Ordinary member has little to say in way community is run		Leadership concern with community problems and interests		Effort by leaders to get approval from members	
	Agree	Disagree	High	Low	Alot	Little
TOTAL	36	42	43	32	43	35
	(352/585)	(502/832)	(651/1092)	(232/387)	(511/850)	(235/389)
Chinese	30	40	35	24	43	29
	(26/65)	(8/25)	(25/66)	(17/46)	(17/39)	(22/62)
German	45	36	42	38	39	32
	(36/65)	(93/160)	(83/143)	(39/72)	(60/108)	(23/47)
Italian	40	50	50	38	48	46
	(125/104)	(213/181)	(260/228)	(95/73)	(204/160)	(98/73)
Jewish	49	44	47	37	45	46
	(51/109)	(96/195)	(129/265)	(20/43)	(106/218)	(27/59)
Portuguese	36	25	31	26	31	26
	(22/56)	(23/57)	(28/66)	(26/65)	(27/69)	(20/46)
Ukrainian	29	34	35	20	40	16
	(23/97)	(48/185)	(61/241)	(15/59)	(48/189)	(17/69)
West Indian	20	22	24	14	27	12
	(70/89)	(21/29)	(66/83)	(21/29)	(48/67)	(28/33)

Table 13.9 presents the percentages who favour taking the issues of cases of discrimination to a community organization among respondents with different perceptions of the community decision-making and leadership. With the first indicator, the relationship is as expected, but is not very strong: those who disagree that members do not have much to say are a little more likely to support the use of ethnic organizational resources than are those who feel they have no influence (42 percent versus 36 percent in the total sample). This result is also seen among the Chinese and Italians (but one of the percentages among Chinese respondents is quite small). There is only a weak or no relationship among Jewish, Ukrainian, and West Indian respondents, and a negative relationship among the Germans and Portuguese.

With the item pertaining to the perceived concern on the part of leaders with community problems, the relationship with the propensity to favour the use of ethnic organizational resources is somewhat stronger: 43 percent versus 32 percent in the sample as a whole. In addition, it is the first item for which the relationship is positive in all groups (although it is weak in two of them: the German and Portuguese).

Similar results are obtained with the third indicator of leader-member relationships, namely the perception of the efforts of leaders to get membership approval. Those who see that they make considerable effort are somewhat more likely to favour ethnic organizational action than those who do not: 43 percent versus 35 percent. The relationship is in the expected direction in five of the seven groups. There is no relationship among Italians and Jews.

Generally, then, the perception that members' interests are incorporated in the decisions of leaders has some bearing on the propensity to favour the use of community organizational resources to deal with issues.

Perception of the Efficacy of Leaders

Are ethnic leaders perceived as capable of bringing about results for their community? Are they perceived as sufficiently well-connected and taken seriously enough for their interventions to matter? It appears reasonable to hypothesize that the evaluation of the community leadership in these regards will be associated with the propensity to turn to community organizations to deal with instances of discrimination or to obtain desired changes in immigration legislation. Three items pertaining to the perceived efficacy of the leaders of one's ethnic community are presented in Table 13.10: (a) whether or not politicians and officials are seen as taking seriously the views expressed by the leaders of ethnic communities; (b) whether or not the leaders have enough connections with important people in business and government to get important results for the community; and (c) whether the group would get more attention from politicians and officials if leaders and their organizations were more active.[12]

To repeat, the items deal with the perceptions of community members. They do not constitute a measure of the actual degree of efficacy of ethnic leaders. In the present context, however, they constitute the relevant kind of data. Indeed, since the concern is with the propensity of members to favour the use of organizational resources in their community, it is their perception of the efficacy of these organizations and their leaders that needs to be considered; in fact, more so than the actual degree of efficacy.

The distribution presented in Table 13.10 shows as much variation among ethnic groups as we observed with the "distance" or "accessibility" items. There is a 54 percent variation among groups in the percentage who *disagrees* that "politicians do not take ethnic leaders seriously" (Table 13.10, Panel A). Jews are the most likely to reject this view (69 percent). The Italians, with 54 percent, are the closest to the Jews on this item. They are followed by the Germans (46 percent) and Ukrainians (51 percent). The Portuguese (33 percent) fall in between these relatively "high" groups and the two that score quite low: the West Indians and Chinese, with 15 percent and 17 percent, respectively.

Table 13.10
Perceived efficacy of community leaders* (percentages)

	Chinese	German	Italian	Jewish	Portuguese	Ukrainian	West Indian	Total
A. POLITICIANS DO NOT TAKE ETHNIC LEADERS SERIOUSLY								
Agree	42	17	28	20	37	41	54	30
Disagree	17	46	54	69	33	41	15	47
Don't know	27	33	13	9	26	15	25	19
B. LEADERS DO NOT HAVE ENOUGH CONNECTIONS								
Agree	55	15	19	7	55	29	65	26
Disagree	15	57	65	83	14	56	17	55
Don't know	22	26	14	8	28	12	18	16
C. EVEN IF MORE ACTIVE, LEADERS AND ORGANIZATIONS WOULD NOT GET MORE ATTENTION								
Agree	35	29	23	23	40	31	37	28
Disagree	40	48	58	65	43	56	34	53
Don't know	14	20	16	8	15	11	24	16
N – weighted	(57)	(173)	(427)	(166)	(67)	(88)	(118)	(1,096)

* The "neutral" and non-responses are not included in the table, but they were included for the calculation of the percentages.

The second item pertains to connections with the larger society (Table 13.10, Panel B). It is again the Jewish respondents who are the most likely to *disagree* that the leaders of their community do not have enough connections with important people in business or government to get results for the community (83 percent). The perception that leaders can be politically efficacious because well-connected is the lowest among the Portuguese (14 percent), the Chinese (15 percent), and the West Indians (17 percent). There is a 69 percent difference between the highest and lowest group in this regard. In between are the Italians, Germans, and Ukrainians, who do not differ markedly, with 65 percent, 57 percent, and 56 percent, respectively.

Finally, the third item concerns the chances of getting more attention from politicians and officials if the leaders and organizations of the community were to be more active. The percentage who *disagrees* is again the highest among Jews (65 percent), who are followed fairly closely by the Italians (58 percent) and Ukrainians (56 percent). The lowest percentage (34 percent) is observed among the West Indians (who also show the highest incidence of "don't know"), and the next lowest occurs among the Chinese. In between are the Germans and Portuguese.

The first two items dealt with the perceived political efficacy of community leaders. The third, however, pertains to the potential that leaders and organizations have not yet tapped, but could, if they were more active. Thus, while Jews are the most likely to perceive their leaders as efficacious, they are also the most likely to think that they have reached the maximum of their potential efficacy. By contrast, among the Portuguese, West Indians, and Chinese, a significant percentage (40, 37, and 35 percent respectively) feels that the community would get more attention if leaders and organizations were more active. These three groups are the ones in which the leadership is the least likely to be perceived as being taken seriously and as well connected.

The relationship between the perception of leadership efficacy and attitude towards the use of ethnic organizational resources is presented in Table 13.11. It shows that, for the sample as a whole, those who agree that politicians and officials do not take the views of ethnic leaders seriously are somewhat less likely to favour ethnic organizational action than those who disagree that such is the situation: 35 percent versus 43 percent in the sample as a whole. Similarly, those who feel that the leaders of their community are poorly connected with important people in business and government are less likely to favour organizational action: 44 percent versus 35 percent.

This pattern does not hold, however, for most group-by-group comparisons. On the first item, the relationship is positive only among Italians. In all the other groups, it is negligible. The perception of the attitudes of

Table 13.11
Per cent favouring ethnic organizational action by perception of ethnic leader's efficacy, total and by ethnic group

	Politicians and officials do not take the views of leaders seriously		Leaders do not have enough connections to get results		Even if leaders were more active, group would not get more attention	
	Agree	Disagree	Agree	Disagree	Agree	Disagree
TOTAL	35	43	35	44	32	45
	(313/532)	(475/789)	(273/485)	(562/921)	(295/519)	(537/876)
Chinese	27	24	33	26	37	28
	(21/56)	(9/24)	(29/74)	(7/21)	(18/43)	(21/59)
German	41	40	51	38	41	38
	(29/51)	(76/142)	(25/45)	(93/168)	(49/88)	(77/133)
Italian	41	48	48	48	35	52
	(107/79)	(210/193)	(75/56)	(254/226)	(96/76)	(226/179)
Jewish	46	46	29	47	34	51
	(33/69)	(110/226)	(12/27)	(132/273)	(39/84)	(104/210)
Portuguese	30	32	32	26	23	33
	(24/59)	(19/46)	(35/84)	(10/28)	(25/62)	(27/66)
Ukrainian	33	30	30	34	28	36
	(35/137)	(33/134)	(24/100)	(47/183)	(26/104)	(47/186)
West Indian	22	26	20	29	20	27
	(63/81)	(17/24)	(73/99)	(19/22)	(43/62)	(35/43)

politicians and officials appears to make little difference in the propensity to favour ethnic organizational action.

On the second item, the relationship is positive among Jews and West Indians. Among them, those who think that leaders are well connected are more likely to favour ethnic organizational action than those who agree that they do not have enough connections. Among Chinese, Germans, and Portuguese the relationship is negative (but the number of cases is sometimes small). It is nil among Italians and Ukrainians.

With the third item, dealing with an untapped potential of influence (at least to the extent of getting attention), the relationship with the propensity to favour ethnic organizational action is a little stronger: 45 percent of those who feel the potential of influence has been attained favour such action, compared with 32 percent of those who feel the opposite. In addition, the relationship is positive in five of the seven groups. The two exceptions are the Chinese (among whom the relationship is negative) and the Germans (among whom there is no relationship).

The perceived efficacy of leaders does seem to make a difference among respondents who declare a high degree of interest in national, provincial, or local issues and politics, but not among the politically uninterested.[13] That is to say, when political interest is low or moderate, the propensity to favour ethnic organizational action is about the same whether leaders are perceived as influential or not. But if interest is high, those who perceive efficacy in the leadership are about 14 percent more likely to favour such action than those who do not (13 percent with one indicator and 15 percent with the other). Similar results are obtained with the third item dealing with the perceived untapped influence potential: there is no association between this perception and the views about ethnic organizational action when political interest is low; only when it is moderate or high.

The measure of political interest used above concerns the affairs of the larger society. The conditional effect, however, is also observed when involvement in the internal affairs of the community is taken into consideration. The indicator used in this case is the respondent's assessment of his/her closeness to the centre of community activities.[14] Perceiving the leadership as efficacious is associated with a greater likelihood of favouring ethnic organizational action among those who describe themselves as close or moderately close to the centre of community activities; not among those who say they are distant from it.

In short, the perceived efficacy of leaders appears to be associated with a positive orientation towards the use of ethnic organizational resources only among those who are politically interested or involved, whether in the affairs of their ethnic community or in the political issues of the larger society.

In addition, the perceived efficacy of leaders is generally associated with the perception that the leaders and organizations are operating at their full potential, and especially so when political interest is high.

Community Cleavages

The third feature of the ethnic community to be considered is the degree of social cohesion or, more precisely, the perceived presence of social cleavages in the group. Respondents were asked about the differences that divide their community in Toronto. The differences they were asked about are as follows: (1) between rich and poor; (2) between political groups; (3) between religious groups; and (4) between members of the group originally coming from different areas.

The percentages who think that each of these differences divides their community "very much" or "somewhat" are presented in Table 13.12. In almost all groups, the economic differentiation is the most significant, as perceived by members of the communities. Ukrainians constitute one exception: it is the division among political groups that they mention the most frequently. Also among Jews and Ukrainians, religious division is mentioned almost as frequently as economic cleavages. Among Portuguese, all four lines of division appear to be almost equally important.

Table 13.12
Perception of factors that divide the community (percentages)

	Chinese	German	Italian	Jewish	Portuguese	Ukrainian	West Indian
A. DIFFERENCES THAT DIVIDE THE GROUP VERY MUCH OR SOMEWHAT							
Between rich and poor	43	39	48	64	22	31	45
Between political groups	35	23	25	29	19	46	27
Between religious groups	14	22	21	63	18	34	22
Between regional groups (in country of origin)	35	22	26	43	23	19	28
B. NUMBER OF PERCEIVED DIVISIONS IN THE COMMUNITY							
Two or more	36	29	35	61	23	38	33
None	33	46	35	16	54	40	37
N – weighted	(56)	(177)	(430)	(167)	(67)	(89)	(117)

There are intergroup differences in the number of differentiating factors, as well as in their nature. Table 13.12 includes the total number of divisions perceived. For each respondent, a count was made of the factors mentioned either as very much or somewhat important. At one extreme, there are those who see all four factors as dividing the community; at the other, there are those who see no factor dividing it. The percentages in Panel B of the table refer to those who mentioned two or more factors as dividing the community somewhat or very much.

This measure yields results similar to those indicated above. The Jewish group is the most frequently perceived by its members as highly divided (61 percent). It is followed by the Ukrainians, the Chinese, and the Italians, with between 35 and 38 percent of the respondents seeing the group as highly divided. Next are the West Indians and Germans (33 and 29 percent respectively). The Portuguese, with 23 percent, show the smallest percentage perceiving internal divisions.

Is the perception of social cleavages related to the propensity to favour organizational action in relation to cases of discrimination? Social cohesion is frequently seen as a facilitator of community action, and a divided community is less able to coordinate itself for effective action.[15] We would therefore expect those who perceive extensive cleavages in their community to be less inclined to favour the use of community organizational resources to deal with problems. However, the lines of social differentiation in a community may become manifest when the community is confronted with problems or events, and when, as a result, a definition of the situation must be established and a course of action identified. From this point of view, it could be argued that cleavages would tend to be more frequently perceived, and organizational action more frequently favoured, in the same communities, since the saliency of social division is, in a way, an indicator of a politically active community. The relation between perceived cleavages and perceived organizational efficacy may, however, differ by type of cleavage. Religious or regional cleavages may reflect organizational vitality in a way that economic divisions do not. Some divisions may not prevent interaction across groupings; on the contrary, the issues that emerge may, by generating debate, increase it. Other cleavages, such as economic ones, may isolate segments of the community from each other.

Table 13.13 tends to support the latter interpretation: in the total sample, the larger the number of perceived cleavages, the more likely the support for ethnic organizational action. This result appeared among Chinese, Portuguese, and Ukrainian respondents. The relationship is in the opposite direction among Jews and West Indians, giving modest support to the first interpretation.

The relationship tends to be curvilinear among the Germans and Italians: in the case of the latter, the propensity to favour the use of community

Table 13.13
Per cent favouring ethnic organizational action and perception of social divisions
in community, by ethnic group

| | Number of perceived lines of social divisions | | |
	None	One	Two or More
TOTAL	35	40	43
	(347/681)	(276/378)	(387/246)
Chinese	23	31	35
	(14/41)	(17/30)	(19/24)
German	36	29	47
	(74/149)	(40/62)	(51/41)
Italian	42	54	48
	(128/119)	(115/74)	(139/50)
Jewish	53	42	46
	(24/82)	(36/78)	(100/43)
Portuguese	21	26	39
	(33/90)	(15/25)	(13/15)
Ukrainian	24	35	38
	(32/141)	(19/81)	(32/47)
West Indian	26	18	16
	(42/59)	(35/28)	(32/26)

organizations is higher among those who perceive *one* cleavage of importance than among those who perceive either none, or two or more. Among
Germans, the propensity towards ethnic action is lower among those who
perceive a single line of social division as important, than it is among the
other two categories. This curvilinear relationship may give support to
both hypotheses simultaneously: the perception of cohesion is a condition
for supporting group action, but at the same time, several manifest cleavages may be an indication of a politically active community. Such an interpretation, however, can only be very tentative. What the data show is that
the relationship between perceived social divisions and the propensity to
favour ethnic action is not unambiguously in one direction. If anything,
the results tend to suggest that, to a certain extent, the perception of
cleavages is an indication of political activity, not of political paralysis.

SUMMARY AND CONCLUSION

This chapter has attempted to describe some of the problems encountered
by ethnic minorities, as perceived by members of the minority groups
themselves and by Majority Canadians. Generally, the rank order of the
groups included in the study is similar with regard to the various instrumental and expressive aspects of social incorporation in Canadian society.
The non-European-origin groups (Chinese and West Indians) and Jews are

Table 13.14
Average rank of groups on items related to problems of social incorporation and cultural loss

	Problems of social incorporation	Problems of cultural loss
Chinese	2.8	3.5
German	6.3	4.2
Italians	4.4	4.7
Jews	2.6	1
Portuguese	4.9	6.7
Ukrainians	5.5	2
West Indians	1.2	6

those who are the most likely to experience problems of social acceptance and job discrimination. Italians and Portuguese tend to be the next most likely to experience problems. Ukrainians and Germans are close to the Majority Canadians and the "English – second and third generation," who are the least likely to face discrimination or social rejection.

With the Portuguese, the non-European-origin groups are also the most likely to perceive their groups as unequally treated by immigration laws. The Jews, however, with the Germans and Ukrainians, are the least likely to perceive difficulties in this area. This response does not mean that they are not concerned with the size of their group in Toronto relative to that of others. On the contrary, the preoccupation with group size is relatively high among Jews, as well as among West Indians and Ukrainians.

The groups that are the most likely to experience problems of incorporation (social acceptance and discrimination) in Canadian society are not necessarily those that are most likely to report problems of cultural maintenance. West Indians are the most likely to declare problems of social incorporation, but are among the least likely to mention problems of cultural loss. The Portuguese show the same pattern, but at the other end of the scale: they rank higher on problems of social incorporation than of cultural loss. The situation is the reverse for Ukrainians: they rank low in the experience of social-incorporation problems, but high on the concern with cultural loss. The Germans show the same pattern (as the Ukrainians), but less pronounced: low on problems of social incorporation, but intermediate on problems of cultural loss. The Jews show the opposite pattern: intermediate on problems of social incorporation, but high on the perception of cultural loss as a problem for their group. Finally, Italians and Chinese occupy almost the same rank on both dimensions. The average rankings on these two sets of items are as given in Table 13.14.

A substantial proportion of members of the different ethnic minorities do not declare that their group experiences problems of cultural loss, but also feel that minority groups should blend into Canadian society. They were referred to as "assimilationists" in orientation. They are like the large proportion of Majority Canadians, who appear to have this orientation. The proportion of "pluralists" is significantly smaller, except in the case of Jews and Ukrainians.

For some members of minority groups, the perception of cultural loss as a problem is not necessarily associated with the desire to form distinct ethnic communities. The preliminary analysis suggested a hypothesis about the attitudes that could underlie the views of these respondents: community formation for protective or defensive purposes rather than for cultural retention as such.

The attitude with regard to different strategies to deal with instances of discrimination and to seek changes in immigration law and procedures was also described. It was found that although respondents tended to favour organizational over individual strategies, they favoured organizations of the larger society much more than those of their ethnic community.

The propensity to favour ethnic organizational resources was found to be related to the perception and experience of problems, to the degree of involvement in the ethnic community, and to the perception of certain sociopolitical features of that community. Table 13.15 presents the rank of the ethnic groups on the items pertaining to participation, to the relationship with leaders, and to the perception of their efficacy. It can be seen that, with a few exceptions here and there, the groups show a similar rank on most items. The Germans and Portuguese show the least consistent pattern.

It can be seen that the average rank of the groups is quite similar on the measures pertaining to the political organization of the community and with regard to the propensity to favour ethnic action on matters of discrimination, and immigration laws and procedures. This similarity suggests that favouring ethnic organizational action is partly a function of the perception of the accessibility of the leadership to the community, of its concern with problems, and of the perceived possibility of making an input into the community decision-making. In addition to the internal political organization of the community, the perceived efficacy of leaders and their organizations in relation to the institutions of the larger society appears to be important.

These results, however, do not come out as clearly when the analysis is carried out at the level of individuals. Weak and inconsistent results are obtained when the perception or experience of problems is related to the propensity to favour ethnic organizational action. This same pattern holds with the measures of involvement in community affairs and of relationships between leaders and members.

The propensity to favour ethnic action, however, seems to be associated with the perception of the leaders' concern for the problems of the

Table 13.15
Average rank of groups on items related to discrimination, group culture, community organization, and views about ethnic organizational action

	Discrimination problems	Immigration laws too restrictive	Cultural concerns	Community participation	Openness of leaders	Efficacy of leaders	Favour ethnic action
Chinese	2.8	3	3.5	5.6	6	7	5
German	6.3	7	4.2	7	4	4	3
Italian	4.4	4	4.7	4.5	3	2	1.5
Jewish	2.6	6	1	2.2	1	1	1.5
Portuguese	4.9	1	6.7	2.7	5	6	6
Ukrainian	5.5	5	2	2.3	2	3	4
West Indian	1.2	2	6	5.2	5	5	7

Note: Rank 1 was assigned to the group with the highest percentage.

community, as well as with the possibility of making an input into the community's public policies. It is also associated with the view that leaders and organizations are operating at their full potential of political efficacy. The respondents who perceive that leaders and organizations are not as active as they could be are less likely to take cases of discrimination to an organization of their ethnic community than those who feel they are. It is not the perceived political efficacy as such that seems to matter, but the perception that leaders are prepared to use all the potential they are seen to have.

Finally, the perception of social divisions in the community is positively associated with the attitude towards ethnic action. It seems that the felt presence of divisions is an indicator of a politically active community. This correlation would, hypothetically, be the reason for the somewhat greater tendency to favour ethnic action when divisions are salient than when they are not.

Another way of summarizing the results is to present the situation of each ethnic group with regard to the various dimensions considered, which is done in the remaining paragraphs.

1 *Chinese*: The problems that the Chinese are the most likely to face in Toronto are ones of discrimination; a significant proportion declare they have experienced discrimination in the past. They are also likely to perceive employers as discriminating against members of their group, a perception with which Majority Canadians tend to agree. Close to a majority of them perceive present immigration laws as making it too difficult for their group to come to Canada. At the same time, issues of social acceptance as relatives, the loss of customs and traditions, and the decreasing use of the language are less likely to be perceived as problems: about a third of the respondents perceived these issues as problems for their group.

Relatively few of the Chinese favour the use of ethnic community organizational resources to deal with the problems faced: a little over a fourth favour the use of such channels to deal with discrimination and to obtain changes in immigration laws and procedures. Consistent with this weak inclination to use community organizational resources is a relatively low involvement in community affairs, a distant relationship with leaders, a fairly negative perception of the community decision-making structure, and a somewhat dim view of the ability of leaders to bring about change. These results suggest that the propensity to favour community action to deal with problems is not only a function of the perception of problems but also of the perception of certain features of the community organization and leadership.

2 *Germans*: Relatively few Germans perceive problems for their group in Toronto with regard to social acceptance, immigration legislation, and discrimination, although about one-third declare having experienced

discrimination themselves in Canada at one time or another, mostly in areas other than work. Group problems in Toronto are more likely to be perceived with regard to the loss of tradition and customs and the decreasing use of the German language.

German respondents show a low level of involvement in ethnic community affairs and a weak relationship with community leaders. However, they are moderately likely to favour the use of ethnic organizational resources to deal with problems of discrimination or immigration legislation and procedures. This propensity does not seem to be associated with their personal relationship with the community, or with a perception of a well-functioning and responsive decision-making structure within the community, including a fairly effective leadership in relation to the elites of the larger community.

3 *Italians*: That present immigration laws make it too difficult for Italians to come to Canada is the phenomenon most frequently perceived as a problem by Italian respondents. They are less likely to either perceive or experience problems of discrimination, although such problems are mentioned by a certain proportion of them (about a fourth). Acceptance as neighbours or as relatives by Majority Canadians appears to be a negligible problem for Italians. Along with discrimination, cultural loss is a problem of intermediate magnitude for them: over one-third appear to be concerned with the loss of customs, tradition, and language among members of the community.

About 40 percent of Italians favour the use of community organizational resources to deal with discrimination or to obtain changes in immigration legislation. A similar percentage is involved in community affairs and has relationships with community leaders. A slightly higher percentage has positive views of the decision-making structure in the community and of the ability of their leaders to obtain results in relation to problems faced by the group.

4 *Jews*: Jewish respondents are quite likely to perceive problems in different areas, the most frequent being problems of cultural maintenance, followed closely by problems of discrimination and of acceptance as relatives. The next frequently mentioned problem is the possibility that their group is getting too small in relation to other groups in Toronto (about one-fourth).

Jews are among the most likely to favour the use of the organizational resources of their community. They are also the most likely to be involved in community affairs, to have relationships with their leaders, to perceive the community decision-making structure as responsive, and to think that their leaders can get results. Some of the other groups included in this study show an awareness of problems facing the community, but their community organization seems to fail to mobilize its members and is perceived as unable to get results. Other groups perceive few problems to be dealt with, but reveal a fairly well-organized community that presumably could launch action in the event that the group became confronted with problems of one sort or another. In the case of the Jews, however, we find a community with both sets of characteristics: it faces a number of problems and shows a willingness to use its organizational resources to deal with them, as is reflected in the high degree of involvement, and in the favourably perceived decision-making structure and leadership.

5 *Portuguese*: The only problem that Portuguese respondents perceived with any significant frequency is that present immigration laws and procedures make it too difficult for members of their group to come to Canada. No other area seems to pose significant problems for the members of this group. In fact, Majority Canadians are more likely than the Portuguese themselves to perceive problems of discrimination for Portuguese or to report difficulties in accepting them socially.

In spite of the high degree of concern with immigration laws and procedures, only about a fourth of the Portuguese respondents favour the use of community organizational action to obtain changes in them. About the same percentage favours such action in relation to problems of job discrimination. In addition, the Portuguese are not particularly involved in the affairs of their community and in relationships with community leaders. They are among the least likely to perceive their leaders as particularly capable of obtaining results and to have a positive view of the responsiveness of the decision-making structure of their community.

6 *Ukrainians*: Few Ukrainian respondents perceive problems for their community: problems of loss of customs and tradition and of discrimination by employers are mentioned by about a fourth of the respondents. A third are concerned that the group is getting too small in relation to other groups in Toronto. Problems of social acceptance are mentioned by a very small proportion of respondents. The problem mentioned the most frequently is the decreasing use of the group's language.

Half of Ukrainian respondents favour the use of community organizational resources to obtain changes in immigration laws and procedures; a slightly lower percentage favours such channels to deal with discrimination problems. As far as community participation and perception of the community decision-making structure and leadership is concerned, it was seen that although Ukrainians do not rate as high as Jews, they (with Italians) come fairly close to them.

7 *West Indians*: In contrast with Ukrainians, West Indians perceive and experience problems in almost all areas, except with regard to cultural maintenance: discrimination; restrictive immigration laws and procedures; the actual experience of discrimination; and problems of social acceptance either as neighbours or as relatives. Majority Canadians tend to share this perception of the situation of West Indians.

By contrast, the propensity to favour ethnic organizational action to deal with problems appears to be relatively low among West Indian respondents. They resemble the Chinese in this regard, although they are a little less likely than the Chinese to favour such action in relation to problems of discrimination.

Involvement in community affairs is fairly low, and relationships with community leaders appear limited. However, compared with most other groups, few West Indian respondents perceive the decision-making structure of their community as responsive (as is the case among Chinese). Also, relatively few perceive their leaders as able to get results in transactions with the representatives of societal institutions (as is also the case among Chinese and Portuguese respondents). In short, the two non-European-origin groups in the study show a similar pattern of experiences and perceptions: they more frequently report experiences of discrimination by individual members and for the group as a whole; a community organizational structure that seems to be lacking in some of the internal features required for effective group action; a leadership that is perceived as being poorly connected with the institutional elites of the larger community and as relatively unable to get responses from them; and, not surprisingly given this context, a fairly low propensity to favour the use of community organizations to deal with the problems encountered.

CHAPTER FOURTEEN

Social Origins of Multiculturalism in Canada*1

Public institutions and their authorities are involved in the distribution of symbolic, as well as material resources. They dispense recognition and honour. They allocate possibilities for identification with purposes that have significance beyond an individual's limited experience. They distribute opportunities for meaningful social roles. These symbolic opportunities or resources can be unequally available to different categories of people, whether they are defined in terms of language, ethnoculture, region, gender, religion, age, or some other socially significant attribute. Accordingly, a well developed symbolic/cultural system can be perceived as inadequate by particular linguistic or ethnocultural groups, in the sense that they feel disadvantaged relative to other groups as far as possibilities of identification, meaningfulness, and recognition are concerned.

In this essay, it will be argued that multiculturalism policy is best understood in this light. Before considering the policy itself, however, it is useful to describe briefly the sociopolitical context in which the condition of ethnocultural groups became a public issue. This context involves various events and circumstances, as well as government activities and sociopolitical processes triggered or accentuated by government actions or by the changing sociopolitical environment.

---

* Abridged from "Multiculturalsim and Canadian Nation-Building," in *The Politics of Gender, Ethnicity and Language in Canada*, edited by A. Cairns and C. Williams (Toronto: University of Toronto Press, 1986), 27–66.

THE SOCIOPOLITICAL CONTEXT OF
MULTICULTURALISM

In recent decades, Canada has experienced a number of symbolic challenges. Among the main ones were those occasioned by the expressed dissatisfaction and claims of linguistic and ethnocultural groups. Several members of these collectivities increasingly perceived and experienced the symbolic (as well as other) dimension of public institutions as inadequate. What some groups questioned was the historically established character of state institutions. Others questioned the interventions to transform that character. The challenge experienced, especially that posed by the Quebec independence movement, had to do with the legitimacy of state institutions. More fundamentally, it pertained to the very conception of Canadian society and the positions that various collectivities were to occupy in the society and in relation to state institutions.

A society is continuously in the process of being constructed and transformed under the impact of a multiplicity of internal and external forces, and actions related to social and institutional interests. There are times, however, when the process is accelerated, when change is precipitated, when a variety of circumstances and interventions converge to generate a significant reorientation or reconstruction of the collective identity and the character of public institutions. It is the contention here that the decades following World War II constituted such a period in Canada, at least as far as the ethnocultural component of the symbolic order is concerned.

In this section, some of the main circumstances, events, and state interventions that characterize that period are briefly reviewed. This overview of the context is essential to understand the underlying dynamics and meaning of multiculturalism as an institutional policy. The relevant context involves a complex interaction of various circumstances and state activity that impinged directly or indirectly on the symbolic/cultural order. A number of the events and circumstances that took place drew the authorities of public institutions into the process of symbolic change, but some of these circumstances were themselves the result of state activity. Sociopolitical processes were triggered that led, in turn, to further pressures on the state, in the form of either opposition to proposed symbolic changes or claims for different kinds of changes.

The section begins with a presentation of a few relevant phenomena, including state activities. This is followed by an examination of the sociopolitical processes involved in redefining the symbolic order and the position of various segments of the society within it.

Immigration was considerable between World War II and 1980. In the 15-year period ending in 1945, immigrants to Canada totalled 219, 494. In each of the two subsequent 15-year periods (1946–60 and 1961–75),

Table 14.1
Population of British Isles, French, and other origins, Canada, 1901–1981

Ethnic origin	1901	1911	1921	1931	1941	1951	1961	1971	1981*
					(thousands)				
British Isles	3,063	3,999	4,869	5,831	5,716	6,710	7,997	9,624	9,674
French	1,649	2,062	2,453	2,928	3,483	4,319	5,540	6,180	6,439
Other	659	1,146	1,466	2,068	2,308	2,981	4,792	5,764	6,370
Multiple origins	–	–	–	–	–	–	–	–	1,600
Total	5,371	7,207	8,788	10,377	11,507	14,009	18,238	21,568	24,084
					(percent)				
British Isles	57.0	55.5	55.4	51.9	49.7	47.9	43.8	44.6	40.2
French	30.7	28.6	27.9	28.2	30.3	30.8	30.4	28.6	26.7
Other	12.2	15.9	16.7	19.9	20.0	21.2	25.8	26.7	26.4
Multiple origins	–	–	–	–	–	–	–	–	6.7
Total	100.0	100.0	100.0	100.0	100.0	100.0	100.0	100.0	100.0

* In the 1981 census, respondents could report more than one ethnic origin: "In earlier censuses, ony the respondent's paternal ancentry was to be reported, theoretically resulting in one ethnic origin per respondent. For 1981, this restriction has been removed and a person may now report more than one ethnic origin" (Statistics Canada, 1984, p. V).

Those whose multiple origins consisted only of "other" origins were added to the "other" category.

It should also be noted that the 6.7 percent of multiple origins can be broken down as follows: 1.8 percent involve British and French origins and 4.9 percent other combinations.

Source: Statistics Canada, *Census of Canada*, various years.

Canada received over 2,000,000 immigrants (2,005,240 and 2,244,081 respectively). In the following 8-year period (1976–83), an estimated 945,668 arrived. During this period, immigration policy and regulations were an object of public debate and change (Hawkins 1972). Among the most significant events were the creation of a Department of Citizenship and Immigration in 1950; the Immigration Act of 1952; the 1962 regulations that removed racial discrimination in the selection of immigrants; the controversial deportation cases of 1964 that led to the commissioning of an independent inquiry, whose recommendations led to the Immigration Appeal Board Act; the White Paper submitted in 1966 and the appointment of a special joint committee of the Senate and House of Commons to examine it; the creation of a new Department of Manpower and Immigration in 1965; the 1967 regulations that introduced the "point system" for the selection of immigrants; the controversial green paper of 1975 and the Senate-Parliamentary committee set up to examine it; and the new Immigration Act of 1977.

One consequence of the immigration flow during that period was to further increase the ethnic diversity of the population. Table 14.1 shows the distribution of the population within three broad categories. The size

Table 14.2
Population by ethnic group, 1871–1971 (percentages)

	1871	1911	1921	1931	1951	1961	1971
Austrian	–	3.8	7.3	2.4	1.1	2.3	0.7
Belgian	–	0.8	1.4	1.3	1.2	1.3	0.9
Czech and Slovak	–	–	0.6	1.5	2.1	1.6	1.4
Dutch	10.1	4.9	8.0	7.2	8.9	9.1	7.4
Finnish	–	1.4	1.5	2.1	1.5	1.3	1.0
German	69.4	35.2	20.1	22.9	20.8	22.3	22.9
Greek	–	0.3	0.4	0.5	0.5	1.2	2.2
Hungarian	–	1.0	0.9	2.0	2.0	2.7	2.3
Italian	0.4	4.0	4.6	4.7	5.1	9.6	12.7
Jewish	–	6.7	8.6	7.6	6.1	3.7	5.2
Lithuanian	–	–	0.1	0.3	0.5	0.6	0.4
Polish	–	2.9	3.6	7.0	7.4	6.9	5.5
Roumanian	–	0.5	0.9	1.4	0.8	0.9	0.5
Russian	0.2	3.9	6.8	4.3	3.1	2.5	1.1
Scandinavian*	0.6	9.8	11.4	11.0	9.5	8.2	6.7
Portuguese**	–	–	–	–	–	–	1.7
Ukrainian	–	6.6	7.3	10.9	13.2	10.1	10.1
Yugoslav	–	–	0.3	0.8	0.7	1.4	1.8
Other European	1.3	0.6	1.2	0.4	1.2	1.9	1.7
Chinese	–	2.4	2.7	2.3	1.1	1.2	2.1
Japanese	–	0.8	1.1	1.1	0.7	0.6	0.6
Other Asiatic	–	0.6	0.7	0.7	0.6	0.7	2.2
Native Indian and Inuit	7.9	9.2	7.8	6.2	5.6	4.7	5.4
Other and not stated	10.1	4.6	2.7	1.4	6.3	5.2	3.5
Totals (other than French and British)	100.0	100.0	100.0	100.0	100.0	100.0	100.0
Number in thousands	293	1,147	1,465	2,068	2,980	4,699	5,764

*Includes Danish, Icelandic, Norwegian and Swedish.
**Included with "Other European" prior to 1971.
Source: Statistics Canada, Perspective Canada (Ottawa: Information Canada, 1974), p. 262.

of the non-British, non-French category as a percentage of the total Canadian population increased from 20 percent in 1941, to 26 percent in 1981.

Changes have also occurred within the "other" ethnic category. First, it has become more diverse over the years, as is indicated by the distributions presented in Table 14.2. Second, members of "other" ethnic groups are somewhat more likely to live in urban centres than they were some decades ago. One implication of this is that with urbanization, the traditional supports of ethnic boundaries – territorial segregation, institutional completeness, cultural identity, and social distance – became insufficient. If it is to maintain itself, urban ethnic pluralism also seems to require a more dynamic regenerational orientation, which includes "dimensions of ideological mythology, historical symbols, charismatic leadership, and social status" (Driedger 1977: 77). The symbolic dimensions of ethnicity become predominant (Burnet 1975).

This predominance is further accentuated by the fact that the white ethnic population is, in large proportion, a middle-class population (Darroch 1979; Blishen 1970; Reitz, Calzavara, and Dasko 1981). Associated with this change is a greater concern with status and social honour relative to material well-being (Collins 1975: chap. 4). It would perhaps be more accurate to say that members of the middle class are preoccupied with the status-enhancing aspects of material objects and pursuits, and take their instrumental features for granted.

The size of the ethnocultural groups and their increasingly urban, middle-class composition have augmented their sociopolitical significance. This was revealed in a special way during Diefenbaker's years in power. Newman notes that a "praiseworthy and realistic historical concern of John Diefenbaker was his view of Canada not as a bi-racial, but as a multi-racial nation. As the first Canadian prime minister who was not of purely British or French stock, Diefenbaker was genuinely sympathetic to the welfare of the two million immigrants who had crossed the Atlantic in the postwar years" (Newman 1963: 187). The following is a significant statement by Diefenbaker (quoted by Newman):

Being of mixed origin myself, I knew something, in my boyhood days in Saskatchewan, of the feeling that was all too apparent in many parts of Canada, that citizenship depended upon surnames, or even upon blood counts. It was then, as a boy on the empty Prairies, that I made the initial determination to eliminate this feeling that being a Canadian was a matter of name and blood. (Newman 1963: 187)

Through Diefenbaker, the political presence of ethnocultural groups was increasingly felt – through his very person as prime minister, his appointments to the Cabinet, and the presence of elected members of his party who belonged to "other" ethnic groups (18 different ethnic origins were represented) (Newman 1963: 188).

The establishment of the Canadian Folk Arts Council in 1964 was another indication of the growing presence of cultural diversity in Canada. The Council, with member organizations in all ten provinces, sponsored a large number of activities and contributed to an increased level of awareness of ethnocultures in Canada.

The American cultural and economic presence in Canada also increased during that period. At the cultural level, this prominence was apparent not only in popular culture, but also in news coverage, and educational materials and personnel. Thus, the growing American presence, which for a long time had been experienced as a threat by Canadians, now presented a new kind of challenge for our collective identity. Its impact was compounded by a shift in identity away from England. It was not the case of a small, young, and independent country submitting to influences from a powerful neighbour. Rather, the growing American influences were experienced by a country that had been economically, culturally, and politically tied to another country, which it considered its mother country. This was primarily the experience of Canadians of British origin. For them, the growing American presence represented a break, as they felt they ceased to be part of something important and meaningful. They felt that their collective and individual identities were at stake.

This sense of loss was accentuated by the decline of the British Empire, a phenomenon that began in the last part of the 19th century, but became evident with World War II (Burnet 1975: 207; Bell-Deutschmann 1978). That important entity, of which many Canadians felt their country to be an integral part, was itself on the decline and could therefore contribute less to Canadians' sense of collective identity and their own historical significance. The Empire was losing its status-giving properties. For some, the decline of the British Empire and its implication for the British cultural presence in Canada was experienced as a loss or a sort of symbolic vacuum. For many, however, it was defined as the normal evolution of the country. It was a new symbolic-cultural opportunity. They felt they were a part of, indeed the makers of, a distinct nation.

One manifestation of this was the symbolic distancing from Britain represented by a number of federal government initiatives. One of the most significant was the Canadian Citizenship Bill of 1946: "Up until then, British nationality, or British 'subjecthood,' had been the basic identity of all peoples under the British Crown; and Canadian citizenship, in so far as it could be said to have existed at all, was simply a minor local variation. The Canadian act completely reversed this order" (Creighton 1976: 129).

There were other manifestations. For instance, in 1949, the Supreme Court of Canada replaced the Judicial Committee of the Privy Council in London as Canada's final court of appeal. The practice of appointing Canadians as Governor General began in 1952 with Vincent Massey. More significant, however, was the federal government's proposal for a distinctive Canadian flag and its expressed wish to adopt "O Canada" rather than "God Save the Queen" as the official national anthem. A flag was adopted in 1965 after a long and intense debate throughout the country (Albinski 1967). The adoption of "O Canada" as the national anthem was to come later, in 1975.

During this period, a new sociopolitical awakening was also taking place among native peoples. Ponting and Gibbins (1980: 25) write that "during the 1960s Indian Affairs in Canada came to be so buffeted by the winds of social change that a climate of confusion and near turmoil prevailed."

Changes took place within the native community, as well as in its relationship with government. The late 1960s saw the formation of the National Indian Brotherhood, and the emergence of a new class of Indian political leaders. These leaders and their organizations have been an important source of pressure for change. Also in the late 1960s, the federal government proposed drastic changes in its relationship with Indians.[2] The 1969 White Paper considered that the best way to deal with the unacceptable conditions in which many Indians found themselves was through "full and equal participation in the cultural, social, economic and political life of Canada" (Canada 1969: 6). Its approach was integrationist, if not assimilationist. Needless to say, the government statement proved to be highly controversial. Opposition to it from a number of sources, especially from Indians, was so strong that the government was forced to retract, and the proposed policy was withdrawn in 1971. It should be noted that this was also the year of the promulgation by the federal government of its multiculturalism policy.

Perhaps the most important phenomenon of the period was the independence movement in Quebec. This was the most serious challenge for public institutions in general, and state institutions in particular, and was perceived as such by a significant proportion of Canadians. Its importance derived not only from its particular objectives but also from its rapid growth and sense of urgency. The movement voiced grievances and frustrations on one hand and aspirations and demands on the other. These brought about a number of government interventions most of which became controversial, if they were not so when initially proposed.

One of the first and most significant interventions was the creation of the Royal Commission on Bilingualism and Biculturalism[3]. The commission itself constituted an important element in the sociopolitical dynamics of the period. Its mandate was

to inquire into and report upon the existing state of bilingualism and biculturalism in Canada and to recommend what steps should be taken to develop the Canadian Confederation on the basis of an equal partnership between the two founding races, taking into account the contribution made by the other ethnic groups to the cultural enrichment of Canada and the measures that should be taken to safeguard that contribution: and in particular

1. to report upon the situation and practice of bilingualism within all branches and agencies of the federal administration – including Crown corporations – and in their communications with the public and to make recommendations designed to ensure the bilingual and basically bicultural character of the federal administration;

2. to report on the role of the public and private organizations, including the mass communications media, in promoting bilingualism, better cultural relations and a more widespread appreciation of the basically bicultural character of our

country and of the subsequent contribution made by the other cultures; and to recommend what should be done to improve that role; and

3. having regard to the fact that constitutional jurisdiction over education is vested in the provinces, to discuss with the provincial governments the opportunities available to Canadians to learn the English and French languages and to recommend what could be done to enable Canadians to become bilingual. (Royal Commission on Bilingualism and Biculturalism 1967: 173–4)

The objective was quite clear. It was to explore how the public institutions of Canada should be modified, instrumentally and symbolically, to better reflect the bilingual and bicultural character of the country, while recognizing the contributions of other groups. The objective was that both English- and French-speaking Canadians be able to consider the national institutions as their own.[4]

The commission made several recommendations, many of which were subsequently adopted and implemented by the government. It is not necessary to review all of these here. The promulgation of the Official Languages Act in 1969 should be mentioned because of its distinctive importance. The main objective of the Act was institutional, not individual, bilingualism. It was to transform national institutions in their functioning and in their symbolic dimension.

These were among the main events and state activities taking place in the ethnocultural field in Canada. Similar movements and events were taking place in the United States (the civil rights movement, for example) and in European countries, in an overall climate of social change. Four phenomena should be mentioned because of their impact on Canadian society at that time.

First, there was considerable economic expansion. The evidence summarized by Bothwell, Drummond, and English reveals

a steady upward progress in output, employment, and prosperity ... Since 1944 most Canadian families have been improving their situations most of the time, and the economy has grown almost fast enough to absorb the rapidly expanding labour force, which rose from 5.2 million in 1945 to nearly 11 million in 1979. Population rose from 11.9 million to 23.6 million, while output rose from $29.7 billion to $126.1 billion in 1978 (in both years outputs are valued at 1971 prices). It is not surprising, then, to find that the average income was much higher by the mid- to late-70s than in the mid-40s. In 1944 it was $2,486 per head; in 1978, $5,388. In 34 years, hardly more than a generation, the average Canadian's living standard doubled. (Bothwell, Drummond, and English 1981: 10)

Second, there was a noticeable increase in state intervention in social, economic, and cultural affairs. This expansion was, to some degree, associated with the population growth and economic prosperity noted earlier, and to some degree also to changes in political philosophy. Government activity is partly reflected in the size of its expenditures. In Canada, real government spending at all levels, as a percent of GNP rose from 28.6 percent in 1947 to 40.0 percent in 1977. The increase was modest at the federal level (from 14.2 to 16.1 percent). It was most significant at the provincial level (from 5.2 to 12.4 percent), a reflection of the substantial expansion in various provincial services, such as education and health care. At the local level, the increase was 4.4 to 8.9 percent (Butler and MacNaughton 1981: 89–92). Employment growth in the public service relative to total employment took place mainly in the 1950s. From 1961 to 1975, it grew by only 1.5 percentage points (from 22.2 to 23.7 percent of total employment). The growth of public service employment in absolute terms over the postwar years reflects the increase in population during that period (Foot 1978).

Third, the baby boom generations[5] started to come of age around the mid-1960s, and to enter post-secondary education or the labour force. These cohorts had already challenged other institutions – those involved with childbirth, daycare, and primary and secondary education – largely due to their sheer numbers in comparison with the preceding generation. As they reached adolescence and young adulthood, their impact was also due to the cultural values and lifestyles they championed.[6]

The relevance of the baby boom generation should be underscored. Its challenge to societal institutions concerned symbolic dimension to a considerable extent. Once the instrumental problems of accommodating the upsurge in numbers had been more or less taken care of, the central issues had to do with recognition, identity, individual and collective expression, and the relative merit of alternative lifestyles. Although they were partly different in specific contents, these were very much the kind of issues on which the ethnic-based movements were focussing. It should be noted in this connection that the baby boom phenomenon took place among Canadians of "other" origins, as well as among those of British and French origins.

Finally, toward the end of the late 1960s, the feminist movement began to gain momentum. A number of organizational activities led to the formation of the Royal Commission on the Status of Women. Its report was tabled in 1967 and published in 1970. In 1972, a conference on the theme "Strategy for Change" was organized which "gave birth to the National Action Committee, an umbrella organization that continues to provide a formal network for Canadian women. Because the NAC speaks for 170 women's organizations across the country it forms the basis of an important pressure group" (Wilson 1982: 127).

The sociopolitical context of the period can be described as a configuration of changing circumstances, events, and state activities, as well as a set of unfolding processes. These processes were an integral part of the evolving situation. They were, so to speak, its underlying dynamics – a dynamics, as noted above, consisting of the interaction between various circumstances, groups pursuing their symbolic interests, and the state pursuing its institutional interests. The following appear to be among the most important of these processes.

Rise in the Salience of Ethnicity

Among the underlying processes were those that raised the salience of ethnicity in public affairs. Ethnicity, like other attributes of social differentiation such as age, gender, religion, or social class, does not always have the same importance in determining what becomes a public issue. Different social, economic, or political conditions can increase or decrease its prominence. The conditions of the 1950s and 1960s heightened its salience.

The rise in immigration affected the prominence of ethnicity, because newcomers understandably attach great importance to their culture of origin. A large inflow of new immigrants tends to revitalize the ethnic community; it provides a new clientele for ethnic organizations and is a source of cultural renewal.

The proposed and actual changes in immigration policy and the public debate surrounding such changes also increased awareness of various ethnic groups and their growing significance in Canadian society. Aside from their economic, social, and demographic consequences, these changes were symbolic events that brought to public consciousness questions concerning the kind of society we are and want to be.

The expression of grievances and aspirations by linguistic and cultural groups brought these social cleavages closer to the centre of public affairs. Moreover, political authorities could not ignore voices from the French-speaking community and from native peoples. Their responses and the public debate they generated further increased the salience of these lines of social affiliation. Public controversies frequently make people more aware of "the side of the ethnocultural fence on which they stand," or lead them to choose sides. The result is frequently an increased consciousness of who one is or is not from an ethnocultural point of view.

Indirectly, economic prosperity also contributed to an increase in the prominence of the symbolic dimension of ethnicity. In periods of prosperity, economic issues tend to be less at the centre of public preoccupations. Other issues can then gain some importance. In contrast, periods of economic decline tend to give relative prominence to the material/instrumental aspects of ethnicity and ethnic relations.

Erosion of the Symbolic Component of Public Institutions

Several of the events mentioned above contributed to the erosion of the symbolic system in its collective identity, cultural traditions, and linguistic dimensions. In this period, a convergence of circumstances seemed to bring the process to a head – increased immigration, the American presence, the decline of the British Empire, government initiatives to reduce Canada's symbolic ties with England, and the Quebec independence movement. It became increasingly clear that the character of public institutions was inadequate in the sense that it corresponded less and less with the character of several segments of the population. The vision of a British type of society was increasingly unrealistic for Canada. A somewhat different view of the Canadian entity and a different collective identity had to be reflected in the cultural character of political, educational, and other public institutions in the language of use in these institutions; in their practices, traditions and way of life; and in the symbols used to represent the society and its people. During the 1960s, it became increasingly evident that the symbolic/cultural character of public institutions needed redefinition and renewal to more adequately correspond to the new realities.

Displacement of the Traditionally Dominant Status Group

Corresponding to the erosion of the symbolic/cultural character of public institutions was the lessening of the cultural dominance of the group that had been fairly successful in the past in defining and controlling the character of those institutions.[7] The decline of the British Empire, particularly after World War II, no doubt contributed to the partial loss of cultural status experienced by Canadians of British origin. However, events within Canada contributed more directly to this status displacement – the independence movement and other expressions of Quebec nationalism, federal initiatives with regard to the French language, the increasingly multicultural character of Canada and the political articulation of the idea of cultural pluralism, and the American economic and cultural presence in Canada.[8]

Ethnic studies and the inclusion in history textbooks of material on the contribution of other ethnic groups were also perceived as a threat by a number of Canadians of British origin. These signs of new awareness of other ethnic groups reflected the loss of cultural dominance by British-origin Canadians, and the fact that they were less in possession of society's symbolic system. Also, ethnic studies inevitably uncover more or less unpleasant events that may tarnish the image that cultural groups construct for themselves and for outsiders. Ethnic studies may build the image of the cultural minorities; what they do for the dominant cultural group is less certain. The political awakening of native peoples is also relevant here, especially their attempts to alert international opinion to their condition of subordination and poverty.

Although the experience of status displacement is almost inevitably accompanied by status anxieties and resistance, it must be noted that the reaction of the British-origin community was positive to a significant degree.[9] This is reflected in the changing attitudes and behaviour of individuals, as well as in institutional accommodations *vis-à-vis* francophones, native peoples, and other ethnic groups. There is still, however, a significant resistance in certain segments of that community.

Intergroup Comparisons and Competition

The events and circumstances also triggered or accentuated intergroup comparison. The expression of aspirations and claims by one group almost inevitably leads other groups to compare them with their own situation. Intergroup comparisons are further accentuated when institutional authorities begin to respond to expressed claims and aspirations. What particular groups seek and obtain from public institutions is closely monitored by the leaders of other groups.

The Quebec nationalist movement in general, and the independence movement in particular, raised numerous questions about the place of the other ethnic groups in the sociopolitical system. What kind of collectivity did the French represent – a founding people and charter group, a nation, or a group like other ethnic groups? If the French collectivity was to be defined as different, what would that imply in terms of political status and prerogatives for itself and other groups? What would be the relative gains and losses of the different groups?

It was inevitable that the Royal Commission on Bilingualism and Biculturalism would become part of the dynamics of intergroup comparisons. Although established by federal authorities to deal with the independence threat, it could not avoid the controversy over the relative position of different groups in society, nor could the government in its subsequent policy proposals. In the controversy, the vision of Canada that was implied by the name and mandate of the commission was questioned. The commission increased the level of ethnic consciousness among the non-British, non-French ethnic groups and led them to compare their situation with that of the French collectivity. Groups looked at each other in terms of their contribution to Canadian society and questioned each other's claims concerning the significance of their contribution. Groups that could not plausibly claim that they had played a special role, simply rejected the historical contribution to the founding and constitution of the society as a legitimate basis for public recognition.

In short, the Quebec independence movement and the royal commission heightened the status anxieties of many members of other ethnic groups. It increased their fear of being defined as second-class citizens, of having their culture and contributions to Canadian society devalued, and of being symbolically cheated or degraded while the status of another group was raised and glorified.

These pressures and counter-pressures led to a shift from biculturalism to multiculturalism – a shift in the allocation of sociopolitical recognition and status among ethnocultural groups. Although the special status of the French collectivity was still acknowledged in the bilingualism policy, the multiculturalism movement and subsequent government policy represented a possible loss of status. In fact, multiculturalism could mean that the French collectivity would eventually be perceived as merely another ethnic group. The independence movement and efforts to assume a more significant place in national institutions can be seen as attempts by the French to raise their status. Their resistance to multiculturalism was an attempt to prevent a loss of whatever sociopolitical status they had succeeded in gaining over the years.

Generally, what has happened in the last few decades is that the sociopolitical context in which groups strive to achieve social recognition and compete with other groups has been modified. Several new social, demographic, political, and economic conditions affecting the means and conditions of status attainment or maintenance have emerged. Foremost among these are the new parameters resulting from changes in the degree and type of government interventions. This is true in several spheres of activity, but is especially the case in the linguistic and ethnocultural fields. Governments in Canada have frequently intervened in the past in regard to languages and ethnocultures. What characterizes the recent period is the extent and especially the content of their interventions.

The growth of state intervention means that groups are not only competing with each other in the marketplace, but increasingly in the political arena as well. This is the case with symbolic as well as material interests. Access to the resources of the state have become more important for the improvement of one's symbolic and material condition.

State interventions provide opportunities and set constraints for the pursuit of symbolic goals. They offer means for groups to compete for status with other groups, but they also define the basic parameters within which the competition is to take place. As mentioned earlier, new policies were introduced, together with associated regulations and programs. These changed the system of status-enhancing opportunities and constraints for linguistic and ethnocultural groups. With a different legislative and organizational apparatus, the cultural status game has to be played quite differently.

Sociopolitical Mobilization

Accompanying the above processes were those of sociopolitical mobilization on an ethnic basis. "While some of the beliefs and propositions underlying the 'ideology' of multiculturalism (if not the term itself) have long been current among Ukrainian Canadians and some other ethnic groups, it was only during the 1960s that this 'ideology' crystallized" (Bociurkiw 1978: 101). Representatives of some groups articulated certain demands or opposed the claims of others. As already indicated, this mobilization took place in the context of a widespread mobilization of groups in the society at large. Moreover, ethnic mobilization in Canada occurred in the context of ethnic mobilization in several other countries.

How widespread and intensive ethnic mobilization for multiculturalism was is difficult to ascertain. Limited research results are available on two aspects of mobilization – popular support and organizational activity. Surveys that could document the existence of grassroots support for multiculturalism do not appear to have been carried out before the early 1970s, when two major studies were undertaken (O'Bryan, Reitz, and Kuplowska 1976; Berry, Kalin, and Taylor 1976). Both found fairly wide support for a multiculturalism policy. This support must be interpreted with caution, however, as both studies found little awareness of the policy. In their 1973 study, O'Bryan and his colleagues asked a sample from ten minority ethnic groups in five cities if they were aware of the policy: "Only 22.3 percent of the respondents said 'yes.' About the same number had some vague knowledge, but more than 50 percent had not heard of the policy" (O'Bryan, Reitz, and Kuplowska 1976: 154). The 1974 study by Berry *et al.*, based on a national sample, found that fewer than one out of five Canadians had any knowledge of the multiculturalism policy that had been in existence for three years.

Berry *et al.* also found that although support for the idea of multiculturalism was high, it was viewed as something that should take place within ethnic communities and not in the public sphere. The view of majority and minority persons tended to be negative with regard to the use of non-official languages in broadcasting and regular school programs; they also tended to reject the use of public funds to support multiculturalism. The study also found that the idea of multiculturalism received the greatest support among Anglo-Saxon respondents, followed by those of "other" ethnic origins, and then by French-Canadians. After reviewing the results of the two surveys, Palmer concludes: "Given the general lack of awareness of the federal multicultural policy, the lukewarm support for multiculturalism as an idea, and the unwillingness to take any positive action in support of multiculturalism, one must conclude that the prevailing Anglo-Canadian attitude toward it is one of indifference" (Palmer 1976b: 60). The results show that his conclusion can be applied to the non-British, non-French groups as well.

Awareness of the government policy may not have been widespread, and support for the idea may not have been strong, but it was nevertheless sufficient to spawn a certain amount of organizational activity. It is this

activity that "crystallized the ideology," making it a public issue by attracting the attention of politicians, civil servants, and the media.[10]

A significant portion of this activity took the form of a protest against
some of the positions of the Royal Commission on Bilingualism and Biculturalism. A number of groups rejected the definition of the situation that
was incorporated in the terms of reference of the commission. Statements
to that effect were made to the media and briefs were submitted to the
commission (Burnet 1984). In his review of this protest, Jaworsky notes that

as the B and B Commission began to hold formal meetings in the prairie provinces,
reaction from the non-Anglo-Saxon and non-French ethnic groups became more
vocal. The vehement statements made by some members of the "other" ethnic
groups were unexpected, and as a result the Commission's co-chairman had to
postpone some of their formal meetings, and had to slow down the work of the
Commission. (Jaworsky 1979: 50)

The protest, however, was not unanimous. Some groups supported the
commission's perspective on the question of language and culture. In
addition, the number of ethnic organizations that submitted briefs was
relatively limited. The commission's report lists 55 briefs from 14 different
ethnic groups, but of those, 32 (about 60 percent) were submitted by
Ukrainian organizations.[11] This does not suggest a widespread mobilization across groups. Finally, there was little or no coordination among the
various groups in the preparation and presentation of their briefs (Jaworsky
1979: 50).

Conferences were also organized to activate public opinion or influence
governmental authorities. An important one was the "Thinkers' Conference on Cultural Rights" held in Toronto in 1968. It was organized by
Senator Yuzyk and was attended by representatives of about 20 different
ethnic groups. In 1970, a campaign consisting primarily of conferences
was launched by the Ukrainian Canadian University Students' Union "to
mobilize grassroots support ... for the policy ... and to stimulate other
ethnic groups to articulate their demands" (Bociurkiw 1978: 108). This
campaign, it should be noted, was financially supported by the federal
government.

This financial assistance indicates that governmental agents and organizations were also actively involved in promoting a shift toward multiculturalism. In addition to giving assistance to ethnic organizations, the
Citizenship Branch also "helped to arrange public meetings across the
country to discuss the work of the B and B Commission, and individual
Branch officers encouraged these (ethnocultural) organizations and interested individuals to prepare and present briefs to the Commission" (Jaworsky
1979: 52).

The government also provided mechanisms through which the views of ethnocultural spokesmen could be expressed and monitored. The ethnic press was reviewed. The minister and his staff held public and private meetings with ethnic group representatives (Jaworsky 1979: 63). The 1970–71 hearings of Parliament's special joint committee on the Constitution was also a channel of communication with governmental authorities on this matter. The committee recommended in favour of multiculturalism (Bociurkiw 1978: 104).

Provincial governments were also part of this movement. The Alberta government announced its multiculturalism policy in July 1971, and Ontario announced in September that it would hold an Ontario Heritage Conference the following year. Such provincial initiatives probably spurred the federal government to move in the direction of multiculturalism.

Another incentive was that multiculturalism turned out to be instrumental to the Trudeau government's political agenda. Indeed, the terms of the royal commission could be interpreted as lending support to the "two nations" view of Canada. A policy of cultural pluralism would help to undermine a notion that was seen as dangerously consistent with the Quebec independence movement (Jaworsky 1979: 59).

In short, the research results on popular attitudes do not indicate a strong and widespread demand for state intervention in the ethnocultural field, except for the symbolic affirmation of Canada as a multicultural rather than bicultural society. The demand for a federal policy of multiculturalism seems to have come primarily from ethnic organizational elites and their supporters, from government agencies and their officers, and from political authorities.

THE FEDERAL MULTICULTURALISM POLICY

Significance of the Policy

It was in a context replete with ethnically related events that the notion of a multicultural ideal for Canadian society entered the public debate. The events of the late 1950s and 1960s had set in motion processes that either led directly to the promulgation of an ethnic policy, or at least provided a climate favourable to a move in that direction. In fact, such a policy was an integral part of the reconstruction of the symbolic system. Public institutions needed to be modified in such a way as to reflect the linguistic and multicultural character of society. As discussed earlier, such reconstruction entails two related tasks.

First, new values, meanings, and identity must be adopted; organizational forms must be transformed or created to embody the new values, cultural traits, and collective identity; and symbols must be invented for their public expression. Such a transformation involves introducing new symbolic forms and eliminating those felt to be offensive or obsolete.

The second task is usually necessitated by the first. Changes in the symbolic/ cultural system generally require a reallocation of status among some of the groups. Symbolic changes that give more recognition to some segments of the population are likely to be perceived as a relative devaluation by others. In their attempts to manage this reallocation, authorities had to intervene on several fronts at the same time – language, ethnocultures, aboriginal rights – and in a variety of ways on each of them.

The contextual changes noted earlier suggest that the climate was propitious for changes in the symbolic order. The immediate motive, however, was the rise of the independence movement and the government's initial response. The transformation of institutional identity, language, and symbols to help members of the French segment of the society recognize themselves generated identification and status concerns, not only among persons of British origin, but among those of non-British, non-French origin as well.

The first manifestations of these concerns by non-British, non-French groups was the reaction of some representatives to the Royal Commission on Bilingualism and Biculturalism. They reacted against the assimilationist orientation of the commission toward "other" ethnic groups and the clearly secondary place they occupied in its preoccupation (Burnet 1984). As the mandate quoted earlier indicates, it was acknowledged that their role was to be taken into account, but it was not seen as a central one.

These reactions led the commission and its staff to attempt "to formulate a scheme in which their members were in no way second-class citizens, a phrase of which the Commissioners had become very weary, but yet the French and English linguistic communities were upheld" (Burnet 1984: 11). The reorientation of the commission was reflected in Book IV of its Report, *The Cultural Contribution of the Other Ethnic Groups,* published in 1970. The federal government's response was the policy of multiculturalism within a bilingual framework.

It seems quite clear that when the policy was introduced, the concerns of the non-British, non-French segment of the society were not primarily with cultural maintenance. Instead, their concerns reflected status anxiety – fear of being defined as second-class citizens, marginal to the identity system being redefined. The policy was thus, in part, a response to the status anxieties voiced in relation to the themes of biculturalism, a two-nation society, charter groups, and founding peoples. One of its objectives was to affirm symbolically that Canadian society is open to all cultural identities, to indicate that it recognizes them all, and that it recognizes them all as equal.[12]

This underlying concern with the public recognition that various components of the society should receive is clearly expressed in the Prime

Minister's statement to the House of Commons in 1971, in which he announced the policy:

In the past, substantial public support has been given largely to the arts and cultural institutions of English-speaking Canada. More recently and largely with the help of the royal commission's earlier recommendations in Volumes I to III, there has been a conscious effort on the government's part to correct any bias against the French language and culture. In the last few months the government has taken steps to provide funds to support cultural-educational centres for native people. The policy I am announcing today accepts the contention of the other cultural communities that they, too, are essential elements in Canada and deserve government assistance in order to contribute to regional and national life in ways that derive from their heritage yet are distinctively Canadian. (House of Commons 1971: 8545–46)

The policy was intended as another element in the shaping of our society. This is reflected, for example, in this excerpt from the same statement to the House:

A policy of multiculturalism within a bilingual framework commends itself to the government as the most suitable means of assuring the cultural freedom of Canadians. Such a policy should help to break down discriminatory attitudes and cultural jealousies. National unity, if it is to mean anything in the deeply personal sense, must be founded on confidence in one's own individual identity; out of this can grow respect for that of others and a willingness to share ideas, attitudes and assumptions. A vigorous policy of multiculturalism will help create this initial confidence. It can form the base of a society which is based on fair play for all. The government will support and encourage the various cultures and ethnic groups that give structure and vitality to our society. They will be encouraged to share their cultural expression and values with other Canadians and so contribute to a richer life for us all. (House of Commons 1971: 8545)

The policy's objective is the incorporation of the "other" ethnic groups in the cultural/symbolic fabric of Canadian society. For instance, the promulgation itself was an important symbolic gesture affirming a particular value – the full acceptance of all members of the society, whatever their cultural background. "A policy of multiculturalism within a bilingual framework" also represents an attempt to accommodate the competing status claims of the various linguistic and ethnocultural groups. In addition, the mechanisms established for consultation, the organizations set up to respond to expressed needs, and the presence of special items in the national budget are themselves symbolic of the greater importance of the "other" ethnic groups in the public affairs of the nation. The apparatus constitutes a symbol, over and above the specific activities carried out, and the cultural contents expressed through it.

The policy is also part of the reconstruction of the symbolic system, in that it was perceived as one of the elements that would counterbalance the Americanization of Canada. It was noted earlier that the American presence accentuates the Canadian collective identity problem. Weinfeld (1981), for instance, writes of the frustration of English-Canadian nationalism "in identifying a uniquely Canadian culture or set of national characteristics. In the absence of any consensus on the substance of Canadian identity or culture, multiculturalism fills a void, defining Canadian culture in terms of the legitimate ancestral cultures which are the legacy of every Canadian: defining the whole through the sum of its parts" (1981: 94). The frequently-heard statement to the effect that Canada does not seek to be a melting pot like the United States, but rather to be a multicultural society, provides informal evidence for that interpretation.[13] Multiculturalism helps to define a distinctive collective identity and thus, to differentiate Canadians from Americans. Viewed from that perspective, it could be said that the growing American presence, together with the decline of the British presence, constituted an opportunity for symbolic innovation.

In short, the multiculturalism policy is a symbolic act that is part of a long and continuing sequence of symbolic transformations in Canadian public life and institutions. In the previous section, several of the symbolic changes in earlier periods were mentioned (e.g., Canadian citizenship, the adoption of a flag and national anthem, the Official Languages Act). The multiculturalism policy represents an additional change to the symbolic/cultural system. This change is in harmony with the previous adaptations to the changing sociopolitical environment.

Moreover, it has already been followed by other significant symbolic events. Among those is the Charter of Rights, part of the new Constitution. In relation to ethnocultures, it states: "This Charter shall be interpreted in a manner consistent with the preservation and enhancement of the multicultural heritage of Canadians" (Article 27). The Special Committee of Parliament on Visible Minorities in Canadian Society constitutes in itself another important symbolic phenomenon. Several of its recommendations deal explicitly with the symbolic dimension of society and public institutions, and with the recognition and status given (or not given) to visible minorities.

Implementation of the Policy

When the multiculturalism policy was announced, four policy directions were indicated:

First, resources permitting, the government will seek to assist all Canadian cultural groups that have demonstrated a desire and effort to continue to develop a capacity to grow and contribute to Canada, and a clear need for assistance, the small and weak groups no less than the strong and highly organized.

Second, the government will assist members of all cultural groups to overcome cultural barriers to full participation in Canadian society.

Third, the government will promote creative encounters and interchange among all Canadian cultural groups in the interest of national unity.

Fourth, the government will continue to assist immigrants to acquire at least one of Canada's official languages in order to become full participants in Canadian society. (House of Commons 1971: 8546)

It should be noted that before the 1971 announcement, the federal government was already pursuing activities in those four areas. Subsequent programs were, to a certain degree, in continuity with previous ones. The new policy nevertheless represented a turning point. With it came a significant shift in the magnitude of programs, the range of pursuits, and the emphasis given to the four areas of implementation.[14]

In the 1950s and early 1960s, the responsible unit was the Canadian Citizenship Branch of the Department of Citizenship and Immigration.[15] Its concerns were the integration of immigrants, citizenship, and intergroup relations. The activities reflecting these concerns included support for language classes set up and operated by provincial departments of education, conferences on citizenship with special reference to the integration of immigrants, and the establishment of a research unit to investigate problems concerning intergroup relations (a recommendation made at a conference). Several publications[16] and films[17] prepared during that period reveal the same preoccupations.

Shortly after announcement of the multiculturalism policy in 1971, organizational innovations were made. The Prime Minister appointed a minister responsible for the implementation of the policy (1972), the Multiculturalism Directorate was established (1972), and the Canadian Consultative Council on Multiculturalism was set up as an advisory body to the minister (1973).

The programs which were added to the existing policy instruments emphasized cultural expression, support to the corresponding community organizations, and the national celebration of ethnocultures. These new emphases were reflected in the array of programs put into operation in the early 1970s:

• Multicultural Grants Program. Through this program, funds are provided to groups and organizations for cultural activities such as festivals, television programs, Saturday schools, literary clubs, and art exhibits.

- Multiculturalism Centres. Grants are provided to ethnic groups for setting up and administering a central facility.
- Ethnic Press Program. This program provides funds for the placement of advertisements in the ethnic press. A monthly digest of reports in the ethnic press is also provided in order to improve government understanding of ethnic communities.
- Third Language Teaching Aids.
- Multicultural Studies Program. Research in the ethnocultural field is supported through this program. The program includes the Ethnic Histories Series.

To administer these programs, it was frequently necessary to establish linkages with ethnocultural organizations. In some instances, the creation of organizations or federations of organizations was encouraged by government officials in order to facilitate communication with the ethnic communities. More often, however, the initiative came from the communities themselves.

Activities were also carried out in other government agencies, as, for example:

- Canadian Centre for Folk Culture Studies – a section in the National Museum of Man that documents the traditional cultures of ethnic groups;
- Ethnic Canadiana Program – the National Library's collection of ethnic newspapers and other publications; and
- National Ethnic Archives – a unit of the National Archives.

Other agencies involved in activities related to multiculturalism are the National Film Board, the Canadian Broadcasting Corporation, the Canadian Radio and Television Commission, and the Canada Council.

In short, the programs in existence in the decades before the multiculturalism policy tended to focus on the integration of immigrants, although the other policy directions listed above were not entirely neglected. Following the policy announcement, the emphasis shifted to the first of the four areas, namely cultural expression, but attention was also given to the others.

RECENT EVOLUTION IN POLICY IMPLEMENTATION

Assistance to ethnic groups for the expression and development of their cultures was the main orientation for about a decade, together with assistance to new immigrants.[18] Recently, however, some changes in the implementation of the policy have been introduced under the impact of a variety of circumstances. Some have to do with the policy instruments adopted, some stem from the limits to governmental intervention in that field, and others pertain to the changing social context.

Although no systematic evidence exists on this question, over the years, a gap began to appear and progressively widen between the multiculturalism ideal and its concrete manifestations. The assistance to cultural groups "to continue to develop a capacity to grow and contribute to Canada" was increasingly perceived as assistance to ethnic folklore. Some began, less flatteringly, to refer to multiculturalism as a "song and dance" affair. The concrete expression of multiculturalism was, to a degree, trivializing the value it was meant to convey. Instead of enhancing the value of cultural diversity and its contribution to Canadian society, multiculturalism ran the risk of producing the opposite effect. To the extent that it was fostering the attitude that ethnocultures were not to be taken seriously, multiculturalism in its concrete form faced the danger of degrading ethnocultures, rather than celebrating them. The need for reorientation was beginning to be felt.

The critics of the policy became more numerous.[19] Some saw the device used by politicians to lure voters and by bureaucrats to maintain or increase their agencies' clientele. Others charged that the underlying intention of those in power with regard to multiculturalism was simply to keep "ethnics" within the confines of their communities, so they would not challenge the existing distribution of power. Finally, those who saw the policy as an attempt to maintain ethnic cultures argued that this was a futile exercise, since the structural conditions for the preservation of ethnocultures – such as parallel institutional systems – did not exist in Canada. They could perhaps exist in relatively isolated rural settings, but it was unrealistic to expect to establish them in cities. Multiculturalism was, therefore, a waste of money. Being ignored, however, is a worse fate than being criticized. Many Canadians of British and French origins (as well as others who had been "assimilated") felt displaced by the symbolic transformation and either resented multiculturalism or considered it a passing fad. Some opposed it openly; others ignored it.

This situation led many to wonder if the prevailing orientation of the policy implementation was having the desire effect. Even those highly favourable to the policy began to ask if the programs were not producing results opposite to those desired. The situation seemed to call for a rethinking of the objectives of the policy and/or of the ways in which it had been implemented.

In addition, there are limitations to be considered. First, as noted earlier, public sentiments are not favourable to the use of public funds for the promotion of ethnocultures. Second, members of ethnic groups do not want to be "locked in" by ethnic boundaries. On this question, what Greeley says about American ethnic differentiation also seems to apply to Canada

– namely, that its most striking aspect "is that by definition ethnic boundaries are *supposed* to be permeable ... Among white ethnic groups in the United States ethnicity has never been primarily a means of separation, much less isolation ... The hyphen denotes equality; it is not a way of withdrawing from the rest of society so much as an institution for dealing oneself into the society" (Greeley 1974: 302). This is an important constraint to activity in the ethnocultural field. In fact, in Canada, this constraint was an integral part of the objective of the policy of "multiculturalism within a bilingual framework":

The individual's freedom would be hampered if he were locked for life within a particular cultural compartment by the accident of birth or language. It is vital, therefore, that every Canadian, whatever his ethnic origin, be given a chance to learn at least one of the two languages in which his country conducts its official business and its politics. (House of Commons 1971: 8545)

Third, in the implementation of a policy, there is always the risk of favouring, or appearing to favour, some ethnic groups over others, and thus, triggering processes of intergroup comparison and rivalry. Finally, through the allocation of subsidies, the government agency and its officials are drawn into the internal politics of the ethnic community. This may entail favouring or appearing to favour some organizations over others (unless grants are given to all organizations). Perhaps more difficult for the managers of programs are the problems that can arise with the use of subsidies – specifically how to devise and administer an adequate system of controls. When receiving grants, ethnic organizations become instruments for the implementation of government policy. Therefore, what they do with the funds at their disposal is of concern to those who administer the policy. The process of verifying and accounting can be a source of tensions, not to mention the fact that the government agency may lose control over the way some of the funds are used.

These problems were exacerbated by the use of grants as the favoured policy instrument during that period. That is, rather than setting up its own structures and organizing its own activities, the government tended to rely heavily on programs mounted by a network of voluntary associations to which it handed out grants. Of course, this was a matter of relative importance, not of all versus none. Other policy instruments were also developed and used in the subsequent period.

The creation of a unit to administer a program provides a number of possibilities of action (in addition to its symbolic role of recognizing the importance of certain groups or activities for the society). However, it also imposes certain limitations. The very fact of being established with a certain mandate within a department or ministry restricts the range of actions that can be initiated without involving other departments. Convincing officials of other departments to initiate certain programs, to include multicultural concerns in their own programs, or to participate in joint programs is certainly an important problem of implementation. This difficulty stems partly from the fact that the Multiculturalism Directorate's field is largely defined in terms of a particular population (i.e., the "other" ethnic groups) rather than in functional terms (as are the fields of most other government departments). Thus, matters of relevance for its clientele often fall under the jurisdiction of other departments.

Finally, the social context has been changing. The context of the late 1970s and early 1980s is different in some significant ways from the one that saw the introduction of the concept and policy of multiculturalism.

Immigration has been somewhat lower in recent years. As immigration from Europe has declined, the proportion of Canadian-born members of ethnic groups of European origin has increased. With the passage of time, the proportion of second-generation members has been increasing in all ethnic groups. Second-generation individuals generally seek to distance themselves from the culture of origin, if not to reject it outright. This is part of their search for full integration in their society – that is, the one in which they were born. This demographic trend is likely to reduce the salience of ethnicity in social life.

In addition, the difficulties of the Canadian and international economies seem to have brought economic and class issues to the foreground, and pushed those related to ethnocultures and national identity to the rear. In this connection, the American presence is perceived not so much as a threat, as an essential element to economic recovery.

Finally, and perhaps most important for the matter under consideration, the independence movement in Quebec is beginning to lose momentum. Things are beginning to quiet down on that front, and some have gone so far as to suggest that nationalism is dying or dead in Quebec. This seems doubtful. What is more likely is that it is in transition, partly disorganized because its future orientation is somewhat uncertain. Be that as it may, it is now subdued compared to its earlier strength. Other groups are therefore less likely to perceive it as a threat to their own public status.

The effect of these contextual changes has been to progressively temper the processes that had operated in an earlier decade. The situation has reduced the salience of "white ethnicity" in public affairs, moderated the competition among cultural groups for public recognition, lowered the concern for national identity, and slowed down sociopolitical mobilization on an ethnic basis. Not that these processes have ceased to operate – rather, they have been moderated by the changing circumstances, just as they were accentuated earlier by other conditions. Moreover, the moderation is progressive – politicians and pressure groups may not be willing or able to

Table 14.3
Population by ethnic group, 1981*

EUROPEAN ORIGINS		ASIAN AND AFRICAN ORIGINS	
Austrian	0.7	Armenian	0.4
Balkans	2.3	African	0.8
Baltic	0.9	Asian Arab	1.1
Belgian	0.7	Chinese	5.1
Czeck and Slovak	1.2	Indo-Chinese	0.8
Dutch	7.2	Indo-Pakistani	3.5
Finnish	0.9	Japanese	0.7
Greek	2.7	Korean	0.4
German	20.2	Lebanese	0.5
Hungarian	2.1	Philippine	1.3
Italian	13.2	Other	0.2
Jewish	4.5		
Polish	4.5	LATIN AMERICAN ORIGINS	
Portuguese	3.3	Caribbean	1.5
Romanian	0.4	Haitian	0.3
Russian	0.9	Other	0.4
Scandinavian	5.0		
Spanish	0.9	OTHER ORIGINS	0.8
Ukrainian	9.4		
Other	0.4	TOTAL	5,642,380

* Because ethnic origin was ascertained differently in the 1981 than in earlier censuses (see note below
Table 14.1) and because of the increase in non-European origins, the distribution for 1981 is
presented separately. Those declaring multiple origins are not included in this table. This accounts
for the different number of "other" ethnic origins in Tables 14.1 and 14.3.
Source: Statistics Canada, Census of Canada, 1981.

abandon some of the items that had been on the public agenda for some
time (e.g., the referendum in Quebec; the patriation of the constitution).
On the other hand, the social context has been characterized by an
increase in the size of "visible minority" groups. As Table 14.3 shows, a
significant proportion of the Canadian population is of non-European
origin. This is the result of the modification of immigration regulations
during the 1960s. In the 1960s and 1970s, the main sources of immigration began to change significantly from European to non-European countries, as shown in Table 14.4. In the 1962–67 period, the United Kingdom,
United States, and European countries provided 80 percent of immigrants; over 1968–76, the percentage dropped to 56 (Canada 1963–77).
A further drop to 42 percent took place in the 1980–82 period (Canada
1983a: 19). Of course, not all immigrants from third world countries are
non-whites. But a significant proportion are, and this is reflected in the
changing composition of the non-British, non-French origin population,
as shown in Table 14.3.

Table 14.4
Ten leading source countries of immigrants to Canada, selected years, 1951–1982

1951	1960	1968	1973	1978	1982
Britain	Italy	Britain	Britain	Britain	Britain
Germany	Britain	United States	United States	United States	United States
Italy	United States	Italy	Hong Kong	India	Poland
Netherlands	Germany	Germany	Portugal	Hong Kong	India
Poland	Netherlands	Hong Kong	Jamaica	Philippines	Hong Kong
France	Portugal	France	India	Jamaica	Vietnam
United States	Greece	Austria	Philippines	Portugal	Philippines
Belgium	France	Greece	Greece	Italy	Germany
Yugoslavia	Poland	Portugal	Italy	Guyana	China
Denmark	Austria	Yugoslavia	Trinidad	France	Guyana

Sources: Canada, Department of Manpower and Immigration, *The Immigration Program* (Ottawa, Information Canada, 1974). p. 84; Department of Employment and Immigration, *1978 Immigration Statistics* (Ottawa: Minister of Supply and Services Canada, 1980); Department of Employment and Immigration, *Background Paper on Future Immigration Levels* (Ottawa: Minister of Supply and Services Canada, 1983).

This change increased the salience of ethnic differentiation on the basis of colour rather than culture and/or language. The shift was accentuated by an increase in incidents of interracial violence, which were highly publicized. Official reports on these incidents were prepared and published (Pitman 1977; Ontario Human Rights Commission 1977; Ubale 1978).[20] The main public issues pertaining to multiculturalism became those related to racism. The full acceptance of visible minorities by society and the participation of these groups in its institutions became major concerns in the ethnocultural field.

New programs, increased awareness of the constraints and limitations of government interventions, and the changing sociopolitical content all have contributed to changes in the emphasis and approach of multiculturalism policy. One such change is a greater emphasis on programs aimed at overcoming barriers to full participation in Canadian society. This shift was prompted by the increase in the visible minorities' population and in incidents of racial discrimination. The new emphasis has meant a greater preoccupation with race relations, as opposed to cultural expression and development. In 1982, a Race Relations Unit was created within the Multiculturalism Directorate, and symposia were held on "Race Relations and the Law" and "Race Relations in the Media." A Special Parliamentary Committee on Visible Minorities in Canadian Society was established in 1983 and submitted its report in 1984 (Canada 1984a).

The shift toward race relations as a significant policy direction of government multicultural activity made those charged with administering multiculturalism more aware of the instrumental dimension of the ethnocultural field – i.e., the removal of discrimination in employment, in relations with the police, and with regard to educational opportunities. The instrumental concern was also reflected in programs to provide immigrant women with language training and other assistance to help them participate in their new environment. For example, a conference on immigrant women was held in 1981.[21]

This does not mean that symbolic problems have disappeared. On the contrary, new ones have emerged, and indeed, a further redefinition of the symbolic character of public institutions has been required. Their character could no longer be primarily British or exclusively bicultural, and being multicultural was not sufficient either. It had to become multiracial. Being a white society is profoundly embedded in the Canadian collective identity, but the changing demographic composition of society and the political articulation of claims by visible minorities challenge the traditional collective self-image and the corresponding character of public institutions. This preoccupation underlies, for example, programs in the field of education in relation to the media. There was yet an additional set of intergroup relations to be managed. Changes to accommodate visible minorities are sometimes interpreted by other groups as decreasing their importance in the eyes of public authorities, and some feel resentment about being considered "invisible." The possibility that visible minorities and race relations may occupy a predominant place in the ethnocultural field is beginning to generate some degree of status anxiety. It is the source of possible tensions. In short, the integration of visible minorities requires accommodations at the symbolic and the instrumental level.

In the field of culture, the late 1970s and the 1980s saw increased attention given to multiculturalism in education at the federal, provincial, and local levels. The teaching of heritage languages became a more important objective. This is perhaps related to the larger size of the second generation within ethnic groups and the need felt by parents to transmit their cultural heritage. Since education is a provincial responsibility, the possibilities of action of federal agencies in this domain are limited. Their action has to be indirect, in the form of conferences (as was organized on heritage languages in 1981), or through funding of community groups and associations, such as the Canadian Council for Multicultural and Intercultural Education. The policy directions here are both cultural transmission and intergroup harmony.

Changes can be noted, not only in policy orientation, but also in the approaches adopted. For example, the target of governmental activity is changing. Instead of focusing almost exclusively on the ethnocultural communities, programs are increasingly oriented toward societal institutions. This move to institutional action was partly due to an increased awareness of its critical importance in relation to policy goals. For example, there is the realization that it is not sufficient to assist groups in fighting discrimination; action must also be aimed at the organizations in which discrimination occurs. The move also appears to be the result of a greater awareness of the pitfalls encountered when several different ethnocultural groups deal with organizations on an individual basis.

The institutional orientation involves both instrumental and symbolic aspects. One of the objectives is to deal with discriminatory or unfair treatment and its consequences. Another is to modify institutions in such a way that they better reflect the changing character of society and its population. In addition to this institutional action, assistance is given to ethnic organizations to fight discrimination and support cultural/symbolic activities.

Action directed at societal institutions has implications for the role of ethnic organizations as instruments of policy implementation. Such action appears to be encouraging interorganizational collaboration across ethnocultural groups. The reason is that joint action is perceived as more effective in bringing about institutional change, and may also serve to reduce intergroup competition and channel efforts toward the attainment of common goals. It is, however, a fairly recent initiative that may or may not be successful.

Finally, in order to overcome the restrictive effects of compartmentalization within a particular ministry, increased attempts are being made to involve other government departments, whenever their domain of activity is relevant for ethnocultural groups.

CONCLUSION

A few points should be underscored. First, the symbolic order is an essential dimension of social and political reality, especially as a component of public institutions. It is important to individuals and groups who aspire to recognize themselves in and be recognized by public institutions. It is also important for society, since it affects the legitimacy of public institutions and their capacity to act effectively.

Second, the relative importance of the symbolic/cultural and the instrumental/material components of reality can shift with changing circumstances over time. This means that sometimes public attention is focussed more on symbolic issues and sometimes more on material issues.

Third, like the economic or instrumental component of reality, the symbolic system can be the object of action by institutions, including the state.

Fourth, the condition of the symbolic system itself can also vary under the impact of changing circumstances. The meaningfulness of its content may differ for different segments of the population. What it signifies for members of society may be rich and satisfying, or poor and underdeveloped. Some of its features may be perceived by particular groups or by the entire society as deficient or inadequate, therefore requiring remedial action. Thus, aspects of the symbolic system become defined as problems requiring intervention. As a result, public authorities may have no choice but to act to modify the symbolic/cultural component of public institutions.

Fifth, interventions to modify the symbolic system, like interventions in economic or other areas, may alienate or antagonize certain segments of the population, generating or accentuating conflicts among different groups. Symbolic innovations entail incorporating new values, lifestyles, traditions, or symbols in the structure and functioning of public institutions. This process almost inevitably requires a reallocation of recognition among social groups. It involves a certain redefinition of the status that groups are to occupy in relation to public institutions. This reallocation is itself a source of tension and conflict which needs to be managed if the eventual result is not to be the opposite of what is desired.

Finally, once government or other public institutions have intervened, a new dynamic begins to operate. A policy field is created or redefined. The way it is structured and the content of the activities that characterize it are partly determined by the parameters of the policy. But to a significant degree, the structure and activities are also determined by the network of government agencies, community groups, and ethnic organizations that come to occupy the field. The evolution of the field in its symbolic as well as its instrumental component is dependent on the social and political forces operating in that interorganizational system. From the point of view of institutional authorities, the management of the symbolic order must now largely be carried out through that interorganizational system.

PART FOUR

Ethnicity and Change in Canada

CHAPTER FIFTEEN

Ethnicity and Change in Canada*[1]

Considerable change has taken place in the relations between ethnic groups in Canada, and between them and the institutions of the society, since the publication of *The Vertical Mosaic* three decades ago. The transformations, as will be seen, are partly a matter of degree, but they also are in some ways changes in the nature of the relationships. In this essay, the evolution of groups and of their societal relationships will be examined for these three major axes of ethnic differentiation in Canada: native peoples in relation to the larger society; English and French relations; and immigrants, their descendants, and the "mainstream" society. This latter section includes the relationship between whites and visible minorities.

In most instances, the process of change was set in motion by the non-dominant groups in the relationship. These groups changed in their demographic composition, in the level of education and socioeconomic achievement of their members, and in their self-conceptions, aspirations, and expectations. The economic and political context also changed, not only in Canada, but in the rest of the world. As a result, the feeling grew among members of ethnic minorities that changes in their relations with other groups and with societal institutions were not only desirable, but possible.

Some of the changes under way in the 1960s are extensively dealt with in *The Vertical Mosaic*. In his monumental study, John Porter devoted considerable attention to the participation of immigrants and ethnic minorities

---

* Abridged from "Ethnicity and Race in Social Organization: Recent Developments in Canadian Society," in *The Vertical Mosaic Revisited*, edited by R. Helmes-Hayes and J. Curtis (Toronto: University of Toronto Press, 1998), 60–115.

in the socioeconomic structure and to the question of ethnic stratification. In fact, this is largely what the title of the book refers to; it is a condensed symbolic expression of his argument. Porter saw the economic and political power structure as dominated primarily by the British charter group, the prevailing theories of race of the time being used to justify this dominance (Porter 1965: 61–8). Other groups were located in lower strata. When economic expansion began after the Second World War, Canada's skilled labour force was inadequate: "the necessity in the 1950s of importing skills from abroad to meet the labour force increment in skilled occupations suggests that Canadian institutions – particularly educational and industrial – were not geared to provide mobility opportunities." While in the United States, the low skill levels of most immigrants "pushed up the existing population to higher educational levels," in Canada, this process was less prevalent because immigration was designed to obtain "skilled and professional workers as an alternative to educational reforms" (ibid: 49). Highly skilled immigrants came primarily from Great Britain and the United States. Others came primarily from Southern and Eastern Europe. The entrance status of these two categories of immigrants was an important factor in the formation and maintenance of a vertical mosaic.

With time, however, those who had entered at the lower echelons of the occupational hierarchy progressively improved their situation, and especially that of their children, leaving the lower positions to new waves of immigrants. This mobility, however, was predicated on "Anglo-conformity," that is, to conformity to the rules of the game established by the charter group and to its values and way of life. This required relinquishing one's ethnic identity, at least in the public domain. Porter saw ethnicity as a problem because it was an obstacle to mobility.[2] He would no doubt have argued that this is even more so when groups are racially different from the charter group.

The other lines of ethnic differentiation were barely touched upon or were dealt with much less extensively by Porter. For instance, his book does not deal with the changes that were beginning to be felt in the relationship of native peoples with the rest of Canadian society. This may have been because, at the time, the momentum for change was just beginning. But it may also have been because sociologists, as other Canadians, saw native peoples as marginal to the mainstream social and political structure. Studies of social inequality, for instance, did not at the time pay much attention to the place of native peoples in the class structure. This was deemed to be the domain of anthropologists.

The relationship between English- and French-speaking Canadians was also beginning to change. One of the manifestations of this change was the resurgence of nationalistic sentiments in Quebec, especially the emergence of a separatist movement at the end of the 1950s. Others were the establishment of the Royal Commission on Bilingualism and Biculturalism in 1963 and the various expressions of grievances and expectations that were part of the Quiet Revolution in Quebec.

These transformations, however, were a secondary component of Porter's analysis of ethnicity and interethnic relations in Canada. While *The Vertical Mosaic* did not address the question of ethnic separatism and its underpinnings, Porter did think that there was some validity to the notion of cultural particularism in the case of Quebec, and he felt that "as Quebec becomes more industrialized it will become culturally more like other industrialized societies," an evolution that would seem to have suggested to him that there was no need for a special accommodation within Canadian federalism, because with time, Quebec's similarities with the other provinces would be far more important than the differences (Porter 1965: 383). This has, in fact, been the nature of socioeconomic change in Quebec. However, the evolution of nationalism and of the independentist movement strongly supports those who criticize social scientists for giving too much importance to economic factors in the shaping of intergroup attitudes and relationships (Connor 1972).

Porter did not deal either with the question of language, and its impact on ethnic stratification and mobility, and on the control of economic institutions in Quebec. This, however, is somewhat understandable, as language was not yet an issue of public policy. It became so in the late 1960s, with the recommendations of the royal commission and with the legislation introduced by the Quebec government in 1968 (Bill-85 concerning the language of education). Porter did, however, address the unfavourable socioeconomic situation of French Canadians (to be considered in a subsequent section).

In concluding this overview of Porter's approach,[3] it is worth mentioning that, generally, his "analyses had little to offer on *relations* among ethnic groups. For the most part he concentrated on the *distributive* aspect of ethnicity, on the question of how people in different ethnic categories were distributed in the system of power and stratification" (Vallee 1981: 640).

NATIVE PEOPLES AND THE LARGER SOCIETY

A little before the publication of *The Vertical Mosaic,* a major reversal had begun in the sociopolitical organization of native peoples, and in their relationship with the larger society and governments. There had been, of course, developments before the 1960s. Political confrontations between whites and Métis occurred in the late 1800s, ending with the rebellion of 1885. Aboriginal political movements sparked by land issues began in British Columbia at the beginning of the 20th century. Indians in other regions eventually joined the movement. The League of Indians of Canada was formed in the interwar years. In the 1930s and 1940s, other organizations were established in British Columbia, Alberta, and Saskatchewan (Miller 1989: 214–19). This organizational expansion was triggered, in part, by the emergence of new issues – agriculture and schooling were added to land claims – and in part, by the Native participation in the First World War and "their understandable tendency afterwards to claim a right to be heard" (Miller 1989: 217).

But in spite of these efforts, the structure and culture of dominance was not seriously challenged. Native communities remained dependencies administered by external agencies under the restrictive Indian Act. The idea that this could be modified in any significant way entered the public agenda only after the Second World War and gained ground at a very slow pace.

The war itself had an impact in launching this process. Indeed, the attitudes of white Canadians were shaken by the systematic racism and atrocities of the war. These events forced Canadians to begin to face the racism embedded in their own institutions, legal practices, and social mores. The Hawthorn Report published in the mid-1960s was one manifestation of this new concern with the conditions of the country's Aboriginal population (Hawthorn 1966–7). By documenting these conditions in a systematic way, the report had the effect of increasing the willingness to accept significant changes. Also, it introduced the notion of "citizens plus" for native peoples, whereby, because of their Aboriginal title and treaty rights, Indians possess certain rights as charter members of the Canadian community, in addition to their normal rights and duties as citizens (Hawthorn 1966–7: 13). This constituted a call for a drastically new relationship between them and the larger society.

The war also had an impact on native peoples themselves. Having contributed to the first war effort, their aspirations were further increased by their participation in the second. Re-establishing control over their own community life and institutions became a significant component of their political agenda (Miller 1989; Ponting and Gibbins 1980). The economic growth and the related exploration for raw materials and energy that followed the war gave a new significance and urgency to the question of land claims. The civil rights movement in the United States also had an impact: Red Power was the slogan that corresponded to Black Power in that country. Another significant element "was the fact that in the later 1960s Indian groups up to and including the National Indian Council were beginning to receive better funding, and, with their better organization and funding ... found themselves able to present their views in a series of cogent, effective arguments" (Miller 1989: 225).

Finally, the 1969 White Paper (Canada, Department of Indian Affairs and Northern Development 1969) generated a sort of crisis, because it put on the public agenda the very fundamental question of the social and political philosophy that was to guide public policies of social and institutional change. One of the basic ideas of the White Paper was that the appalling conditions in which native peoples found themselves were the result of the legal status that kept them apart from the larger society. Thus, it was necessary to dismantle the legal and bureaucratic arrangements that had decimated their traditional social and political organization, kept them in a situation of dependency, and prevented their social, economic, and political development. The remedy envisioned by the White Paper was the elimination of the separate status and the integration of native peoples in the larger social and economic structure. It was *not* to replace the distant, white-controlled bureaucracy by self-administered native organizations and agencies.

The reaction to the White Paper was such as to force the government to withdraw it and to begin, very reluctantly, to explore other avenues of change. As a result, a new process was set in motion, one in which native peoples were very much in the driver's seat, at least in terms of defining the political agenda, if not in terms of actual changes.

Dimensions of Sociopolitical Change

Change is sought and is taking place along six major dimensions. These involve issues pertaining to collective identity, to the social and normative infrastructure of community organization and its territorial and economic basis, and to the social and political participation of women. Such changes require a redistribution of institutional control which, in turn, implies that Aboriginal peoples be recognized as legitimate political actors by the larger society and its institutions, and in the case of women, within the Aboriginal power structure as well. Finally, they require transformations of the institutions of the larger society.

The ultimate objective of these changes is the improvement of the economic and social condition of native peoples – a condition that is among the worst of any groups in Canada. This is so with regard to income, occupational status, labour force participation, educational attainment, and the various manifestations of a poor economic situation, including shorter life expectancies (Siggner 1986; Frideres 1993).

1 *Social Identity:* The construction of a new social identity was essential if Native communities were to be internally transformed and the traditional relationship with the larger society reversed. Indeed, the Indian social identity had definite connotations of inferiority, backwardness, dependency, and irrelevance. "Native peoples" and especially "First Nations" affirm a positive status in relation to the larger polity. The discourse surrounding this identity includes concepts of "citizen plus" mentioned earlier and of inherent rights of self-government within Canada.

Another evolution is the progressive formation of a pan-Aboriginal collective identity, that is, an overarching identity that de-emphasized internal differences and emphasized commonalities.

2 *Institutional Control and the Rebuilding of Community Structures:* Being in a situation of externally administered dependency has weakened considerably the traditional social, economic, and political organization of Aboriginal communities (Frideres 1993). Rebuilding social and organizational structures to cope with the needs and aspirations of their members has been an important component of change.

The drive to rebuild community infrastructures required the control of an increasing range of their institutions. Thus, pressure has built up to end administrative dependency and replace it with administrative autonomy and self-government. In the 1970s, the transfer of the administration from the federal government to native organizations began. Core funding was provided to native organizations. Self-government became a serious issue in the relationship between native peoples and governments.

In recent decades, there have also been a number of developments in building organizations based on insights and the social logic specific to Aboriginal cultures. These have taken place in the fields of political decision-making, education, economic development, the administration of justice, and the rehabilitation of delinquents and criminals, alcoholics and sexual abusers.

Some prominent illustrations are provided by the three Aboriginal communities that have recently won awards for "demonstrating an outstanding collective approach to environmental issues and the social development of their inhabitants" (Valpy 1995). Their success was not due to external support, but rather to the organizational resources and activities of the communities themselves.[4]

3 *Establishing a Territorial and Economic Basis:* Land claims have been one of the main fronts of action in this regard. Control over territory and access to part of the rents from the exploitation of resources are critical to community formation and maintenance. Control of land and of the capital that can be generated from it are essential for the economic development of any community or society. The alternative is integration into the enterprises and the social structure of the community that controls the land and the rents drawn from it.

The question of land control is the fundamental issue raised by the White Paper, and it continues to be part of the public debate, regarding whether native peoples should acquire the means necessary for the building of enterprises and other institutions, or integrate as individuals into the white-controlled institutional system. That is, there are two types of integration involved: corporate and individual. In the first case, the idea is that the Aboriginal communities and organizations are integrated in the larger inter-organizational system (in a way analogous to the way in which municipalities, provinces, and national institutions are part of an integrated whole). In the second, it is individuals and their families that are integrated into the socioeconomic and political structure.

Land has been an issue ever since Europeans came to settle on this continent. At first, because of their skills and environmental knowledge, the Aboriginal population was progressively incorporated into a commercial system shaped by the interests of European trading companies. Defence and culture (i.e., "civilizing" and Christianizing) also shaped the relationship. With time, the settlement ambitions of Europeans led to a growing interest in land and thus, to the displacement and control of the Aboriginal population. To a large extent, the history of Aboriginal-white relationships involves the transfer of land from native to non-native control. Whenever land is needed by the white population – whether for settlement, natural resources, fishing (commercial or recreational), or golf courses – the transfer process from native to non-native ownership and/ or control is set in motion (Valentine 1980).

Recent decades have been characterized by an attempt on the part of native peoples to change this process, so that the transfer becomes an equitable exchange. As a result, native communities have been in regular conflicts with governments, business and industrial corporations, and white communities, who likewise depend on land and the exploitation of natural resources for their vitality and well-being.

4 *Improving the Condition of Aboriginal Women:* The socioeconomic and political situation of Aboriginal women was even worse than that of Aboriginal men: "Indian women come close to matching their male counterparts in educational attainment – only to fall lowest with respect to labour force involvement and income ... In addition ... Indian women who are young suffer especially low labour force participation and high unemployment ... Native females suffer multiple jeopardy on the basis of a number of objective indicators of social and economic well-being" (Gerber 1990: 80).

Significant remedies to these conditions will come about primarily if women organize themselves to deal with them. The general political mobilization of the 1960s and 1970s, especially the women's movement, had a major impact on Aboriginal women. These consciousness-raising movements made Aboriginal women increasingly aware that they could do something to improve their condition, and that improvements would not be the initiative of men, including Aboriginal men.

They were also prompted to organize as a political force in their own right. By the mid-1970s, Native Women's Associations had been formed in virtually all the provinces and territories, as well as at the national level, the first one having been established in 1969 in British Columbia. These regional and national associations included both status and non-status Indians, in contrast to the main male-dominated organizations that were based on legal criteria.

Two national organizations were established, the Native Women's Association of Canada and the National Committee on Indian Rights for Indian Women. The first is primarily a grassroots organization concerned with issues, such as "women's employment opportunities, economic development of Aboriginal communities, alcohol and drug abuse, and child welfare ...; that is, with general community development and in particular, with those aspects of community life that affect women most directly" (Krosenbrink-Gelissen 1993: 344). The objective is also to promote the assumption by women of active roles within their communities. The second is externally oriented: it seeks to combat the sex-discriminatory status regulations in the Indian Act.

5 *Being Recognized as Legitimate Political Actors:* Native peoples assumed that by identifying such goals and working towards them through their organizations and leaders, they would come to be accepted as rightful participants in the policy-making process itself, that is, in the exercise of power. No longer would white governments and corporations devise policies and programmes for them. They wanted more than simply being peripheral pressure groups to whom those in power respond once in a while. They wanted to be full-fledged participants in the polity. To achieve this, for example, to be represented at constitutional conferences, they applied pressure of various kinds: demonstrations, social disruption (e.g., roadblocks), violence, and appeals to the international community.

This last-mentioned tactic has been a critical strategy pursued by native groups. Relationships between Canadian Indians and foreign governments and organizations are not a new phenomenon, but such relations have expanded considerably in the past few decades. This "internationalization" of their affairs has taken many forms. Ponting (1990: 2–4) identified a number of them: (a) the emergence of the concept of "The Fourth World" and the associated reaching out on the part of Canadian Aboriginal people to indigenous groups around the world in similar situations; (b) the cultivation of UN bodies as allies, and their involvement as monitors and lobbyists; (c) appeals to the Queen, and to the British Parliament and court; (d) participation in international fact-finding missions and research projects; and finally, (e) drawing international figures to Canada to observe Indian conditions firsthand and to obtain their moral support (e.g., the Pope).

In the case of Aboriginal women, there is a "double jeopardy" with regard to the political process – just as there is with regard to their socio-economic situation. Indeed, the issue for them is to be recognized as rightful participants in the policy-making process itself, not only by white institutional leaders, but also by male Aboriginal leaders. "Male-dominated national Aboriginal organizations – the National Indian Brotherhood and the Native Council of Canada – appeared not to be concerned with Aboriginal women's views ... and to make it difficult for women to attain leadership in these organizations" (Krosenbrink-Gelissen 1993: 343, 347). For example, an effort by Aboriginal women to change the sex-discriminatory provisions of the Indian Act did not get the wholehearted support of the male-dominated organizations. Thus, in their political fight for changes, native women had to lobby the National Indian Brotherhood and the Native Council of Canada, as well as the federal government.

6 *The Transformation of the Institutions of the Larger Society:* As already noted, native peoples are pulled in two directions at the same time: towards as much participation as possible in distinct, autonomous communities, on the one hand, and towards integration in the larger social structure, on the other. The pull is not the same for all individuals. Some are in situations that limit and even make virtually impossible extensive participation in an indigenous community, while others experience conditions that facilitate such an involvement. For the former, the issue becomes the responsiveness of the institutions of the larger society to their specific needs and cultural distinctiveness, whether these be businesses and industries, labour unions, schools, hospitals, welfare agencies, and so on. For the latter, the issues pertain to the social, economic, and political conditions of community development.

ENGLISH-FRENCH RELATIONS

The dynamics of English-French relations have changed over the past few decades. There has been an evolution in three main areas. First, there has been a movement on the part of francophones from social and institutional isolation to economic and social participation, and to the acquisition of power. Second, the politics of identity and recognition has acquired considerable importance in shaping the relationship between the two collectivities. Third, there has been a change in the dynamics of identification with and attachment to the larger Canadian entity.

From Social and Institutional Isolation to Economic
and Social Participation to the Acquisition of Power

The control of institutions has always been at the centre of the conflicts and accommodations between English- and French-speaking Canadians. Canada is a society segmented into two parallel, linguistically-different institutional systems. To a large extent, the material well-being of English- and French-speaking Canadians depends on the opportunities and services provided by their linguistic sub-societies. Their individual identities tend to be constructed in relation to the cultural features of their respective institutions and nourished by their symbolic activities. Their self-esteem is determined by the societal statues of the linguistic group with which they identify.

Both English- and French-speaking Canadians have established and controlled, and continue to establish and control, separate systems of institutions, each with a distinctive character. Both want their organizational domains to expand so as to provide more opportunities, as the size and aspirations of their populations grow. Both want institutions that embody their culture and religion, and operate in their language. The history of English-French relations in Canada has been, and continues to be, characterized by recurrent power struggles for the control of the means required for society building in its economic, cultural, and linguistic dimensions (Breton 1978; 1988a; Horowitz 1985: Chapter 1).

Accordingly, intergroup clashes have taken place and continue to occur. Initially, these were political, but they took place primarily over the control of the institutional means to maintain language, religion, and cultural practices. The conflicts entailed clashes between divergent ideas, sociopolitical philosophies, and values with regard to the organization of society and different interpretations of history.

1 *The Pressure for Integration in Common Institutions:* For an extensive period, English and French were segregated in the economic sphere. With the expansion of Anglo-Canadian and American enterprises in Quebec, however, the French became progressively part of an economic system constructed by Anglophones, who occupied a position of dominance in it. The federal governmental system was also largely under the control of anglophones (as were the Quebec government and the city of Montreal for a considerable period of time).

Studies carried out by the Royal Commission on Bilingualism and Biculturalism in the 1960s showed that francophones were not only disadvantaged in the economic sphere, but they were also largely absent from the higher levels of decision-making in the federal bureaucracy (Beattie 1975). (The first separatist organization, Le Rassemblement pour l'Indépendance Nationale, was established in the late 1950s by a disgruntled federal civil servant.)

Several reasons for the economically disadvantaged position of French Canadians have been offered by Porter and other authors. First, and perhaps the most frequently mentioned, is the clergy-controlled educational system, which was not "geared to the provision of industrial skills at the managerial or technical level" (Porter 1965: 91–2). Related to this is the "rigidity of French-Canadian class structure, and the authoritarian character of French-Canadian institutions" (ibid: 91). Clark, however, pointed out that Porter may have exaggerated the difference between English- and

French-speaking Canada in this regard: "Members of the British Charter group were admittedly very much on top ... [But] in truth, the rural and working class masses of French Canada were caught up in a social system denying them opportunities for advancement not essentially different from the social system in which the rural and working masses of English-speaking Canada were caught up" (Clark 1975b: 28).

Second, the domination by the British charter group placed restrictions on the mobility of French-Canadians, partly through the imposition of English as the language of work (Porter 1965: 92).

Third, the competition of the large Canadian and American firms reduced the size of the francophone-controlled industries. Contrary to the commonly accepted view, francophones in Quebec were, at the outset, active participants in the process of industrialization. For instance, there were 23,000 small and medium-size manufacturing enterprises in Quebec in 1890, but their number had fallen to 6,948 by 1929 (Bovey 1936). An important reason was that they were too small to withstand the competition by larger Canadian and American firms that benefited from large capital investments.

Porter noted that the disadvantage did not exist in other spheres: "French-Canadian political leaders have ruled Quebec, and, by entering into a series of coalitions with British political leaders within Confederation, have been able to exert a very powerful influence on federal government policy" (Porter 1965: 92). "This seeming contradiction between being a large deprived minority within Canada and having representatives in the structure of power can be explained in terms of the class structure of French Canada which until recently had been pre-modern ..." (Porter 1975: 269). Although the cultural characteristics of the educational system were no doubt a factor, the structure of control of industry and of the governmental bureaucracy must occupy a central place in explaining the pattern of ethnic stratification.

2 *Building and Expanding Institutional Domains:* The Quiet Revolution had economic, as well as political and cultural manifestations. The idea that Quebec had to build and expand its own power base beyond the sociocultural and religious spheres began to be felt and articulated politically. The revolution of rising expectations also included a desire to conquer or reconquer certain institutional spaces, a process that generated confrontations with those who already were in control: the traditional French-Canadian elites, the clergy, and the groups represented by the Duplessis regime; the English-speaking groups dominating the Quebec economy; and the politico-bureaucratic groups controlling the federal government (Pelletier 1990).

The agenda of this category of contending groups was to gain control of the means necessary for organization building, particularly political power and capital, and to displace, partly or completely, those who had traditionally controlled them. This is expressed in the agendas cast in terms of province building, "Quebec Inc.," provincial autonomy, sovereignty, or independence. In the 1960s began a process of acquiring increasing control of business and industry. Enterprises under the control of francophones increased from 47.1 to 61.6 percent between 1961 and 1987. The increase, however, was larger in certain sectors than in others: from 6.5 to 35.0 in mining, from 33.4 (in 1978) to 92.3 in forestry, from 25.8 to 58.2 in finance, from 50.7 to 75.5 in construction, from 21.7 to 39.3 in manufacturing, and from 51.8 to 67.2 in public administration (Vaillancourt 1993: 412). The state took an active role in economic development through the creation and expansion of state enterprises, the most prominent and economically important being Hydro-Québec, and through policies and programs aimed at reinforcing francophone-owned enterprises (Bernier 1993).

Thus, for a segment of the Quebec elite and population, integration in institutions controlled by anglophones is either not sufficient or irrelevant. For many of them, Canadian institutions are necessarily controlled by Anglophones, since they constitute a majority of the population – and a growing majority at that. What is sought is an increasing control of the means of economic production and of the centres of political power within (francophone) Quebec. The issue is institution building and control. This is clearly the objective of sovereignty, whether in its pure form as "sovereignty-association" or some other. This orientation and process could be referred to as *entrepreneurial* nationalism. It is entrepreneurial in the sense of taking advantage of opportunities for institution building and control, and for gaining sovereignty. But it is also *strategic* in the sense that entrepreneurial ambitions are partly pursued through the mobilization of primordial ethnic attachments (that were prominent in survival nationalism) and of past or present grievances (that characterize protest nationalism). It is the strategic use of ethnicity, with its cultural and experiential baggage, in the achievement of economic and, especially, political goals.

In short, there has been, over the years, a progressive shift from a survival to a protest, to an entrepreneurial and strategic nationalism. It is not that there are no longer any concerns about cultural survival or that there are no more grievances, but rather that institution building and control (a "projet de société") are now the central themes of nationalism.

3 *Recent Changes: From Accommodation to Confrontation:* During the 1960s and 1970s, elites throughout the country and a significant segment of the population seemed to agree that francophones in general, and Québécois in particular, had *legitimate grievances* that needed to be rectified. There was considerable disagreement and debate as to what should be done, but a fairly widespread consensus that something ought to be done.

In recent years, the prevailing perception is that, by and large, grievances have been dealt with by shifts of some powers from Ottawa to Quebec City, through language legislation adopted by different levels of government, by economic development policies and programs, by the promotion of bilingualism in the federal civil service, and by the increasing control over sources of capital for institution building within Quebec. In this context, further claims made by Quebec are seen as attempts to grab more and more power, to the detriment of the rest of the country, rather than to deal with inequities.

Much of the response in the rest of Canada is cast in a power framework: no more concessions to Quebec – anything Quebec gets must also be granted to the other provinces. The principles of the equality of the provinces must be maintained. The self-interpretation of Quebec as a "distinct society" is seen by those outside of Quebec as a claim for special status and thus, for more power in the federation. There is also a significant status dimension to this response: it is felt that, even without more constitutionally entrenched power, the recognition of Quebec as a distinct society (or a founding people) would represent a failure to recognize the distinctiveness of other regions and their contribution to the construction of the country.

This is felt also among some ethnic minorities who seek to have their historical participation in the formation and evolution of Canadian society recognized. Some claim that they are also, like the Québécois, "founding peoples;" they also played a critical role in the settlement of a particular region and in its institutional development (Breton 1984: 136).[5]

Attitudes have changed in Quebec, as well. Claims are less and less made on the basis of injustices or violation of rights, but rather in terms of being distinct and not like the other provinces, especially not like the small provinces; in terms of the potential for economic development and organizational efficiency; and in terms of the legitimate aspiration of nations to self-determination. Also, as indicated above, status and recognition are quite central to the dynamics of the relationship between Quebec and the rest of Canada. Even the threat to the language and culture brought about by the fact of being "drowned in a sea of anglophones" has become less prominent in the political discourse surrounding sovereignty or independence, although it is not absent from the debate. Rather, the central elements in that discourse have to do with the failed attempts to modify the constitution in order to enhance Quebec's power to manage its own affairs and to accord it the status it deserves in the country.

Underlying these different positions are two different conceptions of Canada that could be called, respectively, "segmentalist" and "pan-Canadian." The segmentalist approach advocates strengthening the sociopolitical boundaries between the two linguistic communities. It is based on the premise that Quebec is the homeland of the French in North America, that francophone resources and energies should be oriented towards the development of that society. It sees as unrealistic any expectation that the French language and culture can survive and develop elsewhere in Canada in present-day circumstances (except, perhaps, for one or two exceptions such as New Brunswick). Political power is to be built in Quebec through the accumulation of economic, political, and sociocultural resources. Territorial bilingualism (i.e., unilingualism in each territory) is favoured.

The pan-Canadian approach, by contrast, promotes the view that both the francophone and anglophone communities exist in all regions of the country. Thus, it is important that in all regions, whenever numbers warrant it, services be provided for the education of children in the language and culture of the family; that other cultural facilities, such as radio and television stations, be available; and that individuals be able to use, in their own language, the services of at least the federal government – but preferably those of the other levels of government, as well. Institutional bilingualism is what is advocated.

The structural component of this ideological cleavage is that the proponents of each view see their advantages (either economic, political, or cultural-symbolic) as being rooted primarily in the Quebec or in the Canadian institutional system. Most French Quebecers want changes, but different groups favour different programs of change.

4 *The Evolution of Support for Sovereignty:* The consensus among Quebec's elite with regard to the desirability of sovereignty seems to be increasing. There are, however, variations in the extent to which association with the rest of Canada should or should not be part of the sovereignty project. Support for sovereignty is widespread in the political, bureaucratic, and labour elites, as well as in the intelligentsia (e.g., media people, artists, teachers, professors). In the 1980 referendum, 67 percent of intellectuals, 61 percent of other semi-professionals and technicians, and 56 percent of those in liberal professions voted "Yes," in contrast to 38 percent of managers and proprietors, 39 percent of farmers, and 45 percent of workers. The federalist vote, or rather neo-federalist, since the intention was "to set in motion negotiations for a renewed federalism," was more likely to come from managers and proprietors (36 percent were neo-federalists and only 10 percent status quo No's) (Pinard and Hamilton 1984: 22–30). Since then, it seems that support for sovereignty has increased among business-industrial elites, especially those in small and mid-size enterprises.

Popular support for independence[6] has also increased. In the early 1960s, it was 8 percent. It had increased over 40 percent in the early 1990s (with the exception of the two polls in November and December 1990), which showed support at 56 percent. Sovereignty-association was always more favoured (the question began to be asked in the 1970s). In 1970 the support was at 32 percent, and it climbed to between 53 and 61 percent in the early 1990s (65 percent in the November and December polls of 1990) (Pinard 1992).

The terminology used in public opinion surveys has a significant influence on the results. Pinard's analysis of a number of surveys carried out since 1989 revealed that the term "sovereignty" yields the greatest number of positive responses, and "separation" the smallest, with "independence" in-between. On the average, the difference between sovereignty and separation is +11 percentage points (Pinard 1994).

5 *Fragmentation and Competition in the Francophone Collectivity:* A fragmentation occurred among francophones in different parts of the country. Francophones outside Quebec began to think of their communities, not as extensions of Quebec, but as distinct sociopolitical entities. To a certain extent, they also began to see themselves as facing regionally-specific circumstances. In the process, regional identities became more salient (e.g., Acadian, Franco-Ontarian, Franco-Manitoban) and superseded the self-conception as "French Canadian," at least in the younger generations (Juteau-Lee and Lapointe 1982).

This was the result of several phenomena. First, the Quebec-centredness of the independentist movement had much to do with the fragmentation. This was symbolically reflected in the very name of the association that represented "Francophones *outside* Quebec," a denotation that is striking by its negative form (it was changed a few years ago). Second, several of the institutions seen as critical by francophone communities (education, culture, welfare, and municipal administration) are under provincial jurisdictions. The massive expansion of activity in those areas that began in the 1960s, oriented the attention and the action of community groups and leaders towards provincial governments. Finally, the changing attitudes in some segments of English Canada, language policies, and government programs for official language minorities contributed to a new sense of power among francophone minorities, and to the emergence of new elites determined to increase the organizational capacity of francophone communities outside Quebec.

Thus, demands for change were also articulated in provincial arenas. Gains were made. There were, however, considerable variations among the provinces, as governments faced varying degrees of political difficulty in giving increased recognition and institutional services to francophones. Institutional recognition and services are legitmated in reference to the larger pan-Canadian context, but not without meeting much resistance. In all provinces except Quebec and New Brunswick, francophones constitute a small percentage of the total population (frequently smaller than that of other ethnic groups), many of whose members do not see why the French should receive special treatment.

Status Anxieties and the Politics of Recognition

Another dimension of recent changes has been a shift from a concern with cultural survival to a preoccupation with recognition and status. This is a question of emphasis, not an all-or-none matter. It is the quest for respect and endorsement that, almost automatically, accompanies the pursuit of institutional control.

Recognition and a sense of group worth are important for members of a collectivity because self-esteem is, in good measure, a function of the esteem accorded to one's collectivity – the more so if membership in that collectivity is central to one's personal identity (Horowitz 1985: 143). This would be the case, for instance, in "institutionally complete" groups[7] such as Quebec francophones. There is a yearning for a favourable evaluation of the social, cultural, and moral worth of one's group. It is to be expected, then, that people will have an interest in the status bestowed upon their group, its culture and language, by the public institutions of the larger society and by those that they regard as their "significant others" (Mead 1934).

This yearning generates processes of social comparison. Members of groups, minority groups in particular, pay regular attention to how well "we" are doing compared with "them;" how well the system is favouring "them" as opposed to "us." Federal policies, programs, and expenditures in Quebec are compared with those in the rest of the country. The media frequently compare the situation with regard to indicators of economic well-being, social policy, educational achievement, and arts and culture in Quebec, with what is happening in Ontario or in the rest of Canada.

The salience of social evaluations and recognition by others is accentuated by factors, such as intervention by the central state in various domains of activity, integration in larger Canadian and continental economic systems, and intergroup communication through the media. Indeed, all increase the opportunities for intergroup comparisons in terms of economic well-being, political power, and social status (which are, of course, interconnected).

One of the important manifestations of this concern for status is the claim in recent years for recognition as a distinct society, and for sovereignty or sovereignty-association. It also underlies the refusal to be given the same status as other ethnic minorities, and for Quebec to be treated like any other province. Correspondingly, many members of other ethnic minorities and of other provinces consider the recognition of distinctiveness as establishing an inequality in status or a "pecking order" (Kallen 1988) and, accordingly, reject the claim.

But many Quebec francophones experience more than the sense of a simple refusal. There is the perception of a withdrawal of a historically-based status in the federation, namely, that of a "founding people." This is important if one considers that losing something is probably more painful than the failure to acquire it. Similarly, the independentist aspiration is partly motivated by the wish to be recognized by the international community, something that would force the rest of Canada to deal with Quebec, at least formally, on an equal basis.

The concern for status is also manifest in the theme of "humiliation" that comes up regularly in the current political discourse. It was prominent during recent dealings with the question of the Constitution. The vocabulary denouncing the opposition to recent attempts at constitutional change included terms such as "humiliation," "rejection," "isolation," and "being put in one's place." In addition, many of the economic arguments against independence are cast in a framework that exacerbates the status anxieties of many Quebeckers. The idea is to show that remaining in Canada is economically advantageous; but the underlying, and frequently the explicit message is, "Look, you can't make it on your own; you need the rest of Canada." Such a campaign perhaps has – for the status-sensitive segment of the population – an effect *opposite* to the one intended.

Thus, while in English-speaking Canada, as noted above, the constitutional claims of Quebec are perceived as a quest for more power, in French-speaking Quebec, they have as much to do with recognition and status as with power (although these two elements may not be given the same weight by institutional elites and by average citizens). The questioning of and opposition to constitutional change on the part of English-Canadians is perceived as a refusal to recognize Quebec's distinctiveness in terms of culture and institutions.

The Dynamics of Identification and Attachment

Two issues have become salient with the rise and growth of the independentist movement: the nature of the identification with or attachment to Canada and to Quebec, and the possibility of the coexistence of partly different identifications and attachments. What is the basis of identification and attachment to a society? Is it based on economic advantages? On a sense of interdependence and therefore of mutual obligations? On commonalities, such as common descent, historical experience, or cultural traits? Or on a shared sociopolitical philosophy to guide the construction and evolution of the society?

In 1991, an Angus Reid national survey asked respondents about their attachment to Canada. Twenty-two percent of French-origin Quebeckers said they have "a deep emotional attachment to Canada, that they love the country and what it stands for." In contrast, 37 percent said they were attached to Canada, but only as long as it provides a good standard of living. Another 38 percent said they were not attached to Canada and would prefer to see the country split up into two or more smaller countries, or joined to the United States. The corresponding percentages are 64, 24, and 10 in the rest of the sample (non-French origin respondents in Quebec, and all respondents in the rest of Canada).

Why is the attachment of Quebeckers to Canada primarily utilitarian, if it exists at all? More generally, what are the sources of identification to a collectivity in a society that is culturally heterogeneous, that is, where commonalities of descent and culture do not exist? Three can be identified. First, the collectivity provides the conditions and opportunities for the realization of *individual* aspirations and goals. Second, the collectivity provides the conditions and opportunities for the realization of *collective* goals, specifically, organizational, cultural, and status goals. And third, people invest themselves and their resources, and as a result, sense that they are contributing to the construction of the society, to the creation and maintenance of its institutions, its social and material infrastructure, its networks of communication, and to the realization of collective projects (political, social, economic, or technological).

In recent decades, at least, it seems that the public discourse has been appealing primarily to utilitarian motives or to a sense of interdependence (or, as indicated earlier, to a sense of dependence). Is this because there is no other source of identification with Canada to which one can appeal in the case of the Québécois? Or is it the dominant values of our market-oriented culture that make it difficult to perceive any other human motivation except utilitarian? Or both?

Does the public discourse in Canada include references to the contribution of each region to the well-being and development of the society as a whole? Or does it tend to emphasize how each region is being disadvantaged by being part of the federation? (Public opinion polls suggest that a substantial proportion of the population in *each* region of the country feels that their region or province is getting a bad deal.)

Is there a historical role in the building and evolution of the society played by the various collectivities that constitute the country? If so, why do the institutional elites not celebrate it when it is appropriate? Perhaps there is not enough on which to build a convincing mythology; the prevailing view was that English and French would each build their own society and compete for the economic and political power necessary for their attainment of their societal ambitions. As a result, the boundaries of "participatory" identification and attachment and of corresponding obligations would coincide with the linguistic boundaries.

IMMIGRANTS AND ETHNIC MINORITIES

The dynamics of the relations between immigrants, ethnic minorities, and the larger society have also changed since the publication of *The Vertical Mosaic*. Three demographic changes should be underscored.

First, the non-British, non-French component of the population has become more diversified: the proportion of European origin declined from 22.6 percent of the total population in 1961 to 15.4 percent in 1991 (single origins only), while the Asian proportion increased from 0.7 to 6.0 percent, and the proportion of other origins increased from 1.3 to 4.5 percent. This is due to a change in the source countries of immigration. While before 1961, about 95 percent of immigrants came from Europe and the United States, it was about 30 percent in the 1981–91 period. Asia, the Middle East, the Caribbean, South and Central America, Africa, and other parts of the world have become the main regions from which immigrants come to this country now.

Second, the relative size of visible minorities increased significantly. They constituted less than 3 percent of the total population in 1961 (including the Aboriginal groups). "In 1991 the 1.9 million adults in a visible minority in Canada represented 9 percent of the population aged 15 years of age and over, doubling the 1981 proportion" (Kelly 1995: 3). However, the non-white population was still overwhelmingly foreign-born: between 72 and 94 percent for all visible minority groups in 1991, except the Japanese (23 percent) and the Pacific Islanders (63 percent) (Kelly 1995: 4).

Third, as noted above, the proportion of the total population born outside Canada is significant: 16.1 percent in 1991 (about twice the proportion in the United States). Immigrants, however, are far from being evenly distributed across the country. For instance, in 1991, 23.7 percent resided in Ontario, 22.3 in British Columbia, 15.1 in Alberta, 11.0 in the Yukon, 8.7 in Quebec, and 6 percent or less in each of the other provinces. There are, as well, important differences among metropolitan areas: 38 percent in Toronto, 30 percent in Vancouver, 13 cities showing percentages between 13 and 24 percent,[8] four with 7 or 8 percent,[9] and the rest having less than 5 percent (Badets 1993: 10).

Four aspects of the relationship between these groups and mainstream society will be examined: (a) the evolution of ethnic stratification; (b) the tension between universalism and particularism; (c) the extent and modalities of state intervention; and (d) the reactions of "majority Canadians."

The Evolution of Ethnic Stratification

Ethnic stratification was one of Porter's main preoccupations, not only in terms of the overall distribution of groups across occupational and income categories, but also in terms of inclusion in the economic and political elites.

As a result of urbanization, the rise in the levels of education, economic growth, and a combination of growing tolerance and pressure towards Anglo-conformity, minorities have progressively been integrated into the social structure. The institutional rigidities that existed at the time *The*

Vertical Mosaic was published were already breaking down as a result of forces unleashed by the Second World War, and by increasing foreign, especially American, investments in the Canadian economy. A "quiet revolution" took place not only in Quebec, but also in English-speaking Canada: "What emerged after the war was a new Canadian society" (Clark 1975: 29). The educational and industrial institutions that Porter blamed for the lack of mobility opportunities changed: facilities were expanded, at all levels of the educational system, and "new and expanding types of business enterprises emerged ... offering opportunities for rapid economic advancement" (Clark 1975: 29). These were accompanied by massive shifts of population from rural areas to cities, by an increase in the number of women in the labour force, and by an expansion of the middle class (ibid: 29).

These transformations also facilitated the integration of immigrants. If integration was usually partial in the immigrant generation, by the second and especially the third generation, minorities reached and sometimes surpassed the level of socioeconomic attainment of Canadians of British origin (Darroch 1979; Brym and Fox 1989: 103–13; Boyd 1992; Reitz and Breton 1994: 97). This is the case, not only at the mass level, but also at the level of elites (Ogmundson and McLaughlin 1992).

In his analysis of the determinants of a person's position in the social structure, Porter, like other social scientists at that time, paid little attention to gender or to the interaction of ethnicity and gender. The women's movement that emerged in the late 1960s and 1970s was one of the main forces that focused attention on the ways in which and extent to which women are disadvantaged with regard to employment, occupational status, and income, and on the patterns of gender concentration in different occupational categories. Focusing on occupation, Lautard and Guppy observed that the "gendered division of labour is more marked than is the ethnic division of labour; that men and women tend to be clustered in 'sex-typed' jobs more often than members of specific ethnic groups are concentrated in 'ethnic-linked' jobs ..." Also, "typically women in the labour force are paid less but have higher levels of schooling than men" (1990: 204; see also, Reitz 1990).

Many women are subjected to "multiple jeopardy" in seeking to improve their socioeconomic condition. That is, whatever negative impact age, ethnicity, race, or immigrant status might have on socioeconomic disadvantage, it is compounded by the fact of being a woman (Gerber 1990; Labelle 1990; Billson 1991; Boyd 1992). However, just as members of different ethnic or racial groups are not equally advantaged or disadvantaged in the labour market, the degree of jeopardy experienced by women varies, depending on their particular ethnic or racial affiliation. For instance, Gerber observed that Indian women suffered a greater economic disadvantage than Inuit and Métis women (1990: 80). The constraints are also greater for "visible minorities" than for white ethnic groups, although such broad categories may conceal more than they reveal. Indeed, Stasiulis noted that "the combined liability of race and gender in the Canadian labour market varies considerably from one non-white group to another" (1987: 7, quoted in Labelle 1990: 74). Ethnicity or race may be more or less of an asset or more or less of a liability, depending on the group with which one is affiliated (Breton *et al.* 1990: Chapter 1; [Editor's note: Chapter 11 in this volume]), a proposition that would apply to women, as well as to men.

Such variations are partly due to the ways in which those who control resources, especially white men, react to different categories of women. It may also be the result of the ways in which gender identity and roles are defined in different ethnocultural groups. But as Billson pointed out, little attention has been given to "the direct impact of culture on the relative power of men and women ... [to] what it means to be male or female in each culture, in terms of roles, power, permitted versus restricted behaviours, or self-concept" (1991: 52). This underscores the importance, whether for theoretical or policy purposes, of examining patterns of culture-specific gender inequalities.

An important change since the publication of *The Vertical Mosaic* has been the increased number of visible minorities in the Canadian population. A number of these minorities have been in Canada for a long time, but the size of these groups has increased considerably in recent decades, and new ones have been added. This change was brought about by the fact that the supply of labour from European countries was diminishing, many of them having become themselves importers of labour. Changes in Canadian immigration policy were another factor. Indeed, the point system introduced a significant degree of universalism in the selection of immigrants, a process that had, up to then, been largely geared to the recruitment of white immigrants.

Whether or not the overall pattern of socioeconomic mobility for minorities of European origin will repeat itself for visible minorities is not clear. Among immigrants, especially immigrant women, in some visible minorities, socioeconomic achievement is not as high, but neither was it among white immigrants who came in earlier periods (Boyd 1992; Reitz 1990; Reitz and Breton 1994: 97). This is not the case in all visible minorities, some attaining high levels of occupation and income, even in the immigrant generation (Kelly 1995).

The large proportion of members of visible minority groups that are foreign-born raises the question of the long-term effects of "visibility" in ethnic stratification. By and large, "Anglo-conformity" is the model of incorporation of immigrants that has prevailed in Canada. The implicit understanding was that conformity was expected, indeed demanded, and that compliance would increase one's chances of making it in the socio-economic structure. This model assumes that individuals have considerable choice over the social salience of their cultural traits, that is, over what distinguishes them from Anglos, and from what are the expected patterns of appearance and behaviour. The choice is, of course, greater in the second than in the first generation, but it exists to some degree even among immigrants (Palmer 1976). In spite of the rhetoric about the valuation of diversity in Canadian society, this model still prevails today (Reitz and Breton 1994).

Will this model operate when colour is involved, that is, when individuals have no choice in keeping or shedding a distinguishing trait? It is only with data over generations and for different groups that it will be possible to answer these questions in the Canadian context.

Another issue concerns the impact of language differences on ethnic stratification – an issue that is of particular significance in Quebec. In recent decades, public policy, with strong public support, has moved to promote and institutionalize the same model that has prevailed in the rest of North America, except that in this instance, it is "Franco" rather than "Anglo-conformity" that is expected – both linguistically and culturally. However, state intervention is more critical in Quebec than it was and continues to be in the rest of the country. Indeed, the linguistic assimilation of newcomers in English-speaking Canada can be taken for granted. It takes more or less time, but it is virtually inevitable as the demographic, economic, cultural (e.g., mass media), and social forces operating in Canada, in North America, and indeed in the world, all motivate individuals to learn English.

In Montreal (the rest of Quebec is largely ethnically and linguistically homogeneous), the situation is significantly different. The economic, demographic, and sociocultural forces promoting English operate there as well. Thus, in response to these pressures, special measures have been adopted to promote the learning and use of French. Some consist of requirements, such as the obligation for immigrants to send their children to French schools, and the specifications concerning the language of work. Others are climate-creating, such as requirements with regard to commercial signs. Still others are aimed at creating job opportunities that reward the learning and use of French.

Programs have been established for the recruitment of non-francophones in the public service and to fight discrimination. However, it is not clear that the bargain implicit in the Anglo-conformity – a bargain that, as noted, seems to have worked to a considerable extent for white ethnic minorities – is an integral part of the Franco-conformity expected of minorities in Quebec. For instance, some research indicates that the incorporation of minorities in the provincial and municipal public services appears to be quite slow (McAll 1992: 24).

Universalism versus Particularism:
De-ethnicizing or Ethnicizing Public Institutions

Porter was quite concerned with the question of whether or not social resources should be allocated on an ethnic or non-ethnic basis. This question appears in several of his writings (1965, 1972, 1975, 1979). His central concern was that "ethnic differentiation in social structure always creates a high risk of ethnic stratification" (1975: 289). This issue continues to be part of academic concerns and of the public debate about multicultural policies and programs.

Traditionally, a central proposition in the theory of equality of opportunity and in the formulation of related rights has been that individuals should have access to societal resources and should be treated by societal institutions *irrespective* of their ethnicity, race, and national origin. This, it should be noted, was to neutralize the effect of ethnicity: it was to prevent or make it more difficult for ethnic groups advantaged in terms of the historical position in the social structure, in terms of social networks, and in terms of access to centres of decision, to use their ethnic ties against other groups. Because of this, the hypothesis maintained by Porter, among others, was that the maintenance of ethnic or racial boundaries almost inevitably leads to inequality and conflict.

In policies based on the treatment of individuals, irrespective of their ethnicity or race, the incorporation strategy is to "multiculturalize" institutions, that is, to define them as common spaces in which all individuals participate on an equal basis. It is to institutionalize mechanisms such that decisions are made on the basis of professional, economic, artistic, and such standards – not on an ethnic basis.

The underlying view in this approach is that ethnicity is a potentially perverse phenomenon. Ethnicity and ethnic affiliations are viewed by those who belong to dominant groups as strategic resources in the competition for power, wealth, status, and, therefore, advantage. They are means to gain and/or retain control over jobs, positions of power and influence, and decision-making. Ethnicity is seen as a basis of social exclusion, invidious social comparisons, and conflict.

The appropriate strategy, then, is to suppress its operation in social life as much as possible. Otherwise, it will tend to have negative consequences for certain categories of individuals, for communities, the society, and the functioning of institutions. Similarly, the allocation of recognition, influence, and material resources by the state must be opposed. Such allocations invite intergroup comparisons and status competition. They encourage groups to organize in order to influence institutional decisions. The result is to accentuate the social salience of ethnic boundaries and to foster ethnic competition.

In contrast, the social logic of intervention on an ethnic basis is that the distribution of opportunities and resources and of public services will be carried out by *taking into account* ethnic origin and race. In other words, the organization of society becomes progressively institutionalized on an ethnic basis.

The incorporation strategy that flows from taking ethnic boundaries into account can take many forms: (a) the formation of ethnic enclaves within institutions, such as school programs and curricula, and even entire schools, welfare agencies, or cultural organizations designed for specific ethnic or racial groups; (b) basing personnel decisions on ethnic representation; (c) encouraging the persistence of ethnic solidarity and cultural expression in as many institutional spheres as possible; and (d) a process that tends to follow automatically from such schemes, the creation of official ethnic categorizations in order to be able to take into account ethnic diversity in the administration of the various public programs.[10]

In this approach, ethnicity and ethnic affiliations are treated as socially benign phenomena. They constitute an anchorage for individual identity and self-esteem; a basis for social inclusion, community cohesion, and cooperation; and a locus for cultural life and expression. Because ethnicity has such value for individual identity, cultural expression, and social cohesion, the argument is made that it should be supported and even enhanced.

One of the concerns underlying this issue, strongly expressed by Porter, was that fighting discrimination with strategies based on ethnicity or race may have the unintended consequence of reinforcing the very ethnic and racial boundaries that the policy aims at removing or reducing. The risk is the institutionalization rather than the reduction of ethnic and racial competition which, in turn, risks increasing the chances of conflict and of inequalities. On the other hand, the "irrespective of ..." strategy is seen as leading to strategies and programs aimed at all disadvantaged people in some particular respect, whatever their ethnic or racial affiliation.

Porter observed that "for some, the revival of ethnicity has come about precisely because of the failure of universalistic and achievement values to take hold, and thus create a society of equality of opportunity and condition," and that it is understandable that because of this failure, "minorities have had to organize to obtain some measure of distributive justice when deprivation remained concentrated within particular groups" (1975: 295). But he emphasized that "the new instruments focused as they are on groups, and providing what might be called group rights – say, to proportional representation within all institutional hierarchies – constitute a radical departure from a society organized on the principle of individual achievement and universalistic judgments, towards one organized on group claims to representation on the basis of particular rather than universal qualities" (1972: 193–4). The dilemma with regard to the kind of society Canada is to become is still very much on the public agenda.

In concluding her analysis of this societal choice, Burnet (1979) argued that neither alternative can be fully accepted: arrangements that represent compromises between the two sets of principles must be worked out. This would be part of a Canadian tradition. Indeed, even though the principles of universalism and the practices of "irrespective of ethnicity, race, religion" are deeply rooted in our sociopolitical culture, they have not been applied uniformly in our society.

On the contrary, there are several instances of group-based organization or practices in Canadian society. The segmentation of the society into French and British was constitutionally established with the BNA Act, with the Official Languages Act, and through a number of public programs. The segmentation on the basis of Aboriginality was legally established with the Royal Proclamation of 1763, the Indian Act of 1850 and its subsequent modifications, and the maintenance of a separate government department. The right to public support for denominational schools is established in the Constitution. Employment equity legislation seeks to assure a certain representation of groups in the workforce of different institutional sectors. Not surprisingly, given the co-existence of two sets of principles in the culture, all these are more or less strongly contested by some groups and supported by others.

Thus, Canadians have been proclaiming two principles, which are contradictory in some of their institutional implications: the right of all to be treated equally *irrespective* of their .ethnicity, and the right of some to be treated differentially *because* of their ethnicity.

The State and Ethnic and Racial Groups

The state has always intervened in the management of diversity in Canada. It has dealt with the amount and composition of immigration, and to some degree, with immigrants' integration in Canadian society. At different points, it has been actively involved in their settlement. It has taken measures for their linguistic and cultural assimilation. It has kept an eye on the ethnic press and other community organizations. It has segregated and deported members of some groups during war periods.

But in recent decades, beginning at the time of the publication of *The Vertical Mosaic*, state intervention has increased considerably, not only in the provision of services, but also in the structuring of civil society, ethnicity being one of the areas in which this has taken place. Recent decades have witnessed, at all levels of government, the creation of structures for the management of the social organization of ethnicity and of intergroup relations.

The control of immigration remains an important area of government activity. Four areas are relatively new for state intervention, or, if not new, the modalities of intervention are somewhat different.

1 *The Internal Organization of Ethnic Collectivities:* Interventions in this area have to do with the institutional bases of linguistic and cultural maintenance and expression, and organization for the exercise of political influence. The interventions might be intended to strengthen some dimension of the group's culture or structure, to weaken it, or to control its development or evolution.

By legitimizing ethnically-based activities and claims on the state, the multiculturalism policy of the federal government (proclaimed in 1971) provided positive symbolic capital for ethnic mobilization and organization. Furthermore, governmental programs, administrative structures, budgets, and various initiatives (e.g., conferences, ethnic chairs in universities, research programs) provided an opportunity structure for ethnically-based action and organization. Third, subsequent years saw other levels of government and school boards adopt their own policies with regard to ethnocultural diversity.

2 *The Pursuit of Socioeconomic Equality:* There are also interventions aimed at the distribution of income, goods, and services (jobs, education, housing, welfare services, police protection). The main objective is usually to attain greater equality, either of opportunity or of outcome in market and state institutions.

The conception of equality underlying public policies also changed in recent decades, raising at least two issues. First, should public policy pursue equality of opportunity, or equality of results/outcomes? This is the issue underlying the debate on employment equity (or affirmative action/positive discrimination). Second, does equality of treatment mean the same treatment applied to all groups, or different but equivalent treatments to groups who differ in their historical, political, demographic, and socioeconomic situation? This is the issue underlying the debate over the public funding of denominational schools; the recognition of Quebec as a distinct society; self-government for Aboriginal communities; special programs for the French outside Quebec; and special programs for visible minorities.

The pursuit of equality, however defined, seems to have acquired a new urgency in recent years. Indeed, immigrants seem to have new expectations. This has been suggested by West Indian poet Cecil Foster, who said that "the myth of the immigrant experience: first generation immigrants must willingly put up with self-denial for the benefit of their children. This myth does not hold for West Indians like me. While we hope that our kids reap the benefits of our labour, we also want the harvest to start during our lives" (Foster 1994).

The rise in immigrant expectations may be due to the changing higher levels of education of immigrants. It may also be the result of government policies, such as multiculturalism and employment equity, and to the entitlement culture of the providential state. These expectations, however, should be seen in the larger context of individuals and groups pursuing their interests and making claims on society and its institutions – a phenomenon far from being restricted to ethnic and racial minorities. (This is discussed further below.)

Finally, some authors have pointed out that claims for social benefits in Western societies are increasingly made on the basis of status as a victim rather than on status as a citizen. To the extent that one can expect less and less redistribution because of poverty or disadvantage, claims are made for compensation for being a victim of past injustices or present maltreatment. It is not that compensation for injustices is not part of our moral culture. It is. Nor is it that such compensation is not deserved in many instances. The point is that being a victim seems to be acquiring importance for the justification of redistribution, while one's social rights as a citizen seem to carry less weight (Rosanvallon 1995).

3 *The Distribution of Recognition and Status:* Government intervention also has an impact on the distribution of status among groups. The interventions may be to establish the status of a group, to increase that of another, or to change the relative statuses of different groups. The dynamics of the distribution of symbolic resources is different from that of goods and services (although they are related to each other).

4 *The Prevention and Management of Conflict:* Measures aimed at the prevention and management of conflict include measures aimed at shaping intergroup attitudes, the expression of hostility (e.g., hate propaganda), and the control of intergroup confrontations. Several initiatives have been taken in schools and communities, for the mediation of conflicts, and for negotiations over issues dividing communities. The active promotion of the ideology of multiculturalism through education and public relations campaigns has been undertaken to encourage positive attitudes towards diversity.

5 *Symbolic Restructuring:* The definition of the country as "multicultural in a bilingual context" was officially proclaimed and formally established in government organization and programs following the Royal Commission on Bilingualism and Biculturalism. This provided a new framework for interpreting events and their implications for the value attached to different ethnic backgrounds in the cultural-symbolic order. It was a resource for mobilization on an ethnic basis. By legitimizing ethnically based activities and claims on the state, state policies and programs

provided positive symbolic capital for ethnic mobilization and organization. It has been pointed out that the multiculturalism budget has always been quite small. Although this is no doubt true, it is reasonable to suggest that the main capital provided by the state was not financial, but symbolic (Breton 1984, 1986).

Reactions of "Majority Canadians"

The expression "majority Canadians" is in quotation marks because it is an ambiguous denotation in contemporary Canada. Who constitutes the "majority?" Insofar as minorities of European origin are concerned, the majority may still be those of British origin (or of French origin in Quebec). But do visible minorities make a distinction between British origin and other white ethnic groups, or are they all "whites" and therefore all part of the "majority?" This is not a conceptual but a social ambiguity, no doubt due to significant demographic and social change.

1 *Ambivalence vis-à-vis Diversity:* Canadians are ambivalent *vis-à-vis* diversity: they find that it has the potential of adding to the cultural richness of Canada, but that it also harbours potential dangers for its cohesion. One manifestation of this ambivalence is the continuing concern about the extent to which and the ways in which multiculturalism ought to be institutionalized. Another is that the public debate seems, at times, to focus on its positive features, while in other periods, the emphasis is on its problematic aspects.

The latter is the situation today. In contrast to a few years ago, multi-culturalism tends to be seen by many as a source of problems. Because the sociopolitical context has changed in significant ways, multiculturalism is now seen and interpreted differently, that is, as adding to or accentuating the problems confronting our society.

Several contextual changes have taken place: the integration of Canada in a continental and global economy; the critical role of "single issue" interest groups in the political process; the mobilization of collectivities previously at the periphery of the political process (e.g., women, native peoples, and visible minorities); systematic province building in most regions and the accompanying confrontations with the federal government; the magnitude of the providential state and the related "culture of entitlement;" and the continuing presence of the Quebec independentist movement. One of the many impacts of these trends and phenomena is to have created the feeling among many people that hardly anyone is concerned for the state of the society as a whole; that each group is out for the pursuit of its own interest and goals, without much concern for its impact on the larger polity, economy, and society.

A related feeling is that the country is being slowly fragmented; that its cohesion is being undermined; that its capacity to act as a nation is reduced. In this context, multiculturalism is seen as the program of another set of groups seeking their own interest and goals, making claims on the society and its institutions, and accentuating the fragmentation.

In addition, there appears to be confusion as to the ways of interpreting the claims made on society and its institutions. Bellah *et al.* (1985) have noted the difficulty of understanding the complexity of modern social relations; that people they talked to "had real difficulty piecing together a picture of the whole society and how they relate to it" (Bellah *et al.* 1985: 207). They comment that "since we lack a way of making moral sense of significant cultural, social, and economic differences between groups, we also lack means for evaluating the different claims such groups make. The conflict of interest is troubling when we do not know how to evaluate those interests" (ibid: 207).

All these changes have contributed in one way or another to the "devalidation" of the traditional cultural paradigms in our society. There is considerable ambiguity as to how one should think about moral issues, religion, family, social rights, authority, and, of course, ethnicity and its place in the organization of society and public institutions. There is a fair amount of confusion, not to say disorientation, among many segments of the population. It seems to exist, as well, among intellectuals (academics, university professors, teachers, and media people), among institutional managers and their advisers, and among political leaders.

There is ambivalence about the value of ethnic diversity. A Decima survey (sponsored by *Maclean's* magazine), carried out in 1989, asked respondents in Canada and the United States the following question: "What do you think is better for Canada/the US, for new immigrants to be encouraged to maintain their distinct culture and ways, or to change their distinct culture and ways to blend with the larger society?" The overall results showed, first, that in both countries, less than a majority of respondents favour cultural retention: 47 and 34 percent of the American and Canadian samples, respectively, and second, that the results are *opposite* to what one would have expected on the basis of the prevailing Canadian system of belief: 13 percent more Americans than Canadians favour the maintenance of "distinct cultures and ways" (Reitz and Breton 1994: Chapter 2).

Other studies revealed a similar attitude. For example, a variation of the following question was included in surveys carried out in 1976, 1986, and 1988: "People who come to Canada should change their behaviour to be more like us" (Berry *et al.* 1977: 141). In 1976, 50 percent agreed with the statement, in comparison with 60 percent and 62 percent in 1986 and 1988, respectively. Other items, however, suggest the opposite: that Canadians tend to favour cultural maintenance. For instance, in 1976, 64 percent agreed that "it would be good to see that all the ethnic groups in Canada retain their cultures." And in both 1976 and 1986, about half disagreed that "the unity of this country is weakened by ethnic groups sticking to their old ways." The surveys also explored the question of the private versus public manifestations of ethnic cultures: should members of ethnic groups who want to keep their own culture keep it to themselves and not bother other people in the country? In 1976, 49 percent agreed with the item. In 1988, the item was somewhat different: it concluded with "should not display it publicly." The results are accordingly different: 34 percent agreed. These results suggest that some Canadians support cultural maintenance provided that it "fits" well with the ways of other groups. If it is to generate any interference in society, then it should remain private.

There may be a tendency to favour cultural maintenance, but also to wish that people who come here should change their behaviour to be like Canadians; that people retain their culture and be allowed to display it publicly, but not if this is to "bother" others. There appears to be a rejection of assimilation, but also of outright pluralism. In other words, there is a twofold expectation presented to ethnic minorities, an expectation perhaps best captured with the term "integration": on the one hand, become fully part of the society, fit in, adopt our ways of doing things; on the other, do not abandon your cultural background, retain and express your culture, but only if this fits well in the Canadian sociocultural matrix.

2 *Status Anxieties and Relative Deprivation:* Harney has noted that "the two founding nations, the Prairie ethnic blocs, and the new immigrant *ethnies all* thought their piece of the pie and the survival of their cultures were threatened" (Harney 1988: 71). There are two sides to the perceived threat. First, these feelings are a natural reaction to a sense of social displacement, to economic insecurity, declining political power and influence, and/or the erosion of one's cultural world. Second, these social and cultural anxieties are frequently accompanied by envy, resentment, and anger. The anxieties and resentments are, if anything, even more generalized than they were when Harney wrote the above lines. As Spicer said, we live in "an archipelago of envies and anxieties" (quoted by Wilson 1993). These tend to be accompanied by feelings of relative deprivation, which, as research has shown, are related to subjective dissatisfaction, support of particular political candidates and movements, and attitudes towards outgroups (Dion 1986: 176).[11]

There are, first, groups who feel that they are being displaced. These include groups of people of British origin, who feel they are no longer the main definers of the cultural makeup of the society and the main interpreters of events, situations, and problems requiring public action. They also include whites, who increasingly feel that they are in the process of being marginalized by the growing number of visible minorities, at least in certain community settings, if not in the society as a whole.

Second, there are those in the middle of the class structure, who feel that they are paying a disproportionate share of the societal burden and thus resent the "special interest groups." They see the rich as taking care of themselves and the poor as being taken care of by government. They feel relatively deprived in relation to those classes, especially those on welfare, whom they perceive as being better off, even though they have the same or lower educational backgrounds than theirs and certainly do not match them in work ethic. They resent paying taxes to support such groups or seeing them advantaged by government legislation and programs.

Third, there are those who experience a particular kind of status inconsistency. The traditional image of the immigrant is of one who starts at the bottom of the class structure and works hard to climb the socioeconomic hierarchy. The expectation is that they will, in general, occupy a status lower than that of the members of the receiving society.[12] But some immigrants, especially Chinese, appear to be starting quite high up in the structure. Many middle-class people, workers, small business entrepreneurs, and unemployed workers resent the fact that immigrants are economically more successful than they are. Some white parents "complain that school honour rolls are dominated by new immigrants' children, making it difficult for their own, less bookish children to get into the increasingly choosy [universities]." Some are offended by "the Asian kids who have better cars than the teachers do" (Cernetig 1995: D2).

Fourth, there is a generalized fatigue with "special interest groups" as revealed in a recent survey: 77 percent of respondents were fed up with interest groups and governments whining about getting their "fair share" from the federal purse – Ontarians being the most fed up (Ekos Research Associates 1995). A 1991 Angus Reid survey found that 50 percent agree with the statement: "I am sick and tired of some groups complaining about racism being directed at them," and 41 percent with the statement: "I'm tired of ethnic minorities being given special treatment."

Finally, over the past few years, nativistic ideologies have been propounded by political parties and other organizations. These have made it increasingly possible and legitimate to express the status anxieties, sense of relative deprivation, and resentment felt by individuals who feel displaced or threatened in some way. Indeed, nativism is a belief system and a set of attitudes

most likely held by people in social groups that have the same racial, ethnic, and/ or religious characteristics as the dominant class, but not the economic or political power ... [They] generally arise among previously dominant social elements during times of social, political, and economic crisis, suggesting a possible link with relative deprivation. The demand of nativist groups is for increased conformity to the historically based traditions and customs common to the territory. (Harrison 1995: 7, 164)[13]

Nativistic tendencies exist in all parts of the country, although their specific manifestations vary, the main differences being between Quebec and English-Canadian nativism. Ultra-nationalists in Quebec perceive such realities as the English language, federalism, and immigration as threatening the culture and survival of the Quebec "people." Similar groups and individuals in English-speaking Canada see threats to the Canadian identity and character as stemming from immigration, and especially the multiculturalism ideology and policy.

CONCLUSION

Canada has clearly been in a state of transition, during the few past decades, with regard to all axes of ethnic differentiation. The direction in which it is evolving is still uncertain. This change has been taking place in the context of rapid change in many other areas of economic, political, and social life.

Profound changes have been taking place in the relationship between native peoples, Quebec, and francophones elsewhere, immigrants, white ethnic groups, and visible minorities, on the one hand, and relevant segments of the larger society, on the other. In various ways, these groups or categories of people have initiated the process of transforming and even of reversing their traditional condition and status in the society.

The amount of change in the different dimensions of the social structure may be why a relatively low consensus seems to exist in the country with regard to diagnoses and/or remedies around questions of ethnic and racial relations. There is considerable disagreement in Quebec: independentists, federalists, autonomists, all have a certain base of support in the population. Native peoples do not agree on the particular political and administrative arrangements that would be acceptable. Members of other ethnic groups hold different views on whether public institutions should incorporate ethnicity, or should be de-ethnicized as much as possible.

Interethnic relations turned out to be somewhat different from what Porter anticipated in *The Vertical Mosaic*, although his basic theoretical postulates proved to have validity. Porter saw the power structure as dominated primarily by the British charter group, with the other groups located in lower strata. This pattern, however, was partly due to the historical British dominance, but it was also the result of institutional rigidities, that is, of educational and industrial institutions unable to produce opportunities for mobility. Immigration was a substitute for institutional reforms.

But a quiet revolution brought about institutional reforms in English-speaking Canada, as well as in Quebec. The educational and industrial institutions that Porter blamed for the lack of mobility opportunities changed. These transformations facilitated the integration of immigrants and of their descendants. In short, the social order that existed at the time of Porter's analysis has changed, and as a result, the mosaic is not as vertical as it used to be. Whether or not this will occur for non-white immigrants and their descendants is not clear. It may for some of the minorities, but not for others, as their situations differ significantly (Kelly 1995), and as attitudes of whites are not the same *vis-à-vis* all visible minorities, and neither are those of visible minorities *vis-à-vis* each other.

An examination of the contemporary socioeconomic order that adopted Porter's perspective would focus on the possible impact on ethnic stratification of phenomena, such as the globalization of capital, labour and commodity markets, free trade agreements, and the technological transformations in industry, since these are clearly having an impact on the opportunity structure. Thus, the analysis would consider the changes in the occupational structure and in the functioning of labour markets, in the types of jobs and careers being created, and in the distribution of income. Patterns of socioeconomic competition appear to be changing, and this may well have an impact on ethnic stratification. This would be the case for resources distributed by either privately or publicly controlled institutions.[14]

Theory and research by sociologists and other social scientists has also evolved during the past decades, and these have tended to be along the lines of evolution of ethnic and racial realities in the society. It is impossible to summarize all the developments that have taken place in a few pages. However, it is possible to identify a few themes that seem to have received a fair amount of attention.

Ethnicity and Social Inequality

The theme that was prominent in Porter's writings – ethnicity and social inequality – continued to be at the centre of research preoccupations. As noted, the mosaic reflecting inequalities among ethnic groups of European origin seems to have faded considerably over time, a phenomenon that is consistent with part of Porter's analytic framework.

This does not mean, however, that ethnicity has no impact on patterns of inequality. First, birthplace remains a factor in socioeconomic attainment – immigrants, on the average, doing less well than native-born Canadians. Second, ethnic networks and concentrations in occupational niches can be assets, as well as liabilities in socioeconomic mobility. There seems to be no simple relationship between the maintenance of ethnic identity and ties, and lower chances of socioeconomic mobility: sometimes ethnicity is an asset, sometimes a liability (Reitz 1990). Third, contrary to the mosaic versus melting pot ideology, patterns of socioeconomic integration and of acculturation have been largely the same in Canada and in the United States. The same structural (e.g., the functioning of the labour market) and cultural forces (e.g., the "Angloconformity" expectations) appear to be operating in both societal contexts (Reitz and Breton 1994).

Fourth, while ethnicity has decreased in importance, race has become critical in accounting for patterns of inequality. As noted, the colour difference may be of greater significance, since it makes ethnic boundaries more visible. Accordingly, it may lead to more persistent patterns of social exclusion and discrimination than is the case when culture is the prime factor of differentiation. However, earlier immigrants of European origin were also subject to prejudice and discrimination. In fact, even among whites, some minorities used to be seen as racially different and inferior.

During recent years, studies of ethnic inequalities have also paid more attention to the interaction of gender, ethnicity, and immigrant status. Research shows that immigrant women, particularly if they are members of visible minorities, experience multiple jeopardy in terms of socioeconomic attainment.[15] This is also the case for Aboriginal women (Gerber 1990).

An issue that has drawn some attention concerns the impact of employment equity programs on inequality along racial lines. This issue has generated a lot of research, mostly in the United States, but in Canada as well.[16] A key theoretical and empirical point is whether "programs designed to improve the employability of various minority groups will end up with ... a reinforcement of the existing occupational distribution structure" (McAll 1991: 26).

Ethnic Identity and Cultural Maintenance

The study of ethnic identity and retention has been influenced by the concept of "symbolic ethnicity" (Gans 1979) or "affective ethnicity" (Weinfeld 1981). These concepts do not assume that identity and cultural retention necessarily go together; acculturation can take place while ethnic identity remains, although transformed. A related line of research has been on the selective character of ethnic cultural retention (Isajiw 1990). In these developments, the idea is that acculturation is not an all-or-none phenomenon, but one that takes place selectively, depending on the ethnic group and perhaps especially on the social context. What is retained is a function, not only of what is valued by the group itself, but also of what is seen as acceptable or legitimate in the larger cultural context. Ethnicity is largely "situational" (Nagata 1974). It is "not a constant inherited from the past, but the result of a process which continues to unfold." It has relatively little to do with the culture of origin, but much more "with the exigencies of survival and the structure of opportunity" in the adopted country (Yancey *et al.* 1976: 400).

Ethnicity and the State

Recent decades have witnessed massive state intervention in society generally, and in the management of ethnicity and interethnic relations, in particular. Given this reality, it is not surprising that the preoccupation with its impact has also gained importance. A basic theoretical concern has to do with the extent to which and the ways in which government intervention shapes the organization of ethnic communities, either directly or indirectly; affects the saliency of ethnic boundaries and the significance of their role in social relationships and in the functioning of institutions; and stimulates the politics of identity and recognition. The effects could stem directly from the policies of programs themselves, or through the ethnic/racial categorizations produced for the administration of programs, for the distribution of resources, and for public recognition practices. As a result, political power and influence seem to have acquired greater salience than economic issues in shaping intergroup relations. Identity, status, and their symbolic expression – the politics of identity and recognition – have also acquired considerable significance. To a large extent, intergroup competition and tensions are over the allocation of symbolic resources among groups by larger society and its institutions, particularly the state.

Primordialism versus Mobilization

Perhaps one of the most important theoretical developments in recent decades is the counterbalancing of the ascriptive conception of ethnicity with the view of ethnicity as a socially constructed phenomenon. This dual view influenced the study of many aspects of ethnicity, race, and intergroup relations. It is not really that new, since it originates with Weber, who saw ethnic identities and affiliations as mobilizable resources for the control of resources, such as jobs, institutional domains, and state policies (Neuwirth 1969). But beginning about the time of the publication of *The Vertical Mosaic,* this perspective was developed and applied more systematically than it had been up to then (Lyman and Douglas 1973; Cohen 1974; Bell 1975; McKay 1982; Breton 1991a).

Indeed, this view – that ethnicity is not only a matter of primordial ties and identity, but also a base on which to build in social "networking," in organizing for social purposes, in mobilizing in order to influence government or other institutional policies, and generally to be used strategically in improving one's situation in the community or society – is present, as seen above, in the research on social inequality, employment equity, ethnic maintenance, the politics of identity and recognition, and the analysis of state policies with regard to language, race, and ethnicity.

Chronology

1931   Born August 19 in Montmartre, Saskatchewan
1952   BA, University of Manitoba
1958   MA, University of Chicago
1957–59   Assistant Professor of Sociology, University of Montreal
1961   PhD, Sociology, Johns Hopkins University
1961–64   Assistant Professor, McGill University
1964–68   Assistant Professor, Johns Hopkins University
1969–92   Associate Professor and (as of 1971) Full Professor, University of Toronto
1972   Fellow of the Royal Society of Canada
1973–76   Editor, *Canadian Review of Sociology and Anthropology*
1976–81   Program Director, The Institute for Research on Public Policy
1978–86   Co–director (with Professor Robert F. Harney), Ethnic and Immigration Studies Program
1981–83   Member of Committee for the Evaluation of the Official Language Minorities Program, Ottawa: Secretary of State
1982–86   Vice–President, Research Committee on Ethnic and Racial Minorities, International Sociological Association
1987–90   Member of the Academic Board, Multicultural History Society of Ontario
1987–90   Chairman, Ethnic Studies Advisory Committee, Ottawa: Secretary of State
1987–88   Member of Canadian Sociology and Anthropology Association Special Task Force on Priorities and Reform
1988–91   Membre, Comité scientifique du programme "Actions structurantes," Formation de Chercheurs et l'Aide à la Recherche (FCAR), Québec

1990   Outstanding Contribution Award by the Canadian Sociology and
            Anthropology Association
1992–   Professor Emeritus of Sociology, University of Toronto
1994   Doctor of Letters, *honoris causa*, University of Guelph
1994   Hommage pour Contribution à la production et à la diffusion de
            connaissances sociologiques sur le vécu minoritaire – ACFAS, Toronto
2000   Doctor of Letters, *honoris causa*, University of Waterloo
2002   Doctor of Law, *honoris causa*, University of Manitoba

APPENDIX B

Bibliography of Publications

1 AUTHORED BOOKS

1972 *Social and Academic Factors in the Career Decisions of Canadian Youth.* Ottawa: Department of Manpower and Immigration.

1974 *The Social Impact of Changes in Population Size and Composition: An Analysis of Reactions to Patterns of Immigration* (with Jill Armstrong and Les Kennedy). Ottawa: Information Canada.

1977 *The Canadian Condition: A Guide for Research Development.* Montreal: The Institute for Research on Public Policy.

1980 *Why disunity? An Analysis of Linguistic and Regional Cleavages in Canada* (with Albert Breton). Montreal: The Institute for Research on Public Policy.

1980 *Cultural Boundaries and the Cohesion of Canada* (with Jeffrey Reitz, Victor Valentine, and Daiva Stasiulis). Montreal: The Institute for Research on Public Policy.

1981 *La langue de travail au Quebec.* Synthèse de la recherche sur la rencontre de deux langues. Montréal: Institut de Recherches politiques.

1990 *Ethnic Identity and Equality: Varieties of Experience in a Canadian City* (with Jeffrey Reitz, Warren Kalbach, and Wsevolod Isajiw). Toronto: University of Toronto Press.

1991 *The Governance of Ethnic Communities: Political Structures and Processes in Canada.* Westport CT: Greenwood Press.

1992 *Why Meech Failed: Lessons for Canadian Constitution-making.* Toronto: CD Howe Institute.

1994 *The Illusion of Difference: Realities of Ethnicity in Canada and the United States* (with Jeffrey Reitz). Toronto: CD Howe Institute.

2004 *A Fragile Social Fabric? Fairness, Trust and Commitment in Canada* (with Norbert Hartmann, Jos Lennards, and Paul Reed). Montreal: McGill-Queen's University Press.

2   EDITED BOOKS

1974 *Aspects of Canadian Society.* Montreal: Canadian Sociology and Anthropology Association.

1982 *The Quebec and Acadian Diaspora in North America* (with Pierre Savard). Toronto: The Multicultural History Society of Ontario.

1984 *The Dynamics of Government Programs for Urban Indians in the Prairie Provinces* (with Gail Grant). Montreal: The Institute for Research on Public Policy.

1990 *National Survival in Dependent Societies: the Cases of Canada and Poland* (with G. Houle, G. Caldwell, E. Mokrzycki, and E. Wnuk-Lipinski). Ottawa: Carleton University Press.

2003 *Globalization and Society: Processes of Differentiation Examined* (with Jeffrey Reitz). Westport CT: Greenwood Press.

3   JOURNAL ARTICLES

1960 "Group Formation among Immigrants: Criteria and Processes" (with Maurice Pinard), *Canadian Journal of Economics and Political Science* 27: 465–77.

1964 "Institutional Completeness of Ethnic Communities and the Personal Relations of Immigrants," *American Journal of Sociology* 70: 193–205.

1964 "The Challenge of a Technological Culture," *The Social Worker* 32: 24–7.

1968 "School Organization and Student Differences: Some Views of Canadian Educators" (with Stephen Richer), *Canadian Education and Research Digest* 20–37.

1969 "An Economic Theory of Social Movements" (with Albert Breton), *American Economic Review* 54: l98–205.

1970 "Academic Stratification in Secondary Schools and the Educational Plans of Students," *Canadian Review of Sociology and Anthropology* 7: 17–34.

1971 "Output Norms and Productive Behaviour in Non-Cooperative Work Groups: A Study in Computer Simulation," *Simulation and Games.* 45–72.

1972 "The Socio–political Dynamics of the 'October Events'," *Canadian Review of Sociology and Anthropology* 9: 33–56.

1974 "Ethnic Pluralism and Social Equality," *Human Relations* l4: 6–11.

1975 "Research Issues on Canadian Cultures and Ethnic Groups" (in collaboration), *Canadian Review of Sociology and Anthropology* 12: 8l–94.

1977 "L'existence française et canadienne," *Concilium* 121: 63–9.

1978 "Stratification and Conflict between Ethnolinguistic Communities with Different Social Structures," *Canadian Review of Sociology and Anthropology* 15: 148–57.

1979 "From a different perspective: French Canada and the issue of Immigration and Multiculturalism," *TESL Talk* 10: 45–56.

1983 "La communauté ethnique, communauté politique," *Sociologie et Sociétés* 15: 23–37.

1984 "The Production and Allocation of Symbolic Resources: An Analysis of the Linguistic and Ethnocultural Fields in Canada," *Canadian Review of Sociology and Anthropology* 21: 123–44. (Originally presented as the Harry Hawthorne Lecture at the 1983 meetings of the Canadian Sociology and Anthropology Association.)

1985 "L'intégration des francophones hors Québec dans des communautés de langue française," *Revue de l'Université d'Ottawa* 55: 77–90.

1988 "From Ethnic to Civic Nationalism: English Canada and Quebec," *Ethnic and Racial Studies* 11: 85–102.

1989 "Quebec Sociology: Agendas from Society or from Sociologists," *Canadian Review of Sociology and Anthropology* 26: 557–70.

1993 "A Question of Identity: Commentary," *Polyphony* 13: 18–22.

1994 "Modalités d'appartenance aux francophonies minoritaires: Essai de typologie," *Sociologie et Sociétés* 27: 59–69.

1996 "Les nouveaux modes d'organisation ethniques au Canada," *Hommes et Migrations* (juillet): 35–41.

4 CHAPTERS IN BOOKS

1969 "Perception of the Relative Economic and Political Advantages of Ethnic Groups in Canada" (with Howard Roseborough). In *Canadian Society*, 3rd ed., edited by B. Blishen *et al.* Toronto: Macmillan. 269–94.

1969 "Ethnic Differences in Status." In *Canadian Society*, 3rd ed., edited by B. Blishen *et al.* Toronto: Macmillan. 683–701.

1969 "Occupational Preferences of Canadian High School Students" (with J.C. McDonald). In *Canadian Society*, 3rd ed., edited by B. Blishen *et al.* Toronto: Macmillan. 269–94.

1971 "Aspects of Parent–Adolescent Relationships: The Perceptions of Secondary School Students" (with J.C. McDonald). In *The Canadian Family*, edited by K. Ishwaran. Toronto: Holt, Rinehart and Winston. 151–68.

1974 "Le Système scolaire et les transformations sociales." In *Société royale du Canada: Présentations*: 111–18.

1977 "Language and Institutional Control." In *Language, Society and Culture*, edited by W. Coons and F. Vallee. Ottawa: The Canada Council. 90–6.

1978 "The Structure of Relationships between Ethnic Collectivities." In *The Canadian Ethnic Mosaic: A Quest for Identity*, edited by L. Driedger. Toronto: McClelland and Stewart. 55–73.

1979 "Ethnic Stratification Viewed from Three Theoretical Perspectives." In *Social Stratification in Canada*, 2nd ed., edited by J.C. Curtis and W.G. Scott. Toronto: Prentice–Hall. 270–94.

1980 "Social and Political Implications of Language Policies: Observations on the Canadian Experience." In *Politics and Language: Spanish and English in the*

United States, edited by D.J.R. Bruckner. Chicago: The University of Chicago Center for Policy Study. 49–72.

1981 "Regionalism in Canada." In *Regionalism and Supranationalism*, edited by David Cameron. Montreal: Institute for Research on Public Policy. 57–79.

1983 "West Indian, Chinese and European Ethnic Groups in Toronto: Perceptions of Problems and Resources." In *Two Nations, Many Cultures*, edited by J.S. Elliott. Toronto: Prentice–Hall. 425–43.

1986 "Multiculturalism and Canadian Nationbuilding." In *The Politics of Gender, Ethnicity and Language in Canada*, edited by A. Cairns and C. Williams. Toronto: University of Toronto Press. 27–66.

1988 "English–French Relations in Canada." In *Understanding Canadian Society*, edited by L. Tepperman and J. Curtis. Toronto: McGraw-Hill Ryerson. 557–86.

1988 "The Evolution of the Canadian Multicultural Society: the Significance of Government Intervention." In *Canadian Mosaic: Essays on Multiculturalism*, edited by A.J. Fry and Ch. Forceville. Amsterdam: Free University Press. 25–44.

1988 "The Concept of 'Distinct Society and Identity' in the Meech Lake Accord." In *Competing Constitutional Visions*, edited by K.E. Swinton and C.J. Rogerson. Toronto: Carswell. 3–10.

1989 "The Vesting of Ethnic Interests in Societal Institutions." In *Multiculturalism and Intergroup Relations*, edited by James Frideres. New York: Greenwood Press. 35–56.

1990 "Ethnic Groups, Regions, and Nationalism in the Formation of the Canadian and Polish Society." In *National Survival in Dependent Societies: The Cases of Quebec and Poland*, edited by R. Breton *et al.* Ottawa: Carleton University Press.

1990 "Policy decisions and the competition for symbolic resources." In *The Competitive State*, edited by A. Breton, G. Galeotti, P. Salmon, and R. Wintrobe. Dordrecht, The Netherlands: Kluwer Academic Publishers.

1990 "L'étranger dans la ville: Ouverture." In *Les Étrangers dans la Ville: Le regard des Sciences Sociales*, edited by I. Simon-Barouh et P-J. Simon. Paris: Editions l'Harmattan.

1991 "The Political Dimension of Ethnic Community Organization." In *Ethnicity, Structured Inequality, and the State in Canada and the Federal Republic of Germany*, edited by Robin Ostow *et al.* Frankfurt am Main: Peter Lang. 157–66.

1992 "Collective Dimensions of the Cultural Transformation of Ethnic Communities and the Larger Society." In *Migration and the Transformation of Cultures*, edited by Jean Burnet. Toronto: Multicultural History Society of Ontario.

1992 "Dimensions of citizenship," Standing Committee on Social Affairs, Science and Technology, Senate of Canada: Seventh Proceeding (May): 21–35.

1994 "L'appartenance progressive à une société: perspectives sur l'intégration socioculturelle des immigrants." In *Actes du Séminaire sur les indicateurs d'intégration des immigrants*. Montréal: Ministère des Affaires internationales, de l'Immigration et des Communautés culturelles et Centre d'études ethniques, Université de Montréal. 239–52.

1995 "Identification in Transnational Political Communities." In *Rethinking Federalism: Citizens, Markets, and Governments in a Changing World*, edited by Karen Knop, Sylvia Ostry, Richard Simeon, and Katherine Swinton. Vancouver: University of British Columbia Press. 40–58.

1995 "Globalization and the infrastructure of the social order." *Transactions of the Royal Society of Canada*, Series 6, Volume 7: 115–29.

1998 "Ethnicity and Race in Social Organization: Recent Developments in Canadian Society." In *The* Vertical Mosaic *Revisited*, edited by James Curtis and Rick Helmes-Hayes. Toronto: University of Toronto Press.

1998 "Race and Ethnic Relations in Canada." In the *Canadian Encyclopaedia, World Edition*. Toronto: McClelland and Stewart.

1999 "Community Organization." In *Encyclopaedia of Canada's Peoples*. Toronto: University of Toronto Press.

1999 "Intergroup Competition in the Symbolic Construction of Canadian Society." In *Race and Ethnic Relations in Canada*, 2nd ed., edited by Peter Li. Toronto: Oxford University Press.

1999 "Diversity and Homogeneity: The Ambivalence of Canadians: Keynote Address." In *A Sharing of Diversities: Jews, Mennonites and Ukrainians*, edited by Fred Stambrook and Bert Friesen. Regina: Canadians Plains Research Centre, University of Regina.

2001 "La gestion du pluralisme culturel." In *Une Société monde? Les dynamiques sociales de la mondialisation*, edited by Daniel Mercure. Québec: Les Presses de l'Université Laval.

2001 "L'évolution du contexte culturel et socio-politique et la francophonie minoritaire." In *Communautés francophones. Espaces d'Altérité*, edited by Paul Dubé et Pamela Sing. Edmonton: Institut de Recherche de la Faculté Saint-Jean.

5   UNPUBLISHED PAPERS

1981 "The Ethnic Community as a Resource in Relation to Group Problems: Perceptions and Attitudes." Toronto: Centre for Urban and Community Studies, University of Toronto.

1985 "Exchange between Sociology and Economics: Possibilities and Constraints." Ottawa: Economic Council of Canada.

1986 "The Evolution of the Canadian Multicultural Reality: The Significance of Government Intervention." Conference of the Association for Canadian Studies in the Netherlands, Amsterdam.

1989 "The Legitimacy of Language Policies in Canada: Issues and Tensions." Paper presented at the Annual Meetings of the American Sociological Association.

1991 "The Non-State-Non-Market Component of the Social Order and the Production of Social Capital." London, Ontario: University of Western Ontario.

6   RESEARCH REPORTS

1959 *Resources et besoins de la population française de Montréal dans le domaine de la santé mentale* (en collaboration). Montréal: Le Groupe de Recherches Sociales.

1959 *La situation des immigrants à Montreal. Étude sur l'adaptation occupationnelle, les conditions résidentielles et les relations sociales* (en collaboration). Montréal: Le Groupe de Recherches Sociales.

1961 *Ethnic Communities and the Personal Relations of Immigrants.* Montréal: Le Groupe de Recherches Sociales.

1964 *Factors Affecting Levels of Occupation and Income in the Canadian* National Railways (in collaboration). Montréal: Le Groupe de Recherches Sociales.

1965 *A Study of Interethnic Relations in Canada* (in collaboration). Montréal: Le Groupe de Recherches Sociales.

1970 *Social Implications of Selected Demographic Trends.* Institute for the Quantitative Analysis of Social and Economic Policy, University of Toronto.

1972 *A Theory of Public Bureaus* (with Albert Breton and Ronald Wintrobe).

Notes

INTRODUCTION

1 It also suggests that if the relation between aboriginal peoples and the rest of Canadian society had been a major focus for Breton's work, this topic would have preceded the other two. In fact Breton proposed this ordering of topics – first relations between aboriginal peoples and others, then French-English relations, then relations involving immigrant groups – for *Cultural Boundaries and the Cohesion of Canada* (1980).

2 Breton published an article with this title in a 1969 reader edited by Bernard Blishen.

3 See also Breton (1981).

CHAPTER ONE

1 Parallel does not mean that the institutional systems are independent of each other; they do interact and have an impact on each other.

2 Situations of migrant superordination or dominance exhibit a wide variety of patterns. See Mason (1970), especially Part II, for a discussion of different patterns and of the factors related to their emergence.

3 There are exceptions such as the Hutterites and Mennonites. Such groups have followed a different pattern which suggests yet another type of ethnic differentiation that is not discussed here.

4 For a discussion of ethnic boundaries and their maintenance, see Barth (1969: Chapter 1).

5 For a discussion of some differences in patterns of interethnic relationships under the conditions of segmentation and of heterogeneity, see Breton (1978) [Editor's note: Chapter Two in this volume].

6 The role of ethnicity in shaping commercial and financial networks is shown in Handlin (1956), Kriesberg (1955), and Cohen (1969).

7 Examples of the role of ethnicity in occupational structures can be found in Collins (1945), and Carlin (1966: Chapter 2).

8 Campbell (1978) argues that this is the case in Nova Scotia, where there are few associations to maintain ethnic identities and social boundaries, since the social structure is sufficiently organized along ethnic lines to provide such support as a matter of course, so to speak.

9 For an analysis of the impact of formal legitimation in the case of religious educational institutions in Canada, see Westhues (1976b).

10 Smelser defines a social movement as a collective attempt to restore, protect, modify, or create norms or values in the name of a generalized belief. Participants may be trying either to affect norms or values directly or induce some constituted authority to do so. It is a mobilization on the basis of a belief which redefines social action (1963: slightly adapted from pages 8, 270, 313).

11 The continuing role of ascription in "modern" societies and the particular role it plays in them is well argued by Mayhew (1968).

12 The historical resistance of the French to these attempts is also well documented, a resistance that had some degree of success.

13 Multiculturalism as a set of ideas does not appear to explicitly recognize differences among the various collectivities that it presumably encompasses. It does not appear to be formulating different modes of incorporation in the institutional system for the various ethnic collectivities. As an ideological tool, it runs the risk of imposing the same framework on all types of ethnic groupings. Thus, while being an ideology in favour of diversity, it may be ignoring much of the existing ethnic diversity.

CHAPTER TWO

1 This is a revised version of a paper presented at the Poland-Canada seminar held in Warsaw in May 1977. I wish to thank John Jackson, Daiva Stasiulis, and Ralph Matthews for their helpful comments and suggestions.

2 The type of intergroup relationship also affects the pattern of stratification within the ethnolinguistic community. The nature of the relationship with other groups is a determinant of the structure of opportunity available to the members of each community and thus affects the processes of class formation for the pursuit of interests. The consideration of these processes and the resulting intragroup stratification patterns is beyond the scope of this article.

3 These two concepts are similar to those used by Van den Berghe (1969: 67) to define a "plural" society. See also Schermerhorn (1970).

4 The discussion bears on labour markets, but could be extended to other types of organizational memberships, their sources, and mechanisms of recruitment.

5 On the functioning of labour market institutions and their role, see Migué (1970), Granovetter (1974), and Stigler (1962).

6 Language is relevant in two ways: as a symbol of ethnic identification, and as an instrument of communication. Under social and institutional parallelism along linguistic lines, the latter aspect appears more critical than the former.

7 A critical problem is to account for the fact that this interest centres on a particular sphere (cultural, political, economic) rather than another. This is beyond the scope of this paper.

8 If the obstacles to the improvement of the condition of individuals are enormous, there will be an incentive to build a parallel institutional system. However, the existing pattern of dominance may prevent the actualization of such an incentive. For a further discussion, see Albert Breton and Raymond Breton (1980). [Editor's note: for an excerpt, see Chapter Eight in this volume.]

9 See Coleman (1969), and Clark (1973) for a discussion of types of resources and their interrelationships, such as their convertibility into each other.

CHAPTER THREE

1 The author is indebted to Daiva Stasiulus, Jeffrey Reitz, Réjean Lachapelle, and Gail Grant Akian for their willingness to read an earlier draft of this paper under pressures of time, and for their useful comments and suggestions.

2 In his analysis, Westhues (1976a) argues that three major approaches have shaped not only the study of stratification but sociological thinking and research generally, the approaches being differentiated in terms of which is regarded as the most critical decision-making unit in a society: the individual, a class, or an organization. The three approaches discussed in this paper parallel closely the three identified by Westhues. See also Collins' (1971) discussion of the functional and conflict approaches to the study of educational stratification.

3 In a way, the essay is a sort of review of the literature. However, it does not pretend to present a comprehensive analysis of the existing research. No attempt is made to fit most of the existing studies in the analysis. References to studies are presented primarily for purposes of illustration.

4 It could be shown that they also lead to different policy orientations and decisions. But such an analysis is beyond the scope of this paper.

5 On plural or segmented societies see, for example, Smith (1969b), and van den Berghe (1969).

6 In sociology, functionalism is another label for this approach; in economics, it is the approach underlying the marginal productivity of labour theory. The "human capital theory" also falls under this perspective.

7 See, for example, Stigler (1961, 1962), Thurow (1975), McCall (1973), Spence (1973), on the role of information in the labour market.

8 The expression is from Bernard. In judgmental competition, someone decides who the winner is. By contrast, in autonomous competition – a race, for example – the process itself selects the winner (1962: 64).

9 Note that the social networks are treated as an individual resource. Social networks and contacts can be manipulated to achieve certain personal goals. Networks are egocentric (Boissevain 1968; Kapferer 1969).

10 A similar description could be drawn, *mutatis mutandis*, from the vantage of an employer.

11 On the social and cultural characteristics defining the adaptive capacity of any ethnic group, see Wagley and Harris (1958: 264–73).

12 There is an ambiguity that runs through much of the sociological literature regarding ethnicity. On the one hand, ethnicity is frequently given as a prime example of ascription: it is determined by one's birth and early social-ization, and therefore is something beyond one's control. It is not some-thing that one achieves, or shapes, through experience or deliberate action. On the other hand, the literature on acculturation, assimilation, absorption, or integration, or on ethnic retention, maintenance, and especially resur-gence definitely considers ethnicity as being to some degree under individ-ual control. Perhaps the critical distinction is between ethnic origin which is ascriptive, and ethnicity which is achieved, in the sense that it is modifiable through life experiences. But the issue is more complex. There are some ethnic traits which are not modifiable (skin colour), others which are modi-fiable, but with difficulty (language), and still others which are easily modifi-able (cultural customs). Treating ethnicity as an ascriptive phenomenon is ambiguous, not to say misleading.

13 Of course, collective action may not necessarily occur. Other conditions are required.

14 These tendencies may take a long time to manifest themselves. Their visibility would also be affected by factors such as the rate of arrival of new immigrants.

15 This is the Marxist approach which is at the base of a number of Marxist or neo-Marxist models.

16 See, for example, Giddens (1973), Poulantzas (1975), Wright (1976, 1977).

17 Wright provides an analysis of positions which occupy "objectively contradictory locations within class relations." These positions are in a double contradiction: as classes, they are in an antagonistic, contradictory

relation with other classes; but since they share interests with other classes, they "are torn between the basic contradictory class relation" (Wright 1976: 26). Giddens refers to the same phenomenon when he writes of "quasi-class groupings" that "share certain common economic interests, but, for different reasons, stand on the margin of the dominant set of class relationships ..." (1973: 31).

18 See Dahrendorf (1959: 182–9), Tilly (1964), Clark (1975a), and Brym (1977).

19 The expression is from Wright (1976: 26).

20 Wright identifies three sets of "contradictory locations": managers, small employers, and semi-autonomous wage earners (1976: 26–38).

21 Blumer's critique (1965) of the functionalist argument, that with industrialization and the rationalization of socioeconomic processes, ethnicity could eventually disappear as a factor in social organization, seems to be applicable, *mutatis mutandis*, to the argument of the class analysts. Both appear to make the dubious assumption of the dominance of technical and economic factors in shaping a society, rather than examining the interaction that is taking place between those factors and other dynamic forces in social organizations, such as ethnicity.

22 Bonacich's theory throws doubt on the proposition of the deliberate fomenting of ethnic antagonisms for the sheer purpose of weakening the class of sellers of labour. Her theory states that such ethnic antagonisms as do emerge within that class are the result of employers' pursuit of cheap labour. But the proposition that employers have an interest in dividing the other class is certainly consistent with the approach. The question is partly an empirical one: to what extent have employers done so and by what means? It is also partly theoretical: it would seem relatively easy to formulate a theory of conflict in which the attempts of one of the parties to divide its opponents would only serve to strengthen the latter's solidarity.

23 The dual labour market theory and other segmented labour market theories build on this approach. See Stolzenberg (1975), and Cain (1976).

24 E.C. Hughes was one of the first to introduce this concept in the sociology of work (see Hughes and Hughes 1952).

25 The size of the domains can vary considerably. Moreover, domains can be defined in terms of a small set of jobs in a department, of an entire department, or of an organizational level (e.g., management), an occupation, a firm, a set of firms within an industry, or an entire industry.

26 See also Neuwirth (1969), and Cohen (1974c).

27 It should also be noted that Weber does not exclude the possibility of competition among workers. But it occurs within the social enclosure or domain and is regulated more or less severely by the members of the domain.

28 On "gatekeeping," see Anderson (1974: chapter 6).

29 See Brazeau (1958) for further discussion.

30 Such a collectivity can be either a group or a quasi-group. Quasi-groups are "aggregates ... which have no recognizable structure, but whose members have certain interests or modes of behaviour in common, which may at any time lead them to form themselves into definite groups" (Ginsberg 1953: 40). See also, Dahrendorf (1959: 179–89).

31 Individual skills may be a necessary condition, but in this approach they are definitely not sufficient.

32 Social networks are seen as a factor in the social organization for purposive group action. In the first approach, social networks were seen as a set of channels that individuals could manipulate or activate in the pursuit of their individual goals. Here social networks are instruments of concerted action.

33 Weber (1969), Cohen (1974c), Barnet (1974).

34 The argument is not that the dominant group can impose its cultural character in some total way on the society and its institutions. There are other determinants of the characteristics of institutions both from within and from outside the society. The argument is that the dominant group has considerably more impact in shaping institutions than the other ethnic groups.

35 These features of occupations as well as others are discussed by Blalock in his discussion of professional sports and of the blacks' position in athletic occupations (1967: 92–100).

CHAPTER FOUR

1 I am grateful to Jos Lennards, Leslie Laczo, Jeffrey Reitz, and three anonymous CRSA reviewers for helpful comments on an earlier draft.
[The editors of the CRSA are pleased to facilitate the early publication of this revised version of the Harry Hawthorn Lecture, given originally at the CSAA Annual Meetings, Vancouver, June 1983. This manuscript was received September 1983 and accepted January 1984.]

2 For a discussion of this and related questions, see Ogmundson (1980), and Bell and Tepperman (1979).

3 Even analyses of status groups slip into consideration of material interests. Brandmeyer and Denisoff (1969) note, for instance, that authors, such as Lipset and Hofstadter, in their analysis of conflicts between status groups, actually refer to economic, not status interests (as reflected in the cases they present).

4 Conflict theory is, of course, broader than what is implied here, but it has, in fact, been more extensively applied to economic (classes, occupations, regions) than status groupings.

5 By "economisme," Bourdieu refers to the inappropriate use of models based on utilitarian interests to explain social phenomena (1975). See also, Cohen (1974b) for a discussion of such tendencies.

6 This, of course, corresponds to the same broad distinction made in the analysis of economic phenomena. In both areas, the amount and types of resources generated must be considered, as well as their distribution among competing groups.

7 "The state is not merely the government, far less just the central government. The state is a complex of institutions, including government, but also including the bureaucracy (embodied in the civil service as well as public corporations, central banks, regulatory commissions, etc.), the military, the judiciary, representative assemblies, and (very important for Canada) what Miliband calls the sub-central levels of government, that is, provincial executives, legislatures, and bureaucracies, and municipal institutions" (Panitch 1977: 6).

8 See also Warner (1953), and Brody (1982) on the function of symbolic activities for the community.

9 For a discussion of this normative model and of attempts to apply it in contemporary politics, see Young (1976: chapter 3).

10 Bausenhart notes, for example, that "the suppression of the enemy languages press in September 1918 may also be seen as the Federal Government's contribution to a movement which had its beginning in the earlier part of that decade, to establish the supremacy of English in Canada and hence, to abolish bilingual schools. This movement spread from the Ontario side of the Québec border to the Rocky Mountains, with the four central provinces ultimately insisting that English be the sole language of instruction in their public school systems. Legislation to this effect reflected the apprehension of the British majority in each of the four provinces about the large number of non-British immigrants living among them" (1972: 42–3).

11 For a discussion of the relation between cultural security and tolerance, see Turner (1974).

12 Weber states that "the development of status is essentially a question of stratification resting upon usurpation. Such usurpation is the normal origin of almost all status honor" (Gerth and Mills 1958: 188).

13 Heinz (1983) presents an interesting analysis of conflict over symbol production between the New Christian Right and groups associated with what he calls secular humanism and liberal Christianity.

14 This statement is taken from comments by Jos Lennards.

15 On the importance of language in symbolic or status inequalities, see Bourdieu (1975).

16 In a very interesting analysis, Kemper (1979) sees the decline in the quality of municipal sources as a result of the reversal in status between providers and consumers of services. Before the decline, providers had generally a lower social status than consumers: the status relation was in concordance with the service relationship. The shift in population toward black and Hispanic resulted in a discrepancy; consumers were now frequently of

lower status than the providers. The discrepancy affected the quality of
the services.

17 For some English-speaking Canadians, the fact that the French have been
conquered is also important in this connection.

18 Morris and Price (1980) present an interesting analysis of English-Canadian
images or typifications of French-English relations in Montreal and Toronto,
and the role they play in a period of change.

19 Editor's note: this topic is pursued in Chapter Six in this volume.

20 For an overview and critical examination of the policy, see Burnet (1975,
1978).

21 The quest for recognizing as opposed to satisfying adaptive needs may be
accentuated by the changing socioeconomic and generational background
of the population of ethnic collectivities. See, for example, Driedger (1977),
Gans (1979), and Nahirny and Fishman (1965).

22 From a presentation by Rudolph J. Vecoli, Canadian Ethnic Studies
Association, Thunder Bay, 1983.

23 From the same presentation by Vecoli.

24 "Status rights … consist of legitimate normative claims on the behavior of
others which constitute advantages – as rewards or resources – for a social
position" (Meyer and Roth 1970: 97). On this question, see also, Westhues
(1976b).

25 I am indebted to Jos Lennards for drawing my attention to this element of
the situation.

26 Concerning the relative importance of symbolic and material interests
Weber notes that "every technological repercussion and economic transformation threatens stratification by status and pushes the class situation into
the foreground. Epochs and countries in which the naked class situation is
of predominant significance are regularly the periods of technical and economic transformations. And every slowing down of the shifting of economic
transformations leads, in due course, to the growth of status structures and
makes for a resuscitation of the important role of social honor" (Gerth and
Mills 1958: 194).

27 It should be noted that not having a policy (the laissez-faire position) *is* a
policy, whether it has been decided upon consciously or not.

28 The notion of the welfare state should be taken in its broadest sense. One
of its characteristics is that "it is accepted as a legitimate goal of the political system to intervene through governmental institutions in order to create
the conditions under which citizens can pursue their individual goals"
(Janowitz 1976: 3).

29 On the transformation of the structures and processes of representations,
see for example, Meisel (1976), Pross (1982), and Thompson and Stanbury
(1979).

CHAPTER FIVE

1 On the processes of mobilizing power in order to gain access to societal
   rewards or resources, and on the resulting structure of "social closure," see
   Parkin (1979) and Murphy (1984).

2 The main sources for this chapter are: *The Canadian Encyclopedia* (1985);
   Cornell, Hamelin, Ouellet, and Trudel (1967); Careless (1970); Linteau,
   Durocher, and Robert (1979); McInnis (1969); and Silver (1982).

3 For a general discussion of segmentation, see also Smith (1974) and
   Schermerhorn (1970). For its examination in the context of Canadian
   society, see McRae (1974), Ossenberg (1967), and Breton (1978)[Editor's
   note: this is Chapter Two in the present volume; see also Chapter One].

4 About one-third are said to have supported the American troops at the time
   of the revolution, and another third would have been ambivalent. There
   were also several manifestations of unrest against clergy and seigneurs
   (Lanctot 1967). These findings are summarized by Ossenberg (1967: 213).

5 On the emergence of this professional class, see Ouellet (1966).

6 "To risk a broad generalization for a fifty-year interval (the Family
   Compacts) included, characteristically, the heads of departments in the
   colonial administration, judges, most barristers, and the bishop or ranking
   churchman of the Church of England. But this is not all, for closely
   associated with this official hierarchy we find the leaders of the commercial
   and banking community. In the microcosm of colonial society there is no
   clear differentiation between the political and the economic elite" (McRae
   1964: 241).

7 "A government responsible to the representatives of the people, i.e., an
   executive or Cabinet collectively dependent on the votes of a majority of the
   elected legislature. This key principle of responsibility, whereby a government needed the confidence of a Parliament, originated in established
   British practice. But its transfer to British North America gave the colonists
   control of their domestic affairs, since a governor would simply follow the
   advice (i.e., policies) of responsible colonial ministers, except in imperial
   matters" (*Canadian Encyclopedia* 1985: 1579).

8 "For many years, the business groups had been struggling to procure a
   development in transportation, a measure they believed essential to the
   progress of Canada … Since the capitalist group had little means at their
   disposal, the execution of the program fell upon the State. Large investments were needed for enterprises that would bring very little immediate
   return. In short, the political authorities had to realize this need for massive investments in economic development. In addition they had to consent
   to pool resources and credit of both provinces … United Canada assumed
   in its entirety the debt of Upper Canada, which had been contracted with a

view to defraying the cost of the Saint Lawrence canal system" (Ouellet 1966: 232).

9 Between 1840 and 1870, about 200 thousand left for the United States. Another 700 thousand left in the subsequent decades, 1870 to 1930.

10 "The Methodist Church (Canada), the Presbyterian Church in Canada, the Church of England in Canada, and the Baptist Conference of Canada fused out of smaller and less politically effective religious bodies" (Cole 1971: 171).

11 On this matter, see, for example, Watt (1967), Pennefather (1984), and Houston and Smyth (1980).

12 The number of priests increased from one for 1080 persons in 1850 to one for 510 in 1890. Between 1850 and 1901, members of male religious orders increased from 243 to 1984; those of female religious orders increased from 650 to 6628 (Hamelin 1961; Linteau *et al.* 1979).

13 While the French remained largely ethnically homogeneous, the English-speaking population became more heterogeneous: the British origin component constituted a little over 60 percent of the total in 1871 but only about 45 percent in 1971.

14 There were many devices that could be used by the federal government to control and reduce the realm of autonomy of the provinces: "the appointment of a federal supervisor for the provinces (the lieutenant-governor), the disallowance and reservation of provincial statues, and overriding character of federal law in concurrent fields, and the assignment of all residual powers to the central regime. These statutory provisions were freely and deliberately used ..." (Black 1975: 60). For example, Macdonald exercised the power of disallowing provincial legislation "five times during his first term of office and 41 times from 1878 to 1891 when the provinces were beginning to assert their claims to coordinate status with the federal government" (Black 1975: 36).

15 For more information on the sources of these data, see Breton and Stasiulis (1980: 191–2).

16 In 1870, approximately 82 percent of the enumerated population was Métis, the majority being French-speaking and Catholic. The proportion that was from Ontario, the British Isles, and the United States was a little less than 6 percent – a proportion that, twenty years later, had increased to 51 percent. The percentage of Roman Catholics had decreased from 44.6 percent to 13.5 percent in the same period; that of Protestants increased from 39.6 percent to 82.6 percent (Staples 1974: 290–92).

17 The central conflictual factor was that the Quebec government asked Pope Leo XIII to arbitrate its dispute with the Jesuits. This "papist intrusion" was strongly resented by English Protestants.

18 The discussion of the Atlantic arena of French-English relations is restricted to New Brunswick for lack of space. It is also this province in which the most significant events took place.

19 "That [education] was the most critical and most explosive issue in French-English relations between 1880 and 1920 is beyond a doubt. Both the French-speaking and the English-speaking Canadians involved in these disputes clearly recognized that the continuing viability of the French-Canadian's identity outside the province of Quebec was dependent upon the mode and content of instruction given to French-speaking pupils. Both asserted that if that mode and content of instruction was wholly English in character, the 'French fact' in Ontario, Manitoba, and in the Territories soon to become Saskatchewan and Alberta would gradually whither away. Their point of difference was whether that could or should be allowed to happen" (Brown 1969: vii).

20 "For the Orange Order, the increasing number of French Canadians in Ontario signalled danger ahead. Ontario, the stronghold of imperial loyalty and English Protestantism, was being taken over by the French" (Barber 1969: 71).

21 The competition for resources between the French and the Catholic institutional systems continued in subsequent decades (see Jackson 1975).

22 The regulation was erased from the books in 1944.

23 See Hagy (1969) for a description of these organizations. On the independentist movement, see Pinard and Hamilton (1977 1984); Coleman (1984); and Behiels (1985).

24 Editor's note: see Chapter Seven in this volume.

25 In the White Paper published before the linguistic legislation was presented to the National Assembly.

26 For a discussion of those strategies and an examination of their implementation, see McRoberts and Posgate (1980).

27 The case of individuals and enterprises that would have left Quebec or that did not establish themselves there because of the language legislation is an even more difficult question. That there was an exodus seems undeniable; but its size and especially its relationship to the legislation seems impossible to establish with existing evidence. The migration of enterprises and of individuals across provincial boundaries occurs all the time. The legislation may have had an impact on the flow, but other factors were also at work. One thing is sure: the legislation did focus the attention of the media on "the exodus," which, in turn, provided ammunition to interested political groups.

28 Editor's note: see Chapter Four in this volume.

29 For the purposes of their study, Pinard and Hamilton define "intellectuals" as "all those who are engaged in occupational roles concerned with the creation and transmission of culture. More specifically, our notion includes first art creators and performers (novelists, painters, musicians, actors, and other artists); second, all scientists and scholars, whether in academic settings or not (biologists, chemists, economists, sociologists, etc.) ... third, and by far

the largest group numerically, all teachers and professors; finally, all news workers (reporters, journalists, broadcasters, etc.)" (1984: 21).

30 The same pattern was observed over time: in the early development of the movement "support may have been lower but was already coming from all strata, *with the same class differentials that are still prevailing now*" (Pinard and Hamilton 1984: 44; emphasis in original).

CHAPTER SIX

1 See also Cole (1971).
2 Although it is the one on which this essay focuses, it is far from being the only threat considered important. For instance, the economic, cultural, and political pressure of the United States was equally, if not more important.
3 On the two aspects of language, see Jackson (1977).
4 This evolution has also been discussed by McNaught (1966), Nock (1981, 1982), and Breton (1984, 1986 [Editor's note: Chapters Four and Fourteen, respectively, in this volume]).
5 The "survivance" theme was also present in English-Canadian nationalism: "while the theme of survival in English-Canadian history has several variations, it is none the less as all-pervasive as it is in French-Canadian history. Its variants include the struggle for survival against the pressure of the United States, the struggle of a colony to achieve nationhood, and, finally, the struggle to maintain unity" (Cook 1971: 162).
6 It is now necessary to begin to talk in terms of Quebec rather than French-Canadian nationalism. Although the latter has not disappeared and may even gain strength in the future, Québécois nationalism is clearly a distinct reality whose impact affects the great majority of French-Canadians, that is those who live in Quebec.
7 Personal communication to the author.
8 See also Cappon (1974).
9 Reference is made to the perceived threat to language and culture; but this does not mean that this threat was not related in people's minds to their economic and political condition.
10 Dr Camille Laurin, the chief architect of Law 101 when a minister in the Parti Québécois government, has been recently quoted as being quite satisfied with the success of the legislation as far as education is concerned:
   "Ce qui me réjouit le plus, nous a-t-il confié spontanément, c'est de voir que dans certaines de nos écoles françaises, 77% des écoliers sont des nouveaux arrivants." Avant l'adoption de la Charte, rappelle-t-il, 85% des immigrants fréquentaient l'école anglaise. La vapeur a été renversée. (Proulx 1987)
11 "Finally" in the sense that it is the last to be briefly presented here, not in the sense that all other relevant factors have been discussed.

12 For a study about changes in the meaning assigned to the label "Québécois," see Taylor and Sigal (1982).

13 Father Harvey's article in *Relations* (1987) and the debate it generated is a good illustration of this preoccupation. It is also forcefully expressed by Gendron (1987).

CHAPTER SEVEN

1 Revision of a paper presented at the annual meeting of the Canadian Sociology and Anthropology Association, St John's, Newfoundland, June 1971. I wish to express my thanks to Albert Breton, S.D. Clark, Linda Gerber, Jos Lennards, and Maurice Pinard for their helpful comments and suggestions.

2 A precautionary note is in order at this point. The statements made in this essay should be taken as hypothetical, even though this is not always explicitly recognized. Moreover, some pieces of data are presented at different points of the discussion. Although the presentation of these data is not accompanied by a methodological discussion, it is recognized that, like any piece of empirical evidence, they have their limitations.

3 See Dandurand (1970) for a discussion of aspects of the restructuring of power and authority in Quebec's educational system.

4 For example, some analysts have attributed the electoral defeat of the Lesage government in 1966 to the dissatisfaction with the disruption of the local institutions and authority structure by the "technocrats of Quebec City."

5 It also followed ethnic lines. That is, within the English-speaking segment, power was held almost exclusively by people of British origin.

6 These gains have been very uneven. For example, the linguistic composition of the senior levels of the federal bureaucracy does not seem to have changed significantly. Moreover, socially meaningful estimates may be quite unrelated to what is happening in fact. For instance, English-speaking groups who feel threatened tend to exaggerate gains made by French-speaking groups. On the other hand, French-Canadian separatists tend to write off the gain as tokenism and/or to believe that the gains are not real, because they involve people who have sold out.

7 My hypothesis is that a similar process is also taking place to a certain extent in financial, industrial, and commercial sectors, that is a simultaneous expansion of power in Quebec and an increasing integration into the Canadian and North American system.

8 During the entire period 1946–67, a little over 604,000 out of a total of about 2,922,000 immigrants gave Quebec as their intended destination – that is about 20 percent (on the basis of the relative size of the Quebec population, 29 percent was expected).

9 It is my contention that the interest of the French Canadian elite in a high birthrate has always been primarily related to the linguistic balance in the society – that is, essentially a political interest – and that the religious ideology has been used as a means to that end.

10 It is probably obvious to everyone who is following the events in Quebec and Ottawa that there is already a lot going on in the direction of these hypotheses.

11 *Le Magazine MacLean*, nov. 1967; *Maintenant*, mai 1969; *Socialisme 69*, avril-mai-juin, 1969.

12 Many people interpret conflicts within organizations in the process of establishing themselves as a sign of weakness: "They can't even agree among themselves." In some cases, internal conflicts and tensions may disintegrate the embryonic structure, but in other cases, the tensions may be a source of dynamic growth and innovation. There is no doubt, however, that internal tension makes the organization more vulnerable. Opposing groups, for instance, may use strategies aimed at accentuating the conflicts in order to weaken their adversaries. Also, the more organizations have to cope with internal conflicts, the less resources, time, and energy they have for the pursuit of their goals.

13 In Etzioni's typology of organizations, "normative organizations are organizations in which normative power is the major source of control over the participants … Compliance in normative organizations rests primarily on internalization of directives accepted as legitimate. Leadership rituals, manipulation of social and prestige symbols, and resocialization are among the most important techniques of control used" (1961: 40).

14 See, for example, the report on the February meeting of the Party in *Point de Mire*, and a letter to the editor in the same issue (5 mars, 1971). See also the statement of Mr Charron (Parti Québécois deputy) in *Le Devoir* (12 février, 1971), as well as the daily reports on the February meeting. Another illustration is provided by a communication by Charles Gagnon in *Socialisme 69* (April-May-June issue) in which he attacks Réné Lévesque and the Parti Québécois.

15 I have the impression that expressions, such as the "rise of expectations," "the breakdown of traditional values and authority," "a condition of anomie or normlessness," are really meant to refer to the change in people's conceptions of themselves along the sociopolitical ability and autonomy dimensions and the resulting change in their conceptions of the way they should relate to authority, that is to the centres of decision-making in all or in particular institutional spheres.

16 I hope no one will interpret this hypothesis as a way of putting the blame on separatist organizations for the violence of the FLQ. Trying to understand a set of behaviours in terms of various social processes that operate or fail to operate in certain circumstances is *not* the same thing as trying to

decide who is responsible for these behaviours. The confusion about the role of values and ideology in social science is partly a confusion about the issue of the identification of social process versus the assignment of moral responsibility for events and situations.

17 See note 14.

18 The waves referred to here are those identified by Morf in his description of the terrorism between 1963 and 1969. A good chronology of the FLQ's activities also appears in Pelletier's book (1971).

19 The extent to which political and economic elites are responsible for such discontent for having failed to bring about appropriate reforms, and the extent to which the discontent is an unanticipated consequence of the introduction of certain reforms (as seems to be the case with the discontent brought about by educational reforms), is a crucial issue which, however, is beyond the concern of this essay.

20 I am not arguing that the circumstances justified the judgment of an apprehended insurrection, nor am I arguing that they did not justify that judgment. In order to argue this, I would need to know the intentions of the legislators in using the notion of insurrection. Moreover, I am not trying to find out whether or not a notion used in a particular piece of legislation is appropriate for sociological analysis.

21 The present analysis seems to parallel the one made by Mr Claude Ryan during the events. His highly controversial intervention seemed to have been the result of a judgment on his part that the situation was far from being under control.

22 The defensive statement of the government to the effect that it was the only legal means at its disposal to cope with the situation, seems to reveal that "the War Measures Act was not really appropriate for the situation, but ..." A statement by the Prime Minister in the House of Commons on October 16 is clear on this:

> The absence both of adequate time to take other steps and of alternative legislative authority dictated the use of the War Measures Act. After informing the leaders of the opposition parties of our intention to act in this fashion, and following receipt of the letters that I tabled a moment ago, the Government proclaimed the act.
>
> The Government recognizes that the authority contained in the act is much broader than is required in the present situation, notwithstanding the seriousness of the events. For that reason the regulations which were adopted permit the exercise of only a limited number of the powers available under the act. Nevertheless, I wish to make it clear today that the Government regards the use of the War Measures Act as only an interim and, in the sense mentioned above, somewhat unsatisfactory measure. ("Trudeau's explanation in the Commons for invoking the 'War Measures Act,'" *Globe and Mail*, 17 Oct. 1970)

23 The idea of a provisional government, in spite of the rather unfortunate terminology, was not an intrinsically bad idea in this connection. On the contrary, there may be more potential in it than appears at first sight. That is, the formation of a group of "prominent citizens" not involved in the confrontation, at least not directly, to act as mediator or arbitrator may have facilitated the exercise of authority. Of course, it is crucial that such a group be composed of people who are not part of the established political power structure or part of the political opposition and of groups contending for power. For example, the leader of the Parti Québécois, or someone from a municipal administration which had been a target of the FLQ, would be particularly bad choices for such a group.

24 In the last few years, FLQ violence has been instrumental in prompting three acts. The Explosives Act permits searches without warrants. The Fire Investigation Act permits the holding of witnesses without bail, and requires witnesses to give evidence even if it is self-incriminating. The Coroners Act also permits the holding of witnesses without bail and requires giving evidence that may be self-incriminating. Moreover, the coroner is required to state in his verdict if he is of the opinion that a crime has been committed and, if possible, the name of the presumed criminal.

CHAPTER NINE

1 See Geertz (1973).
2 See Raymond Breton (1991b: 97–112).
3 See Kenneth Thompson (1973: 293–302; 1980: 216–36).
4 See Clapp (1969: 120–21).
5 The possible tensions among the principles underlying these different equalities are considered in Chapter 4 of the book from which this essay is taken.
6 The equality of provinces and territories does not seem to be widely accepted yet.
7 See Edelman (1971), and Griswold (1987: 1077–1117).
8 Reports on the language issue in *The Western Report* from April to July 1988 express these criticisms and frustrations in unambiguous terms.
9 In December 1988, the Supreme Court of Canada declared unconstitutional the provision of Quebec's Charter of the French Language – passed in 1977 by the Parti Québécois government – forbidding any language except French on commercial signs. Using the "notwithstanding" clause in the Charter of Rights and Freedoms, which allows provinces to override some of its provisions, the Quebec National Assembly passed a new version of the restriction on languages other than French, which became known as "Bill 178."
10 Gregg and Posner (1990: 44).

11 Reported in *Globe and Mail*, 22 December 1988.

12 For a review of survey results on this matter, see Canada (1990).

13 The survey used a sample of 2,012 respondents. The question was: "Would you classify each of the following regions as better off, less, well-off, or about average?" Interestingly, among respondents who supported the Reform Party, 56 percent thought that Quebec was better off.

14 Quoted in an editorial in *Globe and Mail*, June 4, 1987.

15 See Quebec Liberal Party (1991). The committee's chair was Jean Allaire.

16 This event, which took place in the fall of 1989, was subsequently shown many times on television in Quebec.

17 For a convincing argument that the distinction between power, on the one hand, and acceptance and status, on the other, pervades theoretical thinking in the social sciences, see Kemper and Collins (1990: 32–68).

18 On withdrawal of status, see Hagen (1962).

19 Reported in *Globe and Mail*, November 6, 1991.

20 Northrop Frye wrote that "the main thing wrong with Confederation was its impoverished cultural basis" (*Globe and Mail*, April 15, 1991).

21 See Canada (1991: 9–10).

22 On the allocation of symbolic resources, see Raymond Breton (1984: 123–44). [Editor's note: Chapter Four in this volume.]

23 The suggestion by a provincial premier that all provinces be recognized as distinct societies was, at the time, dismissed out of hand. But it did contain a valuable insight – namely, that status should be allocated equally if the distribution is to have legitimacy. See also Deutsch (1966: 34–5).

24 It seems, for example, that many Canadians are prepared to accept a special status for native peoples on historical grounds.

25 See Peter C. Newman (1991: 20).

26 The Canada Council, Radio-Canada, and the National Film Board are federal initiatives that have played a crucial role in Quebec.

27 *Globe and Mail*, 9 July 1990.

28 On legitimacy and legitimation, see Cipriani (1987), Hirsch (1986: 800–837), and Pfeffer (1981: 1–52).

CHAPTER TEN

1 The material for this article has been taken from the writer's unpublished dissertation, "Ethnic Communities and the Personal Relations of Immigrants" (Baltimore: Johns Hopkins University, 1961). I wish to thank Professors James S. Coleman and Arthur Stinchcombe for their most helpful assistance throughout the study. This study was originally carried out at the Social Research Group in Montreal. It was sponsored by La Fédération des Œuvres de Charité in Montréal and The Canadian Department of Citizenship and Immigration. Their assistance is gratefully acknowledged.

2 The first wave was done during April, May, and June 1958; the second
   during July, August, and September 1959.

3 Ethnic communities classified as "high" in institutional completeness are
   Greek, German, French, Hungarian, Italian, Lithuanian, Polish, Russian,
   Ukrainian. Those classified as "low" are Albanian, American, Austrian,
   Belgian, Bulgarian, Czechoslovak, Danish, Dutch, English, Indian, Irish,
   Latvian, Portuguese, Romanian, Scotch, Spanish, Swedish, Swiss, South
   African, Yugoslavian, West Indian. In referring to degree of institutional
   completeness, what is meant is the *relative degree,* not the absolute degree.
   First of all, not all the organizations are included. The schools, for example, are left out – and what is even more important – so are voluntary associations, which are not only numerous, but also very significant in the social
   life of any ethnic community. However, it seems reasonable to assume that
   the distribution of these associations among the various groups would be
   about the same as the distribution of the organizations presented above.
   Second, there are probably minor errors in the above list. Some ethnic
   groups may have a welfare organization, for example, which was not listed in
   the sources used.

4 No attention is given here to the difference between those with affiliations
   in two or three communities and those whose affiliations are concentrated
   in a single one. Consideration of such differences would be revealing as
   regards both patterns of change over time, and the social and psychological
   impact of the ethnic homogeneity or heterogeneity of affiliations on the
   immigrant personality and behaviour.

5 In order to test the relationship between institutional completeness and the
   composition of personal relations, several factors were held constant: the
   size of the group, its residential concentration, the proportion of professionals in the group, the similarity and difference of the language of the
   group with those of the natives (English and French), the proportion in the
   group who are ignorant of the native languages, years of residence in
   Canada, and occupational status. The relationship held under all these
   controls. The strength of the relationship was reduced by as much as one-
   third in only one case: when the proportion ignorant of the native
   languages was held constant.

6 On the unifying role of social conflict, see Simmel (1955: 13ff).

7 The number of cases in certain cross-classifications did not allow an
   identical break for each type of organization. It was done as a check, and
   the results were in the same direction.

8 The estimate of the effect of the presence of publications remains the same
   when it is computed while holding constant the presence of welfare
   organizations.

9 If there had been no panel dropouts, the proportions changing in each
   direction would probably not have been different. Indeed, if we compare

those who changed address with those who did not, under the assumption that the dropouts were mostly movers, we find that the movers were more likely to change the composition of their personal ties than the non-movers during the period between the two panel waves, but in both directions: among those who had mostly in-group relations at the time of the first panel wave, 13 percent more of movers than non-movers had changed to a majority of out-group contacts by the time of the second wave; among those with a majority of out-group contacts, 11 percent more of movers than of non-movers changed to a majority of in-group relationships.

10 There are two other possibilities: the immigrant may become interpersonally integrated in another immigrant group of an ethnicity different from his own, or he may remain an isolate. These alternatives will be examined elsewhere.

11 Institutional completeness is high in 1 group out of 8 whose language is also spoken by the native community and in 12 out of 22 whose language is different. Also, it is high in 6 of the 13 groups with less than 20 percent ignorant of the native languages and in 6 of the 7 groups with 20 percent or more not knowing these languages. (No data were available for 2 of the ethnic groups with a language other than French or English.)

12 Of 13 ethnic groups with less than 50 percent of their workers in manual occupations, 2 are high on institutional completeness. Of the 14 with 50 percent or more of their workers in manual occupations, 7 have a high degree of institutional completeness. (No occupational information was available for 3 of the ethnic groups.)

13 See Peterson (1958), and Price (1959).

14 The community life-cycle approach to the study of the integration and acculturation of immigrants is well represented by Thomas and Znaniecki (1927), and Galitzi (1929).

CHAPTER ELEVEN

1 Editor's note: the findings are reported in Chapters 2–5 in Breton *et al.* (1990), which also includes information on the history and ethnic composition of Toronto. Excerpts from Breton's Chapter 5 in that volume are included here as Chapter 13.

2 See note 1.

CHAPTER TWELVE

1 On this point, see also Balandier (1969), Swartz (1968), MacKenzie (1967), Bailey (1970), and Crenson (1983).

2 And in an ethnic collectivity.

3 Weick (1969) stresses the fact that individual and collective actors not only react to their environment but also "enact" it. That is to say, they interpret it

creatively, and they attempt to shape it according to their own values and goals.

CHAPTER THIRTEEN

1 For a discussion of ethnic interests in relation to ethnic structure and behaviour, see, for example, Siegel (1970), Cohen (1974c) (especially the papers by Cohen himself, Deshen, Hannerz, and Charlsley), Zielyk (1975), and Breton (1978).
2 The literature on the organizational requirements for collective action is extensive. See, for instance, Dahrendorf (1959), Pinard (1968), Clark (1975a), Tilly (1975), and Brym (1978).
3 The question on acceptance as neighbours or relatives included a number of groups in addition to those in the sample. The results that refer to over-all acceptance (without distinctions as to the degree of acceptance) are as follows. The figures are the percentages of Majority Canadians and of all other groups combined who would accept the groups listed as neighbours and as close relatives. It should be noted that the extent of social accep-tance is lower for the Pakistani than for any other group considered in the study, except among the minority-group respondents, who rate Pakistani with West Indians as relatives.
4 The statements read to respondents were as follows: "Present immigration laws make it too difficult for [group] to come to Canada," and "Present immi-gration laws make it too easy for certain groups to come to Canada." The five response options ranged from "strongly agree" to "strongly disagree."
5 The question was asked as follows: "I'd like to ask the same question about various ethnic groups. Are they now being treated fairly by employers, or do they experience some discrimination or a lot of discrimination? How do they experience some discrimination or a lot of discrimination? How about ... (each group named separately)?" The response options were: "treated fairly," "some discrimination," "a lot of discrimination," "they have an advantage," and "don't know."
6 West Indians may perceive the variety of English they speak as different from the variety of English spoken in Canada, but this matter has not been explored in this study. The question is therefore not applicable in their case.
7 The respondents of British ancestry were asked about "immigrants or members of a minority group."
8 Cultural loss is seen as a problem when either the loss of customs and traditions or the decreasing use of the group's language or both are perceived as very or somewhat serious problems faced by the group.
9 The question is the following: "Do you feel that it is difficult (or a problem) to be both a [group] and a Canadian at the same time?" The response options are: "yes," "no," "depends," "don't know."

10 As will become apparent from the discussion that follows, the notion of resource is used here in its very general sense.

11 The two questions are the following: "Suppose a member of an ethnic group has trouble getting a good job in a company because he is discriminated against. How much do you think the following actions he could take could help to change the situation: very much, somewhat, a little, or not at all?" (The list of actions appears in table 13.5.) "Suppose someone wanted to change Canadian immigration laws or procedures. How much do you think the following actions would help? Very much, somewhat, a little, not at all."

12 Respondents were asked if they agreed or disagreed with the following statements: "In general, politicians and officials do not take seriously the views expressed by the [group] community leaders." "Leaders of the [group] community do not have enough connections with important people in business and government to get important results for the community." "Even if the leaders and organizations of the [group] community in Toronto were more active, we would not get more attention from politicians and government officials."

13 The index of political interest is based on the following two questions: "How interested are you in local issues or events [which do not relate specifically to (group)] such as new bylaws or local politics?" "How about provincial or national affairs? Are you ..." The response options were: "very," "somewhat," "slightly," "not at all."

14 The question asked is the following: "Suppose the circle on this card represented the activities that go on in the [group] community in Toronto. How far or how close from the centre of these activities are you?" Closeness or distance could vary between one and six.

15 On this question, see, for example, Warner (1945), Spiro (1955), and Hannerz (1974).

CHAPTER FOURTEEN

1 This paper was completed in October 1984. I wish to express my appreciation to Drs Alan Cairns, Cynthia Williams, Rick Ponting, Frank Vallee, and Michael Ray for their valuable comments and suggestions concerning several aspects of an earlier draft of this paper. Messrs Kerry Johnston, director, Dhiru Patel, and Eric Lugtigheid of the Multiculturalism Directorate, Ottawa, have provided me with insights and useful information. I thank them for the interest they have shown in this project and for the time they have given me. I am also grateful to Mrs Enakshi Dua for her collaboration in collecting the necessary documentation, to Jean Burnet and Howard Palmer for their help with sources of documentation, to Michèle Breton for her careful editorial work, and to Claire Campbell and Kathryn Hough for their help with administrative arrangements.

2 These changes are outlined in Royal Commission on Bilingualism and Biculturalism (1970).

3 Book IV of the commission's report dealing with the contribution of the other ethnic groups, was published in 1970. See Royal Commission on Bilingualism and Biculturalism (1970).

4 The implications of the commission's mandate for the non-British, non-French groups are discussed later.

5 Jones defines the baby boom generation in the following way: "For two centuries, the birthrate in the United States and the world has steadily declined. It is still declining. There is only one exception: the single, unprecedented aberration we call the postwar baby boom. It was not, as is often thought, a short rise in the birthrate caused by returning GIs making up for lost time. It began that way in 1946, but instead of stopping in the 1950s (as in Europe), the tidal wave of births continued, affecting all races and classes with astonishing uniformity" (Jones 1980: 2). By and large, this definition is applicable to Canada.

6 On the baby boom phenomenon, see Jones (1980), and Kettle (1980).

7 See, for example, Palmer (1976b), Harney (1982), and Bell-Deutschmann (1978; 1979).

8 The anti-American element that underlies English-Canadian nationalism is probably a reaction to the threat of status displacement occasioned by the American presence.

9 The fact that English is the main language of science, industry, and commerce in the world no doubt provides a linguistic security that makes it easier to accept accommodations.

10 Analyses of aspects of ethnic mobilization in Canada during the years preceding the announcement of the policy in 1971 appear in Bociurkiw (1978), Burnet (1984), Jaworsky (1979), and Palmer (1976b).

11 The numbers are inexact, as it is not always possible to identify the ethnic affiliation of an organization by its name. For example, I counted 32 Ukrainian organizations that have submitted briefs, while Bociurkiw mentions 37 (1978: 124).

12 For a further discussion of this point, see Breton (1984). [Editor's note: Chapter Four in the present volume.]

13 Multiculturalism as a value defining the collective identity is underscored by the fact that the actual degree of acculturation of other ethnic groups is not significantly different in the two societies. It is also underscored by occasional statements to the effect that Canada has always opted for multiculturalism, in contrast with the United States. In the light of existing evidence, such statements clearly constitute a rewriting of Canadian history. See, for example, Palmer (1976b; 1982a; 1982b), Abella and Troper (1982), Sunahara (1981), and Bausenhart (1972).

14 The information on programs and activities presented in the following was obtained from interviews with Messrs Johnston, Patel, and Lugtigheid of the Multiculturalism Directorate in Ottawa. In addition, the following sources were consulted: Canada, Secretary of State (1973); Canada, Minister of State for Multiculturalism (1978; 1980; 1983; 1984b; 1984c); Canada, Canadian Consultative Council on Multiculturalism (1982; 1983; undated). The reader should also consult the interesting description and analysis made by Bociurkiw (1978), and by Jaworsky (1979).

15 The branch was transferred back to the Secretary of State in 1966.

16 The following are among the branch's publications during that period: *How to Become a Canadian Citizen; Our Land, Our History, Our Government; Citizen and Citoyen* (provided information and ideas for developing citizenship and related projects); *The Canadian Family Tree; What It Means to Become a Canadian Citizen; Celebrating Dominion Day;* and *Let Us Look at Prejudice and Discrimination.*

17 The films are: *Let's Discuss It* (dealt with techniques for organizing discussion groups); *Threshold* (for organizations involved with the social integration of immigrants); and *A Vote for Michalski* (on the experience of a newcomer to Canada).

18 These programs have not been abandoned. A recent publication of the Multiculturalism Directorate (Canada, Minister of State for Multiculturalism 1984b: 9), lists the following:
• Writing and Publications Program – provides grants for research, writing, translation, and publication of works reflecting the diversity of cultures in Canada.
• Performing and Visual Arts Program – provides funds for production and promotion of performing and visual arts depicting our cultural diversity.
• Canadian Ethnic Studies Program – encourages the study and research of important aspects of cultural pluralism.
• Group Development Program – provides funds for developmental purposes to voluntary organizations representing interests and concerns of ethnocultural communities.
• Intercultural Communications Program – provides funding for those organizations acting collectively on behalf of member groups or organizations and promoting cross-cultural activities.
• Cultural Integration Program – gives assistance primarily for the integration of immigrants into society, and their full participation in the community.
• Cultural Enrichment Program – encourages the learning and retention of heritage languages.

19 See, for example, Porter (1972; 1975), Brotz (1980), Peter (1981), Roberts and Clifton (1982), Smiley (1980), Vano (1981), Harney (1982), and Zolf (1980).

20 For a summary of the studies of this question, see Patel (1980: 7–15).
21 The instrumental preoccupation is also reflected in the brief submitted by
    the Minister of State for Multiculturalism to the Royal Commission on the
    Economic Union and Development Prospects for Canada (Canada, Minister
    of State for Multiculturalism 1984c).

CHAPTER FIFTEEN

1 I wish to thank Professor Rick Helmes-Hayes, James Curtis, Harold Troper,
   and Jeffrey Reitz for their valuable comments on an earlier version of this
   chapter.
2 For an excellent summary and analysis of Porter's views on ethnicity and
   stratification, see Vallee (1981).
3 Some of Porter's ideas are discussed further in what follows.
4 The Friends of the United Nations commissioned a panel of advisors to
   choose 50 model communities: 360 communities were considered, and of
   the 50 winners, three were in Canada: Walpole Island First Nations community near Windsor, Ontario, Sanikiluaq Inuit community in Eastern Hudson
   Bay, and the community of the Oujé-Bougoumou Crees of Northern Quebec
   (Valpy 1995).
5 An illustration is the title of a book on the history of the Finnish
   Organization of Canada: *Builders of Canada* (Eklund 1987).
6 Questions varied from poll to poll, referring to either "separation" or
   "independence" (Pinard 1992: 3).
7 The concept was developed to examine ethnic minorities consisting
   of immigrants and their descendants (Breton 1964 [chapter 10 in this
   volume-Ed.]), but it is eminently applicable to Quebec francophones –
   a collectivity that shows a degree of institutional completeness by far higher
   than that of any other minority in the country.
8 They are Hamilton, Kitchener, Windsor, Calgary, Victoria, St Catharines-
   Niagara, London, Edmonton, Winnipeg, Oshawa, Montreal, Ottawa-Hull,
   and Thunder Bay.
9 They are Regina, Saskatoon, Sudbury, and Halifax.
10 On the impact of social organization on intergroup relations, see Billig and
   Tajfel (1973). For an interesting analysis of official ethnic organizations, see
   Fontaine and Shiose (1991), and Shiose and Fontaine (1995).
11 This is a case for what Runciman (1966) has labelled "fraternalistic relative
   deprivation," which refers to feelings of deprivation not with one's position
   as an individual, but with the position of one's ingroup in society (Dion
   1986: 167).
12 On the social impact of the violation of status expectation, see Hughes
   (1958), and Kemper (1979).

13 See Barrett (1987) on extremist groups promoting racist ideologies.
14 I am grateful to Jeffrey Reitz for alerting me to this dimension of Porter's analysis.
15 For a review of the literature, see Labelle (1990).
16 For a brief review of the literature on this issue, see McAll (1991: 25–7).

References

Abella, Irving, and Harold Troper. 1982. *None Is Too Many.* Toronto: Lester and Orpen Dennys.

Agocs, Carol, and Monica Boyd. 1993. "The Canadian Ethnic Mosaic Recast: Theory, Research and Policy Frameworks for the 1990s." In *Social Inequality in Canada: Patterns, Problems and Policies,* edited by James Curtis, Edward Grabb, and Neil Guppy. Scarborough ON: Prentice-Hall. 330–52.

Albinski, Henry S. 1967. "Politics and Biculturalism in Canada: The Flag Debate," *Australian Journal of Politics and History* 13: 169–88.

Anderson, G.M. 1974. *Networks of Contact: The Portuguese and Toronto.* Waterloo, ON: Wilfrid Laurier University Press.

Andrew, J.V. 1977. *Bilingual Today, French Tomorrow.* Richmond Hill: BMG Publishing.

Bachrach, P., and M. Baratz. 1962. "Two Faces of Power," *Canadian Political Science Review* 59: 947–52.

Badets, Jane. 1993. "Canada's Immigrants: Recent Trends," *Canadian Social Trends* (Summer): 8–11.

Bailey, F.G. 1970. *Strategems and Spoils: A Social Anthropology of Politics.* Oxford: Basil Blackwell.

Balandier, Georges. 1969. *Anthropologie Politique.* Paris: Presses Universitaires de France.

Barber, Marilyn. 1969. "The Ontario Bilingual School Issue: Sources of Conflict." In *Minorities, Schools and Politics,* edited by D.G. Creighton *et al.* Toronto: University of Toronto Press.

Barnett, M.R. 1974. "Creating Political Identity," *Ethnicity* 1: 237–65.

Barrett, Stanley R. 1987. *Is God a Racist? The Right Wing in Canada.* Toronto: University of Toronto Press.

Barth, F. 1969. *Ethnic Groups and Boundaries.* Boston: Little, Brown, 1969.

Baureiss, Gunter. 1980. "Chinese Organizational Development: A Comment," *Canadian Ethnic Studies* 12: 124–30.

– 1982. "Ethnic Resilience and Discrimination: Two Chinese Communities in Canada," *Journal of Ethnic Studies* 10: 69–87.

Bausenhart, Werner A. 1972. "The Ontario German Language Press and its Suppression by Order-in-Council in 1918," *Canadian Ethnic Studies* 4: 35–48.

Beattie, Christopher, *et al.* 1972. *Bureaucratic Careers: Anglophones and Francophones in the Canadian Public Service.* Ottawa: Information Canada.

Beattie, Christopher. 1975. *Minority Men in a Majority Setting.* Toronto: McClelland and Stewart.

Beaujot, Roderic, and Kevin McQuillan. 1982. *Growth and Dualism: The Demographic Development of Canadian Society.* Toronto: Gage Publishing.

Behiels, Michael. 1985. *Prelude to Quebec's Quiet Revolution.* Montreal: McGill-Queen's University Press.

Bell, Daniel. 1975. "Ethnicity and Social Change." In *Ethnicity: Theory and Experience,* edited by Nathan Glazer and Daniel P. Moynihan. Cambridge MA: Harvard University Press. 141–74.

Bell, David, and Lorne Tepperman. 1979. *The Roots of Disunity.* Toronto: McClelland and Stewart.

Bellah, Robert N., Richard Madsen, William M. Sullivan, Ann Swidler, and Steven M. Tipton. 1985. *Habits of the Heart: Individualism and Commitment in American Life.* New York: Harper and Row.

Bell-Deutschmann, Linda. 1978. "Decline of the WASP? Dominant Group Identity in the Ethnic Plural Society." In *Ethnic Canadians: Culture and Education,* edited by Martin L. Kovacs. Regina: University of Regina, Canadian Plains Research Centre. 411–18.

– 1979. "Decline of the WASP? Dominant Group Identity in a Multi-Ethnic Society." PhD dissertation, University of Toronto, Department of Sociology.

Berger, Carl. 1970. *The Sense of Power: Studies in the Ideas of Canadian Imperialism, 1867–1914.* Toronto: The University of Toronto Press.

Berger, Peter L., and Thomas Luckmann. 1966. *The Social Construction of Reality.* Garden City NY: Doubleday.

Berger, Peter. 1966. "Identity as a Problem in the Sociology of Knowledge," *Archives Européennes de Sociologie* 7: 105–15.

Bernard, J. 1962. *American Community Behaviour,* revised edition. New York: Holt, Rinehart and Winston.

Bernier, Luc. 1993. "State-Owned Enterprises in Quebec: The Full Cycle, 1969–1990." In *Quebec: State and Society,* 2nd edition, edited by Alain G. Gagnon. Scarborough ON: Nelson. 243–58.

Berry, John W., Rudolf Kalin, and Donald M. Taylor. 1976. *Multiculturalism and Ethnic Attitudes in Canada.* Ottawa: Minister of Supply and Services Canada.

Billig, Michael, and Henri Tajfel. 1973. "Social Categorization and Similarity in Intergroup Behaviour," *European Journal of Social Psychology* 3: 27–52.

Billson, Janet Mancini. 1991. "Interlocking Identities: Gender, Ethnicity, and Power in the Canadian Context," *International Journal of Canadian Studies* 3: 49–67.

Bissonnette, Lise. 1987. "Quebec Faces a Challenge of the Cradle," *The Globe and Mail,* 25 July.

Black, Edwin R. 1975. *Divided Loyalties: Canadian Concepts of Federalism.* Montreal: McGill-Queen's University Press.

Blalock, H.M., Jr. 1967. *Toward a Theory of Minority-Group Relations.* New York: John Wiley and Sons.

Blishen, Bernard R. 1970. "Social Class and Opportunity in Canada," *Canadian Review of Sociology and Anthropology* 7: 110–27.

Blumer, Herbert. 1962. "Society as Symbolic Interaction." In *Human Behavior and Social Process,* edited by Arnold M. Rose. London: Routledge and Kegan Paul. 179–92.

– 1965. "Industrialization and Race Relations." In *Industrialization and Race Relations,* edited by G. Hunter. New York: Oxford University Press. 1965. 220–53.

Bociurkiw, Bohdan. 1978. "The Federal Policy of Multiculturalism and the Ukrainian Canadian Community." In *Ukrainian Canadians, Multiculturalism,* and *Separatism: An Assessment,* edited by Manolij R. Lupul. Edmonton: University of Alberta Press. 98–129.

Bogardus, E.S. 1928. *Immigration and Race Attitudes.* Boston: Heath.

Boissevain, Jeremy. 1968. "The Place of Non-groups in the Social Sciences," *Man* 3: 542–56.

– 1970. *The Italians of Montreal: Social Adjustment in a Plural Society.* Ottawa: Queen's Printer.

Bonacich, E. 1972. "A Theory of Ethnic Antagonism: The Split Labour Market," *American Sociological Review* 37: 547–59.

– 1973. "A Theory of Middleman Minorities," *American Sociological Review* 38: 583–94.

– 1976. "Advanced Capitalism and Black/White Relations in the United States: A Split Labour Market Interpretation," *American Sociological Review* 41: 34–51.

Borhek, J.T. 1970. "Ethnic Group Cohesion," *American Journal of Sociology* 76: 33–46.

Borrie, W.D. 1959. *The Cultural Integration of Immigrants.* New York: UNESCO.

Bothwell, Robert, Ian Drummond, and John English. 1981. *Canada Since 1945: Power, Politics, and Provincialism.* Toronto: University of Toronto Press.

Bourdieu, Pierre, and Jean-Claude Passeron. 1970. *La Réproduction: Eléments pour une théorie du système d'enseignement.* Paris: Les Editions de Minuit.

Bourdieu, Pierre. 1975. "Le fétichisme de la langue," *Actes de la Recherche en Sciences Sociales* 4: 2–32.

– 1979. "Les trois états du capital culturel," *Actes de la Recherche en Sciences Sociales* 30: 3–6.

Bovey, Wilfrid. 1936. *Canadien: étude sur les Canadiens français*, 3rd edition. London: Dent.

Boyd, Monica. 1992. "Gender, Visible Minority, and Immigrant Earnings Inequality: Reassessing an Employment Equity Premise. In *Deconstructing a Nation: Immigration, Multiculturalism and Racism in the 1990s in Canada*, edited by Vic Satzewich. Toronto: Fernwood. 279–321.

Brandmeyer, Gerard A., and R. Serge Denisoff. 1969. "Status Politics: An Appraisal of the Application of a Concept," *Pacific Sociological Review* 12: 5–12.

Brazeau, Jacques. 1958. "Language Differences and Occupational Experience," *Canadian Journal of Economics and Political Science* 24: 532–40.

– 1964. "Quebec's Emerging Middle Class." In *French-Canadian Society*, edited by Marcel Rioux and Yves Martin. Toronto: McClelland and Stewart.

Breton, Raymond. 1964. "Institutional completeness of ethnic communities and the personal relations of immigrants," *American Journal of Sociology* 70: 193–205.

– 1972. "The Socio-political Dynamics of the October Events," *The Canadian Review of Sociology and Anthropology* 9: 33–56. [Editor's note: Chapter Seven in this volume.]

– 1978. "Stratification and Conflict between Ethnolinguistic Communities with Different Social Structures," *The Canadian Review of Sociology and Anthropology* 15, 2: 148–57. [Editor's note: Chapter Two in this volume.]

– 1981. "Regionalism in Canada." In *Regionalism and Supranationalism*, edited by David M. Cameron. Montreal: Institute for Research on Public Policy. 57–79.

– 1983. "La Communauté ethnique, Communauté politique," *Sociologie et Sociétés* 15: 23–38.

– 1984. "The Production and Allocation of Symbolic Resources: An Analysis of the Linguistic and Ethnocultural Fields in Canada," *The Canadian Review of Sociology and Anthropology* 21, 2: 123–44. [Editor's note: Chapter Four in this volume.]

– 1986. "Multiculturalism and Canadian Nation-Building." In *The Politics of Gender, Ethnicity and Language in Canada*, edited by Alan Cairns and Cynthia Williams. Toronto: The University of Toronto Press. 27–66. [Editor's note: Chapter Fourteen in this volume.]

– 1988a. "English-French Relations in Canada." In *Understanding Canadian Society*, edited by James Curtis and Lorne Tepperman. Toronto: McGraw-Hill Ryerson. 557–86. [Editor's note: Chapter Five in this volume.]

– 1988b. "The Vesting of Ethnic Interests in State Institutions." In *Multiculturalism and Intergroup Relations*, edited by James S. Frideres. New York: Greenwood.

– 1991a. *The Governance of Ethnic Communities: Political Structure and Processes in Canada*. Westport CT: Greenwood.

– 1991b. "Policy Decisions and the Competition for Symbolic Resources." In *The Competitive State*, edited by Albert Breton *et al.* Dordrecht: Kluwer Academic.

Breton, Albert, and Raymond Breton. 1980. *Why Disunity? An Analysis of Linguistic and Regional Cleavages in Canada.* Montreal: Institute for Research on Public Policy.

Breton, Raymond, and Gail Grant. 1981. *La Langue de travail en Québec.* Montreal: L'Institut de Recherches politiques.

Breton, Raymond, Wsevolod Isajiw, Warren Kalbach, and Jeffrey G. Reitz. 1990. *Ethnic Identity and Equality: Varieties of Experience in a Canadian City.* Toronto: University of Toronto Press.

Breton, Raymond, and Howard Roseborough. 1968. "Ethnic, Religious and Regional Representation in the Federal Cabinet, 1867–1966." Unpublished ms.

Breton, Raymond, and Daiva Stasiulis. 1980. "Linguistic Boundaries and the Cohesion of Canada." In *Cultural Boundaries and the Cohesion of Canada,* Part 3, edited by Raymond Breton, Jeffrey G. Reitz, and Victor Valentine. Montreal: The Institute for Research on Public Policy.

Brettel, Caroline B. 1980. "Ethnicity and Entrepreneurs: Portuguese Immigrants in a Canadian City." *In People, Power and Process,* edited by Alexander Himelfarb and C. James Richardson. Toronto: McGraw-Hill Ryerson. 300–08.

Brinton, Mary C., and Victor Nee, eds. 1998. *The New Institutionalism in Sociology.* New York: Russell Sage Foundation.

Brody, M. Kenneth. 1982. "Yankee City and the Bicentennial: Warner's Study of Symbolic Activity in a Contemporary Setting," *Sociological Inquiry* 52: 259–73.

Brotz, Howard. 1980. "Multiculturalism in Canada: A Muddle," *Canadian Public Policy* 6: 41–6.

Brown, Craig. 1969. Introduction. In *Minorities, Schools and Politics,* edited by D.G. Creighton *et al.* Toronto: University of Toronto Press.

Brym, Robert. 1977. "Explaining Variations in Canadian Populist Movements." Paper presented at Canada/Poland Seminar, Warsaw.

– 1978. "Regional Social Structure and Agrarian Radicalism in Canada: Alberta, Saskatchewan, and New Brunswick," *Canadian Review of Sociology and Anthropology* 15: 339–51.

Brym, Robert, with Bonnie J. Fox. 1989. *From Culture to Power: The Sociology of English Canada.* Toronto: Oxford University Press.

Burnet, Jean. 1975. "The Policy of Multiculturalism within a Bilingual Framework: An Interpretation." In *Education of Immigrant Students,* edited by Aaron Wolfgang. Toronto: Ontario Institute for Studies in Education. 205–14.

– 1978. "The Policy of Multiculturalism within a Bilingual Framework: A Stock Taking," *Canadian Ethnic Studies* 10: 107–13.

– 1979. "Separate or Equal: A Dilemma of Multiculturalism." In *The Social Sciences and Public Policy in Canada.* Calgary: Faculty of Social Sciences, University of Calgary. 176–83.

– 1984. "Taking into Account: The Other Ethnic Groups and the Royal Commission on Bilingualism and Biculturalism." Paper presented at Sociology Colloquium, University of Calgary.

Butler, Dan, and Bruce D. MacNaughton. 1981. "Public Sector Growth in Canada: Issues, Explanations and Implications." In *Canadian Politics in the 1980s,* edited by Michael S. Whittington and Glen Williams. Toronto: Methuen. 84–107.

Cain, Glen G. 1976. "The Challenge of Segmented Labour Market Theories to Orthodox Theory," *Journal of Economic Literature* (December): 1215–57.

Cairns, Alan C. 1991. *Disruptions: Constitutional Struggles from the Charter to Meech Lake.* Toronto: McClelland and Stewart.

Campbell, D. 1978. "The Ethnic Literature and the Nova Scotia Experience." In *Banked Fires: The Ethnics of Nora Scotia.* Port Credit ON: The Scribbler's Press. 210–23.

Canada. 1963–77. *Annual Report.* Ottawa: Information Canada, Department of Manpower and Immigration.

– 1969. *Statement of the Government of Canada on Indian Policy.* Ottawa: Department of Indian Affairs and Northern Development.

– 1970. *The Cultural Contribution of the Other Ethnic Groups..* Report, Book IV, Ottawa: Queen's Printer.

– 1973. *A Review of Federal Government Programmes.* (Issued in conjunction with the First Canadian Conference on Multiculturalism.) Ottawa: The Department of the Secretary of State.

– 1974. *The Immigration Program.* Ottawa: Information Canada, Department of Manpower and Immigration.

– 1976. *Multicultural Program Granting Activity, Fiscal 1974–1975.* Ottawa: Secretary of State.

– 1978. *Multiculturalism as State Policy: Proceedings of the Second Canadian Conference on Multiculturalism (1976).* Ottawa: Supply and Services Canada, Minister of State for Multiculturalism.

– 1980a. *1978 Immigration Statistics.* Ottawa: Supply and Services Canada, Department of Employment and Immigration.

– 1980b. *Multiculturalism – A Canadian Reality: Proceedings of the Third Canadian Conference on Multiculturalism (1978).* Ottawa: Supply and Services Canada.

– 1982. *Annual Report, 1980.* Ottawa: Minister of Supply and Services Canada, Canadian Consultative Council on Multiculturalism.

– 1983a. *Annual Report, 1981–82.* Ottawa: Supply and Services Canada.

– 1983b. *Background Paper on Future Immigration Levels.* Ottawa: Supply and Services Canada.

– 1983c. *The Second Decade of Multiculturalism: Opportunities for the Future: Proceedings of the Fourth Canadian Conference on Multiculturalism (1981).* Ottawa: Supply and Services Canada.

– 1984a. *Equality Now! Report of the Special Committee on Visible Minorities in Canadian Society.* Ottawa: Supply and Services Canada.

– 1984b. *Multiculturalism and the Government of Canada.* Ottawa: Supply and Services Canada.

– 1984c. *The Place of Multiculturalism in Canada's Long-Term Economic Development.* Ottawa: Multiculturalism Directorate.

– 1990. *An Analysis of Attitudes towards Official Languages Policy among Anglophones.* Ottawa: Office of the Commissioner of Official Languages, Policy Analysis Branch.

– 1991. *Shaping Canada's Future Together: Proposals.* Ottawa: Supply and Services Canada.

– 1995a. *Basic Departmental Data – 1994.* Ottawa: Supply and Services Canada.

– 1995b. *Profile of the Aboriginal Population of Canada.* Ottawa: Ministry of Industry, Science, and Technology.

– Undated. *National Strategy on Race Relations.* Ottawa: The Multiculturalism Directorate.

Canadian Encyclopedia. 1985. Edmonton: Hurtig Publishers.

Cappon, Paul. 1974. *Conflit entre les Néo-Canadiens et les Francophones de Montreal.* Québec: Les Presses de l'Université Laval.

– 1978. "Nationalism and Inter-Ethnic and Linguistic Conflict in Quebec." In *The Canadian Ethnic Mosaic,* edited by Leo Driedger. Toronto: McClelland and Stewart. 327–39.

Careless, J.M.S. 1970. *Canada: A Story of Challenge.* Toronto: Macmillan of Canada.

Carlin, J.E. 1966. *Lawyers' Ethics.* New York: Russell Sage Foundation.

Cernetig, Miro. 1995. "White Flight, Chinese Distress," *Globe and Mail,* 30 September: D1.

Cheal, David J. 1981. "Ontario Loyalism: A Socio-Religious Ideology in Decline," *Canadian Ethnic Studies* 13: 40–51.

Choquette, Robert. 1975. *Language and Religion: A History of English-French Conflict in Ontario.* Ottawa: University of Ottawa Press.

Cipriani, Roberto, ed. 1987. "The Sociology of Legitimation," *Current Sociology* 35 (special issue).

Clapp, Orrin E. 1969. *The Collective Search for Identity.* New York: Rinehart and Winston.

Clark, S.D. 1962. *The Developing Canadian Community.* Toronto: University of Toronto Press.

– 1975a. "The Political Mobilization of Irish Farmers," *Canadian Review of Sociology and Anthropology* 12: 483–99.

– 1975b. "The Post Second World War Canadian Society," *Canadian Review of Sociology and Anthropology* 12, 1: 25–32.

Clark, T.N. 1973. *Community Power and Policy Outputs: A Review of Urban Research.* Beverley Hills: Sage Publications.

Cohen, Abner. 1969. *Custom and Politics in Urban Africa.* Berkeley: University of California Press.

– 1974a. "Introduction: The Lessons of Ethnicity." In *Urban Ethnicity,* edited by Abner Cohen. London: Tavistock Publications. 1–36.

– 1974b. *Two-Dimensional Man.* London: Routledge and Kegan Paul.

– ed. 1974c. *Urban Ethnicity.* London: Tavistock Publications.

– 1977. "Symbolic Action and the Structure of the Self." In *Symbols and Sentiments,* edited by Ioan Lewis. New York: Academic Press. 117–28.

Cohen, Andrew A. 1990. *A Deal Undone: The Making and Breaking of the Meech Lake Accord.* Vancouver: Douglas and McIntyre.

Cohen, Anthony P. 1985. *The Symbolic Construction of Community.* London: Tavistock.

Cole, Douglas. 1971. "The Problem of 'Nationalism' and 'Imperialism' in British Settlement Colonies," *Journal of British Studies* 10: 160–82.

– 1980. "Introduction," *Canadian Review of Studies in Nationalism* 7: 1–3 (special issue on Anglo-Canadian nationalism and social communication).

Coleman, James S. 1957. *Community Conflict.* Glencoe IL: The Free Press.

– 1964. *Introduction to Mathematical Sociology.* Glencoe IL: The Free Press.

– 1969. "Race Relations and Social Change." In *Race and the Social Sciences,* edited by Irwin Katz and Patricia Gurin. New York: Basic Books. 274–341.

– 1970. "Social Inventions," *Social Forces* 49: 163–73.

Coleman, William. 1984. *The Independence Movement in Quebec.* Toronto: University of Toronto Press.

Collins, O. 1945. "Ethnic Behavior in Industry: Sponsorship and Rejection in a New England Factory," *American Journal of Sociology* 51: 293–8.

Collins, Randall.1971. "Functional and Conflict Theories of Educational Stratification," *American Sociological Review* 36: 1002–19.

– 1975. *Conflict Sociology: Toward an Explanatory Science.* New York: Academic.

Connor, Walker. 1972. "Nation-Building or Nation-Destroying?" *World Politics* 24: 319–55.

Cook, Ramsay. 1971. "La Survivance, English-Canadian Style." In *The Maple Leaf Forever: Essays on Nationalism and Politics in Canada,* edited by Ramsay Cook. Toronto: Macmillan. 141–65.

– 1977. "Nationalist Ideologies in Canada." In *Options, Proceedings of the Conference on the Future of the Canadian Federation.* Toronto: University of Toronto. 81–92.

Cornell, P.G., J. Hamelin, F. Ouellet, and M. Trudel. 1967. *Canada: Unity in Diversity.* Toronto: Holt, Rinehart and Winston.

Creighton, Donald. 1976. *The Forked Road: Canada 1939–1957.* Toronto: McClelland and Stewart.

Crenson, Matthew A. 1983. *Neighborhood Politics.* Cambridge MA: Harvard University Press.

Crispo, John H., and H. W. Arthurs. 1968. "Industrial unrest in Canada: A diagnosis of recent experience," *Relations industrielles* 23: 237–62.

Dahlie, Jorgen, and Tissa Fernando, eds. 1982. *Ethnicity, Power and Politics in Canada.* Toronto: Methuen.

Dahrendorf, R. 1959. *Class and Class Conflict in Industrial Society.* Stanford CA: Stanford University Press.

Dandurand, Pierre. 1970. "Pouvoir et autorité du professeur de l'enseignement public québécois," *Sociologie et Sociétés* 2: 79–106.

Dansereau, Suzanne. 1987. "Ouvrir le Quebec aux Immigrants, à condition qu'ils parlent francais," *Le Devoir,* le 12 aout: 2.

Darroch, Gordon A., and Wilfred G Marston. 1984. "Patterns of Urban Ethnicity: Toward a Revised Ecological Model." In *Urbanism and Urbanization: Views, Aspects and Dimensions,* edited by Noel Iverson. Keiden: E.J. Brill.

Darroch, Gordon A. 1979. "Another Look at Ethnicity, Stratification, and Social Mobility in Canada," *Canadian Journal of Sociology* 4, 1: 1–25.

Dashefsky, Arnold. 1972. "And the search goes on: The Meaning of Religio-ethnic Identity and Identification," *Sociological Analysis* 33, 4: 239–45.

– 1975. "Theoretical Frameworks in the Study of Ethnic Groups: Towards a Social Psychology of Ethnicity," *Ethnicity* 2: 10–18.

Deshen, Shlomo. 1974. "Political Ethnicity and Cultural Ethnicity in Israel during the 1960s." In *Urban Ethnicity,* edited by Abner Cohen. London: Tavistock Publications.

Deutsch, Karl W. 1966. "Political Community and the North Atlantic Area." In *International Political Communities: An Anthology.* Garden City NY: Anchor Books.

Dion, G. 1967. "La concurrence syndicale au Québec," *Relations industrielles* 22: 74–84.

– 1969. "Les Relations patronales-ouvrieres sous la 'révolution tranquille'," *Relations* 344 (décembre): 334–7.

Dion, Kenneth L. 1986. "Responses to Perceived Discrimination and Relative Deprivation." In *Relative Deprivation and Social Comparison,* Ontario Symposium, volume 4, edited by James M. Olson. Hillsdale NJ: Eribaum. 159–79.

Dion, Leon. 1971. "French as an adopted language in Quebec." Lecture delivered at the Colloquium on Languages and Cultures in a Multi-Cultural Society, under the auspices of the Slavic-Canadian Inter-University Committee, Ottawa.

Driedger, Leo, and Glenn Church. 1974. "Residential Segregation and Institutional Completeness: A Comparison of Ethnic Minorities," *Canadian Review of Sociology and Anthropology* 11: 30–52.

Driedger, Leo. 1975. "In Search of Cultural Identity Factors: A Comparison of Ethnic Students," *Canadian Review of Sociology and Anthropology* 12: 150–62.

– 1977. "Toward a Perspective on Canadian Pluralism: Ethnic Identity in Winnipeg," *Canadian Journal of Sociology* 2: 77–96.

– 1978 "Ethnic Boundaries: A Comparison of Two Urban Neighbourhoods," *Sociology and Social Research* 62: 193–211.

du Preez, Peter. 1980. *Social Psychology of Politics.* Oxford: Basil Blackwell.

Duchacek, I.D. 1970. *Comparative Federalism: The Territorial Dimension of Politics.* New York: Holt, Rinehart and Winston.

Duncan, J. D. 1969. *Symbols and Social Theory.* New York: Oxford University Press.

Durkheim, Emile. 1912. *"Les formes élémentaires de la vie religieuse".* Paris: Félix Alcan.

Edelman, Murray. 1964. *The Symbolic Uses of Politics*. Urbana IL: The University of Illinois Press.

– 1971. *Politics as Symbolic Action: Mass Arousal and Quiescence*. New York: Academic Press.

Eisenstadt, S.N. 1952. "The Process of Absorption of New Immigrants in Israel," *Human Relations* 5: 222–31.

– 1954. "Social Mobility and Intergroup Leadership," *Transactions of the Second World Congress of Sociology* 2: 218–30.

– 1955. *The Absorption of Immigrants*. Glencoe IL: The Free Press.

Eklund, William. 1987. *Builders of Canada: History of the Finnish Organization of Canada, 1911–1971*. Toronto: Finnish Organization of Canada.

Ekos Research Associates. 1995. *Rethinking Government '94*. Ottawa: Ekos Research Associates.

Elazar, Daniel J. 1976. *Community and Polity: The Organizational Dynamics of American Jewry*. Philadelphia: Jewish Publication Society of America.

Etzioni, A. 1961. *A Comparative Analysis of Complex Organizations*. New York: The Free Press of Glencoe.

Faucher, Albert, and Maurice Lamontagne. 1953. "History of Industrial Development." In *Essais sur le Québec contemporain; Essays on Contemporary Quebec*, edited by Jean-Charles Falardeau. Québec: Les Presses de l'Université Laval.

Fischer, Claude S. 1975. "Toward a Subcultural Theory of Urbanism," *American Journal of Sociology* 80: 1319–41.

Fishman, J.A. 1965. "Varieties of Ethnicity and Varieties of Language Consciousness." Georgetown University Monographs No. 18.

Flood, M. 1968. *Wildcat Strike in Lake City*. Ottawa: Task Force on Labour Relations, Study no. 15.

Fontaine, Louise, and Yuki Shiose. 1991. "Ni Citoyens, ni Autres: la Catégorie politique 'Communauté culturelle'." In *Citoyenneté et Nationalité: Perspectives en France et au Québec*. Paris: Presses Universitaires de France. 435–43.

Foot, David K. 1978. *Public Employment and Compensation in Canada: Myths and Realities*. Montreal: Institute for Research on Public Policy.

Foster, Cecil. 1994. "The Mood has Soured," *Maclean's* 7 February. 33.

Fox, Paul. 1969. "Regionalism and Confederation." In *Regionalism in the Canadian Community, 1867–1967*, edited by Mason Wade. Toronto: University of Toronto Press.

Frazier, Franklin. 1957. *Race and Culture Contacts in the Modern World*. New York: Knopf.

Frideres, James S. 1993. *Native Peoples in Canada: Contemporary Conflicts*, 4th edition. Scarborough ON: Prentice-Hall.

Friesen, Gerald. 1984. *The Canadian Prairies: A History*. Toronto: University of Toronto Press.

Frye, Northrop. 1991. *Globe and Mail*, 15 April.

Galitzi, E.A. 1929. "A Study of Assimilation among the Roumanians in the United States." PhD dissertation, Columbia University.

Gamson, William A. 1968. *Power and Discontent.* Homewood IL: Dorsey.

Gans, Herbert. 1979. "Symbolic Ethnicity: The Future of Ethnic Groups and Cultures," *Ethnic and Racial Studies* 2: 1–20.

Garrison, W.A. 1968. *Power and Discontent.* Homewood IL: The Dorsey Press.

Geertz, Clifford. 1963. *Old Societies and New States.* New York: The Free Press of Glencoe.

– 1973. *The Interpretation of Cultures.* New York: Basic Books.

Gendron, Gilbert. 1987. "L'immigration est une fausse solution," *Le Devoir,* le 25 juin: 11.

Gerber, Linda. 1979. "The Development of Canadian Indian Communities: A Two-Dimensional Typology Reflecting Strategies of Adaptation to the Outside World," *Canadian Review of Sociology and Anthropology* 16, 4: 123–50.

– 1990. "Multiple Jeopardy: A Socioeconomic Comparison of Men and Women Among the Indian, Métis, and Inuit Peoples of Canada," *Canadian Ethnic Studies* 22, 3: 69–84.

Germani, Gino. 1964. "Social change and Intergroup Conflict." In *The New Sociology,* edited by I.L. Horowitz. New York: Oxford University Press.

Gerth, H.H., and C. Wright Mills, eds. 1958. *From Max Weber: Essays in Sociology.* New York: Oxford University Press.

Gibbins, Roger, and J. Rick Ponting. 1986. "An Assessment of the Probable Impact of Aboriginal Self-Government in Canada." In *The Politics of Gender, Ethnicity, and Language in Canada,* edited by Alan Cairns and Cynthia Williams. Toronto: University of Toronto Press. 171–245.

Giddens, A. 1973. *The Class Structure of the Advanced Societies.* London: Hutchinson.

Ginsberg, M. 1953. *Sociology.* London: Oxford University Press.

Glazer, Nathan, and Daniel P. Moynihan. 1963. *Beyond the Melting Pot.* Cambridge MA: MIT Press.

Globe and Mail. 1987. Toronto, 4 June.

Globe and Mail. 1988. Toronto, 22 December.

Globe and Mail. 1990. Toronto, 9 July.

Globe and Mail. 1991. Toronto. 6 November.

Goffman, Irving. 1959. *The Presentation of Self in Everyday Life.* Garden City NY: Doubleday.

Goodman, Leo. 1961. "Modifications of the Dorn-Stouffer-Tibbits Method for Testing the Significance of Comparisons in Sociological Data," *American Journal of Sociology* 66: 355–63.

Gordon, Milton. 1964. *Assimilation in American Life: The Role of Race, Religion and National Origins.* New York: Oxford University Press.

Granovetter, Mark S. 1974. *Getting a Job: A Study of Contacts and Careers.* Cambridge MA: Harvard University Press.

– 1985. "Economic Action and Social Structure: The Problem of Embeddedness," *American Journal of Sociology* 91: 481–510.

Grant, George. 1965. *Lament for a Nation.* Toronto: McClelland and Stewart.

Grant, John W., ed. 1972. *The Church in the Canadian Era.* Toronto: McGraw-Hill Ryerson.

Greeley, Andrew M. 1974. *Ethnicity in the United States: A Preliminary Reconnaissance.* New York: John Wiley and Sons.

Gregg, Allan, and Michael Posner. 1990. *The Big Picture: What Canadians Think about Almost Anything.* Toronto: Macfarlane Walter and Ross.

Griswold, Wendy. 1987. "The Fabrication of Meaning: Literary Interpretation in the United States, Great Britain, and the West Indies," *American Journal of Sociology* 92: 1077–117.

Guay, J. 1969. "Une presse asservie: des faits," *Socialisme* 69 (avril-mai-juin): 67–73.

Guindon, Hubert. 1964. "Social Unrest, Social Class, and Quebec's Bureaucratic Revolution," *Queen's Quarterly* 70: 150–62.

– 1968. "Two Cultures: An Essay on Nationalism, Class, and Ethnic Tension." In *Contemporary Canada*, edited by R.H. Leach. Toronto: University of Toronto Press. 33–59.

Gusfield, Joseph R. 1981. *The Culture of Public Problems.* Chicago: University of Chicago Press.

Hagan, Everett E. 1962. *On the Theory of Social Change.* Homewood IL: Dorsey Press.

Hagy, James. 1969. "Quebec Separatists: The First Twelve Years," *Queen's Quarterly* 76: 229–38.

Hamelin, Louis-Edmond. 1961. "Evolution Numérique seculaire du clergé catholique clans le Quebec," *Recherches Sociographiques* 2: 189–238.

Hammond, P. E., and R. E. Mitchell. 1965. "Segmentation of radicalism – the case of the Protestant campus minister," *American Journal of Sociology* 71: 133–43.

Handlin, O., and M. Handlin. 1956. "Ethnic Factors in Social Mobility," *Explorations in Entrepreneurial History* 9: 1–7.

Hannerz, Ulf. 1974. "Ethnicity and Opportunity in Urban America." In *Urban Ethnicity*, edited by Abner Cohen. London: Tavistock Publications. 37–76.

Harney, Robert F. 1982. "Ethnic Archival and Library Materials in Canada: Problems of Bibliographic Control and Preservation," *Ethnic Forum* 2: 3–31.

– 1987. "The Effects of Multiculturalism and Ethnic Strategic," Krakow: Conference on Polonia against the Background of Other Ethnic Groups in Canada. Unpublished ms.

– 1988. "'So Great a Heritage as Ours' – Immigration and the Survival of the Canadian Polity," *Daedalus* 117: 51–97.

Harrison, Trevor. 1995. *Of Passionate Interest: Right-Wing Populism and the Reform Party of Canada.* Toronto: University of Toronto Press.

Harvey, Julien. 1987. "Nos Médias sans Immigrants," *Relations* (juillet-aout): 179–80.

Hawkins, Freda. 1972. *Canada and Immigration: Public Policy and Public Concern.* Montreal: McGill-Queen's University Press.

Hawthorne, H.B., ed. 1966–7. *A Survey of the Contemporary Indians of Canada: Economic, Political, Educational Needs and Policies.* 2 vols. Ottawa: Department of Indian Affairs.

Hechter, M. 1978. "Group Formation and the Cultural Division of Labor," *American Journal of Sociology* 84, 2: 293–318.

Heinz, Donald. 1983. "The Struggle to Define America." In *The New Christian Right*, edited by Robert C. Liebman and Robert Wuthnow. New York: Aldine Publishing Co. 133–48.

Helmes-Hayes, Rick, and James Curtis (eds.). 1998. *"The Vertical Mosaic" Revisited*. Toronto: University of Toronto Press.

Henripin, Jacques. 1957. "From Acceptance of Nature to Control: The Demography of the French Canadians since the Seventeenth Century," *Canadian Journal of Economics and Political Science* 23: 10–19.

Hiller, Harry H., and Simon Langlois. 2001. "The Most Important Books/Articles in Canadian Sociology in the Twentieth Century: A Report," *Canadian Journal of Sociology* 26, 3: 513–16.

Hirsch, Paul M. 1972. "Processing Fads and Fashions: An Organization-set Analysis of Cultural Identity Systems," *American Journal of Sociology* 77: 639–59.

– 1986. "From Ambushes to Golden Parachutes: Corporate Takeovers as an Instance of Cultural Framing and Institutional Integration," *American Journal of Sociology* 91: 800–37.

Hirschman, Albert O. 1970. *Exit, Voice, and Loyalty*. Cambridge MA: Harvard University Press.

Hofstadter, Richard. 1944. *Social Darwinism in American Thought*. Boston: Beacon Press.

Horowitz, Donald L. 1985. *Ethnic Groups in Conflict*. Berkeley: University of California Press.

House of Commons. 1971. *Debates*. Vol. 115, No. 187. 3rd Session, 28th Parliament.

Houston, Cecil, and William Smyth. 1980. *The Sash Canada Wore: A Historical Geography of the Orange Order in Canada*. Toronto: University of Toronto Press.

Hughes, Everett C., and Helen MacGill Hughes. 1952. *Where Peoples Meet: Race and Ethnic Frontiers*. Glencoe IL: The Free Press.

Hughes, Everett C. 1945. "Dilemmas and Contradictions of Status," *American Journal of Sociology* 50: 353–9.

– 1958. *Men and Their Work*. New York: Free Press.

Isaacs, Harold R. 1975. "Basic Group Identity: The Idols of the Tribe." In *Ethnicity: Theory and Experience*, edited by Nathan Glazer and Daniel P. Moynihan. Cambridge MA: Harvard University Press.

Isajiw, Wsevolod W. 1974. "Definitions of Ethnicity," *Ethnicity* 1, 2: 111–24.

– 1977. "Olga in Wonderland: Ethnicity in Technological Society," *Canadian Ethnic Studies* 9, 1: 77–85.

– 1990. "Ethnic-Identity Retention." In *Ethnic Identity and Equality: Varieties of Experience in a Canadian City*, by Raymond Breton, Wsevolod W. Isajiw, Warren E. Kalbach, and Jeffrey G. Reitz. Toronto: University of Toronto Press. 34–91.

Jackson, John. 1975. *Community and Conflict: A Study of French-English Relations in Ontario*. Toronto: Holt, Rinehart and Winston.

– 1977. "The Functions of Language in Canada: On the Political Economy of Language." In *The Individual, Language and Society in Canada*, edited by W.H.

Coons, Donald M. Taylor, and Marc-Adelard Tremblay. Ottawa: The Canada Council. 61–76.

Jamieson, S. 1970. "The third wave of labour unrest and industrial conflict in Canada: 1900–1967," *Relations industrielles* 25: 22–31.

Janowitz, Morris. 1976. *Social Control of the Welfare State*. New York: Elsevier.

Jansen, Clifford J. 1981. *The Italians of Vancouver: A Case Study of Internal Differentiation of an Ethnic Group*. Toronto: York University.

Jaszi, O. 1929. *The Dissolution of the Habsburg Monarchy*. Chicago: University of Chicago Press.

Jaworsky, John. 1979. "A Case Study of the Canadian Federal Government's Multiculturalism Policy." MA thesis, Carleton University.

Jenkins, Shirley, ed. 1988. *Ethnic Associations and the Welfare State: Services to Immigrants in Five Countries*. New York: Columbia University Press.

Jones, Landon Y. 1980. *Great Expectations*. New York: Ballantine Books.

Joy, Richard J. 1967. *Languages in Conflict*. Ottawa: published by the author.

Juteau-Lee, Danielle. 1979. "The Evolution of Nationalism in Quebec." In *Two Nations, Many Cultures, Ethnic Groups in Canada*, edited by Jean Leonard Elliott. Scarborough ON: Prentice-Hall of Canada. 60–74.

Juteau-Lee, Danielle, and Jean Lapointe. 1982a. "The Emergence of Franco-Ontarians: New Identities, New Boundaries." In *Two Nations, Many Cultures: Ethnic Groups in Canada*, edited by Jean L. Elliott. Scarborough ON: Prentice-Hall. 99–113.

– 1982b. "From French Canadians to Franco-Ontarians and *Ontarois*: New Boundaries, New Identities." In *Two Nations, Many Cultures*, edited by Jean Elliott. Scarborough ON: Prentice-Hall. 173–86.

Kallen, Evelyn. 1977. *Spanning the Generations: A Study of Jewish Identity*. Don Mills ON: Longmans Canada.

– 1988. "The Meech Lake Accord: Entrenching a Pecking Order of Minority Rights," *Canadian Public Policy* 14: S107–20.

Kapferer, B. 1969. "Norms and the Manipulation of Relationships in a Work Context." In *Social Networks in Urban Situations*, edited by J.C. Mitchell. Manchester: Manchester University Press.

Katzman, M.T. 1969. "Opportunity, Subculture and the Economic Performance of Urban Ethnic Groups," *American Journal of Economics and Sociology* 28: 351–66.

Kelly, Karen. 1995. "Visible Minorities: A Diverse Group," *Canadian Social Trends* 37 (Summer): 2–8.

Kemper, Theodore D., and Randall Collins. 1990. "Dimensions of Micro-interaction," *American Journal of Sociology* 96: 32–68.

Kemper, Theodore D. 1979. "Why are the streets so dirty? Social Psychological and Stratification Factors in the Decline of Municipal Services," *Social Forces* 58: 422–42.

Kettle, John. 1980. *The Big Generation*. Toronto: McClelland and Stewart.

Klapp, Orrin E. 1969. *Collective Search for Identity*. New York: Holt, Rinehart and Winston.

Kotler, Milton. 1969. *Neighborhood Government: The Local Foundations of Political Life.* Indianapolis: Bobbs-Merrill.

Kriesberg, L. 1955. "Occupational Controls among Steel Distributors," *American Journal of Sociology* 61: 203–12.

Krosenbrink-Gelissen, Lilianne Ernestine. 1993. "The Native Women's Association of Canada." In *Native Peoples in Canada: Contemporary Conflicts*, 4th ed., edited by James S. Frideres. Scarborough ON: Prentice-Hall. 335–64.

Labelle, Micheline. 1990. "Femmes et Migrations au Canada: Bilan et Perspectives," *Canadian Ethnic Studies* 22, 1: 67–82.

Lalonde, André. 1982. "Le Patriote de l'Ouest and French Settlement on the Prairies." In *The Quebec and Acadian Diaspora in North America*, edited by Raymond Breton and Pierre Savard. Toronto: The Multicultural History Society of Ontario.

Lanctot, Gustave. 1967. *Canada and the American Revolution, 1774–1783.* London: George G. Harrap.

Lautard, Hugh, and Neil Guppy. 1990. "*The Vertical Mosaic* Revisited: Occupational Differentials among Canadian Ethnic Groups." In *Race and Ethnic Relations in Canada*, edited by Peter Li. Toronto: Oxford University Press. 189–208.

Lavigne, Gilles. 1980. "Le Pouvoir ethnique: ses assises et ses objets." In *Les Transformations du pouvoir au Québec*, edited by Association canadienne des sociologues et anthropologues de langue française. Montréal: Editions coopératives Albert Saint-Martin.

Lavoie, Yoland. 1981. *L'Emigration des Québécois aux Etats-Unis de 1840 à 1930.* Quebec: Editeur Officiel du Québec.

Levitt, Joseph. 1981. "Race and Nation in Canadian Anglophone Historiography," *Canadian Review of Studies in Nationalism* 8: 1–16.

Lewin, Kurt. 1953. "Self-Hatred among Jews." In *Race, Prejudice and Discrimination*, edited by Arnold M. Rose. New York: Alfred A. Knopf. 321–32.

Lieberson, Stanley. 1961a. "The Impact of Residential Segregation on Ethnic Assimilation," *Social Forces* 40: 52–7.

– 1961b. "A Societal Theory of Race and Ethnic Relations," *American Sociological Review* 26: 902–10.

– 1963. *Ethnic Patterns in American Cities.* New York: The Free Press.

– 1980. *A Piece of the Pie: Black and White Immigrants since 1880.* Berkeley: University of California Press.

Linteau, Paul-André, René Durocher, and Jean-Claude Robert. 1979. *Histoire du Québec contemporain: de la Confédération à la Crise.* Québec: Boréal Press.

Little Bear, Leroy, Menno Boldt, and J. Anthony Long, eds. 1984. *Pathways to Self Determination: Canadian Indians and the Canadian State.* Toronto: University of Toronto Press.

Lupul, Manoly. 1970. "Educational Crises in the New Dominion to 1917." In *Canadian Education: A History*, edited by J. Donald Wilson *et al.* Scarborough ON: Prentice-Hall.

Lyman, Stanford M. 1968. "Contrasts in the Community Organization of Chinese and Japanese in North America," *Canadian Review of Sociology and Anthropology* 5: 51–67.

Lyman, Stanford M., and William A. Douglas. 1970. "Ethnicity: Strategies of Collective and Individual Impression Management," *Social Research* 40: 344–65.

Mackenzie, W.J.M. 1967. *Politics and Social Science.* Harmondsworth: Penguin.

MacIver, R.M. 1964. "Subjective meaning in the social situation." In *Sociological Theory,* 2nd ed., edited by L.A. Coser and B. Rosenberg. New York: The Macmillan Company.

Maistre, G. 1971. "Apercu Socio-économique de la presse quotidienne québécoise," *Recherches Sociographiques* 12: 105–15.

Mann, W.E. 1976. "The Canadian Church Union, 1925." In *Religion in Canadian Society,* edited by Stewart Crysdale and L. Wheatcroft. Toronto: Macmillan.

March, James G., and Johan P. Olsen. 1976. *Ambiguity and Choice in Organizations.* Bergen, Norway: Universitetsforlaget.

Marshall, T.H. 1965. *Social Policy in the Twentieth Century.* London: Hutchison.

Mason, P. 1970. *Race Relations.* New York: Oxford University Press.

Mayhew, L. 1968. "Ascription in Modern Societies," *Sociological Inquiry* 38, 2: 105–20.

Mazrui, A.A. 1969. "Pluralism and National Integration." In *Pluralism in Africa,* edited by L. Kuper and M.G. Smith. Berkeley CA: University of California Press. 333–49.

McAll, Christopher. 1991. *Beyond Culture: Immigration in Contemporary Quebec.* Ottawa: Economic Council of Canada, Working Paper No. 25.

McCall, J.J. 1973. *Income Mobility, Racial Discrimination and Economic Growth.* Lexington MA: Lexington Books.

McInnis, Edgar. 1969. *Canada: A Political and Social History.* 3rd ed. Toronto: Holt, Rinehart and Winston.

McKay, James, and Frank Lewins. 1978. "Ethnicity and Ethnic Groups: A Conceptual Analysis and Reformulation," *Ethnic and Racial Studies* 1: 412–27.

McKay, James. 1982. "An Exploratory Synthesis of Primordial and Mobilizationist Approaches to Ethnic Phenomena," *Ethnic and Racial Studies* 54: 395–420.

McNaught, Kenneth. 1966. "The National Outlook of English-speaking Canadians." In *Nationalism in Canada,* edited by Peter Russell. Toronto: McGraw-Hill Ryerson. 61–71.

McRae, Kenneth. 1964. "The Structure of Canadian History." In *The Founding of New Societies,* edited by Louis Hartz. New York: Harcourt, Brace and World.

– 1974. "Consociationalism and the Canadian Political System." In *Consociational Democracies: Political Accommodation in Segmented Societies,* edited by Kenneth McRae. Toronto: McClelland and Stewart.

McRoberts, Kenneth, and Dale Posgate. 1980. *Quebec: Social Change and Political Crisis.* Toronto: McClelland and Stewart.

Mead, George Herbert. 1934. *Mind, Self and Society.* Chicago: University of Chicago Press.

Meisel, John. 1976. "Citizen Demands and Government Response," *Canadian Public Policy* 2: 564–72.

Meyer, John W., and James G. Roth. 1970. "A Reinterpretation of American Status Policies," *Pacific Sociology Review* 13: 95–102.

Migué, J.L. 1970. "Le nationalisme, l'unité nationale et la théorie économique de l'information," *Revue Canadienne d'Economique* 111: 183–98.

Miller, James R. 1989. *Skyscrapers Hide the Heavens: A History of Indian-White Relations in Canada*, 2nd ed. Toronto: University of Toronto Press.

Mills, C.W. *et al.* 1950. The Puerto Rican Journey. New York: Harper and Brothers.

Morf, G. 1970. *Le Terrorisme Québécois*. Montréal: Les Editions de l'Homme.

Morris, Ray, and Kenneth A. Price. 1980. "The Social Construction of Ethnicity in English Montreal and Toronto." Paper presented at the CSAA meetings in Montreal.

Morrison, Bruch R., and C. Roderich Wilson, eds. 1995. *Native Peoples: The Canadian Experience*, 2nd ed. Toronto: McClelland and Stewart.

Murphy, Raymond. 1984. "The Structure of Closure: A Critique and Development of the Theories of Weber, Collins, and Parkin," *The British Journal of Sociology* 35: 547–67.

Nagata, Judith. 1974. "What is a Maly? Situational Selection of Ethnic Identity in a Plural Society," *American Ethnologist* 1: 441–50.

– 1979. "One Vine, Many Branches: Internal Differentiation in Canadian Ethnic Groups." In *Two Nations, Many Cultures: Ethnic Groups in Canada*, edited by Jean Leonard Elliott. Scarborough ON: Prentice-Hall. 173–81.

Nahirny, V., and J.A. Fishman. 1965. "American Immigrant Groups: Ethnic Identification and the Problem of Generations," *Sociological Research* 13: 311–26.

Nettler, Gwynn. 1957. "A Measure of Alienation," *American Sociological Review* 22: 670–7.

Neuwirth, Gertrud. 1969. "A Weberian Outline of a Theory of Community: Its Application to the 'Dark Ghetto,'" *British Journal of Sociology* 20: 148–63.

Newman, Peter C. 1963. *Renegade in Power: The Diefenbaker Years*. Toronto: McClelland and Stewart.

– 1991. "The Closet Federalism of the Parti Québécois," *Maclean's* (30 December).

Nieburg, N.L. 1969. *Political Violence: The Behavioural Process*. New York: St Martin's Press.

Nielsen, Francois. 1985. "Toward a Theory of Ethnic Solidarity in Modern Societies," *American Sociological Review* 50: 133–49.

Nock, David A. 1981. "The Anglican Episcopate and Changing Conceptions of Canadian Identity," *Canadian Review of Studies in Nationalism* 8: 85–100.

– 1982. "Patriotism and Patriarchs: Anglican Archbishops and Canadianization," *Canadian Ethnic Studies* 14: 79–94.

Norris, Mary Jane. 1990. "The Demography of Aboriginal People in Canada." In *Ethnic Demography: Canadian Immigrant, Racial and Cultural Variations*, edited by

Shiva S. Halli, Frank Trovato, and Leo Driedger. Ottawa: Carleton University Press. 33–60.

O'Brien, David J. 1975. *Neighborhood Organization and Interest-Group Processes.* Princeton NJ: Princeton University Press.

O'Bryan, K.G., J.G. Reitz, and O.M. Kuplowska. 1976. *Non-Official Languages: A Study in Canadian Multiculturalism.* Ottawa: Supply and Services Canada.

Ogmundson, Rick, and J. McLaughlin. 1992. "Trends in the Ethnic Origins of Canadian Elites: The Decline of the BRITS?" *Canadian Review of Sociology and Anthropology* 29, 2: 227–38.

Ogmundson, Rick. 1980. "Toward Study of the Endangered Species Known as the Anglophone Canadian," *Canadian Journal of Sociology* 5: 1–12.

Olson, Mancur. 1965. *The Logic of Collective Action.* Cambridge MA: Harvard University Press.

Ontario Human Rights Commission. 1977. *Life-Together: A Report on Human Rights in Ontario.* Toronto: The Ontario Human Rights Commission.

Ormsby, William. 1974. "The Province of Canada: The Emergence of Consociational Politics." In *Consociational Democracy,* edited by Kenneth McRae. Toronto: McClelland and Stewart.

Ossenberg, Richard. 1967. "The Conquest Revisited: Another Look at Canadian Dualism," *The Canadian Review of Sociology and Anthropology* 4: 201–18.

Ouellet, Fernand. 1966. *Histoire économique et sociale du Québec, 1760–1850.* Montreal: Fides.

Paillé, Michel. 1986. *Aspects démolinguistiques de l'Avenir de la Population du Québec.* Québec: Conseil de la Langue française.

Pal, Leslie A. 1993. *Interests of State: The Politics of Language, Multiculturalism, and Feminism in Canada.* Montreal: McGill-Queen's University Press.

Palmer, H., ed. 1974. *Immigration and the Rise of Multi-Culturalism.* Toronto: Copp Clark.

Palmer, H. 1976a. "Mosaic versus Melting Pot? Immigration and Ethnicity in Canada and the United States," *International Journal* 31: 488–528.

– 1976b. "Reluctant Hosts: Anglo-Canadian Views of Multiculturalism in the Twentieth Century." In *Multiculturalism as State Policy: Report of the Second Canadian Conference on Multiculturalism.* Ottawa: Supply and Services Canada. 81–118.

– 1982a. "Canadian Immigration and Ethnic History in the 1970s and 1980s," *Journal of Canadian Studies* 17: 35–50.

– 1982b. *Patterns of Prejudice: A History of Nativism in Alberta.* Toronto: McClelland and Stewart.

Panitch, Leo. 1977. "The Role and Nature of the Canadian State." In *The Canadian State: Political Economy and Political Power,* edited by Leo Panitch. Toronto: University of Toronto Press. 3–27.

Parenti, M. 1969. "Ethnic Politics and Persistence of Ethnic Identification." In *Ethnic Group Politics*, edited by H.A. Bailey, Jr., and E. Katz. Columbus OH: Charles E. Merrill. 267–83.

Parkin, Frank. 1979. *Marxism and Class Theory: A Bourgeois Critique.* London: Tavistock.

Parsons, T. 1960. *Structure and Process in Modern Societies.* New York: The Free Press.

Patel, Dhiru. 1980. *Dealing with Interracial Conflict: Policy Alternatives.* Montreal: Institute for Research on Public Policy.

Pelletier, G. 1971. *La Crise d'Octobre.* Montréal: Les Editions du Jour.

Pelletier, Réjean. 1990. "Social Transformation and Political Change in Quebec Political Parties and the State." In *National Survival in Dependent Societies*, edited by Raymond Breton, Gilles Houle, Gary Caldwell, Edmund Mokrzycki, and Edmund Wnuk-Lipinski. Ottawa: Carleton University Press. 297–322.

Pennefather, R.S. 1984. *The Orange and the Black.* Orange and Black Publications.

Peter, Karl. 1981. "The Myth of Multiculturalism and Other Political Fables." In *Ethnicity, Power and Politics in Canada*, edited by Jorgen Dahlie and Tissa Fernando. Toronto: Methuen. 56–67.

Peterson Royce, Anya. 1982. *Ethnic Identity.* Bloomington: Indiana University Press.

Peterson, W. 1958. "A General Typology of Migration," *American Sociological Review* 23: 256–66.

Pfeffer, Jeffrey. 1981. "Management as Symbolic Action: The Creation and Maintenance of Organizational Paradigms," *Research in Organizational Behavior* 3: 1–52.

Pinard, Maurice. 1968. "Mass Society and Political Movements: A New Formulation," *American Journal of Sociology* 73: 682–90.

– 1992. "The Quebec Independence Movement: A Dramatic Resurgence." Working Paper No. 92–06. Montreal: McGill University, Department of Sociology.

– 1994. "De Meech et Charlottetown au … Québec," *Opinion Canada* 2, 3.

Pinard, Maurice, and Richard Hamilton. 1977. "The Independence Issue and the Polarization of the Electorate: The 1973 Quebec Election," *Canadian Journal of Political Science* 10: 215–59.

– 1984. "The Class Bases of the Quebec Independence Movement: Conjectures and Evidence," *Ethnic and Racial Studies* 7: 19–54.

Pitman, W. 1977. "Now Is Not Too Late." Task Force on Human Relations. Mimeographed. Toronto: Council of Metropolitan Toronto.

Ponting, J. Rick. 1988. "Public Opinion on Aboriginal Peoples' Issues in Canada," *Canadian Social Trends* 11 (Winter): 9–17.

– 1990. "Internationalization: Perspectives on an Emerging Direction in Aboriginal Affairs," *Canadian Ethnic Studies* 22, 3: 85–109.

Ponting, T. Rick, and Roger Gibbins. 1980. *Out of Irrelevance: A Socio-Political Introduction to Indian Affairs in Canada.* Toronto: Butterworth.

Porter, John. 1965. *The Vertical Mosaic: An Analysis of Social Class and Power in Canada.* Toronto: University of Toronto Press.

– 1972. "Dilemmas and Contradictions of a Multi-Ethnic Society." In *Proceedings and Transactions of the Royal Society of Canada*, 4th series, vol. 10: 193–205.

– 1975. "Ethnic Pluralism in Canadian Perspective." In *Ethnicity: Theory and Experience*, edited by Nathan Glazer and Daniel P. Moynihan. Cambridge MA: Harvard University Press. 267–304.

– 1979. "Melting Pot or Mosaic: Revolution of Reversion?" In *The Measure of Canadian Society*, edited by J. Porter. Toronto: Gage. 139–62.

Poulantzas, N. 1975. *Classes in Contemporary Capitalism.* Atlantic Highlands NJ: Humanities Press.

Powell, Walter W., and Paul J. DiMaggio, eds. 1991. *The New Institutionalism in Organizational Analysis.* Chicago: University of Chicago Press.

Price, C.A. 1959. "Immigration and Group Settlement." In The Cultural Integration of Immigrants, edited by W.D. Borrie. New York: UNESCO.

Pross, Paul. 1982. "Space, Function and Interest: The Problem of Legitimacy in the Canadian State." In *The Administration State in Canada*, edited by O.P. Dwivedi. Toronto: University of Toronto Press. 107–29.

– 1986. *Group Politics and Public Policy.* Toronto: Oxford University Press.

Proulx, Jean-Pierre. 1987. "Le scandale est terminé mais il reste l'affichage," *Le Devoir,* le 22 aout: l.

Pye, Lucian W. 1969. "The roots of insurgency and the commencement of rebellions." In *Internal War,* edited by H. Eckstein. New York: The Free Press of Glencoe.

Quebec Liberal Party. 1991. *A Quebec Free to Choose.* Quebec: Quebec Liberal Party Constitutional Committee.

Rayack, E. 1961. "Discrimination and the Occupational Progress of Negroes," *Review of Economics and Statistics* (May): 209–14.

Rea, J.E. 1977. "My main line is the kiddies ... make them good Christians and good Canadians, which is the same thing." In *Identities: The Impact of Ethnicity on Canadian Society,* edited by Wsevolod lsajiw. Toronto: Peter Martin Associates. 3–10.

Reepolds, L.G. 1935. *The British Immigrant.* Toronto: Oxford University Press.

Reitz, Jeffrey G. 1980a. "Immigrants, Their Descendents, and the Cohesion of Canada." In *Cultural Boundaries and the Cohesion of Canada,* by Raymond Breton, Jeffrey G. Reitz, and Victor Valentine. Montreal: Institute for Research on Public Policy. 329–417.

– 1980b. *The Survival of Ethnic Groups.* Toronto: McGraw-Hill Ryerson.

– 1990. "Ethnic Concentrations in Labour Markets and Their Implications for Ethnic Inequality." In *Ethnic Identity and Equality: Varieties of Experience in a Canadian City,* by Raymond Breton, Wsevolod W. Isajiw, Warren E. Kalbach, and Jeffrey G. Reitz. Toronto: University of Toronto Press. 135–86.

Reitz, Jeffrey G., and Raymond Breton. 1994. *The Illusion of Difference: Realities of Ethnicity in Canada and the United States.* Toronto: CD Howe Institute.

Reitz, Jeffrey G., Lorrana Calzavara, and Donna Dasko. 1981. "Ethnic Inequality and Segregation in Jobs." Toronto: University of Toronto, Centre for Urban and Community Studies.

Richmond, Anthony, and Warren E. Kalbach. 1980. *Factors in the Adjustment of Immigrants and their Descendents*. 1971 Census Monograph. Ottawa: Minister of Supply and Services.

Richmond, Anthony. 1964. "Social Mobility of Immigrants in Canada," *Population Studies* 18: 53–69.

– 1967. *Post-War Immigrants in Canada*. Toronto: University of Toronto Press.

Roberge, P. 1969. "Les conflicts intersyndicaux an Québec, 1907–1967," *Relations industrielles* 24: 521–56.

Roberts, Lance W., and Rodney A. Clifton. 1982. "Exploring the Ideology of Canadian Multiculturalism," *Canadian Public Policy* 8: 88–94.

Rosanvallon, Pierre. 1995. *La Nouvelle Question Sociale*. Paris: Seuil.

Rothschild, Joseph. 1981. *Ethnopolitics: A Conceptual Framework*. New York: Columbia University Press.

Royal Commission on Bilingualism and Biculturalism. 1967. *The Official Languages*. Ottawa: Queen's Printer.

– 1969. *The Cultural Contribution of the Other Ethnic Groups*. Ottawa: Queen's Printer.

Runciman, W.G. 1966. *Relative Deprivation and Social Justice*. Berkeley: University of California Press.

Savas, Daniel J. 1987. "Interest Group Leadership and Government Funding: The Federation des Franco-Colombiens – Community Organization or Government Policy Agent?" PhD dissertation. University of British Columbia.

Sayles, L.R. 1952. "Seniority: An Internal Union Problem," *Harvard Business Review* 30: 55–61.

Schermerhorn, R.A. 1970. *Comparative Ethnic Relations: A Framework for Theory and Research*. New York: Random House.

Schneider, March. 1979. *Ethnicity and Politics*. University of North Carolina: Institute for Research in Social Science.

Shils, Edward, and Michael Young. 1953. "The Meaning of the Coronation," *The Sociological Review* 1: 63–81.

Shiose, Yuki, and Louise Fontaine. 1995. "La Construction des Figures de 'l'Autre'" *Revue Canadienne de Sociologie et Anthropologie* 32, 1: 91–110.

Siegel, B.J. 1970. "Defensive Structuring and Environmental Stress," *American Journal of Sociology* 76: 11–32.

Siggner, Andrew J. 1986. "The Socio-Demographic Conditions of Registered Indians." In *Arduous Journey: Canadian Indians and Decolonialization*. Toronto: McClelland and Stewart. 57–83.

Silver, Arthur J. 1982. *The French-Canadian Idea of Confederation, 1864–1900*. Toronto: University of Toronto Press.

Simkin, W.E. 1968. "Refusals to ratify contracts," *Industrial and Labour Relations Review* 21: 518–540.

Simmel, G. 1955. *Conflict and the Web of Group Affiliations*. Glencoe IL: The Free Press.

Smelser, N.J. 1963. *Theory of Collective Behavior*. New York: The Free Press.

Smiley, Donald. 1980. "Reflections on Cultural Nationhood and Political Community in Canada." In *Entering the Eighties: Canada in Crisis,* edited by R. Kenneth Carty and W. Peter Ward. Toronto: Oxford University Press. 20–43.

Smith, Anthony D. 1971. *Theories of Nationalism.* London: Duckworth.

– 1972. "Ethnocentrism, Nationalism and Social Change," *International Journal of Comparative Sociology* 13: 1–20.

Smith, M. G. 1969a. "Institutional and Political Conditions of Pluralism." In *Pluralism in Africa,* edited by L. Kuper and M.G. Smith. Berkeley: University of California Press.

– 1969b. "Some Developments in the Analytic Framework of Pluralism." In *Pluralism in Africa,* edited by L. Kuper and M.G. Smith. Berkeley: University of California Press.

– 1974. *Corporations and Society.* London: Duckworth.

Smith, Whitney, Jr. 1969. "The Study of Political Symbolism." PhD dissertation. Boston University.

Spence, A.M. 1973. "Job Market Signaling," *Quarterly Journal of Economics* 83: 355–74.

Spigelman, Martin. 1975. "Race et religion: Les Acadiens et la hierarchie catholique irlandaise du Nouveau-Brunswick," *Revue d'Histoire de L'Amérique Française* 29: 69–85.

Spiro, Melford E. 1955. "The Acculturation of American Ethnic Groups," *American Anthropologist* 57: 1240–52.

Stanley, George. 1974. "The Federal Bargain: The Contractorian Basis of Confederation." In *Consociational Democracies: Political Accommodation in Segmented Societies,* edited by K.D. McRae. Toronto: McClelland and Stewart.

Staples, Janice. 1974. "Consociationalism at Provincial Level: The Erosion of Dualism in Manitoba, 1870–1890." In *Consociational Democracies: Political Accommodation in Segmented Societies,* edited by K.D. McRae. Toronto: McClelland and Stewart.

Stasiulis, Daiva. 1980. "The Political Structuring of Ethnic Community Action: A Reformulation," *Canadian Ethnic Studies* 11: 19–44.

– 1987. "Rainbow Feminism: Anti-Racist Politics and the Canadian Women's Movement," *Resources for Feminist Research* 16: 1–10.

Statistics Canada. 1963. *Population: Ethnic Groups by Age Groups.* Bulletin 1.3–2. Ottawa: Queen's Printer.

– 1984. *1981 Census of Canada Population: Ethnic Origin.* Ottawa: Minister of Supply and Services Canada.

Stigler, G.J. 1961. "The Economics of Information," *Journal of Political Economy* 69: 213–25.

– 1962. "Information in the labor market," *Journal of Political Economy* 70: 94–105.

Stinchcombe, A. 1975. "A Structural Analysis of Sociology," *American Sociological Review* 10: 57–64.

Stolzenberg. R.M. 1975. "Occupations, Labour Markets and the Process of Wage Attainment," *American Sociological Review* 40: 645–65.

Strauss, Anselm L. 1959. *Mirrors and Masks: The Search for Identity.* Glenroe IL: The Free Press.

Sunahara, M. Ann. 1981. *The Politics of Racism.* Toronto: James Lorimer.

Swartz, Marc J., ed. 1968. *Local-Level Politics: Social and Cultural Perspectives.* Chicago: Aldine.

Tajfel, Henri. 1972. "La Catégorisation sociale." In *Introduction à la psychologie sociale,* edited by S. Moscovici. Paris: Larousse. 272–392.

Taylor, Donald M., and Ronald J. Sigal. 1982. "Defining 'Québécois': The Role of Ethnic Heritage, Language, and Political Orientation," *Canadian Ethnic Studies* 14: 59–70.

Taylor, Ronald L. 1979. "Black Ethnicity and the Persistence of Ethnogenesis," *American Journal of Sociology* 84: 1401–23.

Thomas, William I., and Florian Znaniecki. 1927. *The Polish Peasant in Europe and America.* 2nd ed. New York: Alfred Knopf.

Thompson, Fred, and W.I. Stanbury. 1979. *The Political Economy of Interest Groups in the Legislative Process in Canada.* Occasional Paper No. 9. Montreal: Institute for Research on Public Policy.

Thompson, Kenneth A. 1973. "Religious Organizations: The Cultural Perspective." In *People and Organizations,* edited by Graeme Salaman and Kenneth Thompson. New York: Open University Press.

– 1980. "Organizations as Constructors of Social Reality." In *Control and Ideology in Organizations,* edited by Graeme Salaman and Kenneth Thompson. Cambridge MA: MIT Press.

Thurow, L.C. 1975. *Generating Inequality.* New York: Basic Books.

Tilly, Charles. 1964. *The Vendée.* Cambridge MA.: Harvard University Press.

– 1975. *The Rebellious Century, 1830–1930.* Cambridge MA: Harvard University Press.

Tobin, J. 1965. "On Improving the Economic Status of the Negro," *Daedalus* 94: 78–98.

Torelli, M. 1971. "Conférence sur les événements d'Octobre." Montréal: mimeo.

Touraine, A. 1965. *Sociologie de l'Action.* Paris: Editions du Seuil.

Tremblay, Marc-Adélard. 1984. "The Québécois Identity: Theoretical Perspectives and Trends." Unpublished ms.

Turner, John C. 1974. "Social comparison and social identity: Some prospects for intergroup behaviour," *European Journal of Social Psychology* 5: 5–34.

Turner, Ralph H. 1968. "The Self-Conception in Social Interaction." In *The Self in Social Interaction,* edited by Chad Gordon and Kenneth J. Gergen. New York: John Wiley and Sons. 93–106.

Turner, V.W. 1964. "Symbols in Ndembu Ritual." In *Closed Systems and Open Minds,* edited by Max Gluckman. Edinburgh: Oliver and Boyd.

Ubale, B. 1978. *Equal Opportunity and Public Policy. A report on concerns of the South Asian community regarding their plans in the Canadian mosaic.* Report submitted to the Attorney-General of Ontario.

Vaillancourt, François. 1993. "The Economic Status of the French Language and Francophones in Québec." In *Quebec: State and Society*, 2nd ed., edited by Alain G. Gagnon. Scarborough ON: Nelson. 407–21.

Valentine, Victor. 1980. "Native Peoples and Canadian Society: A Profile of Issues and Trends." In *Cultural Boundaries and the Cohesion of Canada*, by Raymond Breton, Jeffrey G. Reitz, and Victor Valentine. Montreal: Institute for Research on Public Policy. 45–135.

Vallee, Frank G. 1981. "The Sociology of John Porter: Ethnicity as Anachronism," *Canadian Review of Sociology and Anthropology* 18, 5: 639–50.

Vallee, Frank G., and Norman Shulman. 1969. "The Viability of French Groupings Outside Québec." In *Regionalism in the Canadian Community, 1867–1967*, edited by Mason Wade. Toronto: University of Toronto Press. 83–99.

Valpy, Michael. 1995. "Three Award-Winning Communities," *Globe and Mail*, 26 September.

van den Berghe, P.L. 1969. "Pluralism and the Polity: A Theoretical Exploration." In *Pluralism in Africa*, edited by L. Kuper, and M.G. Smith. Berkeley: University of California Press. 67–81.

– 1971. "The Benign Quota: Panacea or Pandora's Box," *The American Sociologist* 6: 40–3.

Vano, Gerard S. 1981. *Neo-Feudalism: The Canadian Dilemma*. Toronto: Anansi.

Vecoli, Rudolph J. 1983. Presentation at Canadian Ethnic Studies Association Meeting. Thunder Bay.

Vipond, Mary. 1982. "Nationalism and Nativism: The Native Sons of Canada in the 1920s," *Canadian Review of Studies in Nationalism* 9: 81–96.

Wagley, C., and M. Harris. 1958. *Minorities in the New World*. New York: Columbia University Press.

Warner, Lloyd. 1953. *American Life*. Chicago: University of Chicago Press.

– 1959. *The Living and the Dead: A Study of the Symbolic Life of America*. New Haven: Yale University Press.

Warner, William L., and Leo Srole. 1945. *The Social Systems of American Ethnic Groups*. New Haven: Yale University Press.

Warren, Roland L., Stephen M. Rose, and Ann F. Bergunder. 1974. *The Structure of Urban Reform*. Lexington MA: Lexington Books.

Watt, James. 1967. "Anti-Catholic Nativism in Canada: The Protestant Protective Association," *The Canadian Historical Review* 48: 45–58.

Weber, M. 1969. *Basic Concepts in Sociology*. New York: Greenwood Press.

Weick, K.E. 1969. *The Social Psychology of Organizing*. Reading MA: Addison-Wesley.

Weinfeld, Morton. 1981. "Myth and Reality in the Canadian Mosaic: 'Affective Ethnicity'," *Canadian Ethnic Studies* 13: 80–100.

Westhues, Kenneth. 1976a. "Class and Organization as Paradigms in Social Science," *American Sociologist* 11: 38–49.

– 1976b. "Public Versus Sectarian Legitimation: The Separate Schools of the Catholic Church," *The Canadian Review of Sociology and Anthropology* 3: 137–51.

– 1980. "Foreign Gods and Nation-States in the Americas," *Canadian Review of Studies in Nationalism* 7: 351–71.

Wiley, N. F. 1967a. "America's Unique Class Politics: The Interplay of the Labour, Credit and Commodity Markets," *American Sociological Review* 32: 529–40.

– 1967b. "The Ethnic Mobility Trap and Stratification Theory," *Social Problems* 15: 147–59.

Willhelm, S.M. 1970. *Who Needs the Negro?* Cambridge MA: Schenkman.

Wilson, V. Seymour. 1993. "The Tapestry Vision of Canadian Multi-Culturalism," *Canadian Journal of Political Science* 26: 645–69.

Wilson. S.J. 1982. *Women, the Family and the Economy.* Toronto: McGraw-Hill Ryerson.

Wittke, C. 1957. *The German-Language Press in America.* Lexington: University of Kentucky Press.

Wolf, E.R. 1966. "Kinship, Friendship, and Patron-Client Relations in Complex Societies," *The Social Anthropology of Complex Societies* (Conference on New Approaches in Social Anthropology), Vol. I.

Wright, E.O., and L. Perrone. 1977. "Marxist Class Categories and Income Inequality," *American Sociological Review* 42: 32–55.

Wright, E.O. 1976. "Class Boundaries in Advanced Capitalist Societies," *New Left Review* 98: 3–41.

Yancey, William B., Eugene P. Erickson, and Richard N. Juliani. 1976. "Emergent Ethnicity: A Review and Reformulation," *American Sociological Review* 41: 391–403.

Young, Crawford. 1976. *The Politics of Cultural Pluralism.* Madison: University of Wisconsin Press.

Zenner, W.P. 1970. "Ethnic Assimilation and Corporate Groups." In *Minority Responses*, edited by M. Kurokawa. New York: Random House. 105–13.

Zielyk, Ihor V. 1975. "Two Types of Ethnic Communities." In *Sounds Canadian: Languages and Cultures in Multi-Ethnic Society*, edited by P. Migus. Toronto: Peter Martin Associates. 147–57.

Zolf, Larry. 1980. "Mulling over Multiculturalism," *Maclean's*, 14 April.

Index

Abella, Irving, 354n13
aboriginal peoples (or groups, or communities), xxi, 291–7, 214; integration of, 293–5, 297; segmentation of, 313; separate status of, 293, 307; whites and relationship to, 295; women among, 295–7, 308–9, 322
Acadia, 78, 79, 80
Acadians, 25, 93–4, 303
acculturation, 39–40, 46, 55, 173, 322; selective, 39, 55
Act of Union (1840), 86, 89
affective ethnicity, 322
Africa, 4, 187, 308
African cultures, 204
Air Canada, 64
Akian, Gail Grant, 335n1
Alberta, 93, 95, 144, 145, 271, 292, 307
Albinski, Harry S., 261

Allaire Committee, 160, 164
Allegheny Mountains, 79
America, 204
American, 105, 108, 112, 317; colonies, 82; culture, 113; enterprise in Quebec, 298, 299; imperialism, 87; investments in Canada, 308; presence in Canada, 260–1, 266, 274, 279; society, 187
American Jewish communities, 203
American Political Science Association, 8
American War of Independence (or American Revolution), 83–4, 103
Americanization of Canada, 271
Anderson, G.M., 337n28
Andrew, J.V., 65
les Anglais, 105, 119

Anglo-Canadian, 298
Anglo-conformity, 107–8, 109, 112, 117, 290, 307, 309, 310, 322
Anglo-Saxon, 269; character, 94; ideology, 107; race, 111; values, 108; white, male, and Protestant, 68
Anglos, 97, 310
anti-separatist, 123, 137
Armée de Libération du Québec, 134
Armée Revolutionnaire du Québec, 134
Arthurs, H.W., 123, 124
Asia, 187, 308
Asian, 319
Asian cultures, 204
Assemblée nationale, 98
assimilation, 39, 46, 86, 101, 108, 110, 116, 119, 169, 188, 272, 277; cultural, 313; linguistic, 125–6, 130, 310, 313; rejection of, 318; typology of, 188